Global Corruption Report: Climate Change

The global response to climate change will demand unprecedented international cooperation, deep economic transformation and resource transfers at a significant scale. Corruption threatens to jeopardize these efforts.

Transparency International's *Global Corruption Report: Climate Change* is the first publication to comprehensively explore major climate-related corruption risks. The book provides essential analysis to help policy-makers, practitioners and other stakeholders understand risks and develop effective responses at a critical moment when the main architecture for climate governance is being developed. More than 50 leading experts and practitioners contribute, covering four key areas:

- Governance: Investigating major governance challenges towards tackling climate change.
- Mitigation: Reducing greenhouse gas emissions with transparency and accountability.
- Adapting to climate change: Identifying corruption risks in climate-proofing development, financing and implementation of adaptation strategies.
- Forestry governance: Responding to the corruption challenges plaguing the forestry sector, and integrating integrity into international strategies to halt deforestation and promote reforestation.

Transparency International (TI) is the global civil society organization leading the fight against corruption. Through more than 90 chapters worldwide and an international secretariat in Berlin, TI raises awareness of the damaging effects of corruption and works with partners in government, business and civil society to develop and implement effective measures to tackle it. For more information, go to www.transparency.org.

Global Corruption Report: Climate Change

TRANSPARENCY INTERNATIONAL
the global coalition against corruption

With support from:

European Investment Bank

BMZ | Federal Ministry for Economic Cooperation and Development

publishing for a sustainable future

London • Washington, DC

First published in 2011 by Earthscan

Earthscan Ltd, Dunstan House, 14a St Cross Street, London EC1N 8XA, UK
Earthscan LLC, 1616 P Street, NW, Washington, DC 20036, USA
Earthscan publishes in association with the International Institute for Environment and Development

For more information on Earthscan publications, see www.earthscan.co.uk or write to earthinfo@earthscan.co.uk

ISBN: 978-1-84971-297-2 hardback
ISBN: 978-1-84971-282-8 paperback

Edited by Gareth Sweeney, Rebecca Dobson, Krina Despota, and Dieter Zinnbauer

Every effort has been made to verify the accuracy of the information contained in this report, including allegations. All information was believed to be correct as of December 2010. Nevertheless, Transparency International cannot guarantee the accuracy and the completeness of the contents. Nor can Transparency International accept responsibility for the consequences of its use for other purposes or in other contexts. Contributions to the *Global Corruption Report 2009* by authors external to Transparency International do not necessarily reflect the view of Transparency International or its national chapters.

Typeset by Saxon Graphics Ltd, Derby
Cover photography by Laurent Weyl, © Laurent Weyl/Collectif Argos
Cover design by Susanne Harris

A catalogue record for this book is available from the British Library

Library of Congress Cataloging-in-Publication Data
Global corruption report : climate change / [compiled by] Transparency International.
        p. cm.
  Includes bibliographical references and index.
  ISBN 978-1-84971-297-2 (hardback) — ISBN 978-1-84971-282-8 (pbk.) 1. Political corruption. 2. Climatic changes. 3. Climatic changes—Political aspects. 4. Climatic changes—Corrupt practices. 5. Environmental policy. I. Transparency International.
  JF1081.G563 2011
    363.738'74—dc22   2010050351

At Earthscan we strive to minimize our environmental impacts and carbon footprint through reducing waste, recycling and offsetting our CO_2 emissions, including those created through publication of this book.
For more details of our environmental policy, see www.earthscan.co.uk.

Printed and bound in the UK by Ashford Colour Press.
The paper used is FSC certified.

Contents

Illustrations

Figures

Tables

Boxes

Preface

Huguette Labelle, Chair, Transparency International

We stand at the threshold of a global challenge: climate change. Governance lies at the heart of this challenge. Implemented with integrity and transparency, policies on climate change will make it possible for people around the world to understand, support and own the changes that will be required of them.

For more than 15 years the work of Transparency International (TI) has demonstrated that, left unchallenged, corruption ruins lives, destroys livelihoods and thwarts attempts at social and economic justice. The same risks apply to climate change. Better governance is the solution, however, and it will be crucial to ensure that the mitigation strategies and adaptation solutions that emerge at local, national and international levels embrace participation, accountability and integrity. With so much at stake, and with urgency of the essence, we must guarantee that climate change policy is just, effective and transparent in its design and implementation.

The *Global Corruption Report: Climate Change* illustrates the immense demands of the task we face. Solutions to climate change must build a bridge of trust between rich and poor countries. At TI we have promoted a similar agenda with the adoption of the UN Convention against Corruption, which reflects a broad, worldwide consensus on our issue.

It is not only governments that are essential to mitigating and adapting to climate change; the private sector also has a key role to play, as the main source of finance for the green economy. TI looks forward to working in partnership with the business community for fair and transparent solutions to climate change, which we see as essential to an ongoing commitment to sustainability that comes with more transparent business practices.

Finally, the climate change challenge brings us closer to others in civil society and the research community. At TI, we are inspired by the many scientists and environmental campaigners who, for decades, have led the charge to bring public awareness and urgency to the issue of climate change. Starting our work in the spirit of partnership, we believe that the pioneering efforts of environmental organizations can be further strengthened by bringing in not just anti-corruption perspectives but also those of human rights, humanitarian assistance, development assistance and consumer advocacy. Drawing together our diverse knowledge and experience can ensure that, as well as tackling the climate challenge, we also move towards better systems of governance and the promotion of sustainable and equitable development.

Foreword

Kumi Naidoo, Executive Director, Greenpeace International

Greenpeace was founded on a prophecy from Canada's First Nation peoples:

> *There will come a time when the Earth grows sick, and when it does a tribe will gather from all the cultures of the world who believe in deeds and not words. They will work to heal it and they will be known as the 'Warriors of the Rainbow'.*

This could just as well be applied to the work of Transparency International, and I am pleased and honoured to introduce this volume of TI's work on climate change.

An unfortunate fact of human nature is that, where there is money to be made, corruption quickly follows. As we face the collective challenge of averting catastrophic climate change and finding development paths that deliver a decent livelihood for all while respecting ecological limits, civil society often finds itself pitted against those who would put personal gain before the good of the planet.

Greenpeace's vision of a sustainable society demands that power be exercised fairly and that those in power be held accountable for their actions. Corruption undermines this vision, by privileging those with power and money over other citizens, allowing them to profit at the expense not only of the rest of us – but of the planet itself.

Greenpeace's experience has shown that corruption does not just drive climate change but undermines economic and social development as well. Africa is one of the richest continents in terms of natural resources and minerals, for example, but, because of what has been termed the 'resource curse', it is the poorest continent when it comes to providing for its own people, as revenues from the wealth of resources are diverted and siphoned off.

Existing forms of corruption that can have a negative impact on efforts to mitigate and adapt to climate change are not difficult to find, whether it is heads of government depriving citizens of any share of their country's resource riches; authorities failing to take real action against corruption in the oil sector, despite losing billions of dollars in revenue; or documented examples of private sector contributions to public officials that result in clear conflicts of interest and interference in the due process of law. All such forms need to be duly considered in the development of a climate policy that will have meaningful effects on the ground.

The *Global Corruption Report: Climate Change* comes at an important time. By mapping risk in a number of rapidly expanding areas and bringing good governance to the forefront of the climate change debate, the report clearly illustrates that decisions made at the global level need to take account of the effects of corruption at all levels in order to pave the way for future success in combating climate change.

Greenpeace is proud to support the first book to make the case comprehensively that fighting for climate justice also means fighting the scourge of corruption.

Foreword

Ashok Khosla, President,
International Union for Conservation of Nature (IUCN)

The everyday face of corruption – bribes, kickbacks, tax avoidance, selling influence – is well known and has distorted economies, demoralized publics and torn asunder the moral fabric of many a society.

Not as well known but perhaps even more destructive are the corrupt practices that lead to the destruction of our natural resources and to the destruction of the people – indigenous populations, tribals, villagers – on whose lands the material resources and sinks of our by-products lie.

The greed and short-sightedness that have landed the world in its current predicaments are in a real sense manifestations of an even deeper corruption in our relationship with each other and with Mother Earth. At no time in history has there been a greater need for a radical rethink of our social and economic goals.

The global climate is undergoing change that is unprecedented in its magnitude and speed. Suddenly, we find ourselves in the fifth great extinction, with species vanishing at rates not seen in millions of years. Soil, water and biological resources that provide the basic supports to all life on the planet are rapidly degrading or disappearing. And each year the gap between the needs of the people and the capacity of the earth to meet these needs keeps on widening.

Who is to blame? And who can help bring about the transformations in our institutions, technologies and, above all, our values that are needed to stabilize the social and environmental systems that have got so out of balance?

In one sense, the answer to both questions is … everyone. But some have greater responsibility than others, both for where we are and for bringing about the reorientation needed in our societies and economies towards where we must go.

One group that must take a solid part of the responsibility for our current predicament is the 'professional' or the 'practitioner', whose knowledge and expertise has enabled the gap between the rich and the poor to grow to where it is today.

In some cases, this might be because of lack of information on the specific, contextual issues to which the professional has been asked to respond. In other cases, it has resulted from lack of knowledge or 'science' regarding the processes and systems that need to be designed, where even the scientist has not been totally successful in internalizing societal values into his or her enterprise. And much of the time, it has been the result of a lack of wisdom – in turn partly because of narrow perspectives engendered by specialized, discipline-based training and partly because of the complexity of the systems we live with.

But ultimately, there is no gainsaying the role of greed and graft. One way to turn back to creed and craft is to reintroduce the pledge that a professional makes to society when graduating from training into professional practice. We now need an extended Hippocratic Oath that promotes the idea that a practitioner's duty is not only 'to do good', but is a doubly extended professional commitment that covers the need for integrity, excellence and relevance.

To set in place a well-designed professional system will require a high degree of vigilance by peers – individuals and organizations – to ensure that development professionals bring to their work the highest possible level of integrity, excellence and relevance. For this effort, the role of civil society, which includes not only the voluntary organizations and NGOs of today but also new kinds of organizations of tomorrow, social enterprises, capable of combining public goals with private motivation, becomes triply important. *Global Corruption Report: Climate Change* should in no small part contribute to defining and strengthening that role.

Acknowledgements

This *Global Corruption Report* on climate change governance is a credit to the collaboration and dedication of its contributors, most notably its authors, whose expertise and commitment have given a richness of perspective to the report.

As Transparency International continues to expand globally, we are grateful for the country-level knowledge and insights of our National Chapters and the contribution they have made by providing detailed and relevant country case studies.

We are grateful for the guidance of a group of distinguished experts who kindly served on our Editorial Advisory Panel: Hansjörg Elshorst, Fiona Harvey, Saleem-ul Huq, David Nussbaum, Hermann Ott, Frances Seymour, Shane Tomlinson, Kevin Watkins, Jake Werksman and Ifthekar Zaman.

We are indebted to our colleagues at the Transparency International Secretariat for their support and insight. We particularly would like to thank the Secretariat's senior management team, and the Transparency International board, as well as Lisa Elges, Michel Gary, Manoj Nadkarni, Farzana Nawaz, Zoe Reiter and David van der Zwaag. The *Global Corruption Report* team would like to express its gratitude to Daniel Abreu for lending his enthusiasm and climate change expertise to the early stages of the project, and Rosie Pinnington and Leah Good for their critical assistance in the final weeks of the report's production.

With the completion of this book, the team is saying goodbye to two valuable editors. We wish to express our huge gratitude to Rebecca Dobson, who contributed to the report with dedication and good humour for the last three years. Her quick thinking, camaraderie and boundless curiosity were enormous assets to the team and she will be deeply missed. Dieter Zinnbauer, chief editor of the Global Corruption Reports 2008 and 2009, also had a fundamental hand in shaping the current report, and pitched in well beyond the call of duty. While he will continue to sit right next door, we'll nevertheless miss his creative approach and his untiring desire to uncover the newest angles in the corruption field.

The hard work and recommendations of our external editors have added tremendously to the quality of the report. Mark Worth's polishing of the text added eloquence and sharpened nuance, and copy-editor Mike Richardson worked against the clock to bring consistency and coherence to our manuscript. We are also thankful, as ever, for astute and perceptive editorial advice and oversight from Robin Hodess.

This year we are very happy to be working with our new publisher, Earthscan, whose team has provided timely, patient and expert assistance throughout the process. We would especially like to thank Nick Bellorini, Veruschka Selbach, Nick Ascroft and Claire Lamont for their generous support.

We would also like to acknowledge a number of individuals from various backgrounds who have employed their expert knowledge and skills to the enormous benefit of the report: Alexios Antypas, Francisco Ascui, Richard Baron, Monika Bauhr, Shikha Bhasin, Tim Bittiger, Jason J. Blackstock, Bernhard Bodenstorfer, Duncan Brack, Rob Bradley, Curtis Brainard, Adam Bumpus, Michelle Chan, Ian Christoplos, Jim Coburn, Simone Cooper, John Crabtree, Delegation of the European Union to Papua New Guinea, Joanna Depledge, Al-Hamndou Dorsouma, Alan Drew, Navroz K. Dubash, Sebastien Duyck, Tejas Ewing, Estelle Fach, Pedro Faria, Dora Fazekas, Jorge Nunez Ferrer, Ivana Gazibara, Arunabha Ghosh, Tamra Gilbertson, Michael Gillenwater, Ruth Golding, Robert Lane Greene, Alberto Guijarro, Lois Guthrie, Mohamed Hamza, Erica Harper, Barbara Hogenboom, David Huberman, Alice Jaraiseh, Maria Ivanova, Patricia Kameri-Mbote, Nalin Kishor, Harvey F. Kline, Andrea Lampis, Magda Lanu, Merrin Layden, Robin Leichenko, Michelle Leighton, Martin Lichtl, Simone Lovera-Bilderbeek, Julio Lumbreras, Michael MacCracken, Darina Malova, María Piedad Martín, Grigorij Mesežnikov, Marcus Moench, John Mulrow, Albert Mumma, Robert Nasi, Siddharth Pathak, Philipp Pattberg, Leo Peskett, Argentino Pessoa, David Proverbs, Gabriela Quimson, Aminur Rahman, Oscar Reyes, James Risbey, Victor Samwinga, Lisa Schipper, Deborah Seligsohn, Winston Shakantu, Anju Sharma, Heidi Siegelbaum, Martin Stadelmann, Wolfgang Sterk, Ian Tellum, Frank Venmans, Erika Weinthal, Laura Williamson, Glenn Wiser, Yin-fang Zhang, Darren Zook, Uchita de Zoysa and Samer Zureikat.

And to those for whom the details are never lost, we would like to thank our tireless and meticulous fact-checkers: Jennifer M. Cruz, Natacha Draghi, Arwen Fleming, Jason Ariel Grullon, Gábor Halmai, Péter Király, Sofia Lindholm, Ariana Mendoza, Andrej Nosko, Leila Peacock and Katherine Stecher.

We continue to receive generous pro-bono libel guidance from Covington and Burling. This year we are particularly grateful for the work of Enrique Armijo, Jason Criss, Laura Flahive Wu, Simon Frankel, Mali Friedman, Eric Hellerman, Gregory Lipper, Candice Plotkin, Eve Pogoriler, Robert Sherman, Lindsey Tonsager and Stephen Weiswasser.

Finally, we would like to express thanks to all of our donors who contribute to the *Global Corruption Report*. Particular thanks are due to the German Federal Ministry for Economic Cooperation and Development (BMZ) and the European Investment Bank, who continue to give generous support. We would also wish to thank the Ministry of Foreign Affairs of Finland, the Canadian Agency for International Development (CIDA) and Swedish International Development Cooperation Agency (Sida) for their contribution to TI's core activities, including the report.

Acronyms and abbreviations

3C	Combat Climate Change
AAU	assigned amount unit
AFB	Adaptation Fund Board
AWG-KP	Ad Hoc Working Group on Further Commitments for Annex I Parties under the Kyoto Protocol
AWG-LCA	Ad Hoc Working Group on Long-term Cooperative Action
BaU	business-as-usual
BAWIN	Bangladesh Water Integrity Initiative
CAIT	Climate Analysis Indicators Tool
CCAP	Center for Clean Air Policy
CCS	carbon capture and sequestration
CCVI	Climate Change Vulnerability Index
CCX	Chicago Climate Exchange
CDM	Clean Development Mechanism
CDP	Carbon Disclosure Project
CEA	Central Environmental Authority
CER	certified emission reduction
CfRN	Coalition for Rainforest Nations
CIFs	Climate Investment Funds
COP	Conference of the Parties
CoST	Construction Sector Transparency Initiative
CPI	Corruption Perceptions Index
CPWC	Co-operative Programme on Water and Climate
CRS	Creditor Reporting System
CSP	concentrated solar power
CTF	Clean Technology Fund
DAC	Development Assistance Committee
DNA	designated national authority
DOE	designated operational entity

EEs	executing entities
EFC	Ethics and Finance Committee
EIA	environmental impact assessment
EITI	Extractive Industries Transparency Initiative
EPA	Environmental Protection Agency
EPI	Environmental Performance Index
ETS	Emissions Trading Scheme
EU	European Union
FDI	foreign direct investment
FMA	Forest Management Agreement
FSC	Forest Stewardship Council
FTC	Federal Trade Commission
GAO	Government Accountability Office
GEF	Global Environment Facility
GHG	greenhouse gas
GIAC	Global Infrastructure Anti-Corruption
GIS	Green Investment Scheme
GS	Gold Standard
ha	hectare
HFC	hydrofluorocarbon
HFC-23	Hydrofluorocarbon-23
ICLEI	Local Governments for Sustainability
IEA	International Energy Agency
IEE	initial environmental examination
IEG	international environmental governance
IIED	International Institute for Environment and Development
IOM	International Organization for Migration
IPCC	Intergovernmental Panel on Climate Change
IRR	internal rate of return
ISO	International Organization for Standardization
IUCN	International Union for the Conservation of Nature
JI	Joint Implementation
JISC	Joint Implementation Supervisory Committee
LDCF	Least Developed Countries Fund
LDCs	least developed countries
LED	light-emitting diode
MARGE	Mediterranean Area Renewable Generation Estimator
MDB	multilateral development bank

MIE	multilateral implementing entity
MOP	Meeting of the Parties
MRV	measuring, reporting and verification
MW	megawatts
NAMA	nationally appropriate mitigation action
NAP	national allocation plan
NAPA	national adaptation programme of action
NGO	non-governmental organization
NIE	national implementing entity
OCHA	Office for the Coordination of Humanitarian Affairs
ODA	official development assistance
OECD	Organisation for Economic Co-operation and Development
OECD-DAC	OECD Development Assistance Committee
OIES	Oxford Institute for Energy Studies
OTC	over-the-counter
PACS	Project Anti-Corruption System
PFCs	perfluorocarbons
PGM	platinum group metal
PNG	Papua New Guinea
PPCR	Pilot Program for Climate Resilience
PPRC	Projects and Programme Review Committee
PV	photovoltaic
QELRO	quantified emissions limitations and reduction obligation
REDD	Reducing Emissions from Deforestation and Forest Degradation
REDD+	Expanded version of REDD (see section 6.2)
RES	renewable energy sources
SBI	Subsidiary Body for Implementation
SBSTA	Subsidiary Body for Scientific and Technological Advice
SCCF	Special Climate Change Fund
SF6	sulphur hexafluoride
SIFORCO	Société Industrielle et Forestière du Congo
SPA	Strategic Priority on Piloting an Operational Approach to Adaptation
STAR	System for Transparent Allocation of Resources
SWIFT	Society for Worldwide Interbank Financial Telecommunication
TI	Transparency International
TWh/y	terawatt-hours per year
UN	United Nations

UNCAC	United Nations Convention against Corruption
UNDP	United Nations Development Programme
UNECE	United Nations Economic Commission for Europe
UNEP	United Nations Environment Programme
UNFCCC	United Nations Framework Convention on Climate Change
UNHCR	UN High Commissioner for Refugees
UNODC	UN Office on Drugs and Crime
USAID	United States Agency for International Development
VVM	Validation and Verification Manual
WHO	World Health Organization
WIN	Water Integrity Network
WRI	World Resources Institute
WTO	World Trade Organization
WWC	World Water Council

Executive Summary
Transparency International

Climate change is arguably the greatest governance challenge the world has ever faced. Addressing it requires a degree of urgency, trust, cooperation and solidarity that tests the limits of conventional mechanisms and institutions to manage public goods. It requires transformational shifts in our economies that may eventually dwarf the dramatic changes brought on by the Industrial Revolution. Climate change affects livelihoods and challenges lifestyles. It exerts immense pressure on the social and political fabric of communities around the world, against the backdrop of tremendous uncertainty about the precise scope and pace of the next steps that will be taken to remedy it, particularly at the global level.

A robust system of climate governance – meaning the processes and relationships at the international, national, corporate and local levels to address the causes and effects of climate change – will be essential for ensuring that the enormous political, social and financial investments by both the public sector and the private sector made in climate change mitigation and adaptation are properly and equitably managed, so that responses to climate change are successful. The stakes are high: we must invest significantly to achieve a low-carbon future, and we must make sure this investment is effective. Despite difficulties in reaching consensus at the international level, states, companies and civil society actors are converging around the need to establish clear rules and compliance mechanisms for addressing climate change. Good governance of the climate can enhance the process, making it more transparent, accessible and equitable for all.

Climate change is not just a challenge to established approaches to governance, however; it also transcends established typologies of corruption. Corruption is defined by Transparency International as the *abuse of entrusted power for private gain*. *Entrusted power* is not only the power a citizen confers to a public office holder. It is the power that future generations have vested in all of us, in our stewardship role for the planet. Likewise, *abuse for private gain* goes beyond corruption in the forms it so often takes – the misappropriation of funds, bribery in the awarding of contracts, and nepotism, all of which undermine good climate governance – and extends to new arenas. These include the distortion of scientific facts, the breach of principles of fair representation and false claims about the green credentials of consumer products – evidence of which is documented in this report. Such practices can be devastating in a policy arena in which uncertainty abounds and trust and cooperation are essential.

Why is corruption, in particular, a risk in addressing climate change? As the *Global Corruption Report* explores at length, the efforts to prevent and respond to climate change will have an enormous price tag. Where huge amounts of money flow through new and untested financial markets and mechanisms, there is always a risk of corruption. Some estimate total climate change investments in mitigation efforts alone at almost US$700 billion by 2020. Public investments of no less than US$250 billion per annum will eventually flow through new, relatively uncoordinated and untested channels. In addition, pressure already exists to 'fast-track' solutions, further enhancing the risk of corruption.

Corruption risks are also high because of the level of complexity, uncertainty and novelty that surrounds many climate issues. Essential concepts, such as what should count as a forest, or how to establish additionality (meaning whether projects could happen in any case without support), are still being debated. Rules for geoengineering, perhaps the most risky and consequential human intervention in our biosphere, are still largely absent. New tools to measure the environmental integrity of carbon offsets are relatively untested. Early evidence presented in this report suggests that there are many regulatory grey zones and loopholes that are at risk of being exploited by corrupt interests. Careful monitoring, quick learning and an active approach to closing entry points for corruption are essential to ensure that strong governance enables the success of these new tools and instruments at this most critical stage.

Another aspect of climate governance that demands urgent attention is the inequality of the current processes for individuals and groups most directly affected by climate change. Contributions to the *Global Corruption Report* shed light on those most adversely affected by climate change: indigenous and rural poor communities in remote locations, the urban poor living in precarious settlements, and displaced persons who require resettlement. All these groups share commonalities. They bear the brunt of the effects of climate change; they are meant to be the main beneficiaries of adaptive action; and yet they are usually the most marginalized voices in the political system. This starkly highlights the need for accountable climate governance.

An overarching message of the *Global Corruption Report* is that *a dramatic strengthening of governance mechanisms can reduce corruption risk and make climate change policy more effective and more successful.* The quality of climate governance – the degree to which policy development and decisions are participatory, accountable, transparent, inclusive and responsive, and respect the rule of law – will help determine how well it addresses inherent corruption risks. The report brings together more than 50 recognized experts to present the first comprehensive analysis of corruption and climate change, and it includes a set of policy recommendations.

Making climate governance work: designing processes for accountability and integrity

The scale and complexity of the climate change challenge and the financial investments required to make it work mean that a well-coordinated system of accountable decision-making is essential.

Important decisions on climate change are taken in many institutional settings – more than the spotlight on some high-profile international meetings would suggest

Overwhelming attention to high-profile intergovernmental meetings on climate change makes their outcomes seem uniquely critical. Although this arena is extremely important, action is dispersed across a multitude of fora and actors from international to local level, reflecting the extraordinary scope and diversity of climate policy issues.

There are currently more than 500 multilateral environmental agreements, many relevant to climate change. Important climate decisions are not deliberated and decided upon only by conferences of state parties in Copenhagen or Cancún. The overall response to climate change is perhaps even more critically shaped in many national and regional venues, from Beijing, Brussels and Brasilia to Delhi and Washington. Many new hybrid initiatives that link public and private stakeholders play a role, and so do cities and local governments that can notch up the standards of commitments – or water them down.

The extent of transparency, accountability and inclusive participation varies widely across these policy-making fora. Standards need to be consistently high to pave the way for sound climate policies that avoid the many potential risks of policy capture and forum-shopping, regulatory arbitrage and hold-ups that are associated with such a dispersed governance landscape and that all have the potential to undermine effective global action.

The attention and record attendance that a few key climate policy processes enjoy make it easy to overlook persistent disparities in influence, even in these settings

High visibility does not equal effective transparency and attendance does not equal proportionate influence. Transparency practices for the United Nations Framework Convention on Climate Change (UNFCCC), the most visible forum for climate policy-making, lag behind established standards practised in other settings. Likewise, record turnout and attention for the Copenhagen summit and a handful of other headline events cannot mask persistent disparities in representation. In Copenhagen, the top five polluting countries were able to field more than three times the number of official delegates than the five countries considered to be most affected by climate change. By 2009 the combined number of registered observer organizations to the UNFCCC from Canada, the UK and the US had reached more than 400, while on the developing country side only Brazil, China and India managed to register more than 10 groups. In sum, high-profile international venues for climate policy-making may garner sufficient attention and raise prospects for better climate governance instruments, but there is a long way to go to achieve an effective and inclusive voice for all stakeholders.

The lobbying landscape is diversifying, and the associated risk of undue influence is higher than ever

The advent of green industries as lobbyists, as a counterweight to lobbying by energy and other sectors dominated by the need for fossil fuels, might suggest that by now a rather balanced spectrum of interests underpins deliberation about climate policies. As the *Global Corruption Report* documents, this is not the full picture. At US national level, oil and gas interests alone outspent the clean energy sector by a factor of eight in lobbying in 2009. In the European Union, business groups contributed more than twice the number of policy positions to an important climate policy deliberation process in 2004 than environmental groups.

Even an equal presence of both green and brown lobbying does not guarantee climate policies in the public interest. As the report shows, double policy capture may occur when a lack of action on polluters exists alongside strong support for influential green interests. Mandatory lobbying registries are still not required in the majority of Organisation for Economic Co-operation and Development (OECD) countries, however, and the quality of internal and external disclosure by businesses on their level of public engagement and activities related to climate change remains mixed.

Elsewhere in the world, the matrix of interests and influence does not bode well for balanced consideration of all interests. In China and India, for example, the actors in the fossil fuel and power sector likely to lose most from progressive climate policies are often large, state-controlled conglomerates with close linkages to the highest echelons of political power. All this requires that close attention be paid in order to avoid policy capture and results that serve the few rather than the many, which would be bad for accountability and bad for the planet.

Mitigation: strategies for reducing carbon emissions

Mitigation efforts aim to slow climate change by reducing the amount of greenhouse gases (GHGs) emitted globally, or increasing the capacity to capture emissions in natural sinks, such as forests, or through technological innovation. Leading mitigation approaches include the establishment of carbon markets, mandated emission standards and energy efficiency policies, and voluntary initiatives to move towards a low-carbon economy. Even though some of these approaches are at relatively early stages of development, adequate governance safeguards should be put in place from the outset to ensure that they can best achieve their objectives.

A robust system for the measuring, reporting and verification (MRV) of emissions is crucial to transparency, and ultimately to the success of mitigation strategies

Accurate MRV is critical, not only to reducing GHG emissions at the national level but also to enable investors to make informed decisions about business sustainability. Although many methods and initiatives are currently in place to measure, report and verify emissions, more resources and training are needed to improve this information. In developing countries, a lack of technical capacity or financial resources makes the development of ongoing emissions data collection difficult, and a lack of expert reviewers may mean that formal reporting on national emissions is not subject to sufficiently robust verification.

Without stringent MRV requirements in developing and developed countries alike, the risks include incentives for industries to exaggerate their baseline emissions data so as to make 'reductions' easier at a later date. The use of unreliable emissions data in carbon markets can result in the over-allocation of carbon credits, making efforts to reduce emissions less ambitious than they ought to be. The result is mitigation strategies that do not reduce emissions and that support the market in the short term only through possible windfall profits for some major polluters, with the climate losing out.

The need to measure, report and verify extends beyond emissions, as the entire industry emerging around the green economy needs to establish the legitimacy of its no- or low-carbon growth credentials. While government attempts to support green technologies are laudable, regulatory oversight must keep pace with expanding industrial activity, as financial incentives have already led some project developers to falsely claim projects to be finished in order to reap heightened profits.

As a critical mechanism for mitigation, carbon markets need safeguards to reduce the risk of corruption, as well as to ensure their sustainability and capacity to reduce greenhouse gas emissions

Carbon markets have been adopted in a number of regions and countries as a method for reducing GHG emissions, and the value of leading carbon markets has now reached some US$144 billion. These initiatives hold the potential to reduce emissions, but they are also politically created and publicly funded markets trading in an intangible commodity.

The European Union's Emissions Trading Scheme (ETS) has shown that carbon markets are susceptible to undue influence from vested interests, which in the case of the ETS may have contributed to the over-allocation of carbon permits. The result was windfall profits of €6–8 billion for Europe's four largest power producers.[1] Weak governance of these critical markets can create a lose-lose scenario, in which over-allocation of permits and the resulting low carbon prices provide a disincentive for business to find new low-carbon means of production, and potentially can bring about market collapse.

The path to a green economy should create opportunity for developing countries by addressing governance concerns directly; the risk if it does not is that global inequalities will be sustained and deepened

The roll-out of renewable energy sources, such as solar and wind power, is crucial to mitigation and requires considerable private investment. According to a recent study in the North Africa region, however, almost 70 per cent of the potential investors interviewed considered regulatory risk, including corruption, to be likely – and a serious impediment to investment.

Significant changes will need to be introduced to bring about a viable low-carbon infrastructure. Many countries believed to be characterized by weak governance or corruption will have a central role to play in this transition. For example, some of the new land required for biofuels, which are slated to comprise 10 per cent of global transport fuels by 2030, is being sought in countries that rank below global averages in the control of corruption, the rule of law and political stability indicators.

Not only land but also minerals such as lithium (demand for which is expected to grow dramatically with the coming of electric cars, for example) are often found in countries that lack strong governance and integrity systems. As these natural resources become crucial to the low-carbon economy, steps must be taken to guarantee transparency in the flows of money that governments receive for access to them. The drive to prevent climate change should not result in a new resource curse, a *green resource curse*, condemning poorer countries to miss the opportunity for economic development while others profit from their wealth in the growth of the green economy. Existing standards such as the Extractive Industries Transparency Initiative (EITI) can play an important role in this regard.[2]

Building effective adaptation to climate change

Strengthening citizen participation is essential to adaptation governance, as adaptation will take place in countries with high corruption risks

Systems need to be put in place to make sure that the planning and prioritization of projects is transparent and encourages local ownership and long-term sustainability by ensuring the participation of those most directly affected. The introduction of 'direct access' to funds through the Kyoto Protocol Adaptation Fund requires that national entities will need to be established for managing adaptation funds, and that they are equipped with the resources and capacity to fulfil their fund allocation and monitoring role. To date, however, only US$200,000 has been designated per country for the development of national adaptation programmes of action (NAPAs) in the least developed countries, and it is still unclear how much money will be provided for capacity-building.

In addition, effective adaptation governance ultimately also depends on the functioning of other checks and balances, including courts, law enforcement and a vigorous media and civil society. Broader systems of governance need to be strengthened in many countries where adaptation is needed most. None of the 20 countries most affected by climate change score higher than 3.6 on the Corruption Perceptions Index, in which 0 is extremely corrupt and 10 is very clean. Strengthening adaptation processes is essential, and yet it must be a part of broader governance reforms.

Oversight at the implementation stage is critical to the success of adaptation programmes

Much adaptation to climate change will consist of large-scale infrastructural development, such as enhancing flood control systems or protecting drinking water from salt water infiltration. In construction costs alone, corruption is currently estimated to cost the developing world some US$18 billion a year. Adaptation without oversight presents a twofold risk of diverted funds *and* substandard work, however, which may put populations at even more risk of climate extremes. In Turkey, where an earthquake killed 11,000 people in 1999, a half of all structures failed to comply with building regulations. Important lessons can be learnt from the humanitarian and development sectors to enhance understanding of how to avoid corruption undermining adaptation efforts, as well as from existing multi-stakeholder initiatives such as the Construction Sector Transparency Initiative (CoST).[3]

Strengthening coordination, mutual accountability and operational transparency in the governance of adaptation funds is essential to building the trust needed for sustainable climate change policy

The disbursement of adaptation funding extends across various bilateral and multilateral streams, including six specific bilateral climate funds, two World Bank Climate Investment Funds and the UNFCCC and Kyoto Protocol funds, including the new Green Climate Fund. All have diverse governance systems and different rules of engagement, making accountability to those affected by climate change rather complicated. Nearly a half of US pledges for fast-start funding made in Copenhagen and Cancún are to be routed through the World Bank in 2011, and therefore subject to its governance frameworks.

An effective common reporting framework for adaptation funding is essential for tagging and tracking funds that come through the system. At present it remains difficult to distinguish between official development assistance and dedicated 'new and additional' adaptation funding. Fixed criteria for 'new and additional' funds will ease measurement and reduce the risks of manipulation. They will also allow the clarity that is necessary for development and adaptation funding to have an impact that is coordinated and of greatest benefit to those most harmed by changes to Earth's climate.

A focus on forestry

Forests play a pivotal role in climate policy, yet a track record of entrenched corruption in the sector demands preventative and proactive action

Enhancing forestry governance is a priority of the highest order to mitigate climate change. High international demand for timber, weak land ownership rights and marginalized indigenous communities present singular challenges to accountable and sustainable forestry. Each year US$10–23 billion worth of timber is illegally felled or produced from suspicious origins. These practices are aided by legal loopholes and deeply engrained corruption schemes, whereby local power brokers use forest assets not only for personal enrichment but also for buying political support or influence.

These factors need to be addressed early on for REDD (Reducing Emissions from Deforestation and Forest Degradation), as the major international initiative to leverage forest policies for climate change. REDD readiness programmes (pledges currently amount to around US$3.5 billion) have the potential to address some of the national-level capacity loopholes, but are not a panacea for addressing corruption in the sector.

Robust systems for monitoring and reporting are essential to reducing corruption risks and ensuring the sustainability of forest projects

Funds of up to US$28 billion a year are expected to flow once REDD programmes are fully operational. As has already been observed in mitigation initiatives such as the UN Clean Development Mechanism (CDM), robust monitoring mechanisms have to be put in place in order to avoid the inappropriate validation of projects, the verification of fictitious projects and the overestimation, double-counting or fraudulent trade of carbon credits. These risks are particularly salient for forestry. Oversight in the forest sector is difficult, since much activity takes place in remote areas. Ensuring the sustainability of forests and the security of carbon credits means that measures need to be put in place to ensure that deforestation does not begin once the financial benefits of REDD have been realized (permanence), or relocate to other areas where REDD programmes are not in place (leakage).

Public participation at the local level is essential to the success of forestry governance

Forest communities' full participation in the REDD process is crucial to make sure that they reap the benefits of the REDD programme and that finances to curb deforestation are not diverted. Putting local communities in charge of managing their forests, or at least giving them a big role in this process, can lead to improved forest conditions and local livelihoods. Forest communities are already becoming victims of fraud as carbon brokers and project developers have moved aggressively to secure carbon rights through non-transparent negotiations with government officials. Increased funding for forests will need to be matched with strong coordination and oversight in order to ensure that the money reaches the communities that need it yet does not increase incentives for corruption.

Actions for sustainable climate governance

The *Global Corruption Report* clearly demonstrates that better climate governance will ultimately require the genuine commitment and cooperation of all stakeholders, from governments and business to non-governmental organizations (NGOs), scientists and society at large. Moreover, integrity in climate policy requires an entire system of interlocking checks and balances. Key ingredients and areas for action include the following.

Generating and making publicly available accurate information

This is in terms of who is responsible for what emissions, who is advocating for what policy, which money goes where and for what, what sized carbon footprint should accompany consumption or investment choices, and so on. This kind of disclosure is essential to assign responsibilities more clearly and improve accountability among stakeholders.

Tracking, benchmarking and comparing the capacity and performance of emitters, regulators, funders and governments

Benchmarking diagnostics generate invaluable pressure for accountability, help detect red flags for corruption and identify priorities for governance reform. Some early examples are described in this report and illustrate how important these mechanisms can be, showing, for example, underperformance on the part of key verification providers in carbon markets and the lack of monitoring capacity for forest carbon issues.

Matching capacity at all levels to the scale of the challenge

A mismatch in enforcement or monitoring capacity means that on-site spot checks are too infrequent – or even completely absent – to be a deterrent, and effectively sanctions corrupt practices. A mismatch between the supply and demand of specialized skills means that key experts end up wearing multiple hats and the potential for conflicts of interests grows. A mismatch between financial flows and the capacity for financial management opens the door to corruption.

Anchoring climate governance firmly in existing frameworks for integrity and accountability

Climate governance must draw on a wide range of existing accountability mechanisms. It can invoke and support the UN Convention against Corruption; it can use and help to develop anti-corruption mechanisms, from ombudsmen to whistleblowing mechanisms; and it can engage with and foster the growing range of social accountability initiatives, from social audits to collaborative monitoring, that are springing up at community level.

A major scaling up of investment and considerable economic change awaits us as a result of climate change. We must accompany this process with the best possible governance we can, to ensure the equitable outcomes we need for the planet and for future generations. Based on the findings of the *Global Corruption Report*, Transparency International makes the following key proposals to climate stakeholders.

Recommended actions for governments

1 Incentivize and design key climate policy instruments so as to promote independence and reduce conflict of interest

Governments need to make sure that relevant oversight bodies are staffed by salaried professionals, with technical expertise, who have proven themselves to be free from conflicts of interest stemming from personal stakes in carbon markets, offset or adaptation projects or additional representative roles in climate negotiations. Governments should also push for project validators to be hired and paid for their services through a centralized fund rather than by project developers. Environmental agencies and government watchdogs cannot act effectively if they offer services to, or have stakes in, the very same bodies they are meant to regulate. The financial crisis showed us that misaligned incentives and conflicts of interest in rating agencies, for example, can bring markets to the brink of collapse. A repeat of this debacle in the carbon markets would spell both financial and climate disaster.

2 Ensure transparency in flows of funding for mitigation and adaptation

State parties to the UNFCCC must develop standard criteria for reporting on the financing of projects. Monitoring, reporting and evaluation systems need to be adaptable to various contexts, while enabling systematic reporting.

International finance mechanisms should provide clear and consistent guidance to national implementing agencies on the required standards for managing adaptation in their countries, from planning processes through to the management of funds, the implementation of projects and final evaluation. States need to ensure that mitigation and adaptation funds also increase national monitoring and reporting capacity. In the context of adaptation, countries with strong national systems should then be in a position to access financing directly from international financing mechanisms in order to fulfil adaptation activities, with an emphasis on domestic accountability – from governments to people – in the determination of funding priorities.

3 Monitor and oversee national climate policy and projects effectively

Government subsidies and support for the development of low-carbon infrastructure must be matched by strong oversight and regulatory institutions in order to protect public funds against fraud, particularly when the introduction of infrastructure is technically complex and requires specialized knowledge. National entities should exist with the capacity to monitor the disbursement and implementation of funds and apply tools for identifying corruption in the implementation of projects. They should also create space for independent civil society input into monitoring efforts.

4 Treat anti-corruption safeguards as integral elements in the design of adaptation and mitigation action

It is essential to build checks and balances into the core structures of climate policies as and when they are built. If the financial crises of recent years offer a central lesson, it is that oversight and regulation find it very difficult to play catch-up and restore order after markets have collapsed and trust has evaporated amid fraudulently inflated asset bubbles. Getting oversight and regulations for the carbon market correct from the start is essential in order to avoid a similar fate. Likewise, the green economy provides a boon for some commodities, from lithium in Bolivia to biofuels in Indonesia and to land for solar energy projects in North Africa. Putting in place public financial management and sound oversight before the revenues start flowing is essential for those countries that stand to profit. The opportunity offered by the green economy must not transform into a green resource course, similar to the pernicious effect that failed governance has had on oil-rich countries.

5 Step up policy coordination and bring key departments into line on climate change issues

Inconsistencies, ambiguities and loopholes in conjunction with poor policy coordination across departments present potential opportunities for exploitation in terms of arbitrage and corruption. Climate change is the archetypical cross-cutting issue and naturally concerns many parts of the executive arm of government; not everyone is walking in the same direction, however. Climate policies and governance are often inconsistent and ill-coordinated at best and subject to explicit inter-departmental power struggles at worst. Strong leadership, clearly assigned responsibilities and vigorous inter-agency coordination are key, and they need to be strengthened everywhere so as to corruption-proof climate governance.

6 *Build robust mechanisms for representation and public engagement that can cope with the increased public demand*

Climate change has entered public consciousness to stay. The ensuing upsurge in attention and engagement is understandable, since everyone is a stakeholder – and a custodian of future generations and our common planet. The 90,000 comments received on a key UNFCCC report and record turnouts for the global climate change summits have strained established mechanisms for consultation and engagement to their limit, however. More educational outreach and capacity-building are required if people are to contribute meaningfully, and if governments are to process, channel and aggregate all this attention.

Recommended actions for business

7 *Be a powerful voice in climate policy through open engagement and disclosure; it is an essential plank of corporate citizenship and a marker of commitment to climate change*

Reporting carbon footprints and carbon policies is not enough. The role of businesses in shaping the response to climate change goes beyond their own emissions. Businesses fight for their interests with lobbying powers that no other interest group can match in scale and sophistication, and they do so increasingly on issues related to climate change. Companies must disclose their climate policy engagement. As important shapers of policy outcomes, they bear responsibility to account for their positions, for the coalitions they participate in and the causes and groups they support. At the international level, business can also play an important part in demanding policy frameworks that set ambitious, fair and sustainable parameters, and should do so openly and in cooperation with other relevant stakeholders.

Once companies know what is expected of them, they are in a position to put more productive energy into how to get there, including disclosing their efforts.

8 *While going green, adhere to strong compliance, an anti-corruption regime and best corporate governance practice*

Business opportunities in adaptation or mitigation activities, such as large-scale infrastructure construction projects or public tenders in other fields, pose many well-known corruption challenges for the private sector. Various tools and action templates to counter these risks effectively are available, from internal training and transparent compliance systems to joint action initiatives such as integrity pacts, the EITI and the CoST to stamp out corruption in specific high-risk situations.

Businesses need to embrace these tools firmly and transfer them to their climate-change-related activities.

Given the high percentage of mitigation costs that will have to be borne by companies participating in the financial markets, the time is right to embed the highest standards for transparency and accountability in these emerging market mechanisms.

9 Commit ample resources to transparency, the disclosure of carbon emissions and green climate action

Good internal oversight mechanisms must include transparency. Major companies are now reporting systematically on emissions, but this reporting needs to be easily interpretable by non-expert groups and mainstreamed into sustainability reporting in order to reach the widest group of stakeholders.

Reporting on green action can also extend to other governance areas, such as internal codes of conduct. Such reporting should include the involvement of the board of directors, be set against benchmarks that measure progress over time, be accessible to stakeholders and the broader public when applicable and include independent processes of verification.

Accurate and publicly accessible reporting needs to be accompanied by a strong commitment not to abuse marketing techniques for 'greenwashing' products in an attempt to make them more palatable to climate-change-aware customers. Lifestyle changes and appropriate consumer choices are critical to avoiding a climate crisis. Companies that misrepresent the climate impact of their products fatally undermine this information flow, stall progress in moving towards a climate-friendly economy and, ultimately, erode consumer trust.

Recommended actions for civil society

10 Undertake independent oversight and monitoring in terms of governance and corruption risk in climate change issues

Increasingly, civil society has a critical role to play in measuring countries' commitments to reduce emissions, including the quality of monitoring and reporting, as well as the disbursement and implementation of climate funding. The fulfilment of these activities could be strengthened by incorporating anti-corruption tools and indicators into existing assessment criteria, however, and promoting 'open budget' and other public sector transparency tools in the climate change arena.

11 *Encourage the public's participation in and oversight of policy development at the local, national and international levels*

Civil society must play a bridging role, ensuring that the public is aware of national climate policies and decision-making on local projects. Civil society also needs to assist communities to engage with international schemes and, in the case of REDD, ensure that local communities understand carbon rights and retain the use of their resources.

Climate governance includes civil society's active engagement in national and international policy development, which goes some way to guarantee that the voices of the most marginalized are heard. Civil society must nonetheless advocate for a more sustained commitment from institutions and businesses that public participation has to be secured in local, national and international decision-making processes, including the UNFCCC.

Civil society in relevant countries should also seek to engage governments in the development of national action plans for adaptation, mitigation actions and their REDD readiness programmes in order to make sure that transparency and accountability are duly incorporated.

12 *Build broader coalitions for integrity in climate governance and ensure that the interests of all stakeholders are represented and taken into account*

Civil society is, arguably, more coordinated and sophisticated in its engagement on climate than on any other global public policy issue. Civil society will be even more effective in the climate change arena, however, if it consolidates its diverse areas of experience, from the environment to development, to humanitarian assistance and human rights, to the anti-corruption movement. With environmental NGOs in the lead, civil society coalitions have already taken great steps forward in presenting a unified voice, but much more can be done to raise visibility and create common approaches that cut across different NGO sectors. Conversely, much more can be done to integrate and mainstream anti-corruption approaches into the work of climate change organizations. It is hoped that the *Global Corruption Report* will contribute to greater NGO cooperation on this urgent issue.

Notes

1. Richard Baldwin, *Regulation Lite: The Rise of Emissions Trading*, Law, Society and Economy Working Paper no. 3/2008 (London: London School of Economics, 2008).
2. See http://eiti.org/.
3. See www.constructiontransparency.org.

PART 1

Introduction

1.0
Defining the challenge
Threats to effective climate governance

Transparency International

Introduction

There will perhaps be no greater challenge to global governance in the 21st century than climate change. Successfully meeting that challenge will require trust and cooperation between countries, across stakeholders, within communities and, fundamentally, in the new institutions and processes created to steer humanity's collective efforts. The difference between success and failure could not be starker.

'Climate governance' is a relatively new term in the development and environmental lexicon, but it is assuming increasingly regular usage. 'Governance' in its broad sense refers to 'a concept that goes beyond the traditional notion of government to focus on the relationships between leaders, public institutions and citizens, including the processes by which they make and implement decisions'.[1] The practice of 'good' governance contains certain core characteristics that promote equity and accountability and minimize opportunities for corruption. Good governance covers a range of practices, including respect for the rule of law, enhanced disclosure and greater participation. Increasingly, good governance also implies sustainable systems – both for governing and for outcomes.

'Climate governance' can be understood as the processes that currently exist at the international, national, corporate and local levels to address the causes and effects of climate change. This is a very wide spectrum, positioned in the framework of international conventions, norms and regulations, and applied through intergovernmental institutions, compliance mechanisms and funding bodies. Climate governance incorporates independent systems of governance in their own right – regional, national and city governance, as well as multi-stakeholder partnerships – thus increasing its complexity.[2]

Good climate governance needs to be at the centre of effective responses to climate change, including the disbursement and use of huge future investments.[3] Currently the system of climate governance is diverse and fragmented, and lacks connectivity – and, by extension, accountability – to those most affected by climate change. Efforts to strengthen the architecture of climate governance will therefore have to build in safeguards against risk, including corruption risks, in order for decisions made to have collective ownership, legitimacy and, ultimately, meaningful effect at the international, national and local levels.

The need for climate governance: science and the impacts of climate change

One starting point for assessing climate governance is to review the science of climate change (see box 1.1).[4] The summary of peer-reviewed scientific knowledge of climate change shows that the problem is acute and that the world has to act immediately.

The scientific summary also shows that those countries least responsible for climate change are those most likely to suffer, and those people who subsist on the land are likely to be least equipped with the capacities to adapt to climate change. In fact, as table 1.1 illustrates, the average per capita greenhouse gas (GHG) emissions in the five countries in the world most vulnerable to climate change are 20 times lower than in developed countries, where the average per capita emissions are more than 11 tonnes per annum.[5]

Country	Global Climate Risk Index score[6] (1990–2008)	Per capita GHG emissions per annum (tonnes CO_2)[7]
Bangladesh	8.00	0.25
Myanmar	8.25	0.25
Honduras	12.00	1.15
Vietnam	18.83	1.10
Nicaragua	21.00	0.79

Table 1.1 Climate risk against per capita emissions

In such countries, it is projected that increasing resilience to climate variation will need to take place just to maintain current levels of development or there is a serious

Box 1.1 Scientific basis of climate change

The synopsis of peer-reviewed science is presented by the Intergovernmental Panel on Climate Change (IPCC), whose 2007 report (its Fourth Assessment Report) found that 'warming of the climate system is unequivocal' and that most of the observed increase is 'very likely [above 90%] due to the observed increase in anthropogenic [man-made] greenhouse gas concentrations'.[8] This has resulted in rises in air temperature of an estimated 0.7°C in the last 100 years, and warming of waters and subsequent sea-level rise of between 2.4mm and 3.8mm per year from 1993 to 2003.

The IPPC developed six possible scenarios in 2000 for measuring the effect of future climate change, depending on the levels of commitment and realization of reducing GHG emissions, in which a worst-case 'business-as-usual' model shows a 6.4°C temperature rise by the end of the century.[9] Such scenarios have resulted in a general consensus among states that the global temperature rise should not exceed 2°C, beyond which climate 'feedback' (secondary changes due to temperature increases) and other events would become unpredictable and the Earth may reach a tipping point, beyond which the effects of climate change cannot be reversed.

Above a 2°C temperature increase, sea levels will continue to rise, oceans will acidify further, sea ice will shrink, precipitation will increase in high latitudes and decrease in subtropical regions, and it is 'very likely that extremes, heat waves and heavy precipitation events will continue to become more frequent'.[10] Discernible impacts are already recorded in biological systems with glacier lake outbursts, a reduced length for growing seasons, losses of coastal wetlands and bleaching of sea corals. With temperature rises exceeding 1.5–2.5°C, 20–30 per cent of plant and animal species are likely to be at increased risk of extinction.

What all this means for human development is difficult to predict, although the IPCC has concluded that it is highly likely that all regions will suffer negative economic effects, with 'developing countries expected to experience larger percentage losses'.[11] The most vulnerable societies will be those whose economies are closely linked to climate-sensitive resources and in areas of rapid urbanization where population growth is already putting stress on scarce resources.

---

risk of undoing progress made under the Millennium Development Goals.[12] The cumulative effect was described by the United Nations Development Programme (UNDP) *Human Development Report 2007/2008* as 'what could be the onset of major human development reversal in our lifetime', consigning 'the poorest 40% of the world's population – some 2.6 billion people – to a future of diminished opportunity'.[13]

The physical effects of climate change are clear. Climate change above 2°C will increase food and water scarcity, as well as leading to the flooding of coastal areas and increasing incidences of conflict over resources. Indigenous, forest and coastal peoples' livelihoods will be irrevocably altered by seasonal shifts, including the submergence of small island states due to sea level rise.[14] According to Care

International, forced displacement and mass migration 'will be in the tens of millions or more'.[15] The most vulnerable are most adversely affected, including women and children. Displacement in turn places huge burdens on neighbouring states, which often are also vulnerable to climate change and other stresses, multiplying governance challenges.

When responses to climate change are then partially or substantially lost to corruption, not only does the quality of projects suffer, but the result is that the ongoing effects of climate change are worst for those who can least afford it. A more strategic, ambitious approach to climate governance will therefore contribute to better outcomes for climate policy and, ultimately, for the planet. Getting it wrong could put a number of solutions at risk.

Evolving climate governance frameworks

The urgent need for international climate policy cooperation was first acknowledged at the UN Conference on Environment and Development (or Earth Summit) in Rio de Janeiro in 1992 with the adoption of the Rio Declaration on Environment and Development[16] for 'a new and equitable global partnership through the creation of new levels of cooperation among states, key sectors of societies and people' (preamble). Recognising the special situation and needs of developing countries and the responsibility of developed countries,[17] the declaration affirmed that 'environmental issues are best handled with [the] participation of all concerned citizens' through access to information and participation in decision-making processes. Agenda 21 of the Earth Summit also delegated nine representative groups to engage with the UN on sustainable development, and the same groupings are today represented in international climate governance.[18] While addressing environmental concerns more broadly, the Rio Declaration also constituted the blueprint for climate governance.

The Earth Summit produced the UN Framework Convention on Climate Change (UNFCCC), which remains the cornerstone of international climate policy, setting mandatory limits on individual states' greenhouse gas emissions according to the 'common but differentiated responsibilities' for industrialized (Annex I) and non-industrialized (non-Annex I) state parties.[19] Among the convention's scant provisions related to governance is one that states should 'encourage the widest participation in [the climate change] process' (article 4(I) (i)), through public access to information on climate change and its effects, and public participation in addressing climate change and its effects and developing adequate responses (article 6).

The UNFCCC's Conference of the Parties (COP) is tasked with reviewing implementation of the convention. It meets annually and comprises the most high-level political forum in climate governance, and may also 'seek and utilize, where appropriate, the services and cooperation of, and information provided by, competent international organizations and intergovernmental and non-governmental bodies'. The COP is supported by the Subsidiary Body for Implementation (SBI) and the Subsidiary Body for Scientific and Technological Advice (SBSTA), both of which play important oversight roles and provide limited access for public participation.

Finally, the convention mandated a Secretariat (often also referred to as the UNFCCC), to make arrangements for the COP and its subsidiary bodies, coordinate with other relevant secretariats and assist states in implementing the convention. Comprising some 400 professional staff with technical expertise, the Secretariat fulfils an important function in the overall system of climate governance.[20]

The Kyoto Protocol, which entered into force in 1997, was the first update to the convention, committing Annex I countries to reduce their GHG emissions by an average of 5 per cent against 1990 levels over the five-year period 2008–2012. It laid out three market-based mechanisms for creating incentives to reduce emissions: emissions trading, offset schemes in developing countries[21] and offset schemes between industrialized countries.[22] The governance of these incentives is spread across the Executive Board of the UN Clean Development Mechanism, the UN Joint Implementation Supervisory Committee, and various regional and national emissions trading schemes, all of which feed into reporting at the international level on efforts to meet Kyoto commitments.

The financing of efforts to address climate change is critical to any chance of future success. A multiplicity of funding mechanisms outside the UNFCCC,[23] administered by the World Bank, the UNDP, the Global Environment Facility (GEF), the European Commission and numerous bilateral donors,[24] some of which are relatively untested, create significant coordination challenges for governance. In addition, new pledges have been made by developed countries at the COP in December 2010 to jointly mobilize (or 'fast track') US$30 billion a year for the period 2010–2012, and US$100 billion a year by 2020 to address the mitigation and adaptation needs of developing countries.[25] The newly established Green Climate Fund, under the interim trusteeship of the World Bank, is expected to administer 'a significant share of new multilateral funding for adaptation'. However, the roles of Green Climate Fund's Transitional Committee still needs to be defined, as well as the creation of a new standing committee to improve coherence and coordination in the delivery of climate financing.[26]

Forestry currently accounts for 15–20 per cent of GHG emissions through deforestation,[27] and yet when forests are left undisturbed they act as an important natural 'sink' for CO_2 emissions. The UN programme for Reducing Emissions from Deforestation and Forest Degradation (REDD), established in September 2008, is the single largest programme to mitigate climate change in forestry, and therefore an important part of the climate governance system. The UN REDD Programme Policy Board provides strategic direction to the programme, and consists of donor and programme countries, intergovernmental agencies and, most notably, the chairperson of the UN Permanent Forum on Indigenous Issues and one civil society representative.[28] The reduction of emissions from deforestation and the enhancement of forest carbon sinks was formally endorsed by the COP in Cancún in December 2010 and REDD funding is already available to assist selected countries in preparing for REDD.

The international climate governance system is rounded out by the Ad Hoc Working Group on Long-term Cooperative Action (AWG-LCA), which was established 'to enable sustained implementation of the Convention beyond 2012 and the end of the Kyoto Protocol', and is therefore of critical importance to the shape of future governance.[29] As this infamously failed to materialize in the 15th COP in Copenhagen last year, the COP extended the mandate of the AWG-LCA to present its conclusions at COP 16 in Cancún, and again at COP 17 in Durban in 2012.

Outside these nominally interconnected instruments and bodies, a further 500 or so multilateral and bilateral agreements add to the scope of climate governance.[30] Although many separate initiatives may advance progressive agendas beyond the 'lowest common denominator' approach of international consensus-building, other processes create conflicting paths.[31] What is clear, however, is that fragmentation needs to be addressed in order to improve the coordination of international climate governance.

A typology of climate corruption risks

It is evident that levels of trust need to be increased for the current format of international climate governance to perform most effectively. The present mistrust is founded on suspicion among states in international negotiations, particularly between those that are historically responsible for climate change and those that are most likely to suffer its effects. The limited provision for public participation in the UNFCCC has also resulted in slow institutional responses to the need for wider engagement and access to information, which would lead to increased public ownership in the process. At the same time, civil society faces its own challenges of ensuring the equitable representation of interests at the international level. Nonetheless, despite slow consensus-building, states have now converged around the need to establish clear rules and compliance mechanisms for mitigation and adaptation, which will serve to strengthen legitimacy and trust.[32]

It is external risks, however, including corruption risks, that pose the most critical challenge to the sustainability and ultimate success of climate governance. From political decision-making and the generation of global financing for adaptation and mitigation to the workings of the carbon markets and national plans to build climate resilience, the following is a typology of cross-cutting corruption risks that represent key challenges to climate governance, all of which are dealt with in detail in the *Global Corruption Report*.

While the COP and many of its subsidiary bodies exhibit openness to public participation to varying degrees, a *lack of transparency and public disclosure* is visible across a number of other important decision-making processes. At the board level of the Clean Development Mechanism (CDM) and the Adaptation Fund, there is no room for any independent oversight of decision-making. In terms of funding, developed states are accused of failing to account for the source of 'new and additional' pledges, leading to accusations that they are diverted from official development assistance (ODA) commitments and double-counted as both development and climate funding. As members of the scientific community look reluctantly at the possible need for intentional manipulation of the Earth's atmosphere, moreover, concerns have been raised at the lack of required disclosure on geoengineering research and funding.

At the national level, the limited participation of stakeholders in the planning and monitoring of adaptation projects is likely to present corruption risks for national climate institutions. Countries that find themselves endowed with green economy resources will also have to take greater steps towards transparency in planning and financing the development of resources, as is already a concern in relation to lithium in Bolivia, for example.[33]

Policy capture and undue influence are fundamental risks. The scale of the transition has created powerful national lobby groups, which can adversely affect progress through undue political influence, media manipulation and the funding of front organizations.[34] In forestry, the risk of policy capture at the international level can affect, for instance, the definition of forests,[35] the issuance of permits and conditionality. Policy capture is also a risk in carbon trading.[36] Where carbon markets have been established, market players are seen to be involved in setting the rules to their benefit. As a result of lobbying activities, the power sector, for example, has a surplus of permits far above its actual emissions in Europe.[37]

Conflict of interest is a pervasive corruption risk in climate governance at the international and national level. In Spain a number of civil servants allegedly authorized licences for photovoltaic plants to companies owned by relatives.[38] At the international level, CDM Executive Board members are not excluded from occupying conflicting positions, such as membership of national approval boards, for example. Validators of CDM or REDD projects may have a potential conflict of interest as they are required to be paid by project developers, rather than out of a common pool, thus raising the risk of actually *increasing* emissions.[39] In the CDM, designated national authorities (DNAs) can, for instance, serve in ministries for industry or finance. In terms of funding, the current relationship between UNFCCC funds and administrators with potential vested interests, such as the World Bank and the Adaptation Fund (for which the World Bank plays an interim trustee role), can result in conflicts of interest, and revolving door policies are a particular problem. Similarly, the administration of short-term funding via the World Bank, derived from commitments in the Copenhagen Accord, has raised concerns about conditionality for what is intended to be unconditional support.

Creative accounting and reporting are serious cross-cutting risks. In some cases the miscounting of emissions is deliberate. Companies regulated under emissions trading schemes may have incentives to inflate their emissions data so as to establish a baseline that makes 'reductions' easier at a later date. In many other cases, however, inaccurate reporting is the result of legal loopholes or gaps in reporting rules. These causes must be addressed, as the use of unreliable data can weaken mitigation strategies and chip away at public confidence.

In the absence of sufficient oversight, creative accounting can lead to the *double-counting of emissions* by companies of their own reported mitigation efforts, which are also sold as credits, thus nullifying the environmental integrity of the emissions reductions. If developing countries adopt voluntary reductions targets, double-counting may also occur: emissions reductions generated from mitigation or REDD projects could be counted against national emissions and sold as credits to allow the same amount of pollution in developed countries.

Under the CDM and REDD initiatives, the same will happen if the additionality principle[40] is not met. If the projects would have taken place regardless of the CDM or REDD, then emission reductions are not 'additional' and cannot produce emissions credits for sale. Proving intent for project implementation is difficult, however, and at least one study suggests that, by 2007, up to 20 per cent of the credits generated for the CDM came from projects for which additionality was unlikely or questionable.[41] Verifying emissions reductions will be particularly difficult for REDD, and there is a real risk of fictitious projects being approved if monitoring is not adequate, as REDD projects are likely to occur in remote locations and be especially hard to measure.

The *mismanagement of public resources* provides perhaps the largest umbrella of corruption risks that threaten climate governance. Under adaptation projects, large amounts of public funds will flow into large-scale construction, a sector rife with corruption risk and issues of sustainability, particularly in countries with weak governance.[42] The need for increased technical specialization and ambiguous definitions of adaptation activities (as opposed to traditional development) make the benefits of adaptation more difficult to monitor, resulting in the potential for massive diversion of funds. From needs assessments, through the preparation and bid design phases, to contractor selection and contract award, to contract implementation and the final auditing phase, corruption is a risk. The effect is, in fact, increased vulnerability to climate change.

In carbon markets, the over-allocation of permits by the European Union's Emissions Trading System (EU ETS) resulted in a situation in which companies stood to profit from an allocation windfall.[43] As the case of Slovakia also shows, with the selling of 15 million tonnes of unused emission permits below the market price, there are strong risks of mismanagement and non-disclosure relating to the use of public resources.[44] Similar risks in terms of undue lobbying, as described above, include collusion to lower the price on allowances by coordinating bidding, while space for non-regulated players in the market raises risks of manipulation and fraud, including VAT fraud and laundering.[45]

In forestry, questions of land tenure, property and user rights can be subject to bribery at the national level. *Embezzlement and misappropriation of funds* are real risks that can occur during the disbursement of funding. Indigenous forest communities are particularly vulnerable to exploitation, as in many places land ownership is based solely on the fact that communities have lived in the forests for centuries. As this land now has 'added value' through carbon rights, unresolved questions of land tenure could lead to corruption, including cases in which private speculators mislead or force communities to sign over rights to the forest.

Finally, the direct effects of climate change on vulnerable populations increase the severity of corruption risks, and with it increase pressure on governance. Further scarcity of resources will increase social inequality and result in conflict or the large-scale displacement of communities. Migration in the tens of millions is likely to lead to increased corruption risks for these communities when they deal with bureaucracies in unfamiliar environments. Responding to climate change impacts in the form of increased humanitarian aid also brings corruption risks as humanitarian aid agencies and governments are faced with an increasing frequency and intensity of disasters.

Environments suffering from disasters are particularly prone to corruption risks and poor governance, with profound effects on their ability to recover.

Towards integrity in facing climate change

The challenges created by corruption in climate change are huge and require concerted action from governments, the private sector and civil society working towards a common goal. The first step in addressing these challenges is to understand the risks involved. The *Global Corruption Report* seeks to map these risks and provide ways to address them.

Part 2 of the report, which follows this one, reviews some of the major policy-making processes that shape climate governance and examines them with regard to the prospects for transparent, inclusive and accountable policy design. Part 3 then identifies the means to move beyond these governance challenges by looking at existing processes and standards for guidance. A national study from Austria assesses accountability and transparency checks in its national climate strategy.

Part 4 assesses the mitigation strategies for combating climate change. It also considers how international agreements can support the measuring, reporting and verification of mitigation activities. Part 4 gives significant attention to carbon markets, one of the most prevalent forms for reducing emissions, examining their design and challenges in governance terms. It then examines the responsibility of private sector actors to be accountable for actions that have a direct impact on mitigating climate change. This material is supported by case studies on carbon markets in Slovakia and Hungary, problematic environmental impact assessments in Sri Lanka, corporate integrity in Columbia, alleged corruption in solar plants in Spain and challenges to governing the extraction of green resources in Bolivia.

Part 5 assesses risks in adapting to climate change. It evaluates the challenges to the financing and monitoring of implementation at the international and national levels and measures increased corruption risks arising from the social and economic impacts of climate change. Case studies are presented on land entitlement issues in Kenya, polical influence in the Philippines and corruption in the world's largest mangrove forest in Bangladesh.

The *Global Corruption Report* concludes with Part 6, which provides a sector-specific focus on forestry. It positions good governance as a prerequisite to the success of REDD, examining REDD's current accountability mechanisms as well as the challenges to be faced in measuring and certifying carbon credits. Country contributions include forestry legislation in Nicaragua and the allocation of offsets in Papua New Guinea.

Notes

1. TI, *The Anti-Corruption Plain Language Guide* (Berlin: TI, 2009).
2. This has been termed the 'transnationalisation of global environmental governance'. Philipp Pattberg, 'Public–Private Partnerships in Global Climate Governance', *Wiley Interdisciplinary Reviews: Climate Change*, vol. 1 (2010), pp. 279–287, p. 280.
3. In developing countries alone, mitigation and adaptation may require funding of some US$250 billion annually, dwarfing total official development assistance (ODA) of US$100 billion a year. World Bank, *World Development Report 2010: Development and Climate Change* (Washington, DC: World Bank, 2009), p. 257.
4. Attempts have been made to claim a lack of objectivity in the findings of the Intergovernmental Panel on Climate Change (IPCC). Nonetheless, the most recent assessment of the legitimacy of the 2007 IPCC report by the Netherlands Environmental Assessment Agency 'found no errors that would undermine the main conclusions in the 2007 report', but found that 'in some instances the foundations for the summary statements should have been made more transparent'. See Netherlands Environmental Assessment Agency, *Assessing an IPCC Assessment: An Analysis of Statements on Projected Regional Impacts in the 2007 Report* (The Hague: Netherlands Environmental Assessment Agency, 2010). The review of the InterAcademy Council in August 2010 addressed reform of the IPCC's management structure, rather than the science, and made a number of recommendations to improve its management structure. See http://reviewipcc.interacademycouncil.net/ReportNewsRelease. html.
5. International Energy Agency (IEA), *CO$_2$ Emissions from Fuel Combustion 2009* (Paris: IEA, 2009).
6. Sven Harmeling, *Global Climate Risk Index 2010: Who Is Most Vulnerable? Weather-Related Loss Events since 1990 and How Copenhagen Needs to Respond* (Bonn: Germanwatch, 2010). Each score is calculated over 10 years according to death toll (1/6), deaths per inhabitants (1/3), absolute losses (1/6), losses per GDP (1/3).
7. IEA (2009).
8. IPCC, 'Summary for Policymakers', in IPCC, *Climate Change 2007: The Physical Science Basis: Contribution of Working Group I to the Fourth Assessment Report of the Intergovernmental Panel on Climate Change* (Cambridge: Cambridge University Press, 2007), pp. 1–18, p. 10. The consideration of remaining uncertainty 'is based on current methodology'.
9. Ibid., p. 13, table SPM 3.
10. Ibid., p. 15.
11. IPCC, 'Summary for Policymakers', in IPCC, *Climate Change 2007: Impacts, Adaptation and Vulnerability. Contribution of Working Group II to the Fourth Assessment Report of the Intergovernmental Panel on Climate Change*, (Cambridge: Cambridge University Press, 2007), p. 17.
12. United Nations Framework Convention on Climate Change (UNFCCC), 'Fact Sheet: The Need for Adaptation' (New York: UNFCCC, 2010).
13. United Nations Development Programme (UNDP), *Human Development Report 2007/2008: Fighting Climate Change: Human Solidarity in a Divided World* (New York: Palgrave Macmillan, 2007), pp. 1–2.
14. Alyson Brody et al., *Gender and Climate Change: Mapping the Linkages: A Scoping Study on Knowledge and Gaps* (Brighton: BRIDGE, Institute of Development Studies, 2008), at www. genanet.de/fileadmin/downloads/themen/climatetalk_life_dec8_2005.pdf.

15. Koko Warner et al., *In Search of Shelter: Mapping the Effects of Climate Change on Human Migration and Displacement* (Washington, DC: Care International, 2009). A Climate Change, Environment and Migration Alliance already exists, with the support of the International Organization for Migration (IOM), at www.ccema-portal.org.

16. The historical basis of climate governance can be linked back to the 1972 Declaration of the United Nations Conference on the Human Environment, which is reaffirmed in the preamble to the Rio Declaration.

17. 'In view of the pressures their societies place on the global environment and of the technologies and financial resources they command' (principle 7).

18. Agenda 21, chapters 23–32, (i) business and industry, (ii) children and youth, (iii) farmers, (iv) indigenous people, (v) local authorities, (vi) NGOs, (vii) scientific and technological community, (viii) women and (ix) workers and trade unions.

19. It should be noted that the Bali Action Plan and the Copenhagen Accord do not categorize countries as industrialized or non-industrialized but, rather, as developed or developing countries. *The Global Corruption Report* applies both categorizations according to the context in which they are being applied.

20. See www.greeningtheblue.org/what-the-un-is-doing/united-nations-framework-convention-climate-change-unfccc.

21. Article 12.

22. Article 6.

23. Only the Adaptation Fund, managed by the Adaptation Fund Board and funded from 2 per cent of the proceeds from CDM projects, currently falls directly under the UNFCCC governance architecture.

24. See www.climatefundsupdate.org/listing.

25. Draft decision -/CP.16, Outcome of the work of the Ad Hoc Working Group on long-term Cooperative Action under the Convention, paragraphs 95 and 98.

26. Draft decision -/CP.16, paragraphs 102–112. For a summary of the current amounts pledged by contributing countries and the amounts committed, see www.faststartfinance.org/content/contributing-countries.

27. The figure is 15 per cent of global emissions, according to G. R. van der Wer et al., 'CO$_2$ Emissions from Forest Loss', *Nature Geoscience*, vol. 2 (2009), pp. 737–738.

28. UN-REDD Programme, *Rules or Procedure and Operational Guidance* (New York: UN-REDD Programme, 2009), paragraph 1.2.3.

29. The AWG-LCA was established as part of the Bali Action Plan, adopted in 2008.

30. See section 2.1 of this volume.

31. For example, the 2005 Asia-Pacific Partnership on Clean Development and Climate departs from key features of the UN climate regime, notably the consideration of climate change impacts and the differentiation between developed and developing countries. See Frank Biermann et al., 'The Fragmentation of Global Governance Architectures: A Framework for Analysis', *Global Environmental Politics*, vol. 9 (2009), pp. 14–40.

32. Farewell statement at the closing plenary of the SBI and the SBSTA, by Yvo de Boer, executive secretary of the UNFCCC, 9 June 2010.

33. See section 4.8.1 of this volume.

34. In one of the most egregious examples, a US lobbying firm acting on behalf of a major coal lobby group sent lawmakers forged letters that claimed to be from the NAACP (National Association for the Advancement of Colored People) and that urged opposition to climate legislation.

35. A narrow definition of deforestation under the Kyoto Protocol means that, if a forest area is cleared but not intended for another land use, this is not considered deforestation and no increases in emissions must be reported.
36. In Australia, for example, where a proposed cap-and-trade bill failed to materialize, an environmental group accused companies of intentionally misleading lawmakers about the damaging consequences of climate change legislation on business. Australian Conservation Foundation, 'Complaint to the Australian Competition and Consumer Commission', 11 June 2009.
37. Richard Baldwin, *Regulation Lite: The Rise of Emissions Trading*, Law, Society and Economy Working Paper no. 3/2008 (London: London School of Economics, 2008), p. 10.
38. See section 4.7.1 of this volume.
39. If project verifiers are over-eager to provide a positive review of the project they are paid to assess, credits generated from these projects allow emissions to occur elsewhere, despite the fact that no corresponding emissions are reduced.
40. The principle of additionality states that mitigation projects are eligible to earn emission credits only if they can be proved to have been implemented specifically for the CDM.
41. See section 4.3 of this volume.
42. The World Bank estimates that between 5 and 30 per cent of construction costs are currently lost to corruption, burdening developing countries to the tune of some US$18 billion a year. Charles Kenny, *Construction, Corruption and Developing Countries*, Policy Research Working Paper no. 4271 (Washington, DC: World Bank, 2007). See also section 5.3 of this volume.
43. Baldwin (2008).
44. See section 4.3.1 of this volume.
45. EuObserver.com, 'EU emissions trading an 'open door' for crime, Europol says', 10 December 2009; *Sydney Morning Herald* (Australia), 'Carbon trading used to launder money', 16 July 2010.

1.1

Mapping the climate change and governance challenge

The big picture

Alyson Warhurst[1]

In which parts of the world are the twin challenges of responding to the impact of climate change and improving governance systems most imminent? The maps presented here explore some of the interrelationships between climate change and corruption. Specifically, they reveal how global risks combine in some countries and suggest that policy responses must consider all the risks at stake and their interrelatedness, rather than look at climate change in isolation. This analysis is crucial, as corruption can undermine efforts to combat the impacts of climate change.

Global climate models predict an increase in the frequency and intensity of extreme hydro-meteorological events, 97 per cent of which occur in developing countries. These events, combined with changing temperature and rainfall patterns, could lead to associated changes in water availability and quality. Agricultural practices are also at risk from climate change as a result of soil erosion and flood-related human displacement, as well as changes in yields, the suitability of certain crops and the distribution of pests.

Figure 1.1 shows how these global risks are not only interlinked but conflate to undermine development gains, particularly in Africa and low- and middle-income countries elsewhere. These interdependencies mean that the ineffective mitigation of climate change and its impacts will make the world more vulnerable to other risks, including energy price shocks, infectious diseases such as malaria, displacement, political instability and even conflict.

Comparing this risk landscape with a world map of perceived corruption illustrates the significant extent to which climate and governance challenges coincide. As figure 1.2 shows, the results are alarming. The countries most vulnerable to the impacts of climate change are also those that face very serious corruption risks.

All five countries most affected by climate change are in the bottom tercile in terms of perceived levels of corruption, and none of the 20 most affected countries score higher than 3.6 on the Corruption Perceptions Index (CPI) scale (ranging from 0, extremely corrupt, to 10, very clean). Certain countries are particularly vulnerable if conflict risk and population growth are included, which is all the more worrying because some are neighbours. These countries include Eritrea, Ethiopia, Somalia and Sudan, as well as Afghanistan, Bangladesh, India, Nepal and Pakistan. Haiti emerges from this analysis as extremely vulnerable.

The twin challenges of climate change and corruption turn out to be even more daunting when it is considered that corruption and climate vulnerability reinforce each other in a number of ways, as many sections in the *Global Corruption Report* demonstrate.

For example, corrupt governments that face conflicts of interest, pander to special interests and are prone to use public money to line their own pockets are less likely to design and implement fair and equitable climate policies. Efforts to increase resilience to the impacts of climate change are more likely to cost more and be ineffective due to corruption. This further inhibits climate change preparedness, by undermining the capital flows necessary for critical infrastructures. In addition, corruption takes money away from essential services such as health systems, clean water delivery, sanitation and flood defences, which are all essential to deal with the fallout from climate change. All this makes the ability to keep corruption in check a critical factor for a country's capabilities to react to climate change.

Figure 1.3 places this institutional dimension of good governance in a broader context. It presents Maplecroft's sub-national Climate Change Vulnerability Index (CCVI) at the global scale. This index uses three indicator clusters to assess the overall capacity of businesses, economies and societies to respond to the risks from the changes in economic, social and environmental conditions that result from climate change. These clusters relate to the risk of exposure to climate change and associated extreme events (drought, cyclones, landslides, flooding and sea-level rise), the degree of current sensitivity to that exposure and the ability of the country to adjust to – or take advantage of existing or anticipated stresses resulting from – climate change.

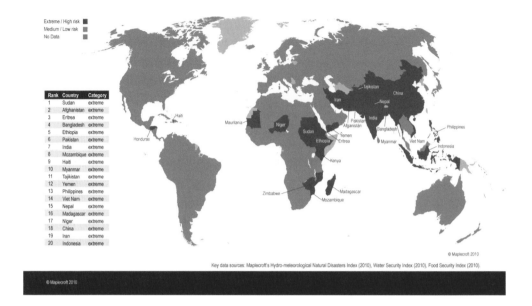

Figure 1.1 Global map of combined risk of hydro-meteorological disasters and water and/or food security 2011

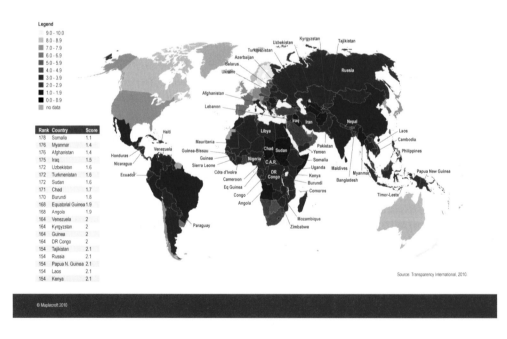

Figure 1.2 Corruption Perceptions Index 2010

The CCVI recognizes that the most serious vulnerabilities to climate change are found in a group of developing countries with socio-economic systems that are ill-equipped to address development challenges such as food and water security, in addition to being burdened by unstable economies and weak institutions. This is the case for a large number of countries, with south Asia and Africa of particular concern. Of the top 20 most at-risk countries in the CCVI, nine are in Africa and eight in south Asia.

A joint perspective on all these risks leaves no doubt: governance risks play an important role in determining the socio-economic vulnerability to climate change. The challenges, in terms of building accountable institutions, expediting development and responding to the impact of climate change, are significant and closely interrelated for many countries around the world. Quite distressingly, the main burden falls on a group of countries that have played almost no part in causing the climate change problem in the first place.

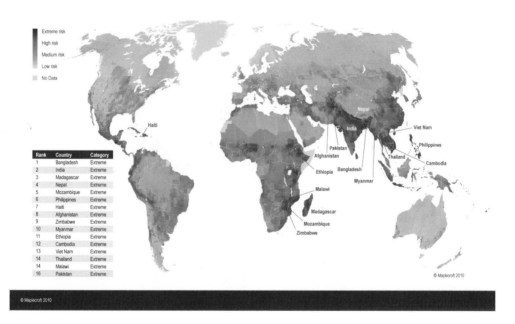

Figure 1.3 Maplecroft's Climate Change Vulnerability Index 2010/11

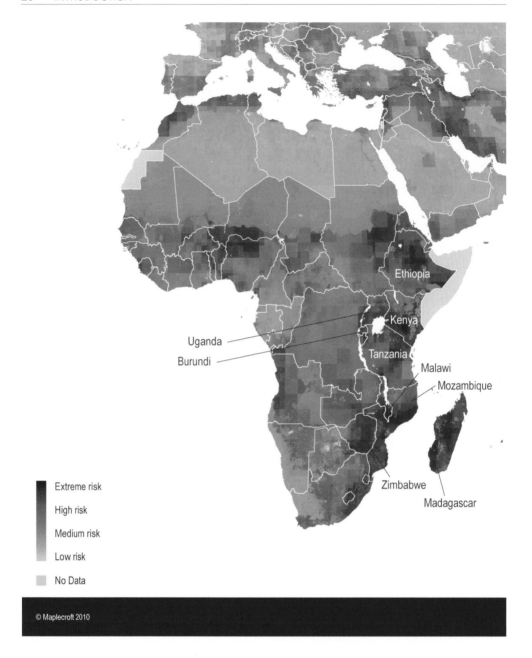

Figure 1.4 Maplecroft's Climate Change Vulnerability Index 2010/11, Africa

Notes

1. Alyson Warhurst is chief executive officer of Maplecroft.

PART 2

The climate policy framework

Examining the effectiveness and accountability of current processes

2.0
The climate policy framework
Examining the effectiveness and accountability of current processes

Essential climate policies are still in the making and the institutional architecture for deciding on specific policy options is vast, diverse and rapidly evolving. The contributions in this part focus on a number of key policy processes at different levels that all play a role in devising the overarching policy frameworks that will shape the global response to climate change. Process matters. The extent to which climate policy-making is organized to be transparent, accountable and inclusive determines how affected by policy capture, undue influence or corruption the eventual policies are likely to be. The analysis shows clearly that despite disproportionate attention to global climate summits, other important decisions are being taken from global to local level. This patchwork of institutions and forums for climate governance is mirrored by a proliferation of collective agreements, estimated to have surpassed 500 over the last 30 years.[1]

The opening contribution by Peter Newell sets the scene and traces the evolution of the most visible segment of global climate policy-making, the series of international summits that gave rise to the United Nations Framework Convention on Climate Change (UNFCCC), the Kyoto Protocol and, more recently the Copenhagen Accord. Newell probes the inclusiveness of the process, the capability of different actors to engage in a meaningful way and – with a view to the events in Copenhagen – discusses the tension between inclusiveness and manageability. Important decisions on the direction of climate policies are also taken at regional level. Progressive policies at European Union (EU) level, for example, can act as pacemaker for positive change. At the same time, failure by the EU to take action offers good cover for others to shirk their responsibilities. The contribution by Anne Therese Gullberg scrutinises two important junctures in EU policy-making with regard to the relative influence that business and green non-governmental organizations (NGOs) managed to bring to the table. Her analysis contributes hard empirical evidence to a debate often characterized by anecdotal or ideologically driven claims.

Honing in on key policy-making processes at national level, Paul Blumenthal provides key figures and a compelling case study to demonstrate how climate lobbying in the US has dramatically increased and may veer towards manipulative, illegal tactics. His contribution also highlights how much more diverse the landscape of interests and influence has become and seeks to provide a first answer to the question of whether this diversification is actually transforming established power balances.

Decision-making processes at city level are easy to underestimate, yet they play a key role in shaping the course of climate policies. The twin challenges of managing urban growth and establishing sound governance systems are evident. None of the 20 urban areas projected to grow fastest between 2006 and 2020 are ranked among the 70 countries perceived to be least corrupt according to the Transparency International (TI) Corruption Perceptions Index 2010.[2] David Dodman and David Satterthwaite present a fascinating account of the role that cities play in both mitigation of and adaptation to climate change, and how these challenges are interlinked with good governance and integrity in decision-making.

Dodman and Satterthwaite's contribution also highlights that, historical responsibilities notwithstanding, policy-making in developing countries assumes an increasingly important role in tackling climate change. This observation is further developed in contributions that look at two of the most important emerging actors on the climate policy scene, India and China. Very often the articulated positions of these countries are simply assumed to reflect an elusive 'national interest', but are rarely traced back to domestic configurations of interests and the decision-making processes that filter and translate these interests into policies. For India, Sudhir Chella Rajan opens this 'black box' of domestic climate policy-making by sketching out the main matrix of interests involved and gauging the prospects for public-interest oriented outcomes in the context of current governance structures. Dieter Zinnbauer, with kind support from Jie Yu, assesses the main configuration of domestic interests in China, as well as important institutional conditions and dynamics and their proneness to policy capture or public-interest accommodation.

The final contribution in this part may seem unusual at first, since it focuses on climate policy-making in a country that may not appear of comparable importance in the context of global climate policies. Yet, Austria is representative of the mitigation challenge and governance context that characterizes smaller industrialized countries. And as Shahanaz Mueller demonstrates in her interesting case study, even for this group of countries there are a series of accountability and responsibility challenges to tackle in order to make climate policies effective.

Notes

1. Frank Biermann et al., 'The Fragmentation of Global Governance Architectures: A Framework for Analysis', paper prepared for the Amsterdam Conference on the Human Dimensions of Global Environmental Change, 2–4 December 2009.
2. See www.citymayors.com/statistics/urban_growth1.html and Transparency International, Corruption Perceptions Index 2010 (2010).

2.1

From global power politics to responsible collective governance

The transparency and inclusiveness of international climate governance institutions and processes

Peter Newell[1]

Issues of transparency, integrity and inclusiveness are central to the effectiveness and legitimacy of the international community's response to climate change. Amid huge disparities in wealth and power, often weak institutional structures and competing claims about rights and responsibilities (and therefore about who should be held to account for what), these issues are at the heart of many key debates about responsibility for action on climate change, even if they are not usually named in those terms.

To understand these challenges it is helpful to give a brief overview of the institutional landscape for climate governance, trace its evolution, and highlight issues of participation and accountability for one of the most pressing global challenges of our time.

The international climate change regime: the main institutions

International negotiations on climate change are organized around a number of key actors, institutions and decision-making processes. Internationally, three institutions are critical to the process of negotiating climate change policy.

The Conference of the Parties (COP) to the UNFCCC and the Kyoto Protocol is the ultimate decision-making body for climate negotiations. It meets annually to review progress on the commitments within these treaties and update them in light of the latest scientific advice.

Second, the UNFCCC Secretariat, based in Bonn since 1996, has a key and often underestimated role to play in shaping the outcomes of the negotiations.[2] It organizes and oversees the negotiations, prepares the necessary documentation and is responsible for overseeing the reporting of emissions profiles and projects funded through the Kyoto Protocol. Guided by the parties to the convention, it provides organizational support and technical expertise to the negotiations and institutions, and facilitates the flow of information on the implementation of the convention. The Secretariat's executive secretary is responsible for guiding the negotiations towards a successful conclusion.

Finally, the Subsidiary Body for Scientific and Technological Advice (SBSTA) and the Subsidiary Body for Implementation (SBI) plus ad hoc working groups take forward negotiations on specific issues that the COP ultimately has to approve. For example there is currently an Ad Hoc Working Group on Further Commitments for Annex I parties under the Kyoto Protocol.

Climate politics in brief

Climate change has progressed from being a cause for concern among scientists to gaining recognition as an issue deserving of a collective global political effort orchestrated by the UN (box 2.1).

Box 2.1 The global governance of climate change: a chronology

1988: World Conference on the Changing Atmosphere: politicians and scientists conclude that 'humanity is conducting an unintended, uncontrolled, globally pervasive experiment whose ultimate consequences could be second only to nuclear war'. The conference recommends reducing CO_2 emissions by 20 per cent by 2005.
1990: The Intergovernmental Panel on Climate Change (IPCC) publishes its First Assessment Report.
1991: The Intergovernmental Negotiating Committee is set up to oversee negotiations towards an international agreement.
1992: 154 countries sign the UNFCCC at the UN Conference on Environment and Development in Rio de Janeiro, which aims to stabilize emissions at 1990 levels by 2000 as part of an overall goal of stabilizing greenhouse gas (GHG) concentrations in the atmosphere at a level that will prevent dangerous interference with the climate system.
1994: The UNFCCC enters into force on 21 March.

1995: The First COP agrees in Berlin that binding commitments by industrialized countries are required to reduce emissions.

1995: The IPCC publishes its Second Assessment Report, which states: 'The balance of evidence suggests a discernible human influence on global climate.'

1996: The Second COP in Geneva sees the US agree to legally binding targets to reduce emissions as long as emissions trading is included in an agreement.

1997: More than 150 countries sign the Kyoto Protocol, which binds 38 industrialized (Annex I) countries to reduce GHG emissions by an average of 5.2 per cent below 1990 levels during the period 2008–2012.

2000: The negotiations at COP 6 in The Hague collapse amid disagreements principally between the US and Europe about the use of the Kyoto Protocol's flexibility mechanisms.

2001: US President George Bush announces that the US is to withdraw from the Kyoto Protocol.

2001: In Marrakesh the final elements of the Kyoto Protocol are worked out, particularly the rules and procedures by which the flexible mechanisms will operate.

2004: The Buenos Aires Programme of Work on Adaptation and Response Measures is agreed upon at COP 10.

2005: The Kyoto Protocol becomes law on 16 February after Russia's ratification pushes the emissions of ratified Annex I countries over the 55 per cent mark.

2005: The first meeting of the Parties to the Kyoto Protocol takes place in Montreal at COP 11.

2006: At the second meeting of the Parties (COP 12), the Nairobi Work Programme on Adaptation and the Nairobi Framework on Capacity-Building for the Clean Development Mechanism (CDM) are agreed upon.

2007: The IPCC publishes its Fourth Assessment Report.

2007: At COP 13 the Bali Action Plan is agreed upon, calling for a long-term goal for emissions reductions; measurable, reportable, verifiable mitigation commitments including nationally appropriate mitigation actions by developing countries as well as enhanced adaptation, action on technology development and transfer, and financial resources and investment to support these measures.

2009: COP 15 takes place in Copenhagen. It ends in controversy with failure to produce a binding accord as hoped. Rather, a Copenhagen Accord is agreed among small number of parties which other governments are encouraged to recognize.

2010: COP 16 takes place in Cancún. While it fails to create a binding international agreement, progress on key areas such as finance, adaptation and technology transfer is made. Decisions taken are agreed by an overwhelming majority in a concerted effort to keep the UN negotiations on track.

The UNFCCC was opened for signature at the UN Conference on Environment and Development summit in Rio de Janeiro in 1992. As the first major milestone in the history of climate diplomacy, the UNFCCC provided a framework for global action on the issue. Given the sharp differences of opinion and the relative lack of momentum behind the issue at the time, the fact that the UNFCCC was agreed upon at all can be regarded as a considerable achievement.

The agreement set an ultimate objective of 'avoiding dangerous interference in the climate system', defined as aiming to stabilize concentrations of greenhouse gases (GHGs) in the atmosphere, and listed policies and measures countries might adopt to achieve this end. Acknowledging the vast differences in contributions to the problem, the convention established the principle of 'common but differentiated responsibility'[3] and recognized that developing countries were not yet in a position to assume their own obligations. The commitments of developing countries towards tackling the issue were made contingent on the receipt of financial resources and technology transfer from industrialized countries that were meant to be 'additional' to existing aid budgets.

Attention then turned to how to realize the general nature of the commitments contained in the UNFCCC. With scientific assessments of the severity of climate change becoming increasingly common and awareness growing of the inadequacy of existing policy responses, momentum built for a follow-up to the convention.[4] The UNFCCC's built-in requirement that the parties review the adequacy of parties' commitments in light of evolving science led to the adoption of the 1995 Berlin Mandate. The COP agreed to negotiate a new set of 'quantified emissions limitations and reduction obligations' (QELROs) – or legally binding targets for industrialized countries to reduce GHG emissions.

The Kyoto Protocol, concluded in 1997, was the outcome of this. Signed by more than 150 countries, it binds 38 industrialized (Annex I) countries to reduce GHG emissions by an average of 5.2 per cent below 1990 levels during the period 2008–2012. It fixes differentiated targets for industrialized countries while setting in train a process to further elaborate joint implementation schemes, set up an emissions trading scheme (ETS) and create the Clean Development Mechanism (CDM).

The process for finalizing the rules and operational details of the Kyoto Protocol was agreed upon at COP 4 in 1998 as part of the Buenos Aires Plan of Action. In November 2000 parties met in The Hague at COP 6 in an effort to complete these negotiations, but they failed amid a growing rift in particular between the EU and the US.[5] Having lobbied hard for including market-based mechanisms that would allow industrialized countries maximum flexibility, the US walked away from the Kyoto Protocol in 2001.

As discussed below, the US refused to ratify Kyoto partly because its economic competitors in the developing world were not required by the protocol to reduce their own emissions. Without US involvement, many assumed the inevitable demise of the Kyoto Protocol. If the largest contributor to the problem and most powerful economy in the world was not on board, what incentive was there for others to sign up? Instead, the absence of the US served to galvanize the EU and the G77+China grouping into further action and, with Russia's ratification of Kyoto, the protocol entered into force in 2005.

Subsequent negotiations have focused on detailed issues concerning the implementation and enforcement of Kyoto and, increasingly, what might replace it as the end of its implementation period (2012) draws ever closer. Agreed upon at COP 7, the Marrakesh Accords established the rules and procedures for operating flexible mechanisms including the CDM, as well as details on reporting and methodologies. Importantly, they also established three new funds: the Least Developed Countries (LDC) Fund, the Special Climate Change Fund and the Adaptation Fund.

This work continued through to the Buenos Aires Programme of Work on Adaptation and Response Measures, agreed upon at COP 10 in 2004. This was followed at COP 11 in Montreal with the creation of the Ad Hoc Working Group on Further Commitments for Annex I parties under the Kyoto Protocol. At COP 12 in Nairobi, dubbed the 'Africa COP', there was significant discussion about financing issues and how to increase the number of CDM projects being hosted by the poorest regions of the world, most notably sub-Saharan Africa. The meeting produced the Nairobi Work Programme on Adaptation and the Nairobi Framework on Capacity-Building for the CDM.[6]

A year later, at COP 13, the Bali Action Plan set the path towards negotiations at Copenhagen by calling for a long-term goal for emissions reductions; measurable, reportable and verifiable mitigation commitments including nationally appropriate mitigation actions by developing countries; enhanced adaptation; action on technology development and transfer; and financial resources and investment to support these measures.[7] COP 15 in Copenhagen in 2009 was expected to 'seal the deal' by concluding a comprehensive legally binding agreement. It failed for reasons discussed below, but did produce a Copenhagen Accord, a short text negotiated by a small number of the world's most powerful countries which other countries were then encouraged to endorse. COP 16 in Cancún in 2010 meanwhile took the accord further, outlining a process for reaching decisions on a new Green Climate Fund, on adaptation and technology transfer and further commitments by developing countries to submit their mitigation actions to international measurement and verification.

Challenges to an open, accountable and inclusive process

Issues of participation and openness in particular will be crucial to a successful outcome for future climate summits. Effective transparency and accountability in international climate politics continue to face a number of considerable challenges, however.

Long chains of delegation

First, long chains of delegation separate citizens from the climate negotiators who represent their countries. This is because, 'lacking significant information about the substance of the discussions, it is virtually impossible, for the ordinary citizen, to make informed choices about who to support, who and what to query, or who to ask for changes to their positions. With many people around the world, and first and foremost the poorest, beginning to feel the heat, or water rising in their house, the accountability gap between decision makers and people affected by climate change seems to widen to an unbridgeable gulf'.[8]

The capability and influence gap

Such problems are compounded by the uneven participation of countries and civil society organizations in the international negotiations. There are inequities in capacity and participation, meaning that most governments from developing countries are not able even to be continuously present throughout the entire negotiation process, let alone adequately represent their citizens' interests in arenas where demands for legal and scientific expertise are high.

While a remarkable 194 countries attended the Copenhagen summit in December 2009, this number masks disparities in effective negotiating capability.[9] For example, the top five polluting countries were able to field more than three times the number of delegates than the five countries considered to be most affected by climate change.[10] Because the delegations of many developing countries lack capacity, they have difficulty effectively participating in the many meetings that are held simultaneously and ensuring their voice is heard. Neither do they have access to the 'informal' meetings held before and during COP meetings, where the major players and contributors to the problem come together to advance progress, but from which most smaller and less influential countries are excluded. We saw this problem come to a head in Copenhagen, where many countries felt aggrieved that the accord was produced by so few countries. Distrust was compounded when a draft accord that a select number of countries had produced was leaked during the first week of the meeting. This experience led to significant efforts by the Mexican presidency at

COP 16 to ensure that negotiations were as transparent as possible and that the texts under negotiation were the only texts on the table.

A fragmented governance landscape

Another major challenge for accountability, openness and transparency derives from the fact that the governance of climate change is highly dispersed and fragmented, reaching well beyond the key institutions introduced earlier. Responsibilities are shared among a multitude of actors operating across numerous scales and in a bewildering number of sites.

Relevant actors include global institutions such as the Intergovernmental Panel on Climate Change (IPCC) and the UNFCCC Secretariat, regional bodies such as the EU, national governments (including trans-governmental networks of environmental regulators), groupings of cities, coalitions of corporate actors and an array of civil society networks. Each is a source of governance in its own right, producing standards and regulations, creating norms of behaviour and developing reporting mechanisms to oversee the implementation of climate-related projects.[11] With such a wide spectrum of actors it is often difficult to specify who is accountable for the governance of which aspect of climate change responses.

In a terrain in which climate politics shifts rapidly and involves a plurality of private and public actors creating formal and informal sites of regulation, challenges of transparency and accountability are heightened – given that traditional channels of representation and participation often do not exist in private and non-state spheres, and that rights to information and consultation are not easily applied to private actors. The spectacular growth in private standards and public–private partnerships as additional important sites and sources of climate governance therefore raises important questions about participation, openness and transparency.[12] Several other articles in the *Global Corruption Report* demonstrate that some forms of private governance allow for more participation, transparency and accountability than others.[13]

A process between openness and manageability

The main negotiation process features a bewildering array of non-government, business and other organizations that are registered to participate alongside the formal negotiations. Though they do not have formal voting rights, they are allowed to intervene and are often admitted onto government delegations, giving them access to all meetings. In many ways these actors are non-governmental 'diplomats' who perform many of the same functions as state delegates, representing the interests of their constituencies, engaging in information exchange, negotiating and providing policy advice.[14]

In principle, this means the decision-making process is considered relatively open to the participation of non-state actors. Nevertheless, what was considered by some to be an excessive degree of direct participation in the process during the plenary sessions at earlier rounds of negotiations resulted in observers being banned from the floor of the UNFCCC meeting room unless they found their way onto government delegations. This turned direct public access to the core negotiations from a general entitlement into a privilege granted by government delegations at their own discretion to a selected few.

This has not reduced demands for participation – a situation that produced a crisis during the Copenhagen summit, when the premises could not accommodate a record 900[15] observer organizations and the security entourage of 196 heads of states joining the talks. Entry passes were rationed – often under chaotic circumstances – and many observers were shut out of the negotiations building, gravely undermining the ambition for an inclusive and open process, and putting into question the feasibility of such a mega-process.

The indispensable role of civil society

These access problems are particularly worrying when we consider the crucial role networks and coalitions of civil society have played in improving the transparency and openness of climate change governance.[16] Some elements of civil society have succeeded in enhancing the degree of transparency of climate change negotiations by working with journalists, adopting protest strategies and publishing their own widely read summaries, briefings and analyses of the negotiations, such as the Climate Action Network's *ECO* newsletter.[17]

This in turn has increased the possibilities of public scrutiny of relevant officials and agencies, helped raise awareness of climate change among different publics, and increased levels of public engagement with the issue in both national and international politics. Civil society groups have led on the issue of evaluating commitments and holding governments accountable for their fulfilment. Finally, in respect of redress, recent climate activism shows a growing interest in using human rights tools as a means to obtain redress for victims of climate change.[18]

Despite these vital functions assumed by civil society groups, a number of concerns remain.

Disparities in effective representation between industrialized and developing countries not only affect state parties, they are also evident among observer organizations. During the Kyoto negotiations only a fourth of the organizations in attendance came from the global South, and many of these could afford to send only one or two observers. Although by summer 2009 more than 1000 organizations from 80 countries had obtained observer status, a closer look reveals that the majority are based in Europe and North America. More than 210 organizations from the US, for example, are registered as observers, alongside 100 groups from the UK and 92 from Canada. Meanwhile, no developing country except for Brazil, China and India manage to bring more than 10 observer organizations to the table.[19]

Issues of internal NGO governance, transparency and stakeholder accountability are also high on the agenda. Influence comes with responsibilities and the legitimate demand for the public to know who is behind specific groups, what agenda they pursue and how well they manage the representational mandate (if any) and financial resources entrusted to them by their supporters. Many groups are not sufficiently proactive in living up to these standards, and these shortcomings have become particularly problematic with the emergence of organizations advancing narrow private interests but claiming to represent public interests in climate policy.[20]

The growing demand for accountability

Challenges of openness, consultation and participation in the climate regime look set to deepen, intensify and evolve as the regime expands to cover more issues, sectors and actors. This is especially true when authority is deferred to new organizations and institutions to create rules and markets to deliver action on climate change. The climate governance landscape is becoming more multifaceted and multilayered and neither the importance nor scale of the accountability gap should be underestimated. As one assessment puts it:

> *Mending the current disjuncture between those involved in the policy formation, negotiating and decision making process, and the citizens who are most vulnerable to climate change is to a significant extent a matter of closing the accountability gap in global climate governance. Accountability on its own will not be sufficient to adequately address the climate change challenge. It is however a fundamental and necessary condition for building a socially and environmentally effective global climate governance system that delivers for people.[21]*

Notes

1. Peter Newell is professor of international development at the University of East Anglia.
2. Joanna Depledge, *The Organization of the Global Negotiations: Constructing the Climate Regime* (London: Earthscan, 2005).

3. UN, *United Nations Framework Convention on Climate Change* (Bonn: UNFCCC Secretariat, 1992), at http://unfccc.int/resources/docs/convkp/conveng.pdf.
4. Michael Grubb et al., *The Kyoto Protocol: A Guide and Assessment* (London: Earthscan and Royal Institute of International Affairs [RIIA], 1999).
5. Michael Grubb and Farhana Yamin, 'Climatic Collapse at The Hague: What Happened, Why, and Where Do We Go From Here?', *International Affairs*, vol. 77 (2001), pp. 261–276.
6. Chukwumerije Okereke et al., *Assessment of Key Negotiating Issues at Nairobi Climate COP/ MOP and What it Means For the Future of the Climate Regime*, Working Paper no. 106 (Norwich: Tyndall Centre for Climate Change Research, 2007).
7. Benito Müller, 'Bali 2007: On the Road Again! Impressions from the Thirteenth UN Climate Change Conference', Oxford Energy and Environment Comment (Oxford: Oxford Institute for Energy Studies [OIES], February 2008); Jennifer Morgan, *Towards a New Global Climate Deal: An Analysis of the Agreements and Politics of the Bali Negotiations* (London: E3G, 2008).
8. One World Trust, 'Beyond Reach? Realizing Accountability in Climate Change Governance', *Accountability in Action* (October 2009), at http://newsletter.electricputty.co.uk/T/ViewEmail/ r/2C4231BBBECAA6E2/FF375D0D1994B87E6A4D01E12DB8921D.
9. List of participants, Conference of the Parties, 15th session, Copenhagen, 7–18 December 2009, http://unfccc.int/resource/docs/2009/cop15/eng/inf01p01.pdf.
10. TI calculations based on COP 15 documentation, pollution data from 2006 (http://unstats. un.org/unsd/environment/air_co2_emissions.htm) and Climate Risk Index 2010 by Germanwatch (www.germanwatch.org/klima/cri2010.pdf).
11. Harriet Bulkeley and Peter Newell, *Governing Climate Change* (London: Routledge, 2010).
12. Karin Bäckstrand, 'Accountability of Networked Climate Governance: The Rise of Transnational Climate Partnerships', *Global Environmental Politics*, vol. 8 (2008), pp. 74–102.
13. See for example, Thomas Marcello, section 4.3.4 in this volume.
14. Michele M. Betsill and Elisabeth Corell (eds), *NGO Diplomacy: The Influence of Nongovernmental Organizations in International Environmental Negotiations* (Cambridge, MA: MIT Press, 2008), p. 3.
15. See http://unfccc.int/resource/docs/2009/cop15/eng/inf01p01.pdf.
16. Peter Newell, *Climate for Change: Non-State Actors and the Global Politics of the Greenhouse* (Cambridge: Cambridge University Press, 2000); Lars Gulbrandsen and Steinar Andresen, 'NGO Influence in the Implementation of the Kyoto Protocol: Compliance, Flexibility Mechanisms and Sinks', *Global Environmental Politics*, vol. 4 (2004), pp. 54–75.
17. Peter Newell, 'Climate for Change: Civil Society and the Politics of Global Warming', in Helmut K. Anheier et al. (eds), *Global Civil Society 2005/6* (London: Sage, 2005), ch. 3.
18. Peter Newell, 'Civil Society, Corporate Accountability and the Politics of Climate change', *Global Environmental Politics*, vol. 8 (2008), pp. 124-155; Peter Newell, 'Climate Change, Human Rights and Corporate Accountability', in S. Humphrey (ed.), *Climate Change and Human Rights* (Cambridge: Cambridge University Press, 2009), pp. 126–159.
19. Kathrin Dombrowski, 'Filling the Gap? An Analysis of NGO Responses to Participation and Representation Deficits in Global Climate Governance', paper prepared for the conference on the Human Dimension of Global Environmental Change, Amsterdam, 2–4 December 2009.
20. See for example, Paul Blumenthal, section 2.2.2 in this volume.
21. One World Trust (October 2009).

2.2

Essential building blocs for Kyoto and beyond

Agreeing on climate commitments at national and regional level

2.2.1

Equal access, unequal voice

Business and NGO lobbying on EU climate policy

Anne Therese Gullberg[1]

The European Union (EU) has for quite some time been considered an agenda-setter in climate policy internationally. In 2007 it adopted three important climate policy aims that came to be known as the '20–20–20' targets: reduce greenhouse gas emissions by 20 per cent compared to 1990 levels; increase the share of energy from renewable sources to 20 per cent; and enhance energy efficiency by 20 per cent – all to be achieved by 2020.

The reputation of the EU's vanguard climate policies was dented somewhat during the Copenhagen negotiations in 2009, however, when EU leadership was overshadowed by other players. Nonetheless, the fact remains: the EU is one of the most important forums for climate policy-making, with a far-reaching impact on the dynamics of international negotiations and national debates in other countries.[2] Risks associated with undue influence by vested interests on EU climate policies can therefore ripple out and slow down action elsewhere. An examination of EU policy-making is therefore imperative for a full understanding of the challenges of accountable climate policy-making in the global system.

How real are such risks of undue influence on EU decision-making? A number of factors shape this assessment.

Formal consultation processes: transparent and rather inclusive, but still a stronger voice for business

Stakeholder consultations have been used as a key mechanism to solicit broader public input during the development of European climate policies. A close look at two of these consultation processes shows that such a mechanism can help make policy development more transparent and inclusive. They are also characterized by disproportionate representation, however.

In 2004 the European Commission invited stakeholders to participate in a process to give input to EU climate policy after 2012. This included the central issue of setting emissions reduction commitments for the period after the expiry of the Kyoto Protocol's first commitment period. The consultation was open to all stakeholders, participation was broad and position papers were submitted by a wide spectrum of groups. The Commission also aimed to have a transparent process, and all the submitted position papers as well as the Commission's summaries of these position papers were open to the public and available online. This openness and diversity did not translate into a balanced spread of input, however. Business and industry organizations mustered resources to submit a total of 78 position papers, more than double the 30 submissions by environmental organizations.[3]

A similar pattern can be discerned for the stakeholder consultation for another centrepiece of EU climate policies: the EU Emissions Trading System (ETS), which is a key instrument to achieve agreed-upon emissions cuts. Questions about which sectors to include or how to allocate permits are central to the efficacy of the entire trading system and its potential to green the European economy, but, more than this, as these questions also determine who wins and loses, they are therefore subject to intense lobbying efforts.[4]

The original ETS was adopted in 2003, and the first trading period started in 2005.[5] As early as that year the Council of Ministers asked the Commission to review the ETS with the aim of improving the system from 2013 onwards. As a first step in the review process, the Commission conducted an internet-based survey that was open to all stakeholders. Log-in data were sent to 517 companies, government bodies, industry associations, market intermediaries and non-governmental organizations (NGOs).[6] A total of 302 organizations responded, and business groups again dwarfed the participation of other groups. Industrial companies accounted for slightly more than a half of all responses, far ahead of associations (25 per cent), NGOs (11 per cent) and government bodies (7 per cent).[7]

The survey was followed by a consultation process that ran from autumn 2006 to summer 2007. This process consisted of four stakeholders' meetings and the possibility of submitting written position papers. Again, the process was transparent and, on the surface, rather inclusive. Both industry and environmental groups participated, and the agendas, participant lists and meeting summaries were made public.

As figures 2.1 and 2.2 show, however, environmental organizations were clearly outnumbered by business groups in all four rounds of consultation.[8]

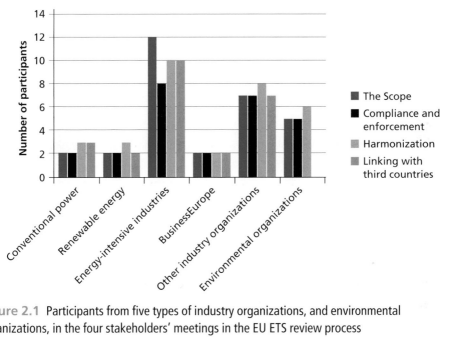

Figure 2.1 Participants from five types of industry organizations, and environmental organizations, in the four stakeholders' meetings in the EU ETS review process

Note: Colour coding refers to the four different topics of the meetings. BusinessEurope's members are 40 central industrial and employers' federations from 34 countries.

The Key Stakeholders Alliance for ETS Review, which consists of organizations representing energy-intensive industries, managed to send 8–12 representatives to each meeting.[9] Thus, these industries alone, not including other industry groups likely to support similar causes, managed to field more representatives than environmental organizations, which sent five or six representatives.[10]

These examples underline the fact that openness does not guarantee equitable representation. Lobbying is far from confined to formal consultations, however. Skewed representation in these official processes may just be a marker of more profound asymmetries in the less visible yet perhaps more informal ways of communicating positions to decision-makers and helping to shape opinions and compelling storylines to further specific interests.

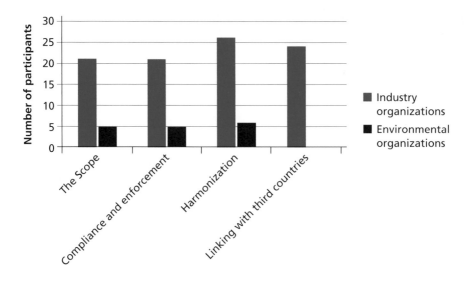

Figure 2.2 Participants from industry organizations and environmental organizations in the four stakeholders' meetings in the EU ETS review process

A multi-level decision-making process that favours well-resourced interests

EU climate policy is handled through the 'co-decision' procedure. This implies that the European Parliament (directly elected by European citizens) and the Council of Ministers (representing EU member states) are joint legislators. The Commission (the EU's quasi-executive arm and guardian of laws) has an exclusive right of legislative initiative in all areas subject to the co-decision procedure. The Commission drafts a legislative proposal and sends it to the Parliament and Council, which then discuss it. If the Parliament and the Council do not agree after a second reading, these two institutions meet in the Conciliation Committee. If the negotiations fail, the proposal is not adopted.

This complex machinery makes influencing EU climate policies a challenging endeavour more conducive to business-style lobbying, in the form of injecting expert information and cultivating longer-term relationships, than to direct action and media mobilization – the traditional domains of NGO advocacy. Establishing a presence and building deeper relationships across all participating institutions is considered a key element for having an effective voice. Such a strategy is expensive, however, and available only to the best-resourced players. Research suggests that environmental groups end up focusing their limited resources on specific policy issues and lobbying the Parliament and the Commission's Environment Directorate, which are both inclined to be relatively sympathetic to their cause.

Business groups, on the other hand, are able to cast a wider web of influence across different directorates. They can afford to lobby friends and foes alike, cultivate longer-term relationships and stay engaged throughout the entire policy-making cycle and related discussions with different directorates and institutions. They therefore wield stronger influence when the essential details of broad policy principles are being thrashed out.

Interviews with all stakeholders corroborate this analysis. Business groups report that they command sufficient resources for their lobbying work. In contrast, environmental groups explicitly complain about a lack of funds, which forces them to focus on specific policy questions and does not allow them to develop more effective comprehensive lobbying strategies like their business counterparts.[11]

Demonstrated impact

These asymmetries in voice and influence leave their mark on policy outcomes. Environmental organizations scored some successes in preventing the EU from cutting back on its relatively ambitious emission reduction targets. When it comes to less visible yet crucial details of policy design and implementation, however, business groups are more influential. Their interests were taken into account both in the Commission's proposal for a revised ETS in January 2008 and in the final decision by the Council and Parliament in December 2008. For example, while the Commission in principle supported the full auctioning of emissions allowances, energy-intensive industries were able to secure an exemption. Industry influence on these and other important parameters are well documented.[12]

In the final analysis, resources and informal access are important to influence open, democratic processes. The resource/access disparities between different stakeholders make participation highly unbalanced, reducing the quality of the democratic processes. Although the Commission sought to address this issue of imbalances in a White Paper on European governance,[13] the dominance of business lobbying is still a great challenge to the EU and its climate policy-making processes.

Notes

1. Anne Therese Gullberg is a researcher at the Center for International Climate and Environmental Research – Oslo (CICERO).
2. Axel Michaelowa, 'The Strength of Different Economic Interests in Shaping EU Climate Policy', *Energy and Environment,* vol. 11 (2000), pp. 277–292; Miranda A. Schreurs and Yves Tiberghien, 'Multi-Level Reinforcement: Explaining European Union Leadership in Climate Change Mitigation', *Global Environmental Politics*, vol. 7 (2007), pp. 19–46.
3. Anne Therese Gullberg, 'Klimapolitikk i EU: Interessegruppenes rolle' [EU Climate Policy: The Role of Interest Groups], *Cicerone*, vol. 16 (2007), pp. 12–13.
4. See Tamra Glibertson and Oscar Reyes, 'Carbon Trading: How it Works and Why it Fails', *Critical Currents*, no. 7 (2009), p. 35.
5. See, for example, Atle C. Christiansen and Jørgen Wettestad, 'The EU as a Frontrunner on Greenhouse Gas Emissions Trading: How Did It Happen and Will the EU Succeed?', *Climate Policy*, vol. 1 (2003), pp. 3–18; Peter Markussen and Gert Tinggaard Svendsen, 'Industry Lobbying and the Political Economy of GHG Trade in the European Union', *Energy Policy*, vol. 33 (2005), pp. 245–255; Jon Birger Skjærseth and Jørgen Wettestad, *EU Emissions Trading: Initiation, Decision-Making and Implementation* (Aldershot: Ashgate, 2008); Gert Tinggaard Svendsen, 'Lobbying and CO_2 Trade in the EU', in B. Hansjürgens (ed.), *Emissions Trading for Climate Policy. US and European Perspectives* (Cambridge: Cambridge University Press, 2005), pp. 150–162; and Gert Tinggaard Svendsen and Morten Vesterdal, 'How to Design Greenhouse Gas Trading in the EU?', *Energy Policy*, vol. 31 (2003), pp. 1531–1539.
6. European Commission, McKinsey & Company and Ecofys, *Review of EU Emissions Trading Scheme: Survey Results* (Brussels: European Commission, 2006).
7. Ibid.
8. For the participant lists, see European Commission, *Emission Trading System (EU ETS): ETS Review* (Brussels: European Commission, 2006), at http://ec.europa.eu/environment/climat/emission/review_en.htm.
9. Anne Therese Gullberg, *The European Electricity Sector and the EU ETS Review*, Working Paper no. 2008:01 (Oslo: CICERO, 2008).
10. In addition, industry and environmental organizations were both represented among the speakers at these stakeholders' meetings.
11. Anne Therese Gullberg, 'Rational Lobbying and EU Climate Policy', *International Environmental Agreements: Politics, Law and Economics*, vol. 8 (2008), pp. 161–178.
12. Peter Markussena and Gert Tinggaard Svendsen, 'Industry Lobbying and the Political Economy of GHG Trade in the European Union', *Energy Policy*, vol. 33 (2005), pp. 245–255.
13. European Commission, *European Governance: A White Paper* (Brussels: European Commission, 2001).

2.2.2

US climate policies

A snapshot of lobbyist influence

Paul Blumenthal[1]

It was like poking a sleeping bear.

> (lobbyist commenting when large anti-climate legislation lobby groups in the United States began to step up their activities)[2]

With the recent Supreme Court ruling, we are in a position to be able to take corporate positions that were not previously available in allowing our voices to be heard.

> (letter from a US coal industry executive to other coal companies)[3]

The prospects for ambitious US climate change legislation have been subject to wild swings in recent years. Hope rose with an incoming president who said he was dedicated to creating a cap-and-trade system similar to that in the EU.

A first milestone was reached when the House of Representatives (the lower chamber of the US Congress) in 2009 passed a scaled-down version of a proposed cap-and-trade law, known as the American Clean Energy and Security Act. By mid-2010, though, this effort had all but collapsed, as the bill was not even put to a vote in the Senate (the upper chamber).

A growing tide of climate lobbying: no balance in sight

The protracted battle and, for the time being, the defeat bear witness to the persistent power of lobbyists and special interests to stall climate policies, even though an outright denial of global warming is not a viable option any more.

Throughout 2009 oil, gas, coal and electricity utilities and alternative energy companies spent a record US$403 million on lobbying the federal government.[4] On top of this, companies from industries as disparate as footwear and computer network server operators have also lobbied on climate policy. In total, more than 2000 lobbyists are registered to lobby on climate legislation in Washington.[5]

Meanwhile, the clean energy lobby has also established itself as a sizeable player in the US capital. In 2009, at the height of the debate on the cap-and-trade bill, environmental groups spent a record US$22.4 million on lobbying federal officials, double their average during the period 2000–2008.[6] This pales in comparison to spending by oil and gas interests, however, which poured US$175 million into influencing policies in 2009.[7]

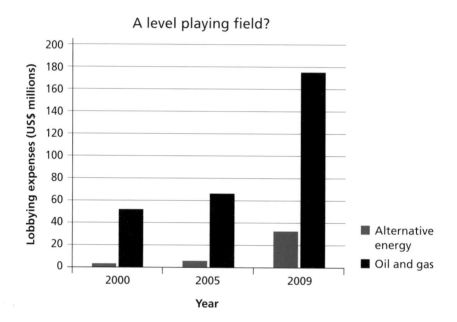

Figure 2.3 Annual lobbying expenses, US

Source: Center for Responsive Politics.

The floodgates for future spending have now been thrown wide open thanks to a US Supreme Court decision in January 2010 that handed a victory to corporations, allowing them to spend freely on election campaign advertising.[8]

A more diverse landscape, more focused on specifics

The interests involved in climate policies have become more differentiated, and coalitions more dynamic. Some major electricity utilities and oil companies have split with traditional industry groups to support cap-and-trade legislation, in the hope that they might benefit from a carbon market. Others have remained in their traditional pose of staunch opposition.

The initial consideration of climate legislation in Congress, for example, saw companies such as Duke Energy, BP, Conoco-Philips, Shell Oil, General Electric, Alcoa and Exelon join climate advocacy groups including the Environmental Defense Fund to create the US Climate Action Partnership, an organization that backs legislation to create a carbon market.[9]

The results have been mixed. Numerous consumer and environmental groups protested the fact that the proposed cap-and-trade legislation gave too many concessions to too many special interests. An initial draft of 648 pages turned into a 1428-page epic brimful with special provisions and exemptions when it was passed by the House of Representatives.[10]

Dubious tools of the trade: feigning grassroots endorsement

Being able to demonstrate that a special interest enjoys broad citizen support is essential in the struggle for influence. At times, the means to achieve this can be very dubious.

In June 2009, for example, before an important vote on the cap-and-trade bill in a House committee, a Washington lobbying firm sent 13 letters to three lawmakers sitting on the committee urging them to oppose the bill. The letters turned out to be forgeries bearing the names of local chapters of the National Association for the Advancement of Colored People (NAACP), among other groups.[11] The lobbying firm was under a US$3 million contract paid through an intermediary by the American Coalition for Clean Coal Electricity, a major coal industry lobby. Two of three lawmakers receiving the fraudulent letters voted against the legislation. According to the implicated lobbying firm, the letters were written by a temporary worker, who was fired after the forgeries came to light. The coal lobby group instructed the lobbying firm to inform the lawmakers of the situation, but by this time the vote had already taken place.[12]

Such incidents, as well as establishing fake grassroots organizations to simulate the appearance of broad public support for a special interest issue (often called 'astroturfing'), bode ill for a sincere debate and an honest representation of interests and viewpoints in US climate policy-making.[13]

Revolving doors: privileged access for special interests of all stripes

In November 2009 a key Senate committee approved a more ambitious piece of climate legislation than the House of Representatives had passed in

June. The lone vote against the bill came from Senator Max Baucus, whose legislative staff exemplifies a phenomenon known as the 'revolving door' – whereby legislative staffers gain experience and establish contacts in Congress and then leave to work as industry lobbyists. Baucus is currently the lawmaker with the most former staffers working as lobbyists; as many as 12 of them lobby on climate and energy policy.[14]

As connections are the main currency in lobbying, these former staffers carry great influence in helping industry get its voice heard in the legislative process. In the case of Baucus, his 12 former staffers who lobby on climate and energy issues represent a broad range of different industry positions. A former chief of staff represents a long list of cap-and-trade opponents, including the American Petroleum Institute and US Business Roundtable.[15] On the other side, Baucus's former policy counsel represents a number of biofuel, bioenergy and alternative energy groups.[16]

Brown and green – not the full spectrum of colours

There is both much to lose and much to win in climate politics, and the stakes are growing all the time. Special interest groups have become more vocal and focused on climate change issues. The days of outright, highly public denial of climate change might be over, yet lobbying has not just persisted but is gathering momentum. It is now down to influencing the arcane, technical details of laws and regulations that actually decide who wins and loses – a battle that is fought with more subtle tactics and is more difficult to monitor.

The emergence of green industry lobbyists and new coalitions makes the front lines more dynamic and the lobbying landscape more diverse. Although this may provide a countervailing force to obstructionists, it should not detract from a number of persistent concerns. Beneficiaries of the status quo far outspend the green industry, by a large factor. In addition, the proliferation of special interest groups does not represent the public interest. The outcome of this may be the sheltering of 'brown' industries from the inevitable transformation of environmental policy and the economy, while dishing out precious subsidies to green players with the most clout rather than those with the greatest future potential. This does not add up to sensible, accountable climate policies in the interest of current and future generations.

Notes

1. Paul Blumenthal is a senior writer at the Sunlight Foundation.
2. *The Economist* (UK), 'Cap and tirade', 3 December 2009.
3. *Lexington Herald-Leader* (US), 'Coal execs hope to spend big to defeat Conway and Chandler', 28 July 2010.
4. Center for Responsive Politics (US), 'Energy and natural resources', 26 July 2010, at www.opensecrets.org/lobby/indus.php?lname=E&year=2009.
5. Marianne Lavelle, 'The Climate Change Lobby Explosion', Center for Public Integrity (US), 24 February 2009.
6. Evan Mackinder, 'Pro-Environment Groups Outmatched, Outspent in Battle Over Climate Change Legislation', Center for Responsive Politics (US), 23 August 2010.
7. Ibid.
8. *New York Times* (US), 'Justices, 5-4, reject corporate spending limit', 21 January 2010.
9. United States Climate Action Partnership, www.us-cap.org/about-us/about-our-members.
10. Marianne Lavelle, 'Tally of Interests on Climate Bill Tops a Thousand', Center for Public Integrity (US), 10 August 2009.
11. *Charlottesville Daily Progress* (US), 'Forged letters to congressman anger local groups', 31 July 2009.
12. *Mother Jones* (US), 'Inside Bonner's climate letter forgeries', 29 October 2009.
13. For more on 'astroturf' groups, see TI, *Global Corruption Report 2009: Corruption and the Private Sector* (Cambridge: Cambridge University Press, 2009), pp. 39–40.
14. Paul Blumenthal, 'The Max Baucus energy and climate lobbyist complex', Sunlight Foundation (US), 9 November 2009.
15. Center for Responsive Politics (US), 'Castagnetti, David: lobbyist profile', at www.opensecrets.org/lobby/lobbyist.php?lname=Castagnetti%2C+David&id=Y00000402241&year=2009.
16. Center for Responsive Politics (US), 'Rich, J Curtis: lobbyist profile', at www.opensecrets.org/lobby/lobbyist.php?lname=Rich%2C+J+Curtis&id=Y00000221901&year=2009.

2.3

Urban governance and climate change policy

David Dodman and David Satterthwaite[1]

Half the world's population lives in urban areas. This is projected to rise to 60 per cent by 2030, with almost all the growth in the world's urban population occurring in low- and middle-income countries.

The industrial activities that occur in cities, and the consumption behaviour and choices of their residents, are important contributors to global emissions of CO_2 and other greenhouse gases (GHGs). In addition, a high proportion of urban areas are very much at risk from climate change. This means that residents of towns and cities, and the municipal authorities responsible for their governance, have a vital role both in climate-related mitigation (reducing atmospheric concentrations of GHGs) and adaptation (building resilience to changing climatic threats).

Urban governance for mitigation

Many GHG-generating activities are concentrated in urban areas. Manufacturing industries, congested roads carrying fossil-fuel-burning vehicles, buildings using energy for heating, cooling and lighting, and high-consumption lifestyles are all major sources of CO_2 emissions. Emission levels vary greatly between urban centres, however; wealthy cities can have GHG emissions per person 50 to 100 times those of urban centres in low-income nations.[2] There are various ways that urban governments can help meet global needs for preventing dangerous climate change.

First, most urban authorities are substantial contributors to emissions, as they are large employers responsible for many buildings and extensive vehicle fleets. They can take initiatives to reduce their carbon footprints, including making buildings more energy-efficient, converting their vehicle fleets to run on electricity or 'green' fuels and improving solid waste management by encouraging waste reduction, recycling and better management of disposal sites. In Cebu City, the Philippines, city authorities have converted their offices' air-conditioning to a more climate-friendly system. In São Paulo, Brazil, the municipal government has obtained carbon credits for reducing methane production at the main landfill site, and is investing the proceeds in social programmes for the surrounding area.

Second, local governments can influence a much broader range of activities taking place within urban boundaries. Although the extent of their powers varies from country to country, they generally have some control over land use, buildings and transportation policy. In Curitiba, Brazil, the municipal government facilitated the transformation of the city by promoting high-density development along linear axes served by more rapid and effective public transport. This helped cut private automobile use (and thus GHG emissions) and provided lower-income groups with easier access to work, among various other social and environmental benefits.

Adaptation as responsive urban governance

Concentrating people and economic activities in urban areas can also concentrate risk and vulnerability. Most of the world's urban population and most of its largest cities are now in Africa, Asia and Latin America. In most urban areas in these regions, infrastructure for water, sanitation and drainage is inadequate to cope with current climatic conditions, and much of the population does not have access to adequate shelter or basic services.[3] In many cities, one- to two-thirds of the population lives in informal settlements – a powerful testament to the incapacity of city governments and/or their lack of accountability to this group of residents.

Without major improvements in drainage, heavier storms will cause increasingly serious flooding. Disasters such as the devastating floods seen recently in many cities in Africa and Asia will become increasingly commonplace. Shifting patterns of rainfall will further stress the capacities of water supply networks, and sea-level rise will cause the loss of land and property in many coastal cities. Table 2.1 highlights the many sectors in which local government's responsibilities are important for reducing risks and responding effectively when a disaster occurs.

Role for city/municipal government	Long-term protection	Pre-disaster damage limitation	Immediate post-disaster response	Rebuilding
Built environment				
Building codes	High		High	High
Land-use regulations and property registration	High	Some		High
Public building construction and maintenance	High	Some		High
Urban planning (including zoning and development controls)	High		High	High
Infrastructure				
Piped water, including treatment	High	Some	High	High
Sanitation	High	Some	High	High
Drainage	High	High	High	High
Roads, bridges and pavements	High		High	High
Electricity	High	Some	High	High
Solid waste disposal facilities	High	Some		High
Wastewater treatment	High			High
Services				
Fire protection	High	Some	High	Some
Public order, police and early warning	Medium	High	High	Some
Solid waste collection	High	High	High	High
Schools	Medium	Medium		
Health care, public health, environmental health and ambulances	Medium	Medium	High	High
Public transport	Medium	High	High	High
Social welfare (including provision for child and old-age care)	Medium	High	High	High
Disaster response (over and above those listed above)			High	High

Table 2.1 The role of city/municipal governments in adapting to climate-change-related disasters

The best-governed cities are generally those most resilient to climate change. Good urban governance should support low-income groups in finding safe, legal accommodation (including acquiring land where they can build their own homes) and ensure they are provided with infrastructure and services. To do so, local political and bureaucratic systems need to be accessible and responsive to the urban poor and other disadvantaged groups.

Good urban practice as an example to the world

In many cases, urban authorities have been at the forefront of recognizing the extent of the climate challenge, and have set themselves ambitious targets for reducing GHG emissions. ICLEI (Local Governments for Sustainability) has challenged local authorities to reduce GHG emissions. More than 1500 local authorities around the world have made commitments to do so: Mexico City has pledged to reduce emissions by 12 per cent of 2000 levels by 2012, Barcelona by 50 per cent of 1990 levels by 2030 and Bangkok by 15 per cent of 2007 levels by 2012.[4]

These commitments are often greater than those agreed by their national governments, and can help to urge responsible climate responses on a much larger scale. In this regard, local authorities can encourage action by other actors, both by lobbying national governments and by developing projects that can show the costs and benefits of responding to climate change.[5]

Local government associations from around the world have also been active in the negotiations within the UN Framework Convention on Climate Change (UNFCCC), and they have developed a Local Government Climate Roadmap that advocates for a strong and comprehensive global agreement on climate change mitigation and adaptation.

The way forward: climate-responsive urban governance

Good climate change adaptation is driven by accountability to the needs and priorities of citizens, especially those most at risk. Some of the most effective adaptation programmes are being implemented by partnerships between urban poor organizations and local governments. Mitigation is also driven by accountability, although to both current and future generations. The bigger picture confirms these linkages. An analysis of more than 400 cities underlines the fact that the quality of governance, including the control of corruption, is clearly associated with better city performance in terms of access to and quality of infrastructure services.[6]

At present, most urban governments in low- and middle-income nations have little accountability to their citizens, and show little interest in reducing climate change risks. This is especially so in the informal settlements that house a high proportion of citizens and businesses and where there are large deficits in necessary protective infrastructure and services. Here, there is the twin challenge of managing urban growth (which includes providing low-income groups with alternatives to informal settlements) and establishing sound governance.

Climate change may act as an incentive for more accountable local government, however. As citizens become increasingly aware of the risks that climate change brings, and as national governments face the need to meet new commitments to reduce emissions and support adaptation, local authorities will be called on to implement both of these agendas.

Strong local democracies and accountable urban governments have been key factors in cities that have progressed on these issues. Cities such as Durban, South Africa, have been leading the way on this front.[7] Led by a highly motivated Environmental Management Department, Durban has developed a locally rooted climate change strategy that has succeeded in mainstreaming climate change concerns, including reducing GHG emissions and reducing vulnerability to climate change risks.

Central to this process has been the building of a recognition that responding to climate change (and, indeed, other environmental challenges) is not a constraint but, rather, an essential underpinning of development. If more urban authorities take this approach, transparent local governance can indeed become a strong force for accountable climate governance.

Notes

1. David Dodman and David Satterthwaite work with the International Institute for Environment and Development (IIED).
2. Daniel Hoornweg et al., 'Cities and Greenhouse Gas Emissions: Moving Forward', *Environment and Urbanization*, vol. 23 (forthcoming).
3. Jane Bicknell, David Dodman and David Satterthwaite (eds), *Adapting Cities to Climate Change: Understanding and Addressing the Development Challenges* (London: Earthscan, 2009).
4. See www.climate-catalogue.org/index.php?id=6870.
5. Harriet Bulkeley and Michele Betsill, *Cities and Climate Change: Urban Sustainability and Global Environmental Governance* (London: Routledge, 2003).
6. Daniel Kaufmann et al., *Governance and the City: An Empirical Exploration into Global Determinants of Urban Performance*, Policy Research Working Paper no. 3712 (Washington, DC: World Bank, 2005).
7. Debra Roberts, 'Thinking Globally, Acting Locally: Institutionalizing Climate Change at the Local Government Level in Durban, South Africa', *Environment and Urbanization*, vol. 20 (2008), pp. 521–537.

2.4

The matrix of interests and influence in key emerging climate countries

2.4.1

Vested or public interest? The case of India

Sudhir Chella Rajan[1]

India has evolved into the fourth largest emitter of greenhouse gases (GHGs) in the world, accounting for 5 per cent of global emissions. If current projections hold true, it will account for up to one-third of the world's energy demand by 2050. As a result, India will assume a greater role in the global climate regime, putting the spotlight on climate policy-making and on the matrix of influences and interests engaging in this process in the world's largest democracy.[2]

Until very recently, climate change was an obscure subject in India, relegated to the back pages of newspapers and remote from the primary concerns of both policy-makers and the general public. The issue began to attract more attention in the popular media only after high-level discussions of India's role began to dominate international summits, such as the G8 and Major Economies Forum, the country's partnering with other major CO_2 emitters to develop the Copenhagen Accord in December 2009 and its prominent role at COP 16 in Cancún in December 2010.

Some business interests and civil society groups have been quietly lobbying the government in recent years to take advantage of important new climate-related financial opportunities, however. These include, in particular, the Kyoto Protocol's Clean Development Mechanism (CDM), which encourages emissions reduction projects in developing countries. At the same time, lobbying by the energy sector, though not associated with climate policy until recently, has a longer history and carries bigger stakes, and crucially shapes the prospects for climate mitigation efforts in India.

A closer look at both these processes sheds an intriguing light on the challenges and opportunities for accountable, public interest-driven climate mitigation policies in India.

India and the Clean Development Mechanism: an interest in lax rules?

India's interest in the CDM[3] was initially cautious during the negotiations over the Kyoto Protocol. Within just a few years, though, the government began to support it earnestly at the international level, and began to develop institutional arrangements to facilitate its own CDM projects. The speed, efficiency and low transaction costs of India's CDM approval process have been remarkable compared to other regulatory agencies. Even so, about 40 per cent of CDM projects rejected worldwide are based in India, raising questions about the soundness of the first-line review by India's National CDM Authority.[4]

Nevertheless, there is a widespread perception among government officials at various levels that the CDM can be an important source of income. At the time of writing, India had 527 registered CDM projects, 22 per cent of the worldwide total and second only to China's 40 per cent.[5] Most of India's certified emissions reductions stem from projects aimed to phase out the highly potent GHG HFC-23. As detailed in Part 4,[6] however, HFC-23 projects can be problematic, because they create perverse incentives to actually encourage the (cheap) production of this gas in order to turn a profit on its subsequent reduction under the CDM. This violates the important criterion that emissions reductions must be 'additional' to a 'business-as-usual' scenario.

As a consequence, Indian businesses that could benefit from HFC-23 projects yet that suffer from high project rejection rates have a strong incentive to lobby for lenient international and domestic interpretations of the 'additionality' rule, and they have been working to influence India's international negotiating stance in this respect. International climate negotiations, in fact, typically include a large delegation of Indian business interests – representing project developers, consultancies and financial institutions – who lobby hard to ensure that any proposed changes to CDM rules would benefit them.

While Indian industry groups are frequently consulted and have close ties to Cabinet-level decision-makers and negotiators, academics and environmental non-governmental organizations (NGOs) are largely kept outside the official realm of international negotiations. The effective influence of business on India's position is further amplified by the comparatively low profile that many Indian NGOs take with regard to international negotiations. As one observer put it: 'Indian civil society – disenchanted with the global process – is dominated by the progressive realist view. While they may be fierce critics of the government at home, they close ranks with them at international climate negotiations and defend against calls for international commitments of any sort.'[7]

This focus on industrialized country commitments is understandable in a country with huge development needs and when considering that India's overall contribution to the global stock of GHGs stands at only 2.3 per cent (compared to an almost 30 per cent US share), while per capita emissions are all but a fraction of the per capita contribution in most other countries, including China (three times higher) and the US (14 times higher).[8]

Legitimate and important as these demands on industrialized countries to live up to their responsibilities may be, it is important to ensure that they do not become a convenient narrative for vested interests and climate polluters at domestic level to delay much-needed action.

Domestic energy reforms: interlocking special interests slow reforms

It is essential for India's coal-reliant electricity industry to become a major focus of the country's climate mitigation policies. The sector is India's largest GHG emitter by far, accounting for 38 per cent of emissions in 2007, up from 28 per cent in 1994. Continued growth potential is huge, as more than 400 million people are still without electricity. India plans to increase coal-fired energy capacity by more than 75 per cent over a 10-year period, and coal-based emissions could more than double by 2030.[9]

Lowering fossil fuel dependence and raising the sector's efficiency are recognized as key ingredients for India's energy future. A web of interlocking interests – including the oil and gas, petrochemical, fertilizer, manufacturing, agriculture and motor vehicle industries – make change to the status quo difficult to achieve, however.

The pricing of fuels and electricity, as well as the extraction of primary energy sources, have long been characterized by subsidies, both for producers and consumers. The issue of providing free or highly subsidized electricity for agricultural irrigation, for example, has received significant attention for more than two decades. Little progress has been made, however, in stemming the enormous increase in subsidized electricity use, the associated growth of groundwater depletion or financial losses for utilities.

While such consumer subsidies were intended primarily to assist the poor, the main beneficiaries, especially agricultural irrigators, have been wealthier farmers, who in large part can afford to pay market prices. In fact, many farmers are believed to pay nothing for electricity, thanks to lobbying by local politicians. Subsidized electricity for farmers alone costs an estimated US$6 billion a year – double the central government's spending on health or rural development – and overall energy subsidies total about US$20 billion.[10]

Reforming such a situation will not be easy, especially since the mainstream Indian energy sector is characterized by large, state-dominated monopolies – a proximity that makes special treatment and interference by particularistic political interests more likely.

An unfinished agenda for transparency and participation

Where private sector engagement has become more prominent, as in oil and gas extraction, concerns have surfaced about undue profiteering through favourable and often less than transparent contracts and concession procedures.[11] A parallel set of conditions was noted in the early days of electricity reform in the 1990s, when independent power producers and distribution companies were given extraordinarily generous terms allowing for the collection of significant rents.[12]

Naturally, the question is open as to whether such arrangements could have been avoided, given the country's infrastructure needs and the scale of the investment required. The government was obligated to err on the side of generosity towards investors with deep pockets in order to make their projects more attractive. The lack of transparency in contracting and relatively lax oversight rules remain troubling, however.

It is encouraging to note that a detailed analysis of electricity governance in India found that significant progress has been made towards opening critical decisions to more public scrutiny, even though much remains to be done. General information about reforms is being more widely disclosed. Effective transparency, systematic engagement with the public and more integration of environmental considerations into electricity governance – all prerequisites for accountable and inclusive climate policies – are far from reality, however, as tables 2.2 and 2.3 indicate.

Indicator PP 14: Quality of public participation during reform or policy decisions	India Low
Public notification	X
Public registries of documents	X
Communication of decisions within one month	X
Use of diverse communication tools	X
Adequate time for public consideration	X
Opportunity for consultation	X
Clear communication on the results of public participation	X
Outreach to vulnerable communities	X
Indicator PP 15: Quality of participation by stakeholders and government responsiveness	*Low*
Quality of participation:	
Quantity of input	X
Breadth of input	X
Responsiveness of policy-maker:	
Notification of public participation by government	X
Summary of public participation	X
Response to public participation	X

Table 2.2 Indicators for quality of participation in India

Indicator ESA 9: Inclusion of environmental considerations in sector reform processes	India *Medium-low reform*
Inclusion of environmental considerations in official documents, before reform	X
Broad framing of environmental issues	X
Access to documents	
Less restrictive confidentiality rules applied to reform-related documents	✓
Adequacy of public comment period	X
Effort to reach affected and less-privileged populations	X
Mechanisms to seek public input	X
Availability of public comments	X
Communication of how public input is incorporated	X

Source: Adapted from Smita Nakhooda et al., *Empowering People, A Governance Analysis of Electricity* (Washington, DC: World Resources Institute [WRI], 2007).

Table 2.3 Indicator of the inclusion of environmental considerations in sector reform processes in India

The future: cause for hope?

The Indian government recently announced plans to reduce its carbon intensity by 20–25 per cent by 2020 compared to 2005 levels, indicating intensified efforts to improve efficiency and promote renewable energy. Proposals include building more wind, solar and geothermal facilities, expanding public transportation and instituting a tax on both domestic and imported coal that would raise money for cleaner energy and technology.

Despite these encouraging signs, India's experience with the CDM and energy reforms indicates that the escalation of energy-related investments will undoubtedly bring new opportunities for rent-seeking. It is therefore imperative that institutional design be improved and public oversight enhanced.

Notes

1. Sudhir Chella Rajan is a professor at the Indian Institute of Technology, Madras.
2. Navroz K. Dubash, 'Climate Politics in India: How Can the Industrialized World Bridge the Trust Deficit?', in David Michel and Amit Pandya (eds), *India Climate Policy: Choices and Challenges* (Washington, DC: Henry L. Stimson Center, 2009), ch. 9; Gudrun Benecke, 'Networking for Climate Change Agency in the Context of Renewable Energy Governance in India', paper presented at the conference on the Human Dimensions of Global Environmental Change, Amsterdam, 3 December 2009.
3. For an introduction on the Clean Development Mechanism and more details on its corruption risk profile, see Lambert Schneider, section 4.3.
4. Gudrun Benecke, 'Varieties of Carbon Governance: Taking Stock of the Local Carbon Market in India', *Journal of Environment and Development*, vol. 18 (2009), pp. 346–370.
5. See http://cdm.unfccc.int/Statistics/index.html.
6. See Lambert Schneider, section 4.3.
7. Navroz K. Dubash, 'Climate Politics in India: How Can the Industrialized World Bridge the Trust Deficit?', in David Michel and Amit Pandya (eds), *India Climate Policy: Choices and Challenges* (Washington, DC: Henry L. Stimson Center, 2009), ch. 9.
8. Ibid.
9. UN Development Programme (UNDP), *Human Development Report 2007/2008: Fighting Climate Change: Human Solidarity in a Divided World* (New York: UNDP, 2008).
10. UN Environment Programme (UNEP), *Reforming Energy Subsidies: Opportunities to Contribute to the Climate Change Agenda* (Nairobi: UNEP, 2008).
11. Ashok Sreenivas and Girish Sant, 'Shortcomings in Governance of the Natural Gas Sector', *Economic and Political Weekly*, vol. 44 (2009), pp. 33–36.
12. Navroz K. Dubash and Sudhir Chella Rajan, 'Power Politics: Process of India's Power Sector Reform', *Economic and Political Weekly*, vol. 36 (2001), pp. 3367–3390.

2.4.2

Climate policies in China

A gradual move towards ambition, more transparency and nascent citizen involvement

Dieter Zinnbauer[1]

Following several decades of rapid economic growth, urbanization and industrialization that has lifted more than 200 million people out of poverty, China is reported to have surpassed the US as the world's largest energy consumer and greenhouse gas (GHG) emitter in 2009 and 2007, respectively – several years earlier than expected.[2] In addition, China's overall energy demand is estimated to double by 2030.[3] This transformation has catapulted China to the forefront of international climate change policy-making, although its per capita share of emissions is still far lower than in industrialized countries, with their voracious appetite for energy-intensive lifestyles.

Now standing with the US at the pivot of global climate policies, China made its role evident for the first time at the Copenhagen talks in December 2009 by expressing its interests more assertively and visibly than ever before. As a result of its heightened position, the interests and players that shape China's own stance and policies towards climate change are also shaping international climate policies. Very different moral and historical responsibilities notwithstanding, the calculus is not dissimilar to the US context: if vested interests can manage to hijack climate policies at the national level, there is a real risk they can do the same at the global level.

Hope and hurdles: can China build on its solid start?

A growing concern about energy security, pollution and the impact of climate change on its economy and society prompted the Chinese leadership to establish targets for reducing energy intensity by 20 per cent from 2006 to 2010. This target has been supported by a diverse and growing array of energy and environmental initiatives, from campaigns to shut down or upgrade outdated production technologies and fuel efficiency standards for vehicles and appliances, to cutting rural GHG emissions, household energy-saving schemes, and government support and feed-in tariffs for green technologies.

These efforts have yielded some significant results, although, at the time of writing, when the economy started recovering from the financial crisis China unexpectedly experienced some difficulties in meeting the energy intensity target. Between 2000 and 2008, however, the country more than doubled its hydropower capacity, more than quadrupled its nuclear power capacity and increased its wind power capacity by a factor of 30.[4] China has evolved into the world's leading supplier of, *inter alia*, certain types of solar panels and water heaters. It has almost twice as much installed capacity for renewable energy production than the US[5] and leads the world in green energy investments with US$34.6 billion in 2009 – nearly double the second-placed

US.[6] In addition, the government is contemplating experiments with programmes such as carbon taxes and carbon trading pilots.

At the 2010 COP 16 in Cancún, China agreed to language establishing an international reporting mechanism for national emissions. One year earlier in Copenhagen it also expressed, among its other aspirations, an intention to reduce its CO_2 emissions per unit of gross domestic product by 40–45 per cent by 2020 compared to 2005 levels, and increase the share of non-fossil fuels in energy consumption to about 15 per cent by 2020.[7]

Opinions differ, however, about the degree of commitment behind these overtures. Many observers were frustrated by what they viewed as China's unproductive insistence on avoiding absolute emissions reduction targets, as well as a stricter emissions reporting and verification mechanism. Others believe these initiatives and commitments show true ambition and signal concessions on important principles that had held up international negotiations, notably the previous resistance to any kind of numerical target or international reporting mechanism.

What experts can agree on is that the road ahead for China's climate policies will be extremely challenging. The low-hanging fruit have already been picked. New promises need to be translated into effective action, and future efforts must be expanded even further to reconcile the country's projected surge in energy demand with requirements to mitigate climate change. It is thus more important than ever to examine the prospects that Chinese climate policy-making can withstand policy capture by vested interests, and whether transparency, accountability and public engagement can be strengthened. At first sight, a number of factors suggest that these prospects are not overly encouraging.

Power confers power: the clout of high-emission energy producers versus environmental institutions

Dramatic improvements in green energy development notwithstanding, China continues to rely heavily on coal, a particularly polluting source of energy, to power its fast-paced development. The country holds 14 per cent of the world's known coal reserves, and in 2009 coal still accounted for 70 per cent of its primary energy needs, representing more than 40 per cent of global coal consumption.[8] This dependence is not expected to lessen significantly in the near future. The share of natural gas, nuclear and renewable energy is expected to expand, yet, at the same time, China is building new coal-fired power plants quickly in order to meet soaring energy demand.

As a result, coal producers and coal-centred power companies, which have worked to slow down green policies in many countries, play a central role in China's energy future and stand to lose from ambitious climate policies.[9] These strong incentives to influence policy can be aided by privileged access to policy-makers. Many of China's large industry groups were derived from government ministries and, as state-owned companies, the major energy companies still enjoy close relationships with state agencies. As one Beijing-based observer put it, 'There don't need to be "lobbyists", when discussions can happen directly through the Party.'[10]

In stark contrast to these well-established coal and energy forces stand environmental policy-makers, who are still building their institutional voice and power base. China's main environmental agency was not granted enforcement powers until the early 1990s, and it was upgraded to ministry status as the Ministry of Environmental Protection (MEP) only in 2008.[11] The ministry has been described as understaffed and underfunded.[12] Likewise, the National Energy Administration, which is responsible for coordinating energy policy, is believed to have insufficient authority over powerful state-owned enterprises.[13]

Fragmented competences, competing policies

Because of China's uneven institutional landscape, policy-making on climate issues has been fragmented, as indicated by table 2.4.

Responsibility	Department
Macro-coordination and control	National Development and Reform Commission
	Ministry of Finance
	Ministry of Foreign Affairs
Pollution control	Ministry of Environmental Protection
Industry and construction	Ministry of Housing and Urban-Rural Development
	Ministry of Industry and Information Technology
Transportation	Ministry of Transport
	Ministry of Railways
Agriculture and forestry	Ministry of Agriculture
	State Forestry Administration
Industrial development	Ministry of Finance
	State Administration of Taxation
	National Development and Reform Commission
	Ministry of Industry and Information Technology
	Ministry of Agriculture
Technology	Ministry of Science and Technology
	Ministry of Environmental Protection
	National Development and Reform Commission

Source: Adapted from UNDP (2010).

Table 2.4 Departments involved in carbon polices in China

As a consequence, China's energy legislation is not fully integrated and it reflects the interests of the particular sectors concerned. China has four partially consistent energy-saving laws, but they exist alongside legislation on electricity and coal that is largely silent on issues of energy-saving and emissions reductions, and is even regarded as an obstacle to the further development of green energy and energy efficiency initiatives.[14]

Central ambition, local discretion

Implementing carbon policies is further complicated by the division of labour between central and local government in the context of a decentralized system that confers considerable powers in terms of implementing and enforcing central administration policies to regional and local authorities.

Climate change governance at local level not only involves environmental protection agencies but also includes a broader range of actors, such as local development and reform commissions. Nevertheless, the experience of environmental protection at local level is indicative of the challenges ahead. A lack of funding and capacity provides a first obstacle to enforcement. For example, most of the 145 energy-saving monitoring centres in China are considered to face weaknesses in staffing, budgeting, equipment and operational specifications.[15]

Abetted by what are often rather unspecific guidelines for implementation, there are instances in which local authorities have been unwilling to curtail the operations of polluting industries that provide significant local employment, fiscal revenues and economic growth and thus help them do well on what continue to be key indicators on which their administrative performance is judged.[16] Incentives for lax enforcement of or direct interference with environmental policies are even stronger when local authorities or individuals within them directly own stakes in these polluting industries.[17]

Similarly, local regulatory agencies, such as environmental protection bureaus, can face considerable conflicts of interest. Often underfunded and lacking sufficient staffing, they are typically organized as 'little treasuries' (*xiao jinku*) – hybrid organizations that are expected to make profits for local governments by selling services to businesses while also being tasked to independently oversee the very same industries that are their clients.[18]

The challenge to implement carbon policies effectively at the local level is further amplified by recent moves by polluting industries to relocate from richer regions, where capacity for enforcement is gradually growing, to poorer provinces further inland, where capacities and resources for enforcement are less adequate.[19]

All this does not bode well for climate policies that truly reflect the societal interest and are implemented effectively without interference from vested interests.

Strong competences and a focus on strengthening environmental authority and green incentives

On a positive note, many of China's leading policy-makers are trained as engineers, scientists or economists and are regarded as having a solid understanding of climate change issues.

Additionally, the growing recognition of energy security and climate issues was reflected by a move in 2010 by the State Council, China's top decision-making institution, to establish a National Energy Commission headed by the premier, Wen Jiabao. This can be seen as a significant effort to ensure a more authoritative voice and greater consistency between related policies and ministries with regard to climate change issues.[20] Similarly, the State Council has been charged with tracking compliance with energy intensity rules. Regional and local officials are required to file progress reports every six months and are offered salary rises and promotions if they can demonstrate progress. Reaching climate-change-related objectives has entered the performance assessments of some local officials, although the strength of these incentives is questionable, since they coexist alongside well-established economic performance criteria. Additionally, Beijing cross checks reported numbers and periodically inspects major energy-using facilities.[21]

A growing embrace of information disclosure

The Ministry of Environmental Protection has pursued information disclosure strongly as a regulatory tool to shore up its enforcement powers. It issued a first batch of rather detailed environmental disclosure obligations for environmental protection departments and specific companies the same day that the national Open Government Information Regulations entered into effect, 1 May 2008.[22] These requirements include proactively publishing detailed environmental information falling within 17 categories and providing a timely response to public requests for environmental information.[23]

With regard to the national energy efficiency goal, performance updates are released annually on the National Development and Reform Commission's official website. Comprehensive and effective transparency is still often hampered, however, by a lack of capacity, fragmented production and maintenance of the data, limited accountability on the part of local officials and the vagueness of some guidelines. One year after the MEP implemented its regulations, a study found that average compliance levels by 113 municipal environmental protection departments were low.[24] Some positive examples illustrate what can be achieved, however. The city of

Ningbo, which earned the highest rank in terms of information disclosure, released more than 600 documents on environmental enforcement on its website in 2008, including all environmental complaints received and the status of processing them.[25]

Opening the doors: broader public engagement and recognition of environmental NGOs

The fact that Ningbo even released information about complaints attests to a gradual opening of environmental policy-making and enforcement processes to broader public involvement. Public hearings for environmental impact assessments are conducted for certain types of projects.[26] Moreover, in recent years draft texts of some energy- and climate-related legislation have been published online in advance and public comments have been invited via e-mail, although details of the discussion and the decision-making process were not disclosed.

On the downside, persistent gaps in effective environmental transparency and limited information on participation procedures and timelines make it difficult for people to participate meaningfully.[27] In addition, provisions for public input are typically less developed for many climate-relevant issues compared with conventional environmental concerns.

These obstacles notwithstanding, environmental NGOs are carefully expanding their engagement – taking on issues ranging from raising awareness on environmental accountability and working with officials and communities on pollution controls to assessing compliance with disclosure rules and assisting pollution victims. Nearly 3500 domestic NGOs are officially registered in China, and international environmental NGOs, including Greenpeace and WWF, have been gradually welcomed since the mid-1980s to undertake projects, including joint initiatives with local groups on climate-related issues.[28]

Although NGOs must navigate burdensome registration rules, fund-raising challenges and political sensibilities, they are assuming a growing role in helping to make environmental and climate policies in China more open and accountable.

Notes

1. Dieter Zinnbauer works on emerging policy issues for Transparency International. This article has benefited from substantial input from Jie Yu, who was formerly the head of the policy and research programme of the Climate Group and is currently an independent climate policy analyst.
2. *Wall Street Journal* (US), 'China tops US in energy use', 18 July 2010.
3. Deborah Seligsohn et al., *CCS in China: Toward an Environmental, Health, and Safety Regulatory Framework* (Washington, DC: World Resources Institute [WRI], 2010).
4. UN Development Programme (UNDP), *China Human Development Report 2009/10: China and a Sustainable Future: Towards a Low Carbon Economy and Society* (Beijing: UNDP, 2010).
5. Jennifer L. Turner, 'China's green energy and environmental policies', testimony before the US–China Economic and Security Review Commission, 8 April 2010.
6. Pew Charitable Trusts, *Who's Winning the Clean Energy Race? Growth, Competition and Opportunity in the World's Largest Economies* (Washington, DC: Pew Charitable Trusts, 2010).
7. Rob Bradley, World Resources Institute, Testimony before the US-China Economic and Security Review Commission on Green Energy Policy in China, 8 April 2010.
8. *Wall Street Journal* (18 July 2010).
9. On a positive note, some companies in this sector, both in China and elsewhere, have begun to explore green energy opportunities, a shift that – thinking optimistically – may at least in the long run reorient their interests towards a greener stance.
10. *Christian Science Monitor* (US), 'China confronts global warming dilemma', 12 November 2009.
11. *Wall Street Journal* (18 July 2010).
12. UNDP (2010).
13. Seligsohn et al. (2010).
14. Ibid.
15. Ibid.
16. Mark Wang et al., 'Rural Industries and Water Pollution in China', *Journal of Environmental Management*, vol. 86 (2008), p. 648.
17. Seligsohn et al. (2010); UNDP (2010).
18. Miriam Schröder, 'Challenging the 'public versus private' dichotomy of environmental governance – lessons learned from the Chinese handling of the international clean development mechanism (CDM)', paper submitted to the Amsterdam Conference on the Human Dimensions of Global Environmental Change, 1–4 December 2009.
19. UNDP (2010).
20. Seligsohn et al. (2010).
21. ChinaFAQs, 'China's measurement and compliance initiatives', 22 October 2009, www.chinafaqs.org/library/chinafaqs-chinas-measurement-compliance-initiatives.
22. Barbara A. Finamore, 'Transparency in China: implications for the environment and climate change', testimony before the US Congressional–Executive Commission on China, Roundtable on Transparency in Environmental Protection and Climate Change in China, 1 April 2010.
23. UNDP (2010).
24. *The China Blog, Time* (US), 'Franz Kafka's China, No.237', 4 June 2009.
25. ChinaFAQs (2009).
26. UNDP (2010).
27. Seligsohn et al. (2010).
28. UNDP (2010).

2.5
Climate policies in Austria
Poor accountability breeds slow progress

Shahanaz Mueller[1]

Austria has committed itself under the Kyoto Protocol and related EU burden-sharing agreements to reduce its greenhouse gas (GHG) emissions by 13 per cent from 1990 levels by 2012. In line with other EU countries, moreover, it has offered to expand these commitments under the Copenhagen Accord to a 20 per cent reduction by 2020 (30 per cent if other developed countries take comparable steps).

A series of related laws and policies in Austria are designed to make these goals possible, centred around a climate strategy devised in 2002 and expanded in 2007.

The success of these measures has been insufficient, however. Austria's Audit Court (Rechnungshof) has raised the alarm by stating that Austria's performance in 2008 was off-track by a significant 25 per cent and that the country is also likely to miss its Kyoto targets unless current efforts are further strengthened.[2]

Non-governmental organization (NGO) observers confirm this picture. Austria was singled out as a particularly poor performer on emission trends in Germanwatch's 2010 Climate Change Performance Index. Its overall performance was ranked in the bottom third of EU countries, and the index noted a particular contrast between policies and actual results.[3]

In short, Austria is off-track with regard to meeting its climate commitments, and a number of governance challenges hamper progress in devising effective climate policies.

Austria's climate strategy: limited coordination and unclear specifics

Austria's Climate Change Strategy 2008–2012, the cornerstone of its climate policy framework, has exhibited significant flaws in policy design. Implementing the strategy is not just a task for the federal government – it also requires active involvement by Austria's states. Unfortunately, ideas for an integrative implementation plan are largely absent, and more specific provisions for states and municipal communities were missing for an extended period.[4]

Similarly, the assignment of reduction targets and the designation of responsible actors are not specific enough to generate real accountability and pressure for reform. It is insufficient simply to state that either the federal government, or states or businesses are responsible for taking specific actions. This leaves open the question of who exactly is accountable if the strategy's implementation is flawed or emissions reduction targets are missed. More broadly, neither oversight responsibilities, mechanisms for review and progress assessment, nor sanctions are spelt out in sufficient detail.[5]

Taken together, these inadequacies leave no doubt that the strategy is actually a political declaration of intent that lacks serious consideration for effective compliance mechanisms and responsibilities. A law enacted in 2008 for ecological modernization (Ökologisierungsgesetz) goes some way towards making certain measures more concrete, but it may come too late for Austria to meet its climate commitments.[6]

Climate project funding: disbursements with poor guidance

Limited clarity has also hampered the disbursement of project funding. A €500 million climate and energy fund was established that committed some €121 million in 2009 to support energy efficiency, renewable energy and other climate-related measures. With so much money at stake, the initiative has attracted considerable public attention, and the verdict is rather negative.[7] Even a half-year after it was created, a strategic planning document, a regional development plan and an annual programme were still absent.[8]

Observers have complained about a lack of guidelines for the disbursement of funds.[9] The availability of information about the actual impact and effectiveness of funded activities has also been judged as poor. It all increases the risk that this large-scale funding programme may end up benefiting various interest groups instead of developing renewable energies.[10]

Project results: poor tracking and accountability

Improving the energy efficiency of buildings is an essential element of Austria's climate policy, yet the Audit Court has lamented, in a harsh assessment, that concrete reduction targets are being missed, guidelines are not coordinated and an efficient monitoring system is not in place.[11]

A similar situation has unfolded with regard to another key instrument of Austria's climate strategy. Higher taxes on fossil fuels yielded €391 million in additional revenues in 2008 that were earmarked for infrastructure and climate-related projects. The Audit Court found that no specific guidelines were in place to ensure that only qualified climate projects would benefit, however. There was no transparency, neither inside the authorities nor to the public, on which projects received funding. No specific targets had been set and no mechanisms for tracking project performance and effectiveness had been put in place.[12]

Time running out for reforms?

Austria's failure to translate commitments into actual performance with regard to emissions reductions speaks very clearly to a transparency and accountability gap that hampers implementation of its climate mitigation policies. Matters are worse on the climate adaptation side, for which a national programme or strategy did not even exist as at the end of 2007.[13]

Little time is left to rectify the situation and implement climate policies with stronger governance dimensions that protect against capture by special interest groups, assign clear responsibilities and track performance in an accountable and transparent manner. Only this will help Austria avoid punitive damages for not meeting its commitments, not to mention the potential costs to its economy and society, and the world as a whole.

Notes

1. Shahanaz Mueller works with Deloitte Forensic & Dispute Services in Austria (Vienna office). This article reflects her personal views only.
2. Der Rechnungshof, 'Bericht des Rechnungshofes', Reihe BUND 2008/11, November 2008; Parlament – Republik Österreich, 'EU-Finanzen und Klima-Maßnahmen auf dem Prüfstand des RH-Ausschusses', Parlamentskorrespondenz no. 24, 21 January 2010.
3. Germanwatch, *The Climate Change Performance Index: Results 2010* (Bonn: Germanwatch, 2009).
4. Comment from Thomas Weninger, general secretary, Austrian League of Towns (Österreichischer Städtebund), March 2007; Wirtschaftskammer Österreichisch, 'Strategie zu Erreichung des Kyoto Zieles 2008/2012' ['Strategy for reaching the Kyoto goals, 2008/2012'], at wko.at/up/enet/stellung/kyotostell.htm; comment from Josef Plank, member of a provincial government.
5. Der Rechnungshof (November 2008), p. 29; comment from Thomas Weninger, general secretary, Austrian League of Towns (Österreichischer Städtebund), March 2007.
6. Der Rechnungshof (November 2008).

7.   ORF (Austria), '500 Millionen – keiner weiß, was geschieht', 17 May 2008, at salzburg.orf.at/stories/276264/; APA-OTS (Austria), 'ÖAMTC: Wo bleibt die Transparenz beim Klimafonds?', 4 April 2008.

8.   Austrian Climate Change Strategy 2008–2012, p. 54; Die Unweltberatung, 'Österreichische Klimaschutzstrategie', 12 October 2010, at www.umweltberatung.at/start.asp?ID=9363; Bundesarbeitskammer Österreich: Anpassung der Klimastrategie Österreichs zur Erreichung des Kyoto-Ziels 2008–2012, Präsident Herbert Tumpel; Klima- und Energiefonds, 'Klima- und Energiefonds Presseinformation', 6 December 2007; Der Rechnungshof (November 2008), p. 5.

9.   ORF (17 May 2008).

10. Der Rechnungshof (November 2008), p. 41.

11. Parlament – Republik Österreich (21 January 2010).

12. Der Rechnungshof, 'Bericht des Rechnungshofes', Reihe BUND 2010/7, June 2010.

13. Der Rechnungshof (November 2008).

PART 3

Key elements to building integrity in decision-making

3.0

Key elements to building integrity in decision-making

This part introduces some of the key principles and elements that need to be in place for what could be termed a climate governance integrity system, a web of interconnected checks and balances that protects against corruption and undue influence. The contributions in this chapter situate such a system in the context of norms, practices and experience of related governance frameworks and environmental regimes, enabling us to learn from and benchmark climate governance against important standards and insights already established. The subsequent chapters then focus on how these principles are applied concretely with regard to adaptation and mitigation policies.

Scientific integrity is the first such element of an integrity architecture for climate governance. All climate policy starts with the science of climate change, and safeguarding the independence, integrity and trust of science is a fundamental prerequisite for the legitimacy and efficacy of climate policy-making. How does climate science fare in this regard, now that outright denial of climate change may have become less tenable? How well does scientific fact-finding cope with unprecedented public attention, as evidenced for example by more than 90,000 review comments that the Fourth Assessment Report has received?[1] Sheila Jasanoff broaches this question and finds ample space for improvements.

Peter Haas expands on the pivotal role of evidence and information by drawing on lessons from other regimes. He reviews insights from 30 years of experience with multilateral environmental governance to help us better understand how information supports effective regimes and under what conditions it can fulfil this function best – important lessons for the current and future design of climate governance.

Taking a similar comparative approach Michael Stanley-Jones elaborates on the principles of transparency, participation and environmental justice as they have been articulated in the Aarhus Convention, which is widely regarded as a standard-setter on access to environmental information and norms of participation in this area. Stanley-Jones also explores to what extent the convention itself may be applicable to climate policies and thus provide a direct building bloc for integrity in climate governance.

The global climate summits might have received more public attention and media coverage than any other environmental decision-making process before them. Yet, does this unparalleled visibility also translate into unparalleled transparency and effective participation? Gareth Sweeney seeks to answer this question by examining how public participation in the United Nations Framework Convention on Climate Change (UNFCCC) subsidiary processes hold up to established practices in other international institutions – and arrives at rather surprising results.

Measuring and benchmarking the performance of countries and other stakeholders with regard to climate policies and the strength of the governance system that underpins them is another essential element for creating accountability for climate policy outcomes. Many performance assessments and rankings have been developed for environmental issues and a new crop of indices is being developed for climate policies. Daniel Abreu in his contribution surveys this landscape of performance indices. He seeks to find out whether and to what extent the major indices in use also consider governance factors, shedding light on important gaps and future development priorities for benchmarking climate policy performance.

Rounding off this comparative examination of essential principles and features for climate governance is a refreshing opinion piece by Anthony Giddens. He presents a bold outlook on a possible development trajectory for climate governance, given near deadlocked negotiations in Copenhagen. This contribution may also provide a glimpse on how the integrity architecture for climate policies may have to evolve to respond to climate politics of the future.

Notes

1. InterAcademy Council, 'Climate Change Assessments: Review of the Processes and Procedures of the IPCC', 30 August 2010.

3.1
Climate science
The world is its jury

Sheila Jasanoff[1]

In November 2009 computer hackers struck what seemed to be a blow for transparency in science. Hundreds of private e-mails and thousands of documents were taken from servers at the University of East Anglia's Climate Research Unit, one of the world's most respected centres for climate science. While university authorities cried foul and stressed the unlawful nature of the disclosure, climate sceptics rejoiced because the evidence, they said, showed collusion among scientists to overstate the case for human-induced climate change. The media, ever ready to pounce on scandal in high places, quickly dubbed the episode 'Climategate', an allusion to the disclosure of dirty doings by the White House under US President Richard Nixon. Enforced transparency in this case had the perverse effect of undermining years of hard-fought scientific consensus-building on a topic that is critically important to human survival on this planet.

The damage caused by these disclosures underlines why transparency, as conventionally understood, is not good enough for climate science or climate policy. To prevent the corruption of scientific knowledge for global policy, we need more than just the opportunity to look behind the façade of expert claims at science in the making. We also need conceptual resources to make sense of what we see when the curtains of power, scientific or political, are pulled aside. With respect to science, we need tools to distinguish legitimate disagreement from illegitimate corruption – and to ask the right questions.

It matters, to begin with, whether disagreement originates from within or outside the scientific enterprise. In this respect the events of 2009 were a far cry from the 1990s, when the carbon lobby more or less openly hired scientists to challenge the mounting evidence that emissions of greenhouse gases from human activity are contributing to a rise in global temperatures. In that phase of the climate controversy, carefully selected scientists were paid to sow doubt. Some industry sponsorship for climate scepticism appears to continue, albeit in a less direct way.[2] A poisonous legacy of the earlier period was to politicize climate science itself, however. Against that background, the hacked e-mails seem to reveal a different kind of advocacy – in defence of ideas and interpretations, not just to satisfy financial sponsors. The messages showcase scientists fiercely committed to their pet interpretations of data, and not above *schadenfreude* when bad things befall their opponents.

Historians and sociologists tell us that passionate belief and fierce debate are part of normal science; but should we worry about such zeal when science seeks to serve policy? Can passions, even the passion for scientific truth, corrupt?

Until a half-century ago, the answer to both questions would have been 'No'. Scientists were deemed to be their own best judges and critics, ensuring quality control through peer review, publication, replication, competitive funding and big rewards, such as Nobel Prizes, for demonstrated excellence. With so many safeguards in place, science was widely seen as incorruptible. Besides, in the end nature was always there as the final arbiter: false claims would eventually be ruled out by nature's refusal to behave as predicted. The Soviet state under Joseph Stalin could not make crops grow in accordance with Trofim Lysenko's optimistic claims.

As society's need for science has risen, however, the mechanisms for securing reliable knowledge have in some respects grown weaker. Today we need a more distributed and participatory approach to the stewardship of science – one that engages scientists, governments and publics in a shared enterprise of responsible knowledge-making. There are three good reasons why a more complex system of accountability needs to be put in place, and they all apply forcefully to climate science.

First, scientists no longer are (if they ever were) disinterested seekers after esoteric knowledge. Modern societies demand that their scientists be ends-directed and instrumental in their uses of expertise. Governments liberally support science and encourage scientists to seek out opportunities to patent and profit from their work. The rationale is that such incentives ultimately serve the public good – by rapidly translating discoveries at the bench into inventions and solutions that further economic growth or meet other social needs. Successful scientists enjoy media attention and often material rewards once accorded only to politicians, film stars and business tycoons. Pulled into closer collaboration with policy leaders, the climate science community has learned to navigate the worlds of politics, hobnobbing with presidents and Cabinet secretaries and campaigning for its findings to be more widely heard. Indeed, across the Western world there has been a rise in the attractiveness of science advice as a career path. In short, science has become another face of politics.

Second, many issues that science addresses demand forms of work that are not easily self-correcting. Policy-relevant knowledge typically grows from interdisciplinary collaborations in which methods and criteria for quality control are not well established in advance but emerge instead from the dynamics of enquiry and assessment. This creates a potential for public misunderstanding and potential corruption, since only those internal to the relevant technical communities can fully appreciate why choices were made in one way and not others. There is no external judge to whom conflicts can be referred or who can act as an impartial arbiter of disagreements. Thus, a body such as the Intergovernmental Panel on Climate Change (IPCC) may take enormous pains, as the IPCC indeed did, to ensure that its reports undergo extensive peer review. Nevertheless, peer critique may never satisfy powerful external sceptics that IPCC findings were not simply the consensus of a narrow and clubby elite. This was an important lesson of 'Climategate'.

Third, nature can no longer be counted on to act as a timely corrective when human judgement fails. This is partly because, in the middle of the 20th century, human societies moved from a preventive to a precautionary posture with respect to many of our expectations from policy. For example, it is no longer acceptable to wait until environmental threats are imminent or people are visibly harmed before undertaking protective action. The costs would be too high: massive loss of life, incalculable property damage, pandemic disease and, in the case of climate change, human survival itself. As environmental policy moves from a reactive to an anticipatory posture, however, it becomes harder to judge whether scientists are crying wolf, whether their predictions are accurate enough and whether public resources are being efficiently targeted towards the most pressing needs.

If we cannot rely on science's self-policing or nature's benign regulation, how can we ensure the integrity of knowledge about urgent global problems such as climate change? The most promising way is to enlarge the circles of accountability within which scientific judgement has to prove itself. It is to supplement mere voyeurism, triggered by malicious disclosure, with systematic opportunities for reasoned criticism and informed give and take.

National legal and administrative systems have developed many mechanisms for enabling publics to question the scientists who advise governments: hearings, consultations, freedom of information, opportunities to contest findings and demand reasons, and even lawsuits for misuse of knowledge. These processes do not seek to establish a singular truth or eliminate all disagreement. Instead, they ensure that experts are honest, that they fairly represent the spectrum of doubts and uncertainties *and* that they are technically skilful at reading nature. Most important, good administrative procedures are two-way streets along which publics can carry their information and analyses to the seats of power, knowing that reasonable arguments must be heard and answered respectfully.[3]

As yet, such mechanisms are thin or missing at the global level, although the need for them is, if anything, more critical. Bodies such as the IPCC must find or invent procedures to allow their judgements to be publicly tested, not only for substance but also for process. A raft of recent, comprehensive assessments of both the IPCC and the incident at the University of East Anglia reject the charge of manipulation and lack of integrity on the part of individual scientists, but they also underscore this demand for more attention to process: more proactive and routine disclosure of data sources, a stronger culture of transparency, and enhanced capacity to respond to public comments during the peer review process.[4] These recommendations go part-way towards meeting the demand for accountability in climate science, but they need to be reinforced. Scientific peer review, however open and transparent, is no substitute for informed citizen participation in all stages of knowledge production – not merely far downstream at the stage of technical review of already drafted consensus documents.

In sum, the integrity of climate science depends on faith more than truth; faith that the best people are using the best of their judgement in pursuit of the best available knowledge. Only if climate scientists can satisfy the jury of the world that they have met those tests will their product rise above the malice of hackers and 'denialists' and prove itself as reliable knowledge for governing the planet.

Notes

1. Sheila Jasanoff is Pforzheimer professor of science and technology studies at Harvard University's John F. Kennedy School of Government.
2. See, for example, *Mother Jones* (US), 'Most credible climate skeptics not so credible after all', 26 February 2010; *Guardian* (UK), 'ExxonMobil continuing to fund climate sceptic groups, records show', 1 July 2009; and *The New Yorker* (US), 'Covert operations', 30 August 2010.
3. For a more extensive elaboration of these arguments, see Sheila Jasanoff, *The Fifth Branch: Science Advisers as Policymakers* (Cambridge, MA: Harvard University Press, 1990).
4. On East Anglia, see UK House of Commons, 'The disclosure of climate data from the Climatic Research Unit at the University of East Anglia', Eighth Report of Session 2009-10, Science and Technology Committee, 31 March 2010; on the IPCC, see Netherlands Environmental Assessment Agency, *Assessing an IPCC Assessment: An Analysis of Statements on Projected Regional Impacts in the 2007 Report* (The Hague: Netherlands Environmental Assessment Agency, 2010) and InterAcademy Council, Climate Change Assessments: *Review of the Processes and Procedures of the IPCC*, pre-publication copy (Amsterdam: InterAcademy Council, 30 August 2010).

3.2

Making climate governance accountable

Reflections on what can be learned from international environmental governance

Peter M. Haas[1]

After more than 30 years of experience with multilateral environmental governance, it is now possible to assess some common assumptions and draw lessons about what makes for effective international environmental governance (IEG). Three broad conclusions can be reached about the nature of IEG.[2]

First, multiple actors are involved in environmental governance. States are no longer the sole legitimate sources of authority in this area. They now share roles and expectations about their behaviour with the private sector, civil society, scientific networks (epistemic communities) and international organizations.[3]

Second, governance entails a number of discrete components. It can be broken down into the analytic categories of agenda-setting, negotiated rule-making and enforcement/compliance.

Third, usable information is a vital element of environmental governance. While most of the research on information has looked at agenda-setting, usable information is also important for contributing to strong rule-making and compliance/ enforcement for all three of these components.

Information and social learning/agenda-setting

Many politicians, policy-makers and private sector decision-makers are ignorant about the environmental effects of their activities, as well as being uncertain about what policies will best mitigate (or provide adaptation for) those environmental threats.

In selective instances – such as dealing with stratospheric ozone, European acid rain and land-based sources of marine pollution – the provision of usable information has led to social learning. Leaders and governments recognized that their traditional foreign policy goals were severely impeded by environmental degradation outside their territorial boundaries, and relied on expert information about how the degradation of global environmental commons affected national well-being. In response they upgraded national goals to promote ecological integrity and sustainable development.

Information and negotiated settlements

Actors are also often ignorant or uncertain about the choices or policies that other actors are likely to make, and thus collective action is difficult without confidence about these features of strategic behaviour.

In order for governments to willingly enter into binding legal agreements, they must have confidence that those agreements are likely to benefit them, and that others are likely to reciprocate their commitments. Thus, usable information is highly valued by decision-makers and negotiators, not only to clarify their own interests but also to advance their understanding about the likely behaviour of others.

Information and compliance/enforcement

Effective governance requires states to convert international obligations into national law (compliance) and to enforce those commitments on domestic society (enforcement).

Those responsible for accelerating the transition to a post-carbon economy require accurate information about the behaviour of markets in key greenhouse-gas-producing countries. Who is funding green projects? Are green technology and greenhouse-gas-reducing projects performing as promised? This information is of value to firms that actually make short-term decisions about technological choices.

The vital role that non-state actors play in enforcement on the ground has also been confirmed. Structured adversarial relations between multinational corporations and civil society set the context in which firms are held accountable for their activities through non-governmental organization (NGO) practices of 'naming and shaming', while green firms are recognized and potentially gain market share.

Experience shows that information about malfeasance will resonate more strongly with consumers when related commitments are formulated through partnerships between civil society and the private sector, rather than purely by the private sector.[4]

What makes information usable? Quality and legitimacy

A key lesson learnt is that for information to fulfil its multiple functions in IEG it must be accurate, legitimate and timely.[5]

For effective agenda-setting, the related information must relate to true threats and not respond prematurely to false alarms. In IEG this typically involves reporting by transnational scientific communities organized into standing research and monitoring networks by international organizations.[6] In climate change this has largely been the purview of the Intergovernmental Panel on Climate Change (IPCC).

Studies of international environmental regimes clearly indicate that legitimacy is crucial in this context. This legitimacy is largely a function of the social authority accorded to the process by which the information is developed and delivered. Are the 'experts' largely impartial and independent of some form of patronage? Is the knowledge base on which they rely transparent?[7] These questions are already playing a prominent role in climate policy-making. As lessons from other environmental governance regimes show, their resolution will be crucial for making climate governance effective.

Notes

1. Peter M. Haas is a professor at the Department of Political Science, University of Massachusetts, Amherst.

2. Norichika Kanie and Peter M. Haas (eds), *Emerging Forces in Environmental Governance* (Tokyo: UNU Press, 2004); Edgar Grande and Louis W. Pauly (eds), *Complex Sovereignty: Reconstituting Political Authority in the Twenty-First Century* (Toronto: University of Toronto Press, 2005); Peter M. Haas (ed.), *International Environmental Governance* (Aldershot: Ashgate, 2008); Peter M. Haas et al. (eds), *Controversies in Globalization* (Washington, DC: CQ Press, 2009).

3. Frank Biermann and Bernd Siebenhüner (eds), *Managers of Global Change* (Cambridge, MA: MIT Press, 2009); Peter M. Haas, 'Introduction: Epistemic Communities and International Policy Coordination', *International Organization*, vol. 46 (1992), pp. 1–37.

4. Benjamin Cashore et al., 'Can Non-State Governance "Ratchet Up" Global Environmental Standards?', *Review of European Community and International Environmental Law*, vol. 16 (2007), pp. 158–172; Benjamin Cashore et al., *Governing Through Markets: Forest Certification and the Emergence of Non-State Authority* (New Haven, CT: Yale University Press, 2004); Sanjeev Khagram, 'Possible Future Architectures of Global Governance', *Global Governance*, vol. 12 (2006), pp. 97–117; Graeme Auld et al., 'The New Corporate Responsibility', *Annual Review of Environment and Resources*, vol. 33 (2006), pp. 413–435.

5. UN Environment Programme (UNEP), *Global Marine Assessment: A Survey of Global and Regional Marine Environmental Assessments and Related Scientific Activities* (Nairobi: UNEP, 2003); Peter M. Haas, 'When Does Power Listen to Truth? A Constructivist Approach to the Policy Process', *Journal of European Public Policy*, vol. 11 (2004), pp. 569–592.

6.   Organizations such as the IPCC, Millennium Ecosystem Assessment, Ozone Trends Panel, Global Environment Fund (GEF) Scientific and Technical Advisory Panels and the Long-Range Transboundary Air Pollution (LRTAP) Working Group on Integrated Assessment Modeling. Efforts are under way to initiate a biodiversity assessment panel through the International Mechanism of Scientific Expertise on Biodiversity (IMoSEB). Ad hoc arrangements were created for the North Sea, Baltic Sea and various marine pollution issues through the Group of Experts on Scientific Aspects of Marine environmental Pollution (GESAMP), and for Antarctica through the Convention on the Conservation of Antarctic Marine Living Resources (CCAMLR).

7.   See Sheila Jasanoff, section 3.1 in this volume.

3.3

The Aarhus Convention

A blueprint for inclusive and accountable climate governance?

Michael Stanley-Jones[1]

Access to information, public participation in decision-making and access to justice are three key dimensions across which climate policy needs to engage the public. One historic legal agreement not only provides an intriguing and progressive template for how these important principles can be elaborated, it is also readily applicable to some aspects of climate change governance.

Known as the UN Economic Commission for Europe (UNECE) Aarhus Convention, it commits 45 European and Central Asian countries to practical principles of environmental justice.[2] The convention's origin can be traced to principle 10 of the Rio Declaration on Environment and Development, adopted at the 1992 Earth Summit in Rio.[3] As the only legally binding instrument that implements this Rio principle, the convention's public participation provisions include access to environmental information, early and ongoing public involvement in decision-making, transparent and user-friendly processes, an obligation that authorities consider public input, a supportive infrastructure and effective means of enforcement and appeal.

The convention also addresses the public's right of access to information, as well as the collection and dissemination of information. The convention's Protocol on Pollutant Release and Transfer Registers[4] seeks to 'enhance public access to information through the establishment of coherent, integrated, nationwide pollutant release and transfer registers', which are also envisaged to capture information on major sources of greenhouse gas (GHG) emissions.

The convention's rights-based approach can also help advance demands for climate justice. Among its climate-related decision-making processes are those related to permits/licences for certain projects involving GHG emissions; and national, provincial or local plans, programmes and policies on climate change and related sectors, e.g. energy, human rights, transportation, agriculture, industry.

Not all climate-related decisions fall within the scope of the convention, however. For example, decision-making on Clean Development Mechanism projects outside the jurisdiction of Aarhus parties may not be covered. This also applies to emissions trading, carbon taxation, eco-labeling, auditing and liability schemes. As a consequence, some observers have called for the convention to be amended to bring its provisions in closer alignment with the demands of the age of climate change.[5]

Progress on these issues would still leave unresolved the fact that the convention is currently regional in focus and binds primarily countries in Europe and central Asia, whereas a truly international approach is required for the global challenge of climate change.

These constraints notwithstanding, the convention sets pioneering standards for progressive participation and rights to information in environmental governance. It is therefore a very important reference point for international agreements on climate governance, which so far fall short of Aarhus on several counts.[6]

Notes

1. Michael Stanley-Jones is public information officer at the United Nations Environment Programme (UNEP). This contribution reflects his personal views only.
2. The Aarhus Convention – formally the UN Economic Commission for Europe (UNECE) Convention on Access to Information, Public Participation in Decision-making and Access to Justice in Environmental Matters – was adopted in Aarhus, Denmark, on 25 June 1998 and entered into force on 30 October 2001. It currently has 44 parties, including the EU as a regional economic integration organization. Two signatories to the convention have not yet ratified the agreement.
3. The UN Conference on Environment and Development, Rio de Janeiro.
4. The Kiev Protocol on Pollutant Release and Transfer Registers to the UNECE Aarhus Convention was adopted on 23 May 2003 and entered into force on 8 October 2009, when it had been ratified by 20 countries and by the European Community. It currently has 26 parties.
5. Jerzy Jendroska (former vice chairperson of the Meeting of the Parties to the Aarhus Convention and professor of law, Opole University, Poland), remarks to the International Conference on the Role of Information in an Age of Climate Change, University of Aarhus, Denmark, 13–14 November 2008.
6. See Daniel Abreu, section 3.5 in this volume.

3.4

Civil society and the climate change process

How does participation compare as a measure of transparency?

Gareth Sweeney[1]

How does public participation in the United Nations Framework Convention on Climate Change (UNFCCC) subsidiary processes[2] hold up to established practices in other international institutions? In terms of the relative size of governing bodies, relevance to the public interest, and level of civil society participation, the human rights arena provides an interesting comparison.

The principle of public participation is duly reflected in article 71 of the United Nations Charter, as well as relevant resolutions and rules of pursuant intergovernmental bodies.[3] Quickly following the formation of the UN, the former UN Human Rights Commission took the early lead in applying article 71, on the grounds that a body whose decisions affected the lives of individuals also needed to heed the voices of individuals. The Commission's 2006 successor, the UN Human Rights Council, has in many ways improved upon the practices for non-governmental organization (NGO) engagement, to the point at which it now provides a good barometer for measuring approaches to participation across multilateral bodies.

In terms of formal engagement, the UN Human Rights Council provides that accredited NGOs[4] can observe all plenary and special sessions. NGOs can submit formal written submissions in advance of the session, which then become part of the official documentation. They can speak on all agenda items of the Council plenary, in principle allowing them to address all thematic and country-specific issues.[5] They may also address questions and comments to independent experts of the Council as well as to the High Commissioner for Human Rights during the interactive dialogues with states. NGO experts are also invited as a matter of course to speak as panellists in formal thematic days of discussion.

Concerning meetings of the Human Rights Council's intergovernmental working groups, NGOs are entitled to attend all sessions, and are generally granted speaking time on all issues. Draft working texts are publicly accessible. In informal meetings on draft resolutions (equivalent to UNFCCC 'contact group' meetings), state sponsors may host open or closed meetings, and in open meetings NGOs may be called upon for interventions. In either case, the status of meetings is announced in advance through bulletins and their accessibility is very seldom subject to change. Side meetings of particular relevance to public participation, such as resolutions on human rights defenders or freedom of expression, are almost always public.

In contrast, the agendas of UNFCCC subsidiary bodies do not have a formal provision for NGO participation. According to the draft rules of procedure of the UNFCCC, the right of NGOs to intervene in the meetings is left to the discretion of the president or the chair of the meeting.[6] The practice of the chairpersons of subsidiary bodies such as the Ad Hoc Working Group on Long Term Cooperative Action has been to allow general statements from NGO constituencies at the outset of each meeting, but not to offer them the floor during substantive discussions. It has also become the norm for informal meetings, during which most of the negotiations take place, to be closed to civil society. The openness of 'contact group' meetings to NGOs is also subject to change at the last minute, through notification on monitors in the conference premises, and in open meetings NGOs may observe but not participate.

In terms of access to information, both the UNFCCC and UN Human Rights Council websites host live and archived webcasts of plenary meetings.[7] The latter also subcategorizes the archived webcast by speaker, however, so that viewers can source individual statements. The secretariat of the UN Human Rights Council also hosts an online 'extranet', which files all statements delivered by Council member and observer states by date and agenda item, as well as all statements by NGOs and national human rights institutions.[8] The extranet is updated daily and is an invaluable means of holding states to account.

The UNFCCC has no such system for organizing and publicizing statements. Aside from uploaded high-level statements, one has to sit through up to three hours of webcasting and then transcribe statements manually. Likewise, while the UN Human Rights Council extranet uploads all draft resolutions, voting records and outcome documents immediately, too often such information is not available on the UNFCCC's website, and thus participating NGOs and states are excluded from having an informed position on developments.

It should be noted that both the UNFCCC secretariat and the UN Human Rights Council secretariat endeavour to provide meeting rooms and office spaces for NGOs, as well as space for side events and exhibits, yet attention has more recently focused on the UNFCCC on account of problems related to NGO entrance to the Conference of the Parties in Copenhagen in December 2009.[9] In response, perhaps the most logical place to begin a reform of engagement should be in the interim subsidiary processes in Bonn, and it is positive at least to hear that the UNFCCC secretariat is currently considering means to improve participation.[10]

How, then, can the UNFCCC process improve? Issues related to access to public documentation, physical accessibility and other logistical matters are the responsibility of the UNFCCC secretariat and can be readily addressed. A good starting point would be to acknowledge and seek to integrate the provisions of the Aarhus Convention as working principles,[11] to assess the working methods of equivalent secretariats in the UN system, such as the UN Human Rights Council, and to subsequently apply best practice as described above.

Questions related to participation in formal and informal meetings rest with states parties to the UNFCCC, specifically the Subsidiary Body on Implementation, and it is more difficult here to arrive at a consensus to revise practices once they have been put in place. The 'beyond 2012' discussions currently under way offer a good opportunity for states to review their commitments and factor in a strengthened role for civil society, however.

The goal should be to arrive at a point where the positions and bargaining tactics of state delegates can be tracked and appraised by the very public that these negotiators are meant to represent, and where civil society is fully informed and can play a meaningful part in collective actions that affect everyone.

Notes

1.   Gareth Sweeney is editor-in-chief of the *Global Corruption Report*.
2.   The term 'subsidiary processes' of the UNFCCC refers to the Ad Hoc Working Group on Long Term Cooperative Action under the Convention (AWG-KP), the Ad Hoc Working Group on Further Commitments for Annex I Parties under the Kyoto Protocol (AWG-LCA), the Subsidiary Body for Scientific and Technological Advice (SBSTA) and the Subsidiary Body for Implementation (SBI). See http://unfccc.int/2860.php.
3.   For example, ECOSOC Resolution 1996/31 (updating ECOSOC Resolution 1296 (XLIV) of 23 May 1968), which addresses the consultative relationship between the UN and non-governmental organizations.
4.   A/HRC/5/1, rules 7 and 8.
5.   Including, for example, the promotion and protection of all human rights (item 4), and human rights situations that require the Council's attention (item 5).

6.   Draft Rules of Procedure of the Conference of the Parties and its Subsidiary Bodies, rule 7, FCCC/CP/1996/2, 22 May 1996.

7.   See http://unfccc.int/press/multimedia/webcasts/items/2777.php and http://www.un.org/webcast/unhrc/archive.asp.

8.   The form to receive the password to access the Human Rights Council extranet is available at www2.ohchr.org/english/bodies/hrcouncil/form.htm.

9.   See, for example, 'NGO shutdown at Copenhagen climate talks', at http://tcktcktck.org/stories/campaign-stories/ngo-shutdown-copenhagen-climate-talks.

10. See www.stakeholderforum.org/sf/index.php?option=com_content&view=article&id=190&Itemid=77.

11. Noting of course that the UNFCCC cannot be party to the Aarhus Convention, there is nonetheless nothing to stop the secretariat from integrating its provisions as principles of good practice.

3.5

Holding commitment to account

The governance dimension in climate change indices

Daniel Abreu[1]

Climate-change-related indices are important public policy tools that help to measure the ability, commitment and performance of a country or an industry with regard to climate change adaptation or mitigation efforts. Such indices make it possible, for example, to benchmark and rank country mitigation action, creating peer pressure for and scrutiny of performance. Similarly, on the adaptation side, climate indices can help map risks, vulnerabilities and adaptation pressures and therefore help prioritize support for adaptive action.

For all such indices to be truly effective and useful, however, they would also have to consider governance issues as an important dimension – such as control of corruption and rule of law at the national level, and the strength of verification and oversight at the sector level. Without governance factors, indices will fail to describe vulnerabilities comprehensively and will offer little confidence about the ability to translate commitments into practice or verify the reported performance. This could lead to a situation in which the trust that is so essential to sustain a global system of mutual promises and commitments is eroded, thus posing serious threats to the overall effectiveness and sustainability of international climate agreements.

Conceptualizing climate indices

Climate change indices generally fall into two categories: those that measure *performance* and those that measure *capacity*. Performance-based indices are the most conventional type, measuring variables such as CO_2 emission levels and energy use. These indices are particularly useful in tracking progress on established climate goals.

Capacity-based indices, on the other hand, are more likely to contain qualitative variables and also to consider governance factors, when measuring the ability of governments or systems to respond to climate change effectively.

An overview of climate indices through the governance lens

The recent generation of adaptation-related indices includes a variety of governance or corruption aspects – for example, HELIO International's Adaptive Capacity Indicators include a civic/governance dimension[2] and, more explicitly, Maplecroft's Climate Change Vulnerability Index[3] includes an index for institutions, governance and social capital.

Additionally, some prominent climate research centres – including the Tyndall Centre for Climate Change Research and the International Institute for Sustainable Development – have developed adaptive capacity proposals that factor in institutional and governance aspects. Two of the most prominent adaptation indices – Germanwatch's Global Climate Risk Index[4] and the United Nations Environment Programme's (UNEP's) Environmental Vulnerability Index[5] – lack clear governance-related factors, however.

Some major mitigation-related indices, such as Yale and Columbia's Environmental Performance Index,[6] the Environmental Indicators of the European Environment Agency and the Environment Indicators of the Organisation for Economic Co-operation and Development (OECD),[7] also exhibit a rather limited regard for governance factors. One notable exception is the World Resources Institute's (WRI's) Climate Analysis Indicators Tool,[8] which includes an aggregated governance indicator. Additionally, WWF's G8 Climate Scorecards[9] aim to assess the 'climate political will' of the G8 countries, though without an explicit indicator for governance-related issues.

Two of the more complex issues related to index design are how governance variables should be weighted and which variables should be included. In this sense, no climate measurement generates primary governance data, but instead all rely upon existing governance metrics. The most commonly used is the World Bank's Worldwide Governance Indicators,[10] which include voice and accountability, political stability and absence of violence, government effectiveness, regulatory quality, rule of law and control of corruption.

Climate focus	Climate index	Description	Governance dimensions
Mitigation	WRI Climate Analysis Indicators Tool (CAIT).	Information and analysis tool focusing on greenhouse gas emissions, and socio-economic and natural factors.	Explicit. Socio-economic indicators include an aggregated governance indicator.
	WWF G8 Climate Scorecards.	Ranking of G8 countries based on energy use, emissions levels and policies for the future.	Not directly, though it assesses a country's level of political commitment.
	Yale/Columbia Environmental Performance Index (EPI).	Tracking of environmental stresses to human health and ecosystem vitality.	Not directly.
Adaptation	Maplecroft Climate Change Vulnerability Index 2009.	Cluster of six indices related to socio-economic and environmental factors.	Explicit. Includes an index with seven indicators focusing on institutions, governance and social capital.
	UNEP Environmental Vulnerability Index.	50 'smart indicators' that capture key elements of environmental vulnerability. Includes a climate change sub-index.	Limited. Measures the number of environmental treaties in force and the number of conflicts.
	Germanwatch Global Climate Risk Index.	Indicators that measure human and material impacts of extreme weather events.	Not directly.

Table 3.1 Governance dimensions in selected climate/environmental indices

The case for more integrated and sector-relevant climate indicators

The links between climate mitigation and adaptation are increasingly being recognized – a dynamic that is also reflected in the development of related indicators. Integrating both capacity and performance oriented elements, the Intergovernmental Panel on Climate Change (IPCC) has more recently proposed the concept of *response capacity*, which includes governance aspects such as the structure of critical institutions, allocation of decision-making authority, stock of social capital, and the credibility and ability of decision-makers to manage information.

This conceptual approach is still in its infancy, however. There is also the need to develop more robust indices that are particularly sensitive to the different measurement issues of diverse climate-sensitive sectors.

Independent of the area or focus of climate indices, governance factors and transparency must be prominent both in substance and methodology if policy relevance and credibility are to be attained.

Notes

1. Daniel Abreu is currently working with the United Nations Children's Fund in the Dominican Republic, and previously worked for Transparency International. This contribution reflects his personal opinion only.
2. See www.helio-international.org/energywatch/indicators.cfm.
3. See www.maplecroft.com/portfolio/climate_change/index_analysis/2010/ccvi_2010.
4. Sven Harmeling, *Global Climate Risk Index 2010: Who Is Most Vulnerable? Weather-Related Loss Events since 1990 and How Copenhagen Needs to Respond*, briefing paper (Bonn: Germanwatch, 2009).
5. See www.vulnerabilityindex.net/EVI_Indicators.htm.
6. Yale Center for Environmental Law and Policy, 'Environmental Performance Index', at http://epi.yale.edu.
7. OECD, *Key Environmental Indicators* (Paris: OECD, 2008).
8. WRI, *CAIT: Indicator Framework Paper* (Washington, DC: WRI, 2009).
9. WWF and Allianz, *G8 Climate Scorecards 2009* (Gland, Switzerland, and Munich: WWF and Allianz, 2009).
10. See info.worldbank.org/governance/wgi/index.asp.

3.6
Personal view
A fresh approach to climate politics?

Anthony Giddens[1]

I am not one of those who felt downhearted by the failure of the climate change meetings held in Copenhagen in December 2009. To be sure there have been some strongly negative consequences. The UN, which staged the whole event, has been weakened. The bickering that occurred between nations and groups of nations undermined the idea that the world is coming together to combat what is probably the greatest set of risks humanity faces this century. The Copenhagen Accord – on the face of things the only tangible result to come from the meetings – is a slim document, put together by a handful of nations and to which countries at least initially committed themselves only in a voluntary way.

However, consider the counterfactual. Suppose the event had been successful and a comprehensive treaty signed by the 192 nations whose representatives attended. Legal obligations to reduce carbon emissions would have been established. Yet such obligations already existed for the developed countries under the Kyoto agreements. A range of such states which had formally signed up more or less ignored them. Since there are no effective punitive sanctions within the international system, nothing could be done to bring the laggards into line. Kyoto took more than seven years from being 'finalized' in 1997 to come into practice. The framework which might have emerged from Copenhagen would have been even more cumbersome and the process of applying it almost certainly would have dragged on even longer.

Will the Copenhagen Accord, by contrast, lead to concrete action on a scale commensurate with the huge task involved? Obviously it could founder. We shall have to wait and see. The 16th Conference of the Parties (COP 16) in Cancún, which will have taken place by the time this account is published, may provide some answers. In the longer term, however, I tend to think that we will come to view the accord as marking a new beginning of potential importance. The accord in principle allowed a much smaller group of countries to move ahead quickly in setting out targets and specify how they will go about achieving them. That group involves the major polluters; it cross-cuts the divide between the developed and developing world, so destructive at Copenhagen. For the first time the leaders of the large developing economies – China, India and Brazil – announced carbon-related reduction targets.

The situation post-Copenhagen also made it clear that a lot of new thinking is needed to make further progress. Some such innovations will have to come at the level of international relations. The accord could provide the anchor, but a variety of bilateral and regional agreements will be needed in order to make real progress. A handful of countries create the vast bulk of carbon emissions, and they should be meeting in a regular way. People get uneasy about a G2 – the US and China working together bilaterally – but in the struggle to contain climate change it is a necessity, since the two states alone contribute over 40 per cent of annual carbon emissions. The same applies to countries suffering from deforestation – thus the ongoing relationship between Brazil and Indonesia should be supported and in some large part externally funded.

There should also be a G3, since the European Union countries collectively are big polluters. The EU was sidelined at Copenhagen because of its leadership problem: who speaks on its behalf? The summit made clear that a single person should be authorized to negotiate on behalf of the EU on climate change matters, either the new High Representative, Cathy Ashton, or someone who is specifically appointed for the task. The accord promised that the rich states will supply funding, building up to US$100 billion a year, to help developing countries either to reduce their emissions or to adapt to the consequences of climate change. The related funding needs made a transnational tax on financial transactions – in all likelihood organized through G20 – no longer look as implausible as it did even a couple of years ago. If set at an appropriate level it could generate that amount and more.

Copenhagen was also insightful as it showed the consequences of putting too much of a focus on costs. It demonstrated that it makes sense to place the emphasis also upon mutual opportunity, wherever it can be found. Self-interest is generally a more powerful motivating force in international politics than appeals to altruism. Most countries now (quite rightly) are worried about future energy security. We should use the overlap with climate change policy as creatively as possible to spread renewable technologies across the world. G20, but also the World Bank, would seem to be the appropriate agencies for encouraging such processes.

Copenhagen also raised the important question of what the role of the UN should be in the future so far as climate change is concerned. The essential weaknesses of the UN were fully on display during the summit. Proceeding by means of full consensus simply is not possible upon issues where there are abiding divisions of interest in the world community. Most of the real action therefore started to migrate elsewhere. Yet, feeble though it is in decision-making terms, the UN is in some respects irreplaceable. Whatever comes from the accord and now Cancún can't be left to the participating countries to monitor. We require a global regime, for example, to assess the emissions of states and track their progress. The logical home for a body set up to carry out such work is the UN, since its participation is the best guarantee of impartiality.

Finally, Copenhagen underscored that activism below the level of nations will play a major role in the struggle against climate change, and some means should be found of giving non-governmental organizations (NGOs) a formal role in international bargaining. Participation by groups below the level of the nation state, as well as transnational collaboration between them – local communities, cities and local states – will be equally important. Depending on one's perspective, the debacle at Copenhagen could be judged to have led to a period of relative quiescence, in which no comprehensive progress was made in pursuing an active climate change policy. I do not think that this will – in the longer run – be remembered as Copenhagen's lasting legacy. The American writer Henry Adams once wrote: 'Chaos often breeds life, when order breeds habit.' He had a point. My hope, and anticipation, is that the impasse reached at Copenhagen will have prompted just that burst of creativity and ingenuity we need, even if its full impact may only unfold after Cancún.

Notes

1. Anthony Giddens is former director of the London School of Economics and a member of the UK House of Lords.

PART 4

Ensuring integrity and transparency in climate change mitigation

4.0

Ensuring integrity and transparency in climate change mitigation

Transparency International

Reducing global greenhouse gas (GHG) emissions will require a transformative shift in energy policy, technological innovation, resource management and consumption habits. Around the world, solutions are being introduced, including developing policies for energy efficiency, implementing market-based mechanisms, such as emissions trading or carbon taxes, and rolling out low-carbon technologies.

Despite the urgent need to reduce global levels of GHG emissions, in 2010 the International Energy Agency (IEA) noted that 'the world has continued to move – and even at an accelerated pace – in the wrong direction'.[1] Reversing this trajectory is possible, but, with little room for error, mitigation solutions must be designed, implemented and managed with the transparency and oversight necessary to guarantee their effectiveness. The authors in this part outline much of the progress that has already been made in reducing opportunities for corruption and improving the accountability of mitigation actions, and identify areas that still have to be addressed.

The rigorous measuring, reporting and verification of emissions are crucial for finding appropriate abatement solutions and measuring progress. Taryn Fransen's opening contribution emphasizes how accounting systems for GHG emissions inform mitigation strategies and determine the effectiveness of emissions reduction efforts. She notes that, although robust systems of GHG accounting have been developed, opportunities for manipulation and gaps in reporting requirements continue to exist.

These concerns take on greater importance as the number of countries measuring, reporting and verifying emissions grows. While developed countries are historically responsible for climate change and must meet binding commitments to reduce emissions, many developing (non-Annex I) countries are also now crafting their own mitigation strategies. Although many of these plans are to be supported by developed countries, trust remains weak. A contribution from Juan Pablo Osornio, Ingmar Schumacher and Krina Despota considers the capacity, commitment and corruption challenges that will need to be addressed for developed and developing countries to collaborate on mitigation strategies. These considerations will become increasingly important in the years ahead, as developing countries now rank among the top global emitters.

While by no means the only path to widespread emissions reductions, a number of contributions in this part consider carbon markets because of their prominence in the debate on mitigation strategies. The introduction under the Kyoto Protocol of market-based mechanisms presents opportunities for the cost-effective reduction of GHG emissions, but also significant risks. Lambert Schneider suggests in his analysis that the European Union's Emissions Trading System (EU ETS), the Clean Development Mechanism (CDM) set up under the Kyoto Protocol, and other carbon markets, while a potentially powerful tool to mitigate climate change and incentivize technological innovation, can be susceptible to conflicts of interest and regulatory weaknesses. Supporting case studies on the government allocation and sale of emissions allowances from Emília Sičáková-Beblavá and Gabriel Šípoš of TI Slovakia and Gábor Baranyai for TI Hungary, respectively, illustrate how failure to transparently manage carbon credits undermines public trust. These are followed by an examination from TI Sri Lanka of shortcomings in the implementation of environmental impact assessments (EIAs), which could carry implications for the environmental sustainability of CDM projects or adaptation activities in that country.

Thomas Marcello traces the recent history of the voluntary carbon markets and, although he notes an increasing trend towards quality on the part of carbon credits, he also identifies opportunities for improving the environmental and social integrity of offset projects. Gernot Wagner, Nathaniel O. Keohane and Annie Petsonk then look towards the future of carbon markets, suggesting that sectoral crediting – in which entire industrial sectors in developing economies meet an emissions cap and sell credits derived from this reduction – will be successful only if the system is designed with integrity from the outset.

Shifting away from markets, this part then focuses on the private sector. The business community holds considerable sway over whether efforts to stop climate change are successful. A transformative shift towards low-carbon infrastructure and technologies threatens the interests of many dominant market players, however, most notably the fossil fuel industry. If these companies cannot identify opportunities for profit in this new context, the risk grows that they will unduly exert their influence to slow mitigation progress. David Levy considers how innovative business models, collaboration between private sector actors and predictable policy signals at local, nation and international levels can keep industry positively engaged in a transition to a low-carbon future.

Ultimately, business responsibility towards climate change solutions must improve. While reducing emissions remains the most crucial mitigation activity that businesses can undertake, it is important to recognize that mitigation outcomes are increasingly shaped by corporate involvement in public climate change policy. Ryan Schuchard and Laura Ediger argue that corporate disclosure that includes the robust reporting of engagement with public climate change policy has a direct impact on the scope and effectiveness of GHG reduction strategies, and is thus a central component of business best practice in the climate change arena.

That message resonates with the anti-corruption community, which has for years worked closely with companies to improve corporate reporting. Transparencia por Colombia provides one example of these efforts, with a summary of a pilot study aimed at improving standards of transparency in corporate governance in private and publicly owned utility companies – an exercise that can contribute to broader expectations for reporting on climate-relevant information, such as energy efficiency.

The extent to which companies represent their actions and products honestly also relates directly to the purchasing choices of consumers – choices that, in turn, have an impact on global emissions. Fred Pearce tracks the ongoing tendency of some companies to mislead consumers about the climate-friendly credentials of products and services, and considers how governments and consumers can step up their efforts to hold companies to account.

As companies make adjustments to mitigate climate change, so too must governments. The move towards a low-carbon future will be marked by the widespread roll-out of renewable energy sources and shifting resource demands. How prepared countries are to manage the governance challenges associated with this transformation will have direct consequences for the public's trust in such initiatives, the interest of the private sector in financing low-carbon projects and, ultimately, the success of a transition to a green economy. Nadejda Komendantova and Anthony Patt present evidence that perceptions of corruption in bureaucratic processes in North Africa could significantly increase the costs of developing renewable energy projects. A case study from TI Spain flips the equation, describing how financial incentives for renewable resources in the form of feed-in tariffs created incentives for fraud in the absence of robust oversight mechanisms.

The development of a green economy will also place intensified demand on natural resources, such as those used in solar installations or hybrid vehicles, among other things. Stefan Bringezu and Raimund Bleischwitz map many of these natural resources against areas of weak governance and consider whether sizeable monetary transfers could trigger a new, green 'resource curse'. Transparencia Bolivia takes a closer look at how one country has so far balanced the development of its lithium reserves with public participation and information-sharing.

Finally, while every effort must continue to be made to reduce global GHG emissions, some scientists are now beginning to consider the possibility of intentional manipulation of the Earth's atmosphere. This continues to be a controversial and an undesirable means of reducing global temperatures, with unpredictable consequences, but one which may nevertheless move ahead. Graeme Wood explores the current lack of accountability surrounding research and governance in connection with geoengineering.

Notes

1. International Energy Agency, *Energy Technology Perspectives 2010: Scenarios and Strategies 2050* (Paris: IEA, 2010), p. 5.

4.1

Greenhouse gas accounting

A foundation for sound climate governance

Taryn Fransen[1]

Formulating, implementing and enforcing policies intended to reduce greenhouse gas (GHG) emissions[2] requires credible and reliable information that shows where emissions come from and who is responsible for them. Just as they are essential for the integrity of the global financial system, standardized accounting frameworks, transparent reporting mechanisms and robust verification systems are vital for effective climate governance.

The consequences – to the environment, communities and markets – of inadvertently inaccurate or intentionally misleading GHG information are significant. The expansion of carbon markets and offset trading has added even more layers of complexity and vulnerability to the integrity of GHG accounting.

Because GHG accounting has many objectives, various accounting approaches have been developed (see box 4.1). For example, the Kyoto Protocol relies on national GHG inventories to determine whether participants meet their agreed-upon emissions limits. Likewise, carbon markets depend on standardized methodologies to ensure that credits translate accurately into tonnes of emissions reduced. Corporate executives and investors rely on corporate GHG inventories to assess the financial or reputational risks associated with emissions. Finally, consumers increasingly have the option to choose among competing products based on their carbon footprint.

Although great strides have been made over the last decade towards standardizing GHG accounting and promoting emissions disclosure, information is still sparse or unreliable for some critical emissions sources. Moreover, the absence of robust rules for some types of GHG accounting leaves certain accounting and reporting systems vulnerable to manipulation.

Because emissions are the result of decisions by a decentralized and diverse set of actors in virtually every sector of the global economy, developing comprehensive GHG information will require time, financial investment and capacity-building.

Box 4.1 Major types of GHG accounting frameworks

National

National GHG inventories, required for parties to the United Nations Framework Convention on Climate Change (UNFCCC), are intended to document all human-caused emissions and removals within a country. Inventory reporting requirements are decided by the Conference of the Parties (COP) to the UNFCCC, and methodologies are developed by the Intergovernmental Panel on Climate Change (IPCC).[3] The Kyoto Protocol has additional accounting rules that determine which sources and sinks[4] count towards a country's assigned amount of permitted emissions. Increasingly, subnational jurisdictions, such as states, provinces and cities, also conduct GHG inventories based on a similar approach.

Corporate

Corporate GHG inventories include a company's direct emissions (from sources owned or controlled by the reporting company) as well as indirect emissions from purchased electricity and other sources not owned or controlled by the reporting company. Companies use inventories to assess risks, identify opportunities to reduce emissions and publicly report emissions information. Standards include the GHG Protocol Corporate Standard and ISO 14064-1 of the International Organization for Standardization (ISO).

Facility

Facility-level accounting includes emissions from a specific industrial installation; facility-level data collection is either a component of corporate GHG inventories or is undertaken to comply with mandatory reporting requirements.

Project

Project-level accounting, which quantifies the impact of GHG mitigation projects, is used to assign credits for offset projects in compliance-driven carbon markets, such as the Clean Development Mechanism (CDM), and in voluntary markets. Rules include the GHG Protocol for Project Accounting, ISO 14064-2 and the Voluntary Carbon Standard, as well as methodologies used in specific markets, most prominently the CDM.

Product

This emerging practice tracks emissions associated with a specific good or service throughout its life cycle – be it a clothes dryer, a loaf of bread or mail delivery. The GHG Protocol and ISO are both developing international standards. The Carbon Trust has developed a standard (PAS-2050) for product life cycle accounting in the UK.

Strengths and weaknesses of the GHG accounting infrastructure

During the last decade five accounting elements have emerged that facilitate a 'true and fair'[5] description of GHG emissions or reductions. They are:

- accounting principles;
- accounting frameworks;
- quantification methods;
- reporting systems; and
- quality assurance and verification.

Each element plays a unique role in ensuring robust and transparent GHG information, but each also has shortcomings or vulnerabilities.

Accounting principles

The principles of accuracy, comparability, completeness, consistency and transparency, used initially by the UNFCCC to guide the development of national GHG inventories, have been modified for other types of GHG accounting, such as at the corporate or project level (see table 4.1).

GHG accounting principles provide guidance to practitioners by applying standards and requirements to specific situations. In some cases, fundamental trade-offs exist between principles. For example, completeness suggests that even small, highly uncertain sources should be included in an inventory, although this could compromise accuracy. Applying GHG accounting principles is therefore more of an art than a science, and more developed accounting frameworks and quantification methods mean that practitioners will need to rely less on subjective interpretation of the principles.

Principle	Definition	National	Corporate	Project
Accuracy	Ensure that GHG emissions are neither systematically over- nor under-quantified; reduce uncertainties as far as practicable.	✓	✓	✓
Comparability	Estimates are comparable between different reporting parties, based on agreed methodologies and formats.	✓		
Completeness	Account for all sources, sinks and gases within inventory boundary; consider all relevant information.	✓	✓	✓
Conservativeness	Use conservative assumptions, values and procedures when uncertainty is high; do not overestimate GHG reductions.			✓
Consistency	Allow meaningful comparisons of emissions estimates over time.	✓	✓	✓
Relevance	Use data, methods, criteria and assumptions that are relevant to the intended use of the information and serve the decision-making needs of users, including external stakeholders.		✓	✓
Transparency	Disclose and explain assumptions and methodologies clearly; disclose and justify any exclusions.	✓	✓	✓

Sources: WRI and World Business Council for Sustainable Development (WBCSD), *The Greenhouse Gas Protocol: A Corporate Accounting and Reporting Standard* (rev. edn.) (Washington, DC: WRI/WBCSD, 2004); WRI and WBCSD, *The Greenhouse Gas Protocol: The GHG Protocol for Project Accounting* (Washington, DC: WRI/WBCSD, 2005); UNFCCC, 'Updated UNFCCC Reporting Guidelines on Annual Inventories following Incorporation of the Provisions of Decision 14/CP.11', Document FCCC/SBSTA/2006/9 (New York: UNFCCC, 2006).

Table 4.1 GHG accounting principles

Accounting frameworks

Accounting frameworks create common expectations regarding the construction of GHG accounts and make it easier to identify potential bias. They delineate which sources should be included in the accounts, determine which entities should account for which emission sources or reductions, and promote the comparability of GHG information between entities and over time.

Certain elements play a fundamental role in limiting opportunities to manipulate GHG accounts, including the following:

● The *inventory boundary*, which establishes all GHG sources that have to be accounted for and limits the possibility of skewing results by arbitrarily including or excluding certain sources from consideration. The comparability of accounts depends critically on standardized rules for determining who accounts for which emissions (for example, the joint ownership of a single facility), and how far up or down the value chain company or project owners should go to account for their effects on emissions.

- The ability to *track emissions over time* consistently from a given base year. A robust accounting framework will not allow a company or country to claim 'reductions' simply by applying a different methodology to the base year compared to the reporting year, or by including sources in the base year that are excluded from the reporting year.
- Emissions reduction projects are compared against a baseline scenario that estimates what an emissions level would be without mitigation efforts. Identifying the baseline scenario involves consideration of hypothetical, counterfactual situations in order to determine whether reductions occurring under the project are 'additional' to those that would have happened anyway. As section 4.3, following, indicates, establishing consistent and objective approaches for this has proved to be difficult.

Despite the safeguards provided by accounting frameworks, two major gaps remain. First, they simply have not been developed or standardized for some situations. For example, no standardized approach yet exists for financial institutions and governments to estimate likely GHG impacts from policies and investments, though some banks and jurisdictions are exploring this.[6] Nor is there yet a commonly accepted framework that balances a company's GHG assets (offsets or other reduction instruments) and liabilities (emissions). Therefore, a company can reduce emissions from a source, sell credits from the resulting reductions and still count these same reductions towards meeting its own voluntary reduction goal, effectively double-counting the reduction. This issue primarily affects corporate accounts under voluntary programmes, and new guidelines are being developed to address it.[7] A similar problem may arise in national GHG accounts, as developing countries that are eligible to host CDM projects are also taking on voluntary reduction targets. No rules prevent CDM or Reducing Emissions from Deforestation and Forest Degradation (REDD) projects from counting against the targets of both buyer and seller countries simultaneously. Moreover, because seller (developing) countries' targets are voluntary in the international context, it is unclear how this might be resolved.

The second shortcoming relates to accounting standards that are insufficiently robust to prevent manipulation. For example, in order to evaluate compliance with national emissions targets, the Kyoto Protocol considers the effects of afforestation, deforestation and reforestation. Because deforestation is narrowly defined, however, emissions from some types of land conversion are not counted against a country's allowed emissions. So, if a forest area is cleared but is not intended for another land use, this does not count as deforestation, and therefore a country's emissions are not debited against the assigned amount – even if the deforested area does not get replanted or regain its original forest cover and carbon storage level.[8]

Quantification methods

Although it is sometimes possible to measure GHG emissions directly from the flue, it is far more common and cost-effective to calculate emissions by multiplying a unit of a commonly tracked activity, such as fuel consumption, by a factor of GHG emissions in terms of that unit, known as an emission factor. The adequacy of this approach depends on the availability of complete and accurate activity data and of appropriate emission factors, which are more widely available for some source types than for others. Carbon dioxide emissions from fossil fuel combustion, for example, can be estimated to a fairly high level of certainty. On the other hand, estimates of nitrous oxide from agricultural soils and transport, methane from landfills, and perfluorocarbons (PFCs), hydrofluorocarbons (HFCs) and sulphur hexafluoride (SF6) are subject to far greater uncertainty,[9] due to technology, local climate or other considerations.

While these factors can compromise the quality of GHG information, robust accounting standards and methodologies limit the potential for exploiting the inherent uncertainty in order to manipulate information. For example, quantification methodologies for offset projects typically require a procedure for calculating emission factors and to estimate reductions conservatively.

Reporting systems

Reporting systems collect GHG information and make it accessible to a range of stakeholders, including regulatory agencies, GHG reporting programmes or the general public. Reporting can be mandatory or voluntary and, although a great deal of reported information is publicly available, it is not comprehensive.

At the national level, UNFCCC parties are required to report their emissions to the secretariat either annually (Annex I countries) or every few years as determined by the COP (non-Annex I countries). While most non-Annex I countries follow IPCC inventory guidelines, they are not required to do so, making reports variable in quality.[10] Under the 2010 Cancún Agreements, however, non-Annex I countries would submit biennial update reports that contain national GHG inventories as well as information on mitigation actions, needs and support received.[11] This revision would greatly enhance the time series of data available, though it is not clear whether it would improve inventory quality.

Capacity is a significant obstacle to comprehensive reporting. Historically, most non-Annex I counties have treated GHG inventories as one-off projects rather than ongoing programmes. This is consistent with the funding mechanism provided through the Global Environmental Facility, which was designed to support individual national communications rather than the establishment of ongoing inventory programmes.[12] Consequently, money has been used to contract experts to prepare single reports rather than invested in establishing permanent data collection processes and programmes.[13] Until funding and technical capacity is scaled up to enable non-Annex I countries to submit regular and comprehensive data, it will be impossible to understand national and regional emissions trends fully.

Subnationally, facility-level reporting is generally required in countries where GHG emissions are or may soon be regulated – namely Australia, Canada, the EU, Japan and, as of 2010, the US. Reporting laws do not cover all sources; regulators typically require reports from sources that produce a significant share of total emissions. Developing countries generally do not require facility-level reporting, although this may change as more countries contemplate new national emissions limitations. Facility-level information can be made public, although some programmes exempt companies if disclosure would compromise confidential business information.

A growing number of companies disclose their emissions voluntarily, a trend driven by stakeholder and investor demands, baseline establishment and protection,[14] and participation in voluntary programmes (see figure 4.1).[15] Voluntary GHG registries include the Climate Registry (North America), Brazil's GHG Protocol Program and similar programmes developed to build capacity, engage the private sector on climate issues and create the political will for mitigation. Some industry associations also run programmes for their members. The quality of information varies by programme; some are more prescriptive than others in terms of adherence to internationally accepted accounting standards and quantification methodologies. Since their focus tends to be on building capacity and engagement in GHG issues, most do not require verification.

Ideally, GHG reporting systems would not only promote comprehensive data collection, but also present it in a manner convenient for a range of audiences to use and interpret. This requires that data be easily accessible – in a public, online database, for instance – and presented in a transparent format that can be aggregated and disaggregated. It also requires thoughtful communication based on a commonly understood terminology. In 2009, for example, the UK Statistics Authority suggested that a report by the Department of Energy and Climate Change fell short of codes of practice for suggesting that emissions had dropped 12.8 per cent without clarifying that almost a third of this represented carbon credit purchases. While the data were correct, the authority pointed out that non-expert readers might misinterpret them.[16]

Overall, the trend is clearly towards increased GHG reporting, both mandatory and voluntary. By the beginning of 2009 only eight non-Annex I countries had submitted national inventories for 2000 data; by mid-2010 25 had done so. Australia and the US have begun requiring facility-level reporting, and Canada has ratcheted down the emission threshold at which reporting becomes mandatory.

At the corporate level, the Carbon Disclosure Project, which acts on behalf of 475 institutional investors to solicit GHG information from companies, found that 83 per cent of its Global 500 respondents reported GHG emissions.[17] Intensifying these efforts requires not just the financial and technical expertise to produce comprehensive and robust reports but also the public pressure to ensure that reporting is a priority.

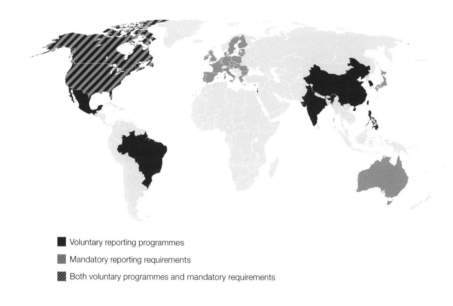

■ Voluntary reporting programmes

▨ Mandatory reporting requirements

▨ Both voluntary programmes and mandatory requirements

This map does not include global voluntary programmes such as the Carbon Disclosure Project or WWF Climate Savers.

Source: Adapted from Taryn Fransen et al., *Measuring to Manage: A Guide to Designing GHG Accounting and Reporting Programs* (Washington, DC: WRI, 2007).

Figure 4.1 Jurisdictions with voluntary, corporate-level GHG accounting programmes

Quality assurance and verification

Quality assurance and verification are essential for ensuring the integrity of GHG reports. A variety of approaches have been piloted and adopted for national inventories, facility-level reporting and crediting mechanisms. Nonetheless, oversight capacity and technical knowledge need to be significantly enhanced to ensure the reliability of GHG information.

At the national level, GHG inventories of Annex I countries are assessed by international experts, who have to pass a qualifying examination. The review process is generally considered adequate, although reviewer capacity is an ongoing challenge.[18] While the UNFCCC has made significant investments in building this capacity, the number of available experts is insufficient to meet review needs, creating a struggle to ensure the integrity of inventories.

Non-Annex I inventories have not historically been subject to technical review, but the Copenhagen Accord and the subsequent Cancún Agreements provide for a process of 'international consultations and analysis' of the biennial update reports.[19] This process, the subject of a highly contentious international debate, aims to enhance transparency of mitigation actions and their effects while avoiding infringements on national sovereignty or taking a view on the appropriateness of domestic policies and measures. While it is not yet clear what form this process will take, some form of technical review would greatly help to enhance transparency and trust in the reported data. It would also provide a channel for feedback to non-Annex I technical experts on how to improve their inventories. Should non-Annex I inventories become subject to an Annex I type of review process, however, the shortage of qualified reviewers will become even more acute.

Similar capacity challenges for verifying mitigation projects include a paucity of technically qualified experts and possible conflicts of interest between offset project developers and those who assess the emissions reductions of those projects (see Lambert Schneider, section 4.3).[20] In response to shortcomings in the third-party verification process, the CDM Executive Board has increased its oversight, scaling up its staff fivefold over the last five years.[21]

Programmes mandating facility-level reporting may also require reporting by accredited third parties or allow spot auditing when non-compliance is suspected. At the national, project or facility level – for programme managers and regulators alike – devising verification and quality assurance requirements is a matter of balancing risk with cost. Comprehensive verification can be resource-intensive, requiring extensive time investment by technical experts. Some steps can be taken to overcome this hurdle: Japan, for example, is developing an electronic data system to faciliate data collection at the corporate and national levels.[22]

For voluntary corporate inventories, some programmes and companies have indicated that the value they receive from verification does not justify the cost. Although most programmes typically do not require third-party verification, some, such as the Climate Registry, the Brazil GHG Protocol Program and the Mexico GHG Program, offer differentiated recognition to companies that report verified information. Other voluntary programmes emphasize technical assistance, capacity-building and inventory management planning – focusing on facilitating rather than verifying information accuracy. Honest misreporting can still happen. In 2009 an energy company familiar with GHG reporting systems nevertheless misclassified 70 million tonnes of carbon.[23] Verification can therefore provide an extra layer of protection from reputational risk.

Certainly, steps are being taken across various GHG accounting initiatives to improve quality assurance. Accreditation schemes now certify competent verifiers, and the ISO has developed standards for verifying GHG and accrediting verifiers.[24] While these relatively new efforts provide valuable guidance on identifying competent verifiers, broader reforms may be needed to protect against conflicts of interest.

Moving forward

Driven by the emphasis on 'measurable, reportable and verifiable' mitigation actions in the international policy framework, and by private sector interest in managing GHG-related risks all along supply chains, there is tremendous momentum towards more comprehensive and robust GHG information. As reporting becomes more widely mandated and encouraged, capacity has begun to replace political will as the prominent constraint. Technical and financial support, new accounting frameworks, enhanced data collection and user-friendly quantification tools will contribute to building the necessary capacity.

Countries and companies that are major sources of emissions require technical support to develop data sets and adopt methodologies to prepare reliable inventories. The technical knowledge of reviewers and verifiers must be enhanced, and the number of experts filling these roles considerably expanded, in order to meet the needs of both private sector accounting initiatives and national GHG inventories. For the national inventories of developing countries, assistance in building technical capacity should be matched by financial support from the international community so as to develop more frequent and robust inventories.

Increasing stakeholder access to GHG information will be enhanced by identifying and prioritizing gaps in accounting frameworks and implementing multi-stakeholder processes to fill these gaps. Candidates include 'balance sheet' frameworks and new approaches for governments and international financial institutions, including multilateral development banks, to account for the GHG impact of their policies and investments.

Enhanced data collection is also needed. By building on existing non-GHG data collection systems, it should be possible to ensure consistency while promoting synergies and saving resources. For example, China collects energy data to support its Top 1000 Energy-Consuming Enterprises programme. GHG data could be collected simultaneously through relatively simple amendments.[25]

Developing a comprehensive and user-friendly database of emission factors and GHG quantification methodologies for inventory developers would facilitate data quantification. Such a resource could build on the current IPCC emission factor database, but its mandate should be broader than national inventories in order to include corporate, facility and life cycle accounting, and it should contain user-friendly guidance on selecting appropriate emission factors for various sources and applications.

While building capacity, policy-makers and civil society must remain vigilant to ensure that the emerging policy architecture builds on existing systems so as to address GHG accounting, reporting and verification needs adequately. This is especially important given the uncertain future of the Kyoto Protocol and its associated emissions-tracking infrastructure.

The global community needs to work towards improved practices in reporting emissions and removals from land-use change. Common standards are also necessary for national registries to track inventories, reduction units and associated transactions. The role of civil society organizations in demanding access to GHG information and deploying it to call attention to best and worst practices is also critical; these organizations should seek opportunities to enhance their technical capacity.

Taken together, these steps would greatly enhance the availability and utility of GHG information for decision-making and accountability purposes.

Notes

1.   Taryn Fransen is a senior associate with the Climate and Energy Program at the World Resources Institute (WRI).
2.   Throughout this contribution, the term 'emissions' refers both to emissions of GHGs to the atmosphere and to the removal of carbon from the atmosphere through carbon sequestration; 'emissions reductions' refers to increases in emissions removals.

3. IPCC Task Force on National Greenhouse Gas Inventories: see www.ipcc-nggip.iges.or.jp.

4. According to the Fourth Assessment Report of the IPCC, a source is any process, activity or mechanism that releases a GHG, an aerosol or a precursor of a GHG or aerosol into the atmosphere, and a sink is any process, activity or mechanism that removes a GHG, an aerosol or a precursor of a GHG or aerosol from the atmosphere. See www.ipcc.ch/pdf/assessment-report/ar4/wg1/ar4-wg1-annexes.pdf.

5. The term 'true and fair' is a financial accounting convention to signify that accounting reports represent correct and complete information about a business's financial situation.

6. See, for example, go.worldbank.org/SCH4V8MXE0.

7. For more information on the forthcoming guidelines, see www.ghgprotocol.org/performance-tracking-guidelines.

8. Florence Daviet, *Forests in the Balance Sheet: Lessons from Developed Country Land Use Change and Forestry Greenhouse Gas Accounting and Reporting*, working paper (Washington, DC: WRI, 2009).

9. Kristin Rypdal and Wilfried Winiwarter, 'Uncertainties in Greenhouse Gas Emission Inventories: Evaluation, Comparability and Implications', *Environmental Science and Policy*, vol. 4 (2001), pp. 107–116.

10. Taryn Fransen, *Enhancing Today's MRV Framework to Meet Tomorrow's Needs: The Role of National Communications and Inventories*, working paper (Washington, DC: WRI, 2009).

11. UNFCCC, 'Draft Decision -/CP.16: Outcome of the work of the Ad Hoc Working Group on long-term Cooperative Action under the Convention.'

12. Clare Breidenich and Daniel Bodansky, *Measurement, Reporting and Verification in a Post-2012 Climate Agreement* (Arlington, VA: Pew Center on Global Climate Change, 2009), pp. 13–14.

13. Ibid.

14. Companies operating in countries where emissions are not yet regulated sometimes anticipate that regulators will eventually allocate emissions allowances based on historical emissions levels. This possibility can create a perverse incentive that discourages companies from taking early, voluntary action to improve efficiency. Some companies view the establishment of GHG inventories as a means to document their baseline emissions and avoid being penalized with lower permit allocations under eventual regulation.

15. See Samantha Putt del Pino et al., *Sharpening the Cutting Edge: Corporate Action for a Strong, Low-Carbon Economy* (Washington, DC, WRI, 2009).

16. Correspondence from Sir Michael Scholar, UK Statistics Authority, to Tim Yeo, MP, 'Reporting of UK emissions under the EU trading scheme', 19 October 2009.

17. PricewaterhouseCoopers (PwC), *Carbon Disclosure Project 2009: Global 500 Report* (London: PwC, 2009).

18. See Fransen (2009), pp. 3-5.

19. UNFCCC, 'Draft Decision -/CP.15: Copenhagen Accord', 18 December 2009; UNFCCC, 'Draft Decision -/CP.16: Outcome of the work of the Ad Hoc Working Group on long-term Cooperative Action under the Convention.'

20. Mark Schapiro, 'Conning the Climate: Inside the Carbon-Trading Shell Game', *Harper's Magazine*, February 2010, pp. 31–39; Emma Lund, 'Dysfunctional Delegation: Why the Design of the CDM's Supervisory System Is Fundamentally Flawed', *Climate Policy*, vol. 10 (2010), pp. 277–288.

21. Schapiro (2010).

22. International Carbon Action Partnership (ICAP), *Summary Report on the First Global Carbon Market Forum on Monitoring, Reporting, Verification, Compliance and Enforcement: 'Backbone of a Robust Carbon Market'* (Berlin: ICAP, 2008).
23. *Recharge* (Norway), 'Carbon hole the size of Denmark', 11 December 2009.
24. ISO 14064-3 ('Specification with guidance for the validation and verification of greenhouse gas assertions'); 14065 ('Requirements for greenhouse gas validation and verification bodies for use in accreditation or other forms of recognition'); 14066 ('Competence requirements for conducting greenhouse gas validation and verification engagements with guidance for evaluation').
25. Michelle Zhao, 'On common ground: a CO_2 calculation tool based on China's *Energy Utilization Status Report*', unpublished paper prepared for the WRI, 2009.

4.2

Measuring, reporting and verification of NAMAs and their support

Considering capacity, corruption and commitments

Juan Pablo Osornio, Ingmar Schumacher and Krina Despota[1]

Although industrialized nations are widely agreed to be historically responsible for climate change, it has become increasingly evident that mitigation efforts by these countries alone will be insufficient to ensure that greenhouse gases (GHGs) do not cause a global temperature rise of more than 2°C above pre-industrial levels. GHG emissions from developing and emerging economies (non-Annex I countries) are growing rapidly. In absolute quantities, China is now the world's largest emitter,[2] and projections suggest that, by 2025, emissions from developing countries including Brazil, China, India and Mexico could outpace those of developed countries.[3]

While the principle of 'common but differentiated responsibilities' has been interpreted to mean that developed countries should take the lead on emissions reductions, international negotiations have in recent years recognized that developing countries[4] also need to work towards reducing emissions and developing their infrastructure along a low-carbon pathway. The 2007 Bali Action Plan called for developing countries to consider undertaking measurable, reportable and verifiable (MRV) 'nationally appropriate mitigation actions' (NAMAs).[5] The agreements reached at COP 16 in Cancún in 2010, called the Cancún Agreements, reconfirm that commitment by clearly stating that developing countries will introduce NAMAs to achieve a deviation in emissions relative to business-as-usual emissions in 2020. Unlike the somewhat ambiguous acceptance of the Copenhagen Accord, the Cancún

Agreements' broad support boosts emerging countries' incentives to design and implement mitigation actions.

The Cancún Agreements also provide the tools needed for NAMAs to be accomplished. They call for a registry to match finance, technology and capacity-building support from developed countries, with NAMAs from developing countries – also to be listed in the registry – that require the international support. The Cancún Agreements further agreed that NAMAs receiving international support would be subject to domestic and international MRV following guidelines still to be developed, while NAMAs that required no international support would be subject to domestic MRV also following as yet undetermined guidelines.

How these terms – NAMA and MRV – are developed in practice continues to be discussed in the international arena, just as they are being operationalized in many national and local contexts. Broadly speaking, NAMAs can be any range of activities by a developing country to reduce GHG emissions, from cap-and-trade programmes or carbon taxes to technology deployment programmes or sustainable development initiatives. Although more precise categories continue to be negotiated, three general types might be envisaged: unilateral NAMAs, requiring no international funding; supported NAMAs, using international financing, capacity-building or technology support from developed countries; and credited NAMAs, earning credits from the international carbon market.[6]

Box 4.2 Major sources of public financing for developing-country mitigation

Public support for mitigation financing currently comes through a variety of channels. Bilateral support from developed countries (Annex II)[7] under the United Nations Framework Convention on Climate Change is reported through national communications,[8] or via the Global Environment Facility (GEF). Between 2003 and 2006 the GEF's annual funding to climate change projects was about US$163 million, and between 2003 and 2007 OECD Development Assistance Committee members contributed an annual average of US$3.5 billion specifically for climate change mitigation.[9] Multilateral development banks (MDBs) also fund climate change mitigation in various ways: average annual commitments to clean energy and energy efficiency in developing countries totalled some US$4 billion annually in 2006 and 2007,[10] and the World Bank also purchases GHG emissions reductions credits derived from mitigation projects based in developing countries.

The MDBs, via the World Bank, also contribute to the Climate Investment Funds (CIFs) – financing instruments aimed at driving low-carbon and climate-resilient development. By July 2010 the Clean Technology Fund (CTF), one programme under the CIF umbrella, had allocated over US$4 billion to investment projects related to 13 investment plans in countries that are ODA-eligible.[11] Plans include the development of wind power (Egypt), concentrated solar power

(Middle East and North Africa), energy-efficient transport (Mexico) and geothermal energy (Indonesia).[12] Non-governmental organizations (NGOs) have noted a lack of transparency in the process used to select country investment plans, and have called for greater involvement from civil society in the development of investment plans.[13] The newer Scaling-up Renewable Energy Programme in Low-income Countries, established at the Copenhagen conference in December 2009, had received almost US$300 million in pledges by mid-2010.[14] Discussion regarding the governance and transparency of bilateral funding and the CIFs – which also include funds for adaptation – are discussed more broadly in part 5 (see Rebecca Dobson, section 5.1.1).

Towards greater trust and cooperation

Though progress was made in Cancún, international negotiations over MRV systems have been particularly contentious. Although, historically, reporting has been a common feature in multilateral environmental agreements, the verification of such data has not.[15] Implementing MRV systems could be seen to be leading developing countries towards the eventual introduction of binding emissions reductions targets,[16] or placing undue hardship on developing countries.[17] Acknowledging these potential problems, the Cancún Agreements explicitly decided that content and frequency of national communications from non-Annex I parties would 'not be more onerous than for [Annex I States]'. To achieve this, as has been the case with national communications, developed countries will provide financial support for developing countries' reporting. One would view this as the first and basic step that ensures trust-building and signals commitment towards cooperation.

Robust implementation of MRV systems should be welcomed as a tool for enhancing trust between both Annex I and non-Annex I countries and between citizens and their governments. It is also important to acknowledge that a number of countries that are likely to rely on external support for mitigation activities are also those for which perceptions of corruption are high.[18] For developed countries, therefore, a robust MRV system may provide assurances that resources for mitigation actions will be managed responsibly, even in countries or regions sometimes perceived as demonstrating lower levels of government accountability. Further, within countries that will receive international support for NAMAs, MRV may provide citizens with an added layer of accountability to ensure that their governments are implementing effective mitigation strategies and programmes.

Developing countries also stand to benefit from an MRV system that keeps closer tabs on support from developed countries. Experience from development aid demonstrates that support often has been delivered against timescales ill-suited to their intended projects and that allocation may be managed by multilateral organizations that inadequately represent the interests of developing countries.[19] Tracking commitments in the context of climate change can be particularly difficult. One study examining pledges for mitigation and adaptation made by the European Union in 2001 found that it was impossible to say with any certainty whether commitments had been met by 2009.[20] A strong MRV system that links mitigation actions to specific funding commitments will help alleviate much of the financing uncertainty faced by developing countries. For both parties, rigorous measuring, reporting and verifying of NAMAs and of their support should help develop trust and facilitate cooperation. Creating such a system presents some challenges, however.

Overcoming challenges in measuring, reporting and verifying NAMAs and their support

Developing capacity

Among the biggest challenges for implementing MRV systems for NAMAs will be obtaining sufficient financing and technological support to ensure reliability and accuracy and to enable the development of in-country expertise. At the national level, the experience of self-reporting in other governance regimes suggests that developing in-country expertise in monitoring and reporting can fall short even after decades. For example, 20 years after the World Trade Organization's (WTO's) Trade Policy Review Mechanism was introduced, only one-fifth of 70 developing countries had independent agencies to undertake policy reviews.[21]

Within the climate regime, developing and developed countries alike have struggled with accuracy in their national communications, and long delays between submissions have not been uncommon.[22] Funding and support for developing countries' national communications have been sporadic, making it difficult to develop ongoing systems for monitoring and reporting on emissions.[23] With regards to reporting frequency, the Cancún Agreements state that non-Annex I parties will submit national communications and inventories every four years, along with biennial update reports on GHGs (least developed countries and small island developing States will have greater flexibility in meeting these timelines). While the Agreements state that this should be done according to capacity, enhanced reporting can be expected to place strain on a country's financial and technical resources. In mid-2010, the expert group[24] that provides technical support for the development of national communications noted a lack of technical support for non-Annex I countries undertaking their third national communications.[25] Thus, as guidelines for domestic and international MRV are developed, a simultaneous challenge will be to ensure that national institutions tasked with measuring, reporting and verifying mitigation actions in developing countries are given the support they need – both from developed countries and civil society – to build domestic-capacity.

For supported NAMAs, international MRV systems could include in-country visits by expert reviewers, allowing for more accurate verification of emissions and policy actions, though this would require significant resources.[26] Centralized reviews, which the UNFCCC currently coordinates for Annex I countries, will need further resources for reliably gauging mitigation policies in developed and developing countries. Insufficient capacity to support international or domestic MRV systems will result in lower accuracy in tracking the progress of mitigation efforts.

Designing adaptable MRV models

A second challenge for the years ahead will be to develop MRV guidelines that accurately capture diverse mitigation efforts and low-carbon development strategies. Some mitigation actions will not lend themselves to measurement against emissions targets – a plan to implement broad multi-sector energy efficiency policies, for instance. Ensuring that these efforts are nevertheless subject to measurement and review that allows comparison between countries, while allowing for differences in national contexts, will be crucial to ensuring that MRV systems are both relevant and fair.[27] Efficient and complete reporting will play a critical role in this aspect.

NAMAs that allow the measurement of emissions impacts may also stretch the boundaries of the current structures in place for accounting and verifying emissions. Credited NAMAs, for example, would present a threat of double-counting if a mitigation project was counted both as a reduction in a developing country's emissions while simultaneously creating emissions reductions credits used by an Annex I nation to count against its own emissions. Proposals to avoid this outcome include 'walling off' the emissions reductions from pre-existing Clean Development Mechanism (CDM) projects so that they cannot count against the emissions reductions goals of supported NAMAs.[28]

If proposals for the crediting of NAMAs move forward (see Wagner, Keohane and Petsonk, section 4.3.5 in this volume), entire industrial sectors in developing countries will be expected to reduce emissions collectively. This approach could present a number of challenges for MRV systems. In China, for instance, an estimated 1200 companies make up the iron and steel sector, the largest of which provided only 6 per cent of domestic crude steel production in 2007.[29] Relying on so many small producers to provide the data necessary to determine emissions reductions could present significant accuracy and resource challenges for MRV. Rules for the measurement and reporting of a broad menu of mitigation actions must be agile enough to accurately address such nuances.

Addressing external and internal corruption

As NAMAs become operational, internal and external corruption and accountability risks are likely to present themselves. The establishment of CDM projects throughout the developing world has already highlighted examples of independent verification companies undertaking lax or inaccurate assessments of mitigation projects (see section 4.3 in this volume). There are also concerns that criteria determined by the host countries to assess the sustainable development benefits of CDM projects are vague, that the approval process is vulnerable to corruption and that, in some cases, conflicts of interest are a risk if the authorities entrusted to review CDM projects can also advise on project proposals.[30]

NAMAs that have no direct emission reduction target should nevertheless have quantifiable milestones for project implementation. MRV of these projects could thus create a more structured system of oversight that increases project accountability. Failure to design measurements that are objective and demonstrable could increase the incentives for those engaged in the project to siphon off funding for personal gain at the cost of project effectiveness. Large-scale mitigation projects involving significant financial flows may also prove susceptible to corruption throughout the project cycle if domestic verifiers have an incentive to create favourable reports. A truly independent system with public oversight will need to be implemented to ensure that MRV systems do not become the final stage of complicity in a corrupt process.

As the form of mitigation actions expands in developing countries, corruption risks may also multiply. Sectoral crediting that commits entire sectors of industry to an emissions cap could, in a worst-case scenario, lead to collusion among businesses in establishing an inflated emissions baseline or manipulating emissions measurements and reports. Such activities would not be unique to developing countries; in 1998 the US Environmental Protection Agency (EPA) agreed a settlement with companies in the diesel engine industry for over US$1 billion for selling engines equipped with software that disabled the engine's emissions control system during highway driving.[31] Especially in countries where technical expertise is lacking to monitor and measure mitigation technologies adequately, such risks may be expected to increase.

Confronting these risks in order to ensure a reliable reflection of emissions will require a similar arsenal of tools to those used by anti-corruption practitioners. The implementation and enforcement of the United Nations Convention against Corruption (UNCAC) and regional anti-corruption conventions can contribute to the penalization of corruption while sending a clear message of zero tolerance with regard to corruption to private sector actors. Integrity pacts, in which both government departments and bidding parties for a public sector contract agree not to accept or offer bribes or engage in collusion, have been used successfully in Asia, Latin America and Europe to discourage corruption in public procurement. Such tools could be modified to stimulate a culture of trust and transparency in developing and implementing NAMAs, or to ensure that any verifying agencies that are established adhere to high standards of integrity. Although citizen oversight may prove difficult in an area as technically complex as GHG emissions, citizen monitoring may help ensure that international funding for NAMAs is appropriately accounted for at national and local levels or that milestones for project completion are met. In this regard the registry established by the Cancún Agreements could provide a basis for comparing project milestones and costs and thereby help in identifying potential sources of corruption.

Creating transparency and predictability in financing

In the climate change arena, resources provided by developed countries to developing countries have proved to be difficult to track. UNFCCC guidelines for reporting climate financing have not been updated in over a decade, parties use various budget and accounting methods and they may have an unclear assessment of their climate financing if it is provided through multiple government agencies.[32] Other channels for reporting climate funding, such as the OECD's Development Assistance Committee (DAC) Creditor Reporting System (CRS), are unable to capture a full picture of financing: aid is recorded on the basis of intent rather than project implementation; multilateral organizations do not always report to the OECD; and financing passing through multilateral organizations often separates donors from specified projects or aid objectives.[33]

A number of suggestions have been made for improving reporting guidelines. These include incorporating the OECD's Rio Markers – designed to help identify official development assistance targeted for climate change mitigation[34] – for use in national communications from developed countries, thus allowing cross-checking with the OECD's CRS;[35] development of an alternative marker system for classifying funds; and introduction of a standardized format for non-Annex I countries to report on assistance needs and sources in national communications.[36] Relating to the importance of capacity-building outlined above, it has also been noted that improving capacity must extend to the development of enhanced financial reporting structures in both developed and developing countries to enable cross-checking of financial commitments.[37] Most urgently, perhaps, pledges from donor countries should be specific and time-bound, offering greater certainty and accountability to developing countries relying on such funding.

Encouragingly, the Cancún Agreements reflect some of these suggestions and concerns, calling for enhanced reporting on financial, technological and capacity-building support to developing countries, which would include reporting under a common framework. Civil society and academic groups can also play a key role in developing tools that keep track of whether developed countries are meeting their support commitments. Initiatives that create oversight in the public sphere can provide added accountability. Websites that enable visitors to search levels of aid assistance by donor countries or by specific sectors or project type provide a strong model that could be tailored directly to developed country support of NAMAs.

Prepared for change?

Although the Cancún Agreements lay the foundations for an enhanced reporting system for NAMAs and their support, the question for the years ahead is whether rigorous MRV systems can be introduced and implemented in a way that is sufficiently fair, transparent and flexible to be meaningful for a wide range of needs and projects. By anticipating some of the challenges today, relating to capacity, corruption and commitments, MRV systems can be designed to be robust. The challenges are significant – but so are the rewards: an effective MRV system can increase trust between industrialized and developing nations and between developing nations and their citizens. That trust ultimately fuels enhanced mitigation ambitions and enables long-term planning for mitigation strategies.

Notes

1. At the time of writing Juan Pablo Osornio was manager of sectoral projects for Mexico at the Center for Clean Air Policy. Ingmar Schumacher is currently an economist at the Banque centrale du Luxembourg. The authors have written this article in their personal capacity and the opinions expressed are not necessarily shared by CCAP or the Banque centrale du Luxembourg. Krina Despota is a contributing editor to the *Global Corruption Report*.
2. It merits mention that Chinese per capita emissions remain below those of developed countries, and it is also worth noting that almost a quarter of China's emissions were produced in the manufacture of goods that are ultimately exported. See National Public Radio (US), 'For developing nations, exports boost CO_2 emissions', 8 March 2010.
3. Kevin Baumert et al., 'Navigating the Numbers: Greenhouse Gas Data and International Climate Policy' (Washington, DC: WRI, 2005), p. 18.
4. These are referred to in the UN Framework Convention on Climate Change (UNFCCC) as non-Annex I parties.

5. While the scope of this paper is limited to MRV in the context of NAMAs and their support, it is important to note that the Bali Action Plan also called for the MRV of mitigation commitments or actions from developed country parties.

6. See, for example, Center for Clean Air Policy (CCAP), *Nationally Appropriate Mitigation Actions by Developing Countries: Architecture and Key Issues* (Washington, DC: CCAP, 2009), pp. 7–10.

7. Annex II parties consist of the Organisation for Economic Co-operation and Development (OECD) members of Annex I, except those countries with economies in transition.

8. National communications include information on emissions and removals of GHGs, as well as information on what steps the party has taken to implement the convention. National communications might include, *inter alia*, information on national circumstances, vulnerability assessments, financial resources, and public education and awareness.

9. Jan Corfee-Morlot, Bruno Guay and Kate M. Larsen, *Financing Climate Change Mitigation: Towards a Framework for Measurement, Reporting and Verification* (Paris: OECD/ International Energy Agency, 2009, pp. 17-18).

10. Ibid., p. 23.

11. Bretton Woods Project, 'Update on the climate investment funds' (London: Bretton Woods Project, July 2010), p. 4.

12. See www.climateinvestmentfunds.org.

13. CCAP (2009); Smita Nakhooda, *The Clean Technology Fund: Insights for Development and Climate Finance*, working paper (Washington, DC: WRI, 2010), p. 8.

14. Bretton Woods Project (July 2010), p. 1.

15. Clare Breidenich and Daniel Bodansky, *Measurement, Reporting and Verification in a Post-2012 Climate Agreement* (Arlington, VA: Pew Center on Global Climate Change, 2009), p. 7.

16. See Arunabha Ghosh and Ngaire Woods, *Governing Climate Change: Lessons from Other Governance Regimes*, working paper 2009/51, Global Economic Governance Programme, Oxford University. A final version of the article is included in Dieter Helm and Cameron Hepburn (eds), *The Economics and Politics of Climate Change* (Oxford: Oxford University Press, 2009), pp. 454–477.

17. Third World Network (TWN), 'Developing Countries Mitigation and MRV – Call for Balance in Negotiations', TWN Bonn News Update no. 10 (Penang, Malaysia: TWN, 5 June 2010).

18. David Frame and Cameron Hepburn, 'An Issue of Trust: State Corruption, Responsibility and Greenhouse Gas Emissions', *Environmental Research Letters*, vol. 5 (2010).

19. Ngaire Woods, 'Making Climate Financing Work: What Might Climate Change Experts Learn from the Experience of Development Assistance?', in Richard Stewart et al. (eds), *Climate Finance: Regulatory and Funding Strategies for Climate Change and Global Development* (New York: New York University Press, 2009), pp. 206–210.

20. Marc Pallemaerts and Jonathan Armstrong, *Financial Support to Developing Countries for Climate Change Mitigation and Adaptation: Is the European Union Meeting Its Earlier Commitments?* (London: Institute for European Environmental Policy, 2009), p. 16.

21. Arunabha Ghosh and Ngaire Woods (2009), p. 16; for more, see Arunabha Ghosh, 'Developing Countries in the WTO Trade Policy Review Mechanism', *World Trade Review*, vol. 9 (2010), pp. 419–455.

22. Ghosh and Woods (2009), p. 15.

23. Breidenich and Bodansky (2009), pp 13–14.

24. Under the UNFCCC, the Consultative Group of Experts on National Communications from Parties not included in Annex I was established to improve the process of national communication development by non-Annex I parties.

25. UNFCCC, 'Progress Report on the Work of the Consultative Group of Experts on National Communications from Parties Not Included in Annex I to the Convention', Document FCCC/SBI/2010/INF.2, 10 May 2010.
26. Breidenich and Bodansky (2009), p. 23.
27. Ibid., pp. 21–22.
28. See Ellina Levina and Ned Helme, *Nationally Appropriate Mitigation Actions by Developing Countries: Architecture and Key Issues* (Washington, DC: CCAP, 2009), p. 4.
29. Ned Helme et al., *Global Sectoral Study: Final Report* (Washington, DC: CCAP, 2010), p. 30.
30. Aaron Cosbey et al., *Realizing the Development Dividend: Making the CDM Work for Developing Countries: Phase 1 Report* (Winnipeg: International Institute for Sustainable Development, 2005), pp. 43–44; Jørund Buen and Axel Michaelowa, 'View from the Inside – Markets for Carbon Credits to Fight Climate Change: Addressing Corruption Risks Proactively', in TI (ed.), *Global Corruption Report 2009* (Cambridge: Cambridge University Press, 2009), pp. 41–45; *Financial Times* (UK), 'Beijing races to profit from fledgling trade', 2 December 2009. The last article cites the example of an individual who serves on the expert group approving CDM proposals in China while simultaneously acting as a consultant for CDM projects in the country. It is worth noting that this article only highlights the conflict of interest risk associated with serving these dual purposes simultaneously, making no suggestion that the individual has acted inappropriately in either capacity.
31. EPA, 'DOJ, EPA announce one billion dollar settlement with diesel engine industry for clean air violations', press release, 22 October 1998.
32. Dennis Tirpak, *Guidelines for Reporting Information on Climate Finance*, working paper (Washington, DC: WRI, 2010), pp. 4, 6; Breidenich and Bodansky (2009), p. 16.
33. Dennis Tirpak (2010), p. 9.
34. See, for example, OECD, 'Measuring Aid Targeting the Objective of the United Nations Framework Convention on Climate Change' (Paris: OECD, 2009), at: www.oecd.org/dac/stats/rioconventions.
35. Breidenich and Bodansky (2009), p. 26.
36. Tirpak (2010), p. 9.
37. See Remi Moncel et al., 'Counting the Cash: Elements of a Framework for the Measurement, Reporting and Verification of Climate Finance' working paper (Washington, DC: WRI, 2009), pp. 13–14.

4.3

The trade-offs of trade

Realities and risks of carbon markets

Lambert Schneider[1]

Over the past decade, carbon markets have become an important instrument to reduce global greenhouse gas (GHG) emissions. The main advantage of market instruments is that they can help achieve emissions reductions in a cost-effective manner. The carbon market provides regulated entities – regions, countries, companies – with flexibility as to where and how they reduce emissions: an entity with the opportunity to reduce emissions at low costs can implement more GHG abatement measures and sell its excess allowances to an entity that faces higher costs, thereby reducing the overall costs to achieve an emissions reduction target. Effective and robust carbon markets will, over time, see the price of carbon increase, creating incentives to reduce emissions, and signalling to investors and industry the necessity for long-term investment in low-carbon technologies.

Carbon markets were introduced under the Kyoto Protocol and have emerged in various regions. They have been used most prominently by the European Union (EU) and emerging economies, but markets were also established in the northeastern states of the US and in New Zealand. Carbon markets have significantly changed emissions trends in some sectors and contributed to the unlocking of new mitigation potentials. They also helped create awareness on climate change, in particular in developing countries. Despite these successes, they have also been criticized for various reasons, including that their oversight is problematic, that they have not resulted in the emissions reductions envisaged by proponents and that they have not helped developing countries sufficiently in achieving sustainable development.

Varieties of carbon markets

In 1997 the Kyoto Protocol introduced three market mechanisms: emissions trading, the Clean Development Mechanism (CDM) and Joint Implementation (JI). Broadly speaking, carbon markets take two forms: cap-and-trade and offsetting. Under cap-and-trade or emissions trading systems, governments or intergovernmental bodies determine a cap on the total amount of GHGs that can be emitted by participating regions, countries or companies and then auction or freely distribute allowances to participants. The entities must surrender an allowance for each tonne of GHG they emit. Participants that reduce their emissions beyond the allowances they hold may sell their unused allowances to companies or countries that need additional allowances to cover their emissions.

The 40 developed countries that agreed under the Kyoto Protocol to place a cap on their national GHG emissions were issued assigned amount units (AAUs), corresponding to their emissions reductions targets, which they may trade among themselves. In addition to this international trading scheme under the Kyoto Protocol, several countries and regions have introduced trading schemes under which emissions are capped at an installation or company level.

By far the largest such scheme is the EU's Emissions Trading Scheme (EU ETS), which began in 2005 and covers nearly a half of European CO_2 emissions. In 2009 the total value of EU ETS trading rose to nearly US$119 billion, making it the largest carbon market currently in operation.[2] The EU ETS includes major emitting sources in the 27 EU member states and Norway, such as energy providers, refineries and cement, iron and steel plants. Other cap-and-trade markets exist in New Zealand and in northeastern states in the US. Additional regional, national or city-based schemes are under development or discussion in Australia, Japan, South Korea, Switzerland and the US.

Cap-and-trade systems can be amended by offsetting mechanisms: the entities regulated by an emissions cap can then offset their emissions by purchasing credits generated by emissions reductions from uncapped sources, such as projects to reduce emissions in the developing world.

The CDM is the most prominent offsetting mechanism. Under this system, projects that reduce emissions in developing countries can earn certified emission reductions (CERs). These can be purchased by industrialized countries in order to meet emissions reduction targets set under the Kyoto Protocol. In addition, schemes such as the EU ETS allow participants to use CERs in order to partially fulfil their emissions reduction commitments. By August 2010 the CDM had registered over 2300 projects, and was expected to deliver about 1 billion credits up to 2012. In

2008 direct investment in CDM projects was worth US$6.5 billion, although this fell to US$2.7 billion in 2009 with the advent of the financial crisis and the lack of an international agreement on a post-2012 climate regime.[3] Similar to the CDM but smaller in scope, JI enables an industrialized country (or a private entity within that country) committed to an emissions cap to finance a GHG reduction project in another country that also has an emissions cap.

Governing carbon markets with transparency

Carbon markets are unique in a few crucial ways. First, the commodity that is traded – GHG emissions allowances – exists only on account of a political regulation, with the initial distribution of the commodity being politically defined. Furthermore, as a new market, regulatory oversight mechanisms have to be built from scratch. These factors can create opportunities for vested interests to influence the design of the markets and regulatory institutions.

Unlike other markets, neither buyer nor seller has an inherent interest in the quality of the commodity. While buyers face reputational risks, they do not face compliance risks if they purchase allowances with a low quality: the allowances entitle the buyer to emit a certain amount of greenhouse gas (CO_2 or CO_2 equivalents) whether or not these allowances represent actual emissions reductions that have occurred elsewhere.

These unique circumstances make it especially important that, in both the design and operation of carbon markets, the highest standards of oversight, transparency and effective enforcement are in place to ensure that the market works in a stable and predictable manner and fulfils its objective of providing real emissions reductions. The early lessons from carbon markets already in operation offer insights into how carbon markets will need to be improved and developed in the future to achieve real emissions reductions and instil public trust.

Setting an ambitious cap

Setting an ambitious – low – emissions cap is a prerequisite for achieving real emissions reductions. An emissions cap set too high creates an abundance of permits and does not provide incentives for investments in low-carbon technologies. For some regulated industries, though, conforming to an emissions cap may be unwelcome. The regulated entities have incentives to lobby for a generous cap and influence the design of the scheme. At its extreme, an overly generous cap can lead to no emission reductions at all and a collapse in the price for allowances, and thus the carbon market itself.

Two years after the introduction of the EU ETS, in 2007, the price for allowances fell close to zero. The collapse was precipitated by the release of emissions data from regulated companies, which demonstrated that market regulators had over-allocated permits, inadvertently driving down the price of carbon and lowering the incentives for business to take steps to reduce emissions. Some observers believe it is plausible that regulated businesses would have tried to influence the ministries allocating allowances by emphasizing the competitive disadvantage the cap-and-trade scheme imposed – activities that potentially led to an inflated cap.[4]

Implementing a sufficiently ambitious and long-term cap is imperative to ensure the stability of the market. The early collection of data on the actual GHG emissions of regulated entities helps establish realistic caps, but these data also need to be accurate and verifiable. The unintended over-allocation of allowances could be avoided by introducing a minimum price for auctioning emissions allowances, as proposed by the UK and US.[5]

Issuing allowances: auctioning versus free distribution

Once an emissions cap has been set, industries regulated by a cap-and-trade system either receive emissions allowances via auction or for free, or through some combination of the two. One of the advantages of auctioning allowances is that it ensures that the polluter pays for the carbon it emits. It avoids establishing rules for the free allocation of emissions allowances, which are often controversial and difficult to establish in a fair and non-discriminatory manner. The auctioning of emissions allowances can also generate considerable revenues, which can be used for different purposes, including for mitigation and adaptation activities.

The auctioning of emissions allowances can also face risks, however. When carbon markets have limited coverage, the additional costs for auctioning emissions allowances can potentially result in 'carbon leakage' – that is, the shift of production from installations covered under emissions trading to installations outside emissions trading schemes. Moreover, the auctioning process needs to be designed carefully in order to avoid actors in the market colluding to lower the price on allowances by coordinating bidding. More frequent auctions would limit the impact of any single auction on market prices, reducing the opportunities for manipulation while creating a more stable carbon price.

When distributing emission allowances for free, two main approaches have been followed so far: grandfathering, the allocation of emissions allowances according to an entities' historical emissions; and benchmarking, the allocation of emissions allowances on the basis of an emission performance benchmark, usually expressed as tonnes of GHG per production. Grandfathering is problematic, because it undermines the 'polluter pays' principle.

Besides ignoring a moral argument that the industries should pay to emit greenhouse gases, free distribution is problematic because allowances represent a considerable asset that can yield windfall profits for regulated industries. In the ETS's first phase, free distribution and over-allocation resulted in profits of €6–8 billion for the EU's four largest power producers, which attributed a monetary value to the allowances they received for free but then passed them on as a cost to consumers.[6]

Benchmarking – distributing allowances on the basis of the performance of the most efficient installations in a given sector – does not violate the 'polluter pays' principle and provides a fairer means of allocating allowances. Entities that have implemented GHG abatement measures in the past are not punished but benefit, and entities that pollute more must purchase additional allowances. Beginning in 2013, EU ETS will distribute about one-half of allowances via benchmarking and the other half by auction.

Clearly, the regulated industries have incentives to lobby for the free allocation of emission allowances. For example, in 2009, before proposed cap-and-trade legislation failed in Australia, the Australian Conservation Foundation asked the Competition and Consumer Commission to investigate whether six companies engaged in 'misleading or deceptive conduct', alleging they exaggerated the damaging consequences of climate change legislation in order to gain free emissions permits.[7]

Offsets: demonstrating additionality

A key requirement for offsets is that the emissions reductions they generate must be 'additional', meaning that projects to reduce emissions must be proved not to have been implemented without the revenues earned from selling offset allowances. Offset allowances that violate this principle actually increase total carbon emissions, since they entitle the entity that purchases the allowance to increase emissions, while the emissions reduction from the offset project would have taken place regardless.

Under the CDM, the world's largest offsetting scheme, the current approach to demonstrate additionality mostly requires project participants to demonstrate under which conditions they would be able to proceed with the project activity. Proving additionality largely becomes a question of demonstrating the intention of the project developer in taking investment decisions. The rationale as to why projects rely on funding for offset allowances may be quite vaguely argued, however. Practical experience suggests that the current approach fails to identify the additionality of projects reliably, with several analyses suggesting that a significant number of registered projects are probably not additional.[8] The fact that, by October 2008,

76 per cent of all projects registered under the CDM had been completely constructed prior to being approved for credits calls further into question whether offset projects really relied on CDM-related financing.[9] In an effort to make the demonstration of additionality less subjective and more transparent, over the last two years the CDM Executive Board has adopted guidance that aims to assess in a more objective manner whether projects can be economically viable without revenues from offset credits, if the project is impeded by too many barriers without the CDM or if the CDM was seriously considered in the decision to proceed with a project.[10]

All the same, rules could be improved or replaced. For example, emissions benchmarks can be used to measure the performance of a specific type of CDM project: the average emissions rate of top-performing plants for a given project type could be used as a benchmark, and only projects that have a better performance than the benchmark would be eligible for credits.[11] For benchmarks to be effective, however, they must be updated regularly to reflect improvements in industry standards over time. Establishing benchmarks can be challenging, since industry performance data may be unavailable or confidential and because some sectors produce various products, necessitating multiple benchmarks. Market penetration rates, which can be used to judge the extent to which a technology is used within a sector, may also be used to determine whether or not projects are likely to be additional. While both are improvements over more subjective claims of additionality, however, neither can fully avoid the 'free-riding' of projects that would have been implemented regardless of the CDM.

Another proposed method to improve the environmental integrity of offset credits is to move beyond an offsetting mechanism by crediting only part of the emissions reductions. For example, for 2 tonnes of emissions reductions only one offset credit may be issued.[12] This option was proposed recently by the European Commission and in draft legislation for an emissions trading scheme in the US.

Box 4.3 HFC-23: a case of perverse incentives under the CDM

Hydrofluorocarbon-23 (HFC-23) is a powerful GHG generated as a by-product of manufacturing hydrochlorofluorocarbon-22 (HCFC-22). In developing countries HFC-23 is usually vented into the atmosphere, which has led to the capture and elimination of this chemical becoming the largest project type under the CDM. Nineteen registered HFC-23 projects are expected to deliver 476 million CERs by 2012, comprising about a half of the emissions reductions expected from the more than 2300 other CDM projects. With the abatement cost for eliminating HFC-23 less than US$1 per tonne of emitted CO_2 equivalent, revenues from CDM projects can easily exceed the revenue from HCFC-22 sales.[13]

Recent analysis of these plants indicates that such large revenues created perverse incentives for plant operators to produce more HCFC-22 and HFC-23 than they would have without the CDM.[14] Although the methodology for determining credits includes safeguards to prevent this, these were found to be ineffective, and CDM HCFC-22 plants were intentionally operated to maximize offset credits. Two plants reduced HFC-23 generation while they were ineligible for credits and increased it once they could again claim credits. One plant stopped HCFC-22 production when it was not allowed to claim further offset credits and resumed operation when it again became eligible. Moreover, several plants were found to be producing exactly the amount of HCFC-22 and HFC-23 for which they were allowed to claim credits, whereas production was lower or varied year to year before offset credits were rewarded.

In mid-2010 the non-governmental organization CDM Watch submitted a formal request to the CDM Executive Board to revise the crediting methodology. The proposed revision would introduce an ambitious emission benchmark and cut the credits claimed for eliminating HFC-23 by more than 90 per cent, reducing the incentive to increase HCFC-22 production or HFC-23 generation.

The chair of the CDM's Methodologies Panel recommended putting the methodology on hold, and CDM Watch noted that CDM Executive Board members who were reluctant to review the methodology often came from countries that had a direct stake in HFC-23 projects, such as Japan, where the government is associated with eight such projects, China, which hosts 11 of the registered projects and charges a 65 per cent levy on all HFC-23 credits, and India, which hosts seven projects.[15] While the methodology was not put on hold, the executive board decided to start an investigation into the issue and put the issuance of credits on hold. The World Bank, which contracted CERs from HFC-23 projects worth about US$1 billion, claimed that there was not sufficient evidence to support the allegations.[16]

Offsets: demonstrating sustainability

Under the CDM, as well as for voluntary standards that approve carbon credits for sale outside the compliance market, another requirement is that offset projects should contribute to sustainable development. A CDM project requires the host-country government to confirm that the project assists in achieving sustainable development goals, but leaves determination for what constitutes sustainable development to the discretion of that government. National authorities have little incentive to reject projects that have no or only a few sustainable development benefits, however, as this results in lost revenue for their country. Indeed, studies examining the sustainable development benefits of CDM projects suggest that the contribution of the CDM to sustainable development is low.[17] Sweeping reforms could call for an internationally agreed methodological standard for the assessment of the sustainable development benefit of offset projects.[18] Alternatively, a positive or negative list of project types could be agreed on the basis of commonly expected sustainable development benefits. Several experts have also proposed the discounting of CERs – issuing fewer credits than correspond directly to the tonnes of carbon released – from projects with less sustainable development benefit, thereby giving sustainable development benefits a monetary value.[19]

Third-party verification: building capacity and strengthening independence

Under all carbon market mechanisms, private accredited companies or individuals are responsible for ensuring the quality of the commodity by validating projects and verifying that emissions or emissions reductions correspond to the claims of the involved entities. These entities must make sure that all the requirements set out by the authorities governing the carbon market mechanism are met. Ensuring the quality of third-party verification is central to any carbon market, and the quality of the validation and verification under the CDM and JI may have consequences for non-compliance markets (see Thomas Marcello, section 4.3.4 in this volume). Despite this role being crucially important for the integrity of the carbon market, the track record of verification agencies is varied.

Verifiers of CDM projects – designated operational entities (DOEs) – are accredited by the CDM Executive Board. DOEs are paid directly by project developers. This may undermine their independence in conducting their verification functions. In the past two years the CDM Executive Board has temporarily suspended the accreditation of four DOEs,[20] including the three largest market players. The board found either that DOE personnel lacked competence, that DOEs did not appear to have undertaken independent technical reviews or that the verifying companies did not follow internal review or audit procedures adequately to ensure project quality.[21] This suggests that there are deep-rooted problems in the validation and verification process. Moreover, fewer than half the DOE-validated projects pass the board without any corrections.[22] In an independent rating of DOEs on an A to F scale ('A' indicating a very strong performance, 'F' representing a very poor performance), the top-scoring DOE received a 'D', with all others scoring below this.[23] Other assessments suggest that 'DOEs are willing to rubberstamp project documents containing unverifiable and highly dubious claims',[24] and that in some cases documents presented to DOEs have been falsified, and verifying document authenticity is difficult.[25]

The capacity of personnel has been cited as a significant problem, with some verifying agencies reporting difficulties in hiring and retaining qualified staff. In some cases, staff members of verifiers who had acquired a basic level of expertise moved on to become project developers, creating a potential for conflicts of interest.[26] Another problem is that the guidance by the CDM Executive Board is in some cases not fully clear, leading to differences of interpretation between the board and DOEs. Moreover, the accreditation process has relied strongly on formal requirements and is not very transparent, given that relevant documentation, such as assessments of DOEs by the CDM Executive Board, is not made publicly available. Increased transparency would serve as a learning tool for verifiers, and the public scrutiny could provide added incentives for verifying companies to improve their internal operations.

In recent years the CDM Executive Board has initiated different actions to improve the validation and verification process. A Validation and Verification Manual (VVM) was adopted by the CDM Executive Board in November 2008, followed by an accreditation standard. The UNFCCC Secretariat is starting to conduct trainings for DOEs. Furthermore, the board has decided to implement a policy framework to oversee DOEs systematically, which includes monitoring of their performance and which may trigger spot checks at the DOEs. As part of this new system, performance indicators have been calculated and made available to the CDM Executive Board – though not yet to the public. The board is also considering how DOEs can be made liable in case of over-issuance of CERs.

In addition to these efforts to address the shortcomings in the current validation and verification process, a broader set of penalties could also be implemented to address non-compliance on the part of verifiers, including financial sanctions and compulsory training and exams for the personnel of DOEs.

In the case of the CDM and for other offset programmes, a more fundamental reform could be that verifiers are paid out of a common fund to which project developers contribute, rather than being commissioned and paid directly by the project developers. This would diminish the opportunities for conflicts of interest.

Reporting emissions and tracking allowances: avoiding double-counting and ensuring transparency

Carbon markets require proper bookkeeping of the issuing and trading of emissions allowances in order to avoid any double-counting of emissions (when the same allowances are used by various entities to meet their emissions reduction targets). In the spring of 2010 the Hungarian government sold CERs that had been surrendered by companies participating in the EU ETS to an intermediary company.[27] Despite claims that the CERs would be kept out of EU carbon exchanges, the 'recycled' credits were soon traded on the EU market without buyers realizing that they could not be used for compliance within the EU ETS. This led to the suspension of CER trade in European exchanges and a change in the European registry regulation to close this loophole.

In addition to avoiding such double-counting, it is key for the integrity of the market that regulated entities in emissions trading schemes report their GHG emissions in an accurate, conservative and transparent manner in order to assess compliance (see Taryn Fransen, section 4.1 in this volume). In the EU ETS, GHG emission data are reported according to well-established protocols, which usually have a low potential for gaming and require verification by third parties that may be held liable in cases of fraud. Generally, the introduction of trading schemes can significantly enhance the transparency of GHG emissions. Frequent reporting on GHG emissions, as well as on offsets and allowances, will enable the public to track the GHG emissions and compliance efforts of companies.

Implementing accountable and effective market oversight

Institutions responsible for overseeing carbon markets must be independent and accountable, and possess the technical knowledge necessary to make informed and reliable decisions.

Avoiding conflicts of interest and ensuring accountability

Within the oversight structures for carbon markets, conflicts of interest are a particularly salient concern. The CDM and Joint Implementation (JI) are overseen by the CDM Executive Board and the JI Supervisory Committee (JISC), respectively, each of which consists of 10 members elected by the parties to the UNFCCC and the Kyoto Protocol. Although members are instructed to act in their personal capacity, many hold multiple roles, such as serving as climate change negotiators for their country, representing their country's national authority (which gives national permission for CDM projects) or managing large government CDM purchasing programmes.[28] While the CDM Executive Board requires members to declare conflicts of interest,[29] members 'exercise personal discretion in deciding whether s/he has a real or perceived conflict'. Some members make formal statements regarding conflicts of interests, but others do not.[30]

A newspaper report suggests that, in closed-door meetings, board members have in some instances aggressively promoted projects that benefit their home countries or companies from their countries.[31] A statistical evaluation of all decisions by the CDM Executive Board suggests that, after quality criteria, political/economic variables also drive decisions. For instance, a project has a better chance of being approved if the host country is also represented by a board member. Similarly, the involvement of powerful players such as the World Bank improves the probability of success.[32] While such examples may be the exception rather than the rule, the lack of defined conflict of interest guidelines leaves board members vulnerable to perceptions of conflict of interest. To address the problem more radically, it has been considered that staff for such positions should be full-time salaried professionals, rather than appointees.[33]

In the case of offsetting mechanisms such as the CDM and JI, many stakeholders, including project developers, have called for board meetings to be open, requested clarity on how decisions are made, and called for better substantiation of decisions and more direct communication with board members.[34] Ensuring sufficient accountability in carbon market governance requires proper consultation and communication with stakeholders before and after decisions are taken. A significant criticism of the CDM process was the lack of an appeals process for board decisions, which the Executive Board is working on.

Ensuring compliance, protecting against fraud

Central to any market are enforcement mechanisms that make sure that regulations are followed and that market integrity is safeguarded. In the EU ETS, a fine of €100 per allowance must be paid if an entity does not surrender the necessary amount of allowances.[35] This fine has, so far, successfully ensured broad compliance on the part of the regulated entities. Regulators also have to pay attention in order to prevent market manipulation and fraud, however, by ensuring sufficiently rigorous oversight, adopting penalties for offenders and providing regular in-depth information on the market. Strong oversight may be particularly important in the early stages of market development. In 2009 European regulators struggled to control VAT fraud, in which people opened trading accounts in a national carbon registry, purchased allowances VAT-free, sold the allowances on with VAT and then absconded prior to paying VAT to the tax authority. Such issues are not unique to the carbon markets, but will have to be regulated against vigilantly so as to bolster public trust in existing and emerging markets.

Managing public assets and revenues from the carbon market

Depending on how assets generated by carbon markets are distributed at the outset of the market, some or all of them might initially be held in public coffers. These assets can provide a significant source of revenue for governments and must be managed with the accountability expected of any public resource. This did not happen in 2009, when a Slovakian environment minister was forced to resign after selling a portion of that country's AAUs at below-market prices and withholding details of the sale (see the Slovakia case study which follows this section).

The use of funds generated from sales of allowances also matters. Allowance auctions for the third phase of the EU ETS will generate significant revenue, 50 per cent of which is earmarked for climate programmes such as renewable energy and energy efficiency, reducing deforestation and funding adaptation to climate change. The Regional Greenhouse Gas Initiative in the eastern US also auctions allowances and uses revenues to boost investment for energy efficiency and renewable sources of power. In addition, 2 per cent of offset credits from the CDM are directed towards the UNFCCC's Adaptation Fund, and revenues derived from the sale of assigned amount units may also be invested in environmentally oriented projects – so-called Green Investment Schemes (GISs). This last practice could be quite important in the case of eastern European countries, which under the Kyoto Protocol were allocated emissions targets exceeding their actual emissions. The resulting surplus AAUs, referred to as 'hot air', can be sold on to other countries or carried over to subsequent commitment periods, considerably undermining the overall efforts to reduce GHG emissions if the allowances are used. A contentious debate has arisen as to how the carry-over of surplus AAUs can be prevented in a post-2012 climate regime.

In all cases, governments are entrusted with both an environmental and a financial asset, and have to manage these proceeds responsibly, transparently and accountably.

Robust carbon markets: a collective responsibility

As a leading tool for mitigating climate change, carbon markets must be designed carefully, and they require strong, transparent and accountable oversight. The lessons from existing carbon markets suggest that several loopholes were created in establishing new policy instruments, which stifled the potential of carbon markets to mitigate global GHG emissions. It is imperative that these lessons be considered in establishing new markets, and used to improve and reform the existing mechanisms.

Notes

1. Lambert Schneider worked previously for the Öko-Institut in Germany and as an independent researcher. In October 2010 he joined the UNFCCC Secretariat. This article was written before that appointment.
2. Alexandre Kossoy and Philippe Ambrosi, *State and Trends of the Carbon Market 2010* (Washington, DC: World Bank, 2010), p. 1.
3. Ibid., pp. 1–2.

4. Tamra Gilbertson and Oscar Reyes, *Carbon Trading: How It Works and Why It Fails*, Critical Currents Occasional Paper no. 7 (Uppsala: Dag Hammarskjöld Foundation, 2009), p. 35.

5. In the US, a price ceiling was proposed in the Waxman–Markey bill and the Kerry–Boxer bill; PointCarbon.com, 'UK govt calls for carbon floor price', 12 May 2010.

6. Richard Baldwin, *Regulation Lite: The Rise of Emissions Trading*, Law, Society and Economy Working Paper no. 3/2008 (London: London School of Economics, 2008), p. 10.

7. RechargeNews.com, 'Six Australian companies accused of carbon fraud', 15 June 2009; see also Australian Conservation Foundation, 'Complaint to the Australian Competition and Consumer Commission', 11 June 2009.

8. See Lambert Schneider, 'Assessing the Additionality of CDM Projects: Practical Experiences and Lessons Learned', *Climate Policy*, vol. 9 (2009), pp. 242–254; Martin Cames et al., *Long-Term Prospects of CDM and JI*, Climate Change Research Report no. 12–07 (Dessau: Federal Environmental Agency of Germany, 2007); Axel Michaelowa and Pallav Purohit, *Additionality Determination of Indian CDM projects. Can Indian CDM Project Developers Outwit the CDM Executive Board?* (Zurich: University of Zurich, 2007); David Victor and Michael Wara, *A Realistic Policy on International Carbon Offsets*, working paper no. 74 (Stanford, CA: Stanford Universty, 2008).

9. International Rivers, 'Rip-Offsets: The Failure of the Kyoto Protocol's Clean Development Mechanism' (Berkeley, CA: International Rivers, 2008).

10. Meeting report of the 39th meeting of the CDM Executive Board, annex 35; meeting report of the 41st meeting of the CDM Executive Board, annex 46; meeting report of the 50th meeting of the CDM Executive Board, annex 13.

11. Lambert Schneider, *Is the CDM Fulfilling Its Environmental and Sustainable Development Objectives? An Evaluation of the CDM and Options for Improvement* (Berlin: Öko-Institut, 2007), p. 58.

12. See Stefan Bakker et al., 'Differentiation in the CDM: Options and Impacts' (Bilthoven: Netherlands Environmental Assessment Agency, 2009); Sonja Butzengeiger-Geyer et al., 'Options for Utilizing the CDM for Global Emission Reductions', final report to the German Federal Environment Agency (Zurich and Berlin: University of Zurich, Perspectives GmbH, Öko-Institut and Point Carbon, 2010); Paula Castro and Axel Michaelowa, 'The Impact of CER Discounting on the Competitiveness of Different CDM Host Countries', *Ecological Economics*, vol. 70 (2009), pp. 34–42; Rae Kwon Chung, 'A CER Discounting Scheme Could Save Climate Change Regime after 2012', *Climate Policy*, vol. 7 (2007), pp. 171–176; and Lambert Schneider, 'A Clean Development Mechanism with Global Atmospheric Benefits for a Post-2012 Climate Regime', *International Environmental Agreements*, vol. 9 (2009), pp. 95–111.

13. UNFCCC, 'Issues arising from the implementation of potential project activities under the clean development mechanism: the case of incineration of HFC-23 waste streams from HCFC-22 production', FCCC/TP/2005/1; Lambert Schneider et al. 'Implications of the Clean Development Mechanism under the Kyoto Protocol on other Conventions. The Case of HFC-23 Destruction' *Environmental Law Network International Review* (2005); Technology and Economic Assessment Panel (TEAP)/IPCC, *Safeguarding the Ozone Layer and the Global Climate System: Issues Related to Hydrofluorocarbons and Perfluorocarbons* (Cambridge: Cambridge University Press, 2005), p. 427; TEAP, *Report of the Task Force on HCFC Issues (With Particular Focus on the Impact of the Clean Development Mechanism) and Emissions Reduction Benefits Arising from Earlier HCFC Phase-Out and Other Practical Measures – Response to Decision XVIII/12*, 2007, p. 57.

14. See request for revision REV0186, submitted by CDM Watch to the CDM Executive Board, available at http://cdm.unfccc.int, and Lambert Schneider, 'Perverse Incentives under the Clean Development Mechanism (CDM): An Evaluation of HFC-23 Destruction Projects', accepted by *Climate Policy* (forthcoming).

15. Environmental Investigation Agency (EIA), 'UN delays action on carbon market scandal', press release, 30 July 2010.

16. World Bank, 'Q&A for CDM HFC-23 incineration projects', 5 August 2010.

17. See Karen H. Olsen, 'The Clean Development Mechanism's Contribution to Sustainable Development: A Review of the Literature', *Climatic Change*, vol. 84 (2007), pp. 59–73.

18. See, for example, Karen H. Olsen and Jørgen Fenhann, 'Sustainable Development Benefits of Clean Development Mechanism Projects. A New Methodology for Sustainability Assessment Based on Text Analysis of the Project Design Documents Submitted for Validation', *Energy Policy*, vol. 36 (2008), pp. 2773–2784; Cristoph Sutter, *Sustainability Check-up for CDM Projects: How to Assess the Sustainability of International Projects under the Kyoto Protocol* (Berlin: Wissenschaftlicher Verlag, 2003); and SouthSouthNorth, *SouthSouthNorth CDM Toolkit* (Cape Town: SouthSouthNorth, 2004).

19. Bakker et al. (2009); PointCarbon.com (2010); Castro and Michaelowa (2009); Chung (2007); Schneider (2009: 'A Clean Development Mechanism').

20. These were DNV (Det Norske Veritas), KEMCO, SGS and TÜV-SÜD. At present there are over 30 DOEs.

21. Meeting report of the 44th meeting of the CDM Executive Board, annex 2, and meeting report of the 49th meeting of the CDM Executive Board, annex 2. The CDM Executive Board implemented a systematic monitoring of the performance of DOEs; the results of this performance assessment have not yet been made publicly available, however.

22. Lambert Schneider and Lennart Mohr, *2010 Rating of Designated Operational Entities (DOEs) Accredited under the Clean Development Mechanism (CDM)* (Berlin: Öko-Institut, 2010).

23. Ibid.

24. Lori Pottinger, *Bad Deal for the Planet: Why Carbon Offsets Aren't Working... and How to Create a Fair Global Climate Accord* (Berkeley, CA: International Rivers, 2008).

25. Jørund Buen and Axel Michaelowa, 'View from the Inside – Markets for Carbon Credits to Fight Climate Change: Addressing Corruption Risks Proactively', in TI (ed.), *Global Corruption Report 2009: Corruption and the Private Sector* (Cambridge: Cambridge University Press, 2009), pp. 41–45.

26. Mark Schapiro, 'Conning the Climate: Inside the Carbon-Trading Shell Game', *Harper's Magazine*, February 2010, pp. 31–39.

27. BusinessGreen.com, 'Carbon traders voice fears over recycled carbon credits', 17 March 2010.

28. Charlotte Streck and Jolene Lin, 'Making Markets Work: A Review of CDM Performance and the Need for Reform', *European Journal of International Law*, vol. 19 (2008), pp. 409–442.

29. Report of the 47th meeting of the CDM Executive Board, annex 62.

30. The meeting reports of the CDM Executive Board contain conflict of interest statements for some but not all members.

31. *New York Times* (US), 'Secret UN Board Awards Lucrative Credits with Few Rules Barring Conflicts', 7 April 2009.

32. Florens Flues et al., *UN Approval of Greenhouse Gas Emission Reduction Projects in Developing Countries: The Political Economy of the CDM Executive Board*, working paper no. 35 (Zurich: Center for Comparative and International Studies, 2008).

33. Streck and Lin (2008).

34. Ibid.; International Emissions Trading Association (IETA), 'The Joint Implementation Mechanism Post-2012', position paper (Geneva: IETA, 2009).

35. Directive 2003/87/EC of the European Parliament and of the Council of 13 October 2003 establishing a scheme for greenhouse gas emission allowance trading within the Community and amending Council Directive 96/61/EC.

4.3.1

Slovak public see no credit in government's carbon trading

Emília Sičáková-Beblavá and Gabriel Šípoš[1]

Under article 17 of the Kyoto Protocol, most industrialized countries and some economies in transition are permitted to sell 'unused' emission permits (assigned amount units: AAUs) to countries that exceed their agreed-upon emissions targets (see Lambert Schneider, section 4.3 above).[2] Slovakia, with average emissions for 2003–2007 that were 32 per cent lower than its 1990 Kyoto target, held a considerable amount of saleable emissions quotas by 2008.[3] In November of that year the Slovak government sold 15 million tonnes of its AAUs to Interblue Group, a US-based company headquartered in Washington state.[4] As a public resource, many would argue that these permits should have been sold transparently and at a fair market price. The Ministry of Environment, as the ministry responsible for allocating permits, chose not to organize any public tender or auction, however, and instead directly allocated the contract to Interblue.[5] When the media started questioning the transaction, in December 2008, it became clear that neither the contract nor the sale price was publicly available.[6]

Calls from the media and members of the opposition parties to make the contract public were refused by the then environment minister, Jan Chrbet, who argued that Interblue considered the information to be a trade secret.[7] By May 2009 journalists had discovered from secondary sources that Slovakia may well have sold its quotas at half the market price, representing an estimated €75 million in lost revenue.[8]

Further investigations found that Interblue had been formed only shortly before the transaction took place.[9] Later it was discovered that an individual involved in the sale had other relationships with the ministry of the environment: an Interblue project manager had worked as an adviser for the ministry under both Chrbet and his predecessor.[10]

The prime minister rejected accusations made in the press that the government had sold the permits below the market price, but forced Chrbet to resign in May 2009 on the grounds that he had demonstrated a lack of political responsibility in failing to defend the contract.[11] The new environment minister, Viliam Turský, published the contract, but the sale price, volume of emissions and the name of Interblue's representative were omitted. Turský claimed that, 'based on the Act on Freedom of Information and the Act on Protection of Personal Data, we had the right to whiten it out', emphasizing that the buyer would have to agree to publish the full contract.[12] The act states, however, that if public resources are at stake such information is to be made available, and court precedent would seem to support this.[13]

Facing continued pressure from the media and non-governmental organizations, the ministry published the contract's full text in June 2009, revealing a sale price of €5.05 per tonne.[14] Analysts found that, at around the same time as the Slovak sale to Interblue, countries including Ukraine, the Czech Republic and Latvia had sold AAUs at approximately €10 per tonne.[15]

Journalists further discovered that the Japanese government had been close to buying Slovakia's AAUs at a price twice that paid by Interblue.[16]

Interblue subsequently sold the AAUs at a minimum of €8 per tonne, earning at least €45 million.[17] The Interblue contract also gave the company the right of first refusal for a further 35 million tonnes of Slovakia's AAUs at the same price of €5.05.[18]

Elements of the media and others called on the government to cancel the contract and, if possible, reverse the sale of the first batch of permits.[19] In July 2009 Turský began to reconsider the agreement.[20] In the months that followed, negotiations were complicated by the fact that Interblue had ceased to exist, reportedly succeeded by Interblue Group Europe. This company has publicly offered to cancel the deal, yet the ministry of the environment did not recognize it to be a legal successor to Interblue and therefore expressed unwillingness to negotiate.[21]

Although the prosecutor general has initiated an investigation into the case on the grounds of misuse of power by public officials, no one had been charged as of mid-2010.[22] Media and civil society scrutiny might have brought the case to the forefront of public attention, but the authorities have made no formal, long-term changes to their practices for AAU sales. The opposition victory in the 12 June 2010 general election and the installation of a new government brought promises to cancel the contract that had given Interblue the right to acquire additional AAUs; as of mid-August 2010, however, no progress had been announced.

In a market characterized by opacity, with little information publicly available about the pricing or structures of AAU transactions, the risk persists that citizens could lose out because of innocent – or deliberate – mismanagement.

Notes

1. Emília Sičáková-Beblavá is programme director at TI Slovakia and Gabriel Šípoš is director of the organization.
2. Kyoto Protocol to the United Nations Framework Convention on Climate Change, 1997.
3. European Environment Agency (EEA), 'GHG Trends and Projections in the Slovak Republic', in EEA, *Greenhouse Gas Emission Trends and Projections in Europe 2008: Tracking Progress towards Kyoto Targets* (Copenhagen: EEA, 2008), pp. 164–165.
4. ETrend.sk (Slovakia), 'Slovenské pozadie veľkého kšeftu', 22 April 2009; ETrend.sk (Slovakia), 'Ďalší kšeft SNS: Horúci vzduch', 3 December 2008. While early media reports suggested that 10 million tonnes of AAUs had been sold, the actual figure was 15 million tonnes of AAUs.
5. Etrend.sk (3 December 2008).
6. Ibid.
7. Ekonomika.sme.sk (Slovakia), 'Chrbet kryje Interblue Group', 24 April 2009.
8. ETrend.sk (Slovakia), 'Emisie: obludný škandál', 26 May 2009.
9. ETrend.sk (3 December 2008).
10. *Slovenská Tlačová Agentúra* (English-language) (Slovakia), 'HZDS alleges organized group stands behind AAU emissions sale', 26 March 2010; Ekonomika.sme.sk (Slovakia), 'Vláda predala emisie poradcovi', 25 March 2010.
11. DNES.sk (Slovakia), 'Fico: strašiakov vo vláde nepotrebujem. Chrbet končí', 5 May 2009.
12. *Slovak Spectator*, 'Slovak environment minister releases no additional info on Interblue Group', 3 June 2009.
13. *SME* (Slovakia), 'Chrbet zverejní zmluvu', 30 April 2009. The article states, that in the past, the courts have ruled that documents of public concern, unless explicitly closed by law, should be made available by public authorities upon request.
14. Ekonomika.sme.sk (Slovakia), 'Štát ustúpil a zverejnil celú emisnú zmluvu', 15 June 2009.
15. Ekonomika.sme.sk (Slovakia), 'Emisný škandál zaujal aj Švajčiarov', 21 November 2009.
16. Hnonline.sk (Slovakia), 'Japonci chceli emisie. Dali by dvakrát viac', 13 August 2009.
17. *Slovak Spectator*, 'New revelations blow lid on Interblue puzzle', 29 March 2010.
18. *Tlačová Agentúra Slovenskej Republiky* (Slovakia), 'Interblue Group Europe has new person in charge', 29 March 2010; *Slovak Spectator* (29 March 2010).
19. Spravy.pravda.sk (Slovakia), 'Dzurinda žiada zrušiť zmluvu s Interblue Group o predaji emisií', 16 June 2009; Ekonomika.sme.sk (Slovakia), 'Premiér kľučkuje pred emisiami (16 naj Ficových výrokov k téme)', 10 November 2009.
20. Hnonline.sk, 'Turský pre HN: S Interblue budeme určite rokovať, 8 July 2009.
21. Spravy.pravda.sk (Slovakia), 'Medveď: Interblue Group Europe nie je pre ministerstvo partner', 7 April 2010.
22. Hnonline.sk (Slovakia), 'Emisie. V hre je "práčka"', 7 June 2010.

4.3.2

Permit politics

Hungary's CO$_2$ allowances

Gábor Baranyai[1]

As the largest cap-and-trade market in the world, the European Union's (EU's) carbon emission trading system (ETS)[2] has received both praise and criticism. One early concern related to the allocation of emissions allowances. If allocated to regulated industries in excess of actual emissions, these permits can constitute hidden state aid; and, when distributed in a non-transparent manner, allowances can be a powerful tool to disburse unjustified subsidies, potentially becoming a hotbed for political favouritism.

Under the first two phases of the EU ETS (2005–2007 and 2008–2012), the allocation of permits was managed by each EU member state. National allocation plans (NAPs), which outline the number of allowances given to each regulated facility, were submitted by member state governments and approved by the European Commission. The relative discretion of member states to determine allocation methodology, the potential uncertainty of emissions data and lobbying pressures[3] in many countries resulted in the adoption of excessively generous allocation plans.

Hungary's misallocation of allowances

The preparation of Hungary's NAP for 2008–2012 was susceptible to industry lobbying. Political instability further complicated matters, with the position of environment minister – who oversees emissions allocations – reappointed three times within three years. Each subsequent minister was approached with new requests and proposals for more allowances for certain sectors and companies. Once the drafts had left the ministries involved, additional interests appeared at the Cabinet level, making oversight of the process increasingly difficult.[4]

In April 2007 the European Commission identified faults with the first 2008–2012 NAP submitted by Hungary,[5] including the over-allocation of emissions allowances. The Commission cut Hungary's emission ceiling for regulated facilities by 12 per cent, stating that methodological information used to determine allowance allocation was insufficiently substantiated and that Hungary had not demonstrated that information provided by regulated companies had been 'systematically verified by independent experts'.[6]

The Commission also found a system of built-in benefits for existing CO_2-emitting facilities. Under the NAP, these facilities would have been guaranteed access to extra allowances even in cases of production fluctuations, amounting to an ex-post adjustment of the emissions cap.[7] Therefore, these companies would have benefited financially from reduced emissions by selling allowances on the market, while essentially transferring the costs of increased production and higher emissions to the government by obtaining free allowances upon demand.

The 12 per cent cut in overall emissions, as ordered by the Commission, meant that Hungary's entire allocation had to be recalculated, undoing previous political and industry agreements and creating new incentives for lobbying.

The justification for subsequent reallocation was not always clear. Journalists reported in 2009 that the state-owned Vértes power plant was to receive an additional 400,000 allowances over what had originally been allocated, at an estimated market price of €6 million. Media sources suggested the plant was given the additional allowances under favourable conditions not justified by the emissions data.[8]

Flaws in the reallocation process were exacerbated by weak application of measures intended to enhance transparency. During the preparation of the amended NAP the government reduced the consultation timeframes from 15–30 days to 5–10 days.[9] This rendered the consultation process largely ineffective, depriving companies and the public of the chance to review and comment on the final allocation figures.

An EU-wide issue

Many of the problems that arose in Hungary were manifest throughout the EU. One researcher found that short timeframes in phase I (2005–2007) and complex allocation rules meant that 'most member state regulators had little

time in which to process and verify large volumes of representations and pleadings from industry'.[10] Because these problems remained unresolved for phase 2 of the ETS (2008–2012), and on account of the global industrial downturn, 70 per cent of ETS participants received unneeded emissions allocations in 2009.[11] The same year Hungary had a surplus of allowances for more than 1 million tonnes of carbon emissions.[12]

The fundamental challenges were recognized by the Commission, leading to an early and radical amendment of the allocation model: starting in 2013, the emissions cap will be determined at the EU level.[13] While national governments will have much less direct influence on allocation decisions, the future distribution of allowances may nevertheless be subject to lobbying at the Commission level.

The emissions allocation experience of Hungary and other EU countries will be instructive for establishing and reforming existing and future emissions trading schemes. Curbing undue influence will require mechanisms that enable transparency, such as publishing clear criteria for allocation, adequate timeframes for implementation, and the introduction of robust and mandatory lobbying registries to tie corporate interests more closely to policy interactions.

Notes

1. Gábor Baranyai is former head of department, Ombudsman for Future Generations, Hungary. He has written this article in his personal capacity, on behalf of TI Hungary.
2. See Lambert Schneider (section 4.3 of this volume) for a more detailed description of emissions trading schemes.
3. Markus Wråke, *Emissions Trading: the Ugly Duckling in European Climate Policy?*, Report no. B1856 (Stockholm: Swedish Environmental Research Institute, 2009).
4. Personal observation of the author.
5. Commission of the European Communities, 'Commission decision concerning the national allocation plan for the allocation of greenhouse gas emission allowances notified by Hungary in accordance with Directive 2003/87/EC of the European Parliament and of the Council', Commission Decision of 16 April 2007, Brussels, Recitals (17)–(28).
6. Ibid.
7. Ibid.
8. *Index* (Hungary), 'Szén-dioxiddal is kistafírozták Kapolyit', 14 January 2009.
9. By government decrees: 14/2008. (I. 30.) Korm. rendelet az üvegházhatású gázok kibocsátási egységeinek kereskedelméről szóló 2005. évi XV. törvény végrehajtásának egyes szabályairól szóló 213/2006. (X. 27.) Korm. rendelet módosításáról, section 3. Effective as of 30 January 2008.
10. Robert Baldwin, *Regulation Lite: The Rise of Emissions Trading*, Law, Society and Economy Working Paper no. 3/2008 (London: London School of Economics and Political Science, 2008).
11. Sandbag, *Rescuing the EU ETS from Redundancy* (London: Sandbag, April 2010).
12. Sandbag, 'Emissions map', at www.sandbag.org.uk/etsmap.
13. Directive 2009/29/EC of the European Parliament and of the Council amending Directive 2003/87/EC so as to improve and extend the greenhouse gas emission allowance trading scheme of the Community, *Official Journal of the European Union,* L 140, 5 June 2009.

4.3.3

Shortcomings and short cuts

Sri Lanka's environmental impact assessments

Transparency International Sri Lanka

Environmental impact assessments (EIAs) can be expected to have growing relevance for climate change mitigation and adaptation activities in a number of countries. EIAs are considered to be useful tools to strengthen provisions for adaptation measures such as climate-proofing in development projects,[1] and, under the rules of the Clean Development Mechanism (CDM), host countries can require project developers to produce an EIA if they believe a mitigation project could have significant environmental impacts.[2] To date, Sri Lanka has registered seven CDM projects – a low number compared to other Asian countries but higher than many participating countries outside the region. If mitigation and adaptation projects are scaled up in Sri Lanka, considerable efforts – by citizens, non-governmental organizations (NGOs) and the government – will be needed to ensure that the criteria used to assess the environmental integrity of these projects is robust and open to public oversight.

In Sri Lanka, though, EIAs may be a weak indicator of environmental sustainability. EIAs have been required for years in order to obtain development approval for ventures that could present adverse impacts on the environment, such as airports, industrial facilities, power stations or hotels.[3] The documented shortcomings are numerous, however: conflicts of interest, a lack of clear guidelines, challenges to public oversight and a failure to monitor impacts have all been attributed to the EIA process. These issues are worth examining, since they may reflect some of the challenges the government will have to overcome in order to assess adequately the environmental ramifications of large-scale mitigation projects or adaptation activities.

A litany of challenges

Twenty-two government institutions are designated as approval agencies for EIA applications, with the Sri Lankan Central Environmental Authority (CEA) overseeing the process.[4] These agencies are responsible for determining the potential environmental impacts of proposed projects, soliciting participation from affected parties and deciding whether an EIA or a less comprehensive evaluation is required.

Ambiguity regarding the application of environmental assessments was illustrated in 2004, when the Environmental Foundation Ltd (EFL), a leading environmental NGO in Sri Lanka, brought a case against the CEA, challenging the validity of its approval of a mini-hydropower plant.[5] The EFL objected that approval had been granted on the basis of an initial environmental examination (IEE) report rather than an EIA report. IEEs are comparatively short and simple studies; unlike EIAs, they require neither public notification of project requests nor a public comment period. The case revealed that the project was ultimately approved on the basis of the proponent's answers to an 'environmental questionnaire' and a letter from the Department of Forest Conservation, rather than on an IEE or EIA. Among a number of errors the presiding justices found to have been made by the CEA was its reasoning that an environmental questionnaire could be equated with an IEE or an EIA.[6]

In Sri Lanka, the development of EIAs as well as their evaluation may also be susceptible to conflicts of interest.[7] Project developers employ consultancy firms of their own choosing to conduct the EIA,[8] potentially undermining the capacity for these firms to formulate unbiased assessments. State agencies financing projects may also propose that their parent ministry review the EIA, potentially adversely impacting objectivity.[9]

Public review, a crucial element of the EIA process, has mixed success. All EIAs are announced in national papers, and the public may make observations or submit queries over 30 days. If proposals prove controversial, the approving agency and the CEA hold public hearings. In the best cases, public oversight has led to the protection of lands inappropriately slated for development; in 2007 a massive public campaign led the CEA to reject an EIA that proposed an 800-hectare site of farmland and marshland be acquired for the construction of a new airport.[10]

Despite oversight provisions, however, the ability of the public to access and interpret EIAs can be compromised. In Sri Lanka, there is no provision to determine whether the proponent has justifiably responded to the concerns raised by the public.[11] The content of EIAs may also vary considerably, creating challenges for the public and reviewing committees alike: data may be scant, inconclusive or improperly analysed; alternative sites may be inadequately considered; and facts may deliberately be slanted towards a favourable outcome.[12] Overly detailed description of unwanted or irrelevant data on impacts[13] can force the public and evaluation committees to sift through mountains of data in search of relevant information.

The variable quality of EIAs can have direct impacts on the country's biodiversity and ecosystems. One study of 130 EIAs and IEEs completed in Sri Lanka found that almost one-fifth made no mention of ecological impacts, while over 40 per cent discussed impacts in only a few sentences.[14] The study further found that environmental assessments concentrated only on the direct ecological impacts of projects and not on indirect or secondary impacts. This could relate to the researchers' further finding – that, while the professional credentials of ecological consultants are often adequate, time and resources may be limited, making inputs on ecological impacts to EIAs and IEEs little more than tokenistic.[15] Follow-up monitoring also appears to be weak. In the above study, less than a third of environmental assessments included plans for monitoring the ecological impacts of the proposed development, but none made commitments to monitoring.[16]

Towards a reliable, robust process

If left unaddressed, these and other issues associated with the EIA process will have corrosive effects on both the natural environment and public trust. In too many instances, the media in Sri Lanka are not free to report independently, and public apathy means that citizen oversight can be insufficient. Despite these obstacles, steps must be taken to improve the EIA process. For both CDM projects, and the incorporation of climate resilience into new infrastructure development, these issues must be tackled. Although on paper EIA procedures are strong, their implementation can be improved. Taking the initiative to do so would be the first step the government could take to ensure that rigorous environmental safeguards underpin the development of all projects in Sri Lanka, climate-change-related or not.

Notes

1.   Peter King, *Mainstreaming Climate Change into National Development Planning: A Training Manual* (Apia, Samoa: Secretariat of the Pacific Regional Environment Programme, 2010); Asian Development Bank (ADB), *Climate Proofing: A Risk-Based Approach to Adaptation* (Manila: ADB, 2005).
2.   UNFCCC, 3CMP.1, paragraph 37(c); see FCCC/KP/CMP/2005/8/Add.1. Under the 2001 Marrakesh Accords, it is the responsibility of the host country to define the criteria for sustainability and determine whether proposed CDM projects meet these requirements. It is worth noting that there is currently no legislation in Sri Lanka that stipulates that all CDM projects must be accompanied by an EIA.
3.   National Environmental (Procedure for approval of projects) Regulation no. 1 of 1993, Gazette Notification Number 772/22, dated 24 June 1993.
4.   Specifying the State Agencies which are PAAs (EIA), Gazette Notification Number 859/14, dated 23 February 1995.
5.   Environmental Foundation Ltd v. Central Environmental Authority and others; Application no. 1556/2004 in the Court of Appeal.
6.   EFL v CEA and others, 1556/2004, Court of Appeal.
7.   Lareef Zubair, 'Challenges for Environmental Impact Assessment in Sri Lanka', *Environmental Impact Assessment Review*, vol. 21 (2001), pp. 469–478.
8.   Jagath Gunawardena, senior environmental lawyer, interview with author, 22 August 2009.
9.   Zubair (2001).
10.   *The Nation* (Sri Lanka), 'Weerawila airport too far out', 27 January 2008.
11.   Gunawardena interview, 22 August 2009.
12.   Dekshika Kodituwakku, 'The Environmental Impact Assessment Process in Sri Lanka', *SARID Journal of South Asian Affairs*, vol. 1 (2004).
13.   Deputy Director General of CEA, Ramani Ellepola, at www.penta-eu.net/docs/Ramani_Ellepola.ppt.
14.   The study's sample was taken from the 463 environmental assessments completed between 1981 and 2005. Two-thirds of these were IEEs and one-third EIAs. Miriya Samarakoon and John Rowan, 'A Critical Review of Environmental Impact Statements in Sri Lanka with Particular Reference to Ecological Impact Assessment', *Environmental Management*, vol. 41 (2008), pp. 441–460.
15.   Ibid., pp. 455-456.
16.   Ibid., p. 456.

4.3.4

Voluntary carbon markets

Successes and shortfalls

Thomas Marcello[1]

A maturing market landscape

Unlike in government-mandated cap-and-trade systems, participants in voluntary carbon markets are not driven by mandatory emissions reduction schemes. Actors include businesses that anticipate having to reduce emissions under an eventual compliance system; companies that wish to offset their current emissions as part of larger corporate responsibility efforts; governments seeking to institute net-zero emissions initiatives; and individuals hoping to offset their carbon footprint.

Trading takes place through over-the-counter (OTC) trading or exchanges. The OTC market comprises deals between buyers and sellers for credits generated from emissions reduction projects, known as offsets, and purchased voluntarily. The exchange market is dominated by the US-based Chicago Climate Exchange (CCX), the world's only voluntary cap-and-trade system. It offers a voluntary but legally binding cap-and-trade system in which members agree to reduce emissions against a baseline that can be met with both offsets and allowances.

Conservation-oriented non-profit organizations dominated the voluntary market throughout the 1990s, typically using carbon finance to fund forestry-related projects. As media attention, public awareness and corporate interest in climate change increased, however, private enterprise supplanted philanthropy as the underlying market driver. The private sector's share of the voluntary OTC market has risen significantly since 2002, standing at 91 per cent as of 2009 (see figure 4.2).[2] The overall market value increased sevenfold from 2006 to 2008 before falling by nearly 50 per cent to US$387 in 2009, on account of the economic recession (see figure 4.3).[3]

Percentage share

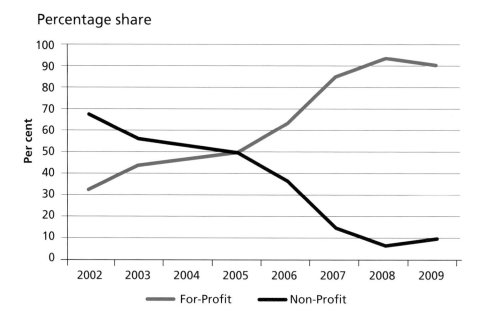

Figure 4.2 Non-profit versus private sector share of voluntary OTC market, 2002–2009

Source: Ecosystem Marketplace, Bloomberg New Energy Finance.

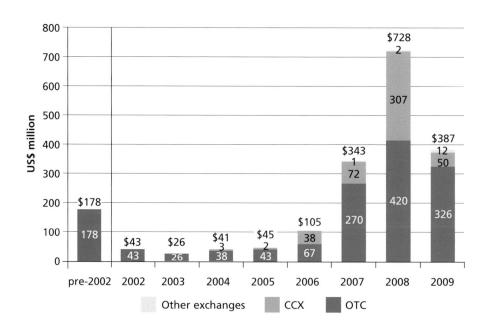

Figure 4.3 Historical annual value of the voluntary carbon markets

Although the voluntary carbon market is unregulated, it has progressively adopted best practices, standards, third-party verification and registries since 2006, coinciding with increasing private sector participation and extraordinary market growth. Despite this laudable progress, the voluntary market still has to address some transparency and accountability challenges in order to help ensure effective and credible operation.

Encouragingly, despite recent market contraction, the development of oversight and regulatory mechanisms to ensure offset quality has continued. In 2006 and 2007 myriad standards emerged to provide credibility to offsets sold on the voluntary market; by 2009 more than 90 per cent of offset credits met third-party standards.

Today, though the trend is towards consolidation of standards, with three third-party standards dominating the market,[4] more than 15 standards exist that focus on how carbon credits should be developed. Among other things, these standards might outline methodologies for making sure that projects provide net emissions reduction benefits, quantify emissions reductions from certain types of emissions reduction projects and define verification criteria.[5] This move towards the standardization of best practices for offset project developers was a necessary first step to ensure that market participants adhere to core principles, including the following:

- *Additionality*, which requires overall emissions reductions generated by offset projects to go beyond 'business-as-usual', addressing the question 'Would the offset project have been developed without the promise of financial benefits accrued from selling offset credits?'
- *Measurement*, which calls for the accurate and complete measurement of emissions reductions in order to award offset credits to projects, and ensure quality.
- *Prevention of leakage*, which addresses the risk that offset projects cause increased emissions elsewhere. For example, deforestation projects that are avoided may simply encourage deforestation in other areas. Offset projects, therefore, should not trigger leakage.
- *Permanence*, which refers to carbon benefits accrued that are irreversible. A forest offset project, for example, would be impermanent if it lacked an insurance mechanism to replace any carbon lost due to forest fire.

While adherence to these principles led to improvements in offset quality, without a central database of offset projects there were no mechanisms to prevent offset suppliers from selling the same emissions reduction to multiple buyers. Therefore, in 2008 standards organizations – the Climate Action Reserve, the Gold Standard (GS) and the Voluntary Carbon Standard (VCS) – created partnerships with third-party registry platform providers, which assign a unique serial number to each third-party-verified offset to allow market participants to track offset ownership throughout the project life cycle. Registry providers also check other offset registries to guard against a project being listed in more than one registry. Starting in 2009, major registry infrastructure providers APX and Markit adopted the Society for Worldwide Interbank Financial Telecommunication (SWIFT) messaging system to track offset transfers across multiple registries.[6]

Pre-registered CDM projects: a credibility threat?

Even with quality criteria and market infrastructure in place, threats to the voluntary market's credibility remain. Criticism of the Clean Development Mechanism (CDM) accounts for some of this scepticism, as two of the most popular voluntary market standards, the VCS and GS, are based on the CDM methodologies.

Some research has led to scrutiny of the CDM. For example, by one estimate, additionality was 'unlikely or questionable' for 40 per cent of CDM projects registered by mid-July 2007,[7] though the figure could be even higher.[8] Verifiers and validators for non-CDM offset credits are often the same private sector companies accredited by the CDM, raising concerns that conflicts of interest and a lack of technical competence associated with CDM offsets could spill into the voluntary market.[9]

Pre-registered CDM projects – projects that have been submitted for review by the CDM Executive Board and may have already begun generating emissions reductions – can apply to the VCS and GS offset programmes in order to monetize emissions reductions while awaiting CDM approval. As of April 2009, of the 19.2 million tonnes of issued voluntary offset credits sourced from CDM-eligible nations, 53 per cent originated from pre-registered CDM projects.[10]

Although pre-registered CDM projects that are accepted by voluntary programmes might damage public perception of voluntary markets, the impact is mitigated by an increasingly knowledgeable customer base. The widespread use of offset registries increases transparency and enables buyers to determine offset quality and set bids accordingly.

Integrity shortfalls

For private sector buyers, both corporate social responsibility and public relations are typically identified as primary motivations for purchasing voluntary offset credits. The risk, however, is that companies that seek projects with 'storytelling appeal'[11] may overlook their commitments to due diligence. While the social and environmental quality of offset projects is increasingly important, project integrity varies. The Chicago Climate Exchange has come under scrutiny for selling offsets with allegedly questionable integrity; the exchange was criticized for offering to pay US landowners for offset projects, such as no-tillage farming, even though the projects had already occurred.[12]

Perhaps most often when project integrity falls short, it is due to conflict over land between offset developers and local residents. Even where no laws are broken, developing offset projects may violate the 'do no harm' principles of many of the standards established for the voluntary carbon market. Examples of problematic situations include the following:

- For a number of years, controversy surrounded a tree-planting project financed by Netherlands-based FACE (Forests Absorbing Carbon-dioxide Emissions),[13] which took place in an area at the centre of a violent dispute between people who had been evicted from land designated as a national park, and park rangers from the Ugandan Wildlife Authority. Although the offset project could not be held to be directly responsible for the conflict, one researcher argued that 'funding generated by the project likely provided additional incentives and justifications to administer evictions and violently patrol the area'.[14] FACE stated that it would stop planting trees in the area until the issue was resolved.[15] That the project was certified by the Forest Stewardship Council (FSC) may suggest the need for an added layer of oversight.

- In 2010 a wind energy developer was accused of damaging the livelihoods of native populations in India after it cut down some 12,000 trees and clashed with locals in connection with taking over farmland in order to construct windmills. The conflict ended with police tear-gassing and arresting the protesting farmers, who later expressed increasing hardship associated with the loss of land.[16]

Social and environmental risks are more pronounced in the forest sector because many projects require large tracts of land in developing nations, where land rights may not be clearly defined and where many indigenous populations may not have the means to challenge projects they oppose (see section 6.2 of this volume).

Wrongdoing in the voluntary market can also take the form of direct corruption, for example by the sale of credits for carbon emissions reductions that have not taken place and will never take place.[17] Although registries can prevent such fraud, counterfeiting carbon does occur. In one case, Hungarian company KlimaFa presented carbon credits to the Vatican, promising to plant trees and make the Vatican the world's first-carbon-neutral territory. The company offered offsets for sale but according to news sources never actually planted any trees.[18]

Market infrastructure alone will not surmount the challenges faced by the voluntary carbon market. Media exposure of poor offset practices is bad publicity for suppliers and buyers alike. Individuals who are inclined to offset emissions associated with frequent travel or other lifestyle choices will probably avoid purchasing offsets if they believe they are a marketing ploy backed by minimal environmental benefit. A desire to adhere to strong corporate responsibility practices may also have motivated some offset buyers, such as Nike, to forsake credits in favour of less controversial methods for minimizing their carbon footprint, such as reducing corporate travel and increasing energy efficiency.[19] For other private sector buyers, reputational risk creates an incentive to become knowledgeable about the marketplace and ask questions about the source of offsets.

Since its inception, the voluntary market has made tremendous strides towards improving the quality and reliability of carbon offsets, but much work remains to be done. Knowledgeable buyers, media oversight and enhanced market governance can continue to expose and reject shoddy or unjust offset projects. It is in the long-term interest of offset project developers and carbon credit suppliers to develop, demonstrate and demand integrity in the voluntary carbon market.

Notes

1. Thomas Marcello is a senior carbon analyst with Bloomberg New Energy Finance.
2. Kate Hamilton et al., *Building Bridges: State of the Voluntary Carbon Markets 2010* (New York and Washington, DC: Ecosystem Marketplace and Bloomberg New Energy Finance, 2010), pp. 27–28.
3. Ibid., p. 20.
4. The Voluntary Carbon Standard (VCS), the Climate Action Reserve and the CCX, which together hold 78 per cent of the market.
5. Hamilton et al. (2010), pp. 57–68.
6. Although SWIFT does not hold accounts, clear or settle transactions, its ability to transmit secure financial messaging among financial institutions worldwide is sufficient to track offset ownership considering they are intangible goods.
7. Lambert Schneider, *Is the CDM Fulfilling its Environmental and Sustainable Development Objectives? An Evaluation of the CDM and Options for Improvement*, report prepared for WWF (Berlin: Öko Institut, 2007), p. 44.
8. Madhusree Mukerjee, 'Is a Popular Carbon-Offset Method Just a Lot of Hot Air?', *Scientific American*, June 2009.
9. See also Hamilton et al. (2010), p. 57.
10. Bloomberg New Energy Finance, 'Will the supply glut of voluntary credits drive down carbon prices?', April 2009.
11. Hamilton et al. (2010), pp. 58, 96.
12. ClimateWire (US), 'Sale of Chicago Climate Exchange to ICE reinforces weak carbon market', 3 May 2010.

13. See *Inter-Press Service (Italy)*, 'Uganda: Mount Elgon eviction has reduced us to beggars', 13 November 2009; ActionAid, 'Benet under massive eviction from their homeland' (London: ActionAid, 2008), at www.actionaid.org/kenya/index.aspx?PageID=2661.

14. Melissa Checker, 'Double Jeopardy: Carbon Offsets and Human Rights Abuses', *Synthesis/Regeneration*, no. 51 (2010).

15. Stephan Faris, 'The Other Side of Carbon Trading', *Fortune Magazine*, 29 August 2007, at http://money.cnn.com/2007/08/27/news/international/uganda_carbon_trading.fortune.

16. *Christian Science Monitor* (US), 'Carbon offsets: Green project offends Indian farmers who lose land to windmills', 20 April 2010.

17. This does not refer to forward sales of offsets that schedule for future generation.

18. *Christian Science Monitor* (US), 'Carbon offsets: How a Vatican forest failed to reduce global warming', 20 April 2010.

19. GreenBiz.com (US), 'Nike shrinks GHG footprint to 2007 levels and dumps carbon offsets', 22 January 2010.

4.3.5

Sectoral crediting

Getting governance right from the beginning

Gernot Wagner, Nathaniel O. Keohane and Annie Petsonk[1]

Several pathways lead into a low-carbon, high-efficiency future. Many go through something commonly called 'sectoral crediting', by which developing economies would both adopt emission reduction goals for entire economic sectors and allow reductions to be sold, via permits, into industrialized countries' compliance carbon markets. These twin elements of sectoral crediting contrast with project-by-project crediting, as is currently seen under the Clean Development Mechanism (CDM), and sector-level emission standards not linked to any market mechanism.

Properly designed and operated, sectoral crediting could unleash substantial investment in efficient emissions reductions across entire sectors. A quick look at the numbers makes the appeal of and need for sectoral crediting clear. The world now emits roughly 45,000 million CO_2-equivalent tonnes of greenhouse gases annually.[2] In order to avoid the most dangerous consequences of climate change, that number needs to decrease swiftly, and by at least one-half to two-thirds by mid-century.[3] Neither the market-based project-by-project approach of the CDM nor sectoral non-market standards on their own are likely to achieve this goal.

According to the World Bank's State and Trends of the Carbon Market 2010 report, the CDM accounted for 200 million tonnes of reductions below business-as-usual (BaU) levels in 2009, down from 400 the previous year.[4] Total CDM reductions are estimated to reach 1 billion tonnes by 2012 – far short of the amount needed.[5] Moreover, the benefits of these reductions are offset by their transfer to cover industrialized nations' emissions increases, and even if one project in any given sector in a particular country reduces emissions, that gain could be offset by increases elsewhere in the same sector or elsewhere in the economy.

Mandated sectoral standards can be useful, but they have clear limits. Emissions reductions occur only up to the standard and often no further. Most importantly, standards usually take the form of limiting rates of emissions, or prescribing specific technologies. Rates may go down, but total emissions can still go up as output increases. Without a market component, there is little incentive for investors to seek reductions in total emissions.

Market-based sectoral crediting is gaining ground in some policy circles because it has the potential to move beyond the confines and risks of the CDM and standards, catalysing a faster, more effective transition to clean development. The Chinese steel sector provides an instructive example. McKinsey & Company estimates that by 2030 its emissions reduction potential could be as much as 350 million tonnes below BaU projections.[6] If other industrial sectors, such as chemicals and cement, are also included, the numbers quickly rise above 1 billion tonnes for China alone – equal to all CDM reductions by 2012.

Introducing some portion of these reductions as credits in carbon markets presents not just enormous opportunities but also some serious risks. With entire sectors capped, the consequences of unreliable or manipulated emissions reports, tainted verification processes, poor crediting methodology, or inadequate domestic legal and regulatory systems more broadly, grow exponentially. These risks make it crucial to get governance right in at least four areas.

First and foremost is the environmental integrity of the system. CDM projects that fail to reduce emissions exacerbate climate change. Non-performing sectoral crediting could have the same effect on a much larger scale. Credible measurement and reporting and conflict-of-interest-free, independent verification and enforcement are crucial for environmental integrity and a robust carbon market. Although industries may raise concerns about disclosing commercially sensitive information, experience in industrialized and emerging economies shows that emissions data – including greenhouse gas (GHG) emissions – can be disclosed in ways that promote transparency and protect trade secrets.[7]

Second are risks associated with the CDM model of issuing credits for reductions below BaU. If sectoral approaches are premised on this model, they will not lead us toward sufficient global emissions reductions to avert dangerous climate change. At a minimum, industrialized countries have to adopt more stringent targets to absorb the growing number of credits. Discounting should also be introduced, by which a certain portion of sectoral credits would be automatically retired from the market, guaranteeing a net reduction of emissions credits, rather than 'emissions shifting', thus ensuring environmental benefits. Moreover, BaU is a projection and, thus, inherently unverifiable. Awarding credits for reductions below BaU creates incentives to inflate BaU projections – maximizing crediting at the expense of the environment. This is especially true for fast-growing sectors and countries, whose emissions will increase rapidly with large uncertainties around BaU projections. Consequently, the governance of sectoral crediting must shift away from BaU, to a fundamentally different model: the negotiation of sector-wide, country-specific baselines, based on historical emissions data and always keeping the environmental implications in mind, with credits awarded for reductions below those baselines. Lastly, there is a clear need for countries to develop the capacity to ensure accuracy in measuring, reporting and verifying the absolute tonnes of their emissions reductions.

Risks are also associated with crediting reductions in 'intensity' rather than in absolute emissions. Crediting intensity reductions – i.e. emissions per unit of economic output or per unit of energy output – risks minting 'credits' that are actually emissions increases if intensity declines occur amid high growth in output and energy use. Reducing total emissions is what matters

to the atmosphere. Sectoral credits ought to be made, measured and reported in absolute tonnes of reductions from an absolute baseline. Absolute measurements are also useful in highly heterogeneous sectors, in which firms use a host of different technologies to produce similar products.

Finally, risks come with carbon markets themselves. Any market requires proper infrastructure, regulatory guidance and oversight. Especially in their early stages, markets can experience volatility and the occasional start-up woes. We learnt important structural lessons from the European Union's Emissions Trading Scheme (EU ETS).[8] In April 2006 EU ETS prices dropped by a half within five days as the first official figures were published, revealing that overall emissions were lower than had previously been assumed, and that credits had therefore been over-allocated. In April 2010 the EU published official data for 2009, showing that emissions had fallen by over 10 per cent. The market hardly budged. Prices already reflected expectations of lower emissions, based partly on the economic crisis and partly on the effectiveness of the ETS. The lesson: timely data, a liquid market, policy certainty and the ability to save reductions over time – the 'banking' of credits – also matter.

Proper market governance is similarly crucial. In both industrialized and developing countries, transparent and accountable agencies must be responsible for maintaining mutually recognizable registries to track transactions and fund flows. Firms that monitor emissions and calculate baselines should be prohibited from marketing credits to avoid conflicts of interest. Such structural transparency offers important co-benefits – public participation in policy processes and better institutions for development – that reinforce the durability of the reductions achieved and the sustainability of the market itself.

Private investors may face additional risks under sectoral approaches compared to CDM. The role for policy here is not to eliminate risk, but to create the appropriate incentives to ensure that private capital and insurance markets can manage and mitigate it.

Sectoral crediting is not a goal in itself. The goal is to enable a rapid transition to enforceable, absolute emissions limits for all major emitting sectors, powered by a broad carbon market made up of global or linked national or regional emissions trading systems.

The first sectoral credit has yet to be issued. That allows us to get governance right and keep the goal in sight from the beginning. It is a tall yet not insurmountable order, and a step we ought to take to ensure that, if sectoral crediting moves ahead, a system is created that ultimately stabilizes the climate and helps transform the over US$5,000 billion-a-year fossil-fuel-based energy sector into a cleaner, greener future.[9]

Notes

1. The authors are, respectively, an economist, the chief economist, and an international counsel at Environmental Defense Fund.
2. See the World Resource Institute's (WRI's) Climate Analysis Indicators Tool (CAIT) database, cait.wri.org, for the most comprehensive emissions data.
3. Environmental Defense Fund (EDF), *Turn toward Climate Safety* (New York: EDF, 2009).
4. Alexandre Kossoy and Philippe Ambrosi, *State and Trends of the Carbon Market 2010* (Washington, DC: World Bank, 2010).
5. EDF analysis of UNEP Risø's CDM pipeline spreadsheet, at http://cdmpipeline.org/publications/CDMPipeline.xlsx; Kossoy and Ambrosi, 2010.
6. McKinsey & Company, *China's Green Revolution: Prioritizing Technologies to Achieve Energy and Environmental Stability* (New York: McKinsey & Company, 2009), p. 91, exhibit 37.
7. See, for example, US Environmental Protection Agency 40 Code of Federal Regulations (CFR) part 2, 'Proposed Confidentiality Determinations for Data Required Under the Mandatory Greenhouse Gas Reporting Rule and Proposed Amendment to Special Rules Governing Certain Information Obtained Under the Clean Air Act; Proposed Rule' (28 June 2010); Mexican Environmental Agency, *Informe Nacional de Emisiones y Transferencias de Contaminantes*, at http://app1.semarnat.gob.mx/retc/index.html.
8. For the most comprehensive review of EU ETS to date, see Denny Ellerman et al., *Pricing Carbon: The European Union Emissions Trading Scheme* (Cambridge: Cambridge University Press, 2010).
9. Fred Krupp and Miriam Horn, *Earth: The Sequel* (New York: W. W. Norton, 2008), p. 12.

4.4

Climate change, corporate change

Shifting business models towards the climate agenda

David L. Levy[1]

A global transition to a low-carbon economy requires the large scale mobilization of financial, technological and organizational resources, many of which are concentrated in the hands of large multinational corporations. Of the US$500 billion in annual global investment needed over the coming decades to keep warming within a 2°C limit, more than 80 per cent will have to come from private sources.[2] Climate change presents a profound strategic challenge to business, however. Measures to control the emissions of greenhouse gases (GHGs) most directly threaten sectors that produce and depend on fossil fuels, such as oil, power and transportation. Managers in energy-intensive industries, including cement, chemicals, paper and metals, have also been concerned – understandably – with the regulatory risk of higher costs for fuels and lower demand for energy-intensive products.

During the 1990s energy-intensive sectors responded aggressively to the prospect of mandatory GHG limits, and their influence on policy, especially in the US, constituted a virtual veto on regulation. In the last decade, government incentives, competitive pressures and non-governmental organization (NGO) campaigns have led many firms, in varying degrees, to craft business models that exploit potential market opportunities in low-carbon products and services. This shift in corporate political and market strategy has created a virtuous cycle, in which strengthened business coalitions have grown supportive of more stringent climate policy and widened the political space for action. This cycle is fragile, however, and, without opportunities to transform climate risks into business opportunities, it is possible that undue corporate influence could again hinder mitigation efforts.

The momentum of this corporate conversion is already in danger of stalling. Climate change creates considerable competitive risk, as changes in prices, technologies and demand patterns disrupt traditional business models. Investing in new technologies can be a treacherous business. Automobile manufacturers, for example, find that they are dependent on existing infrastructure, creating barriers for electric vehicles, which require a network of charging stations. Multiple clean energy technologies are in competition, such as solar thermal versus photovoltaics, and 'thin film' versus 'crystalline silicon' solar cells, making it hard to pick winners.

Moreover, companies successful in one area of business cannot easily transition to new products and markets. Corporate managers know that the key lesson of business strategy is to stick to your 'core competences'. Exxon lost money when it tried to diversify in the 1970s energy crisis,[3] and now understands that its expertise lies in geology, hydrocarbon chemistry, extraction and distribution. Rather than embrace radical change, it has enhanced its capacity in related low-carbon technologies. In 2009 Exxon announced a US$600 million algae biofuels project with a biotech company, and a US$41 billion acquisition of a major player in the shale gas sector.[4] These investments represent a better strategic fit than solar or wind, though they entail cross-industry partnerships to acquire external capabilities.

Similarly, oil and gas companies have befriended the coal industry as proponents of carbon capture and sequestration (CCS) technology,[5] as the expertise to extract fluid fuels is closely related to that required to re-inject CO_2 underground. Although many of these emerging technologies will have to be proved to be environmentally safe and financially feasible, the model for cross-industry collaboration is strong, allowing companies to share risks, gain capabilities and shoulder the fixed costs of research and development.

Climate change presents a host of strategic uncertainties regarding the unfolding science, regulation, technological developments and competitor reactions. Thus, when British oil company BP committed itself to investing in solar and wind energy in 2000, it was competing in the same global oil market as Exxon, but perceived the risks very differently. BP plotted a strategy for a world in which mandatory emission controls appeared inevitable, carbon would carry a price tag, and consumers would demand low-emission products. A decade later, though, with growing regulatory uncertainty and its solar business far from profitable, BP has pulled back from its renewable energy investments, instead increasing its investments in Canadian oil sands.[6]

National and regional authorities have a vital role to play by implementing policies that provide incentives for positive corporate action. Bolstered by tax policies in Denmark and Israel, the company Better Place is developing a national replaceable battery infrastructure for pure electric vehicles that allows consumers to pay according to driving distance.[7] The Vélib bike rental system in Paris and the US-based Zipcar car rental firm similarly engage business and government in partnerships that transform markets and overcome systemic obstacles in infrastructure, scale and incentives.[8]

These initiatives move towards a service- rather than product-based business model. Moreover, they trigger competitive dynamics with far-reaching effects. Better Place has signed a deal with Renault–Nissan to supply the electric cars, and other car companies, fearful of falling behind, are accelerating their own plans for plug-in hybrids and pure electric vehicles.

Major companies in the US power sector have adopted a more proactive position on climate change in recent years. Duke Energy, Exelon and PG&E have joined initiatives led by the US Climate Action Partnership and the Pew Center on Global Climate Change that aim at emissions reductions by deploying renewables, boosting generation efficiency and implementing demand-side management policies.[9] These companies might anticipate a future national cap-and-trade regime and carbon price, but they face more immediate and local pressures, notably escalating renewable or alternative energy portfolio standards in more than 30 US states.[10]

US states are also attempting to restructure power markets to provide incentives for energy efficiency. Most frequently, this takes the form of small 'benefit charges' being added to bills, which are used to subsidize consumer efficiency upgrades.[11] Several states are also examining California's experience with rate decoupling, which rewards utilities with higher power prices for implementing energy efficiency and demand-side management measures.[12]

The lesson for public policy here is the importance of structuring incentives and managing expectations to shape business models and channel corporate resources in a positive rather than counterproductive way. In the face of global policy uncertainty, a key task is to maintain momentum by creating a predictable business and regulatory environment.

Business realizes the dangers of the proliferation of multiple regulations, standards and carbon trading schemes, and large firms are joining groups that press for clear, predictable and coherent climate policy. In 2007 more than 60 of the world's largest companies, including BP, Siemens, GE and Unilever, launched Combat Climate Change (3C), with the goal of developing 'a worldwide policy framework to replace the Kyoto Protocol from 2013 and onwards'. In December 2009, as the negotiations mired in Copenhagen, Lars Josefsson, CEO of Swedish power company Vattenfall and chairman of 3C, warned that large-scale business investment was contingent on a binding international treaty and coordinated national initiatives.[13] In the absence of an international treaty, the onus falls on the private sector, along with local and national governments, to seek novel business models that stimulate the transition to a low-carbon future.

Notes

1. David L. Levy is chair of the Department of Management and Marketing at the University of Massachusetts, Boston, and director of its Center for Sustainable Enterprise and Regional Competitiveness.
2. International Energy Agency (IEA), *World Energy Outlook 2009: Executive Summary* (Paris: IEA, 2009), p. 14.
3. *Wall Street Journal* (US) 'Exxon chief makes a cold calculation on global warming', 15 June 2005.
4. MarketWatch.com, 'Exxon Mobil lays $600 million on the line for algae fuels', 14 July 2009; CNNMoney.com, 'Exxon to buy XTO in $41 billion deal', 14 December 2009.
5. See, for example, www.globalccsinstitute.com.
6. BusinessGreen.com (UK), 'BP shrugs off anti-tar sands shareholder resolution', 16 April 2010.
7. See Betterplace.com.
8. NPR.org (US), 'Paris' popular bike program may inspire others', 15 September, 2009; Government-fleet.com (US), 'City of Baltimore launches car sharing program', 1 July 2010.
9. See www.us-cap.org/about-us/about-our-members and www.pewclimate.org/business/belc/members.
10. Pew Center on Global Climate Change, *Climate Change 101: State Action* (Arlington, VA: Pew Center on Global Climate Change, 2009).
11. Ibid.
12. See Pew Center on Global Climate Change, 'Decoupling in detail', at www.pewclimate.org/what_s_being_done/in_the_states/decoupling_detail.
13. *Financial Times* (UK), 'Business coalition calls for firm CO_2 treaty', 23 November 2009.

4.5

Policy engagement

A missing link in corporate climate reporting

Ryan Schuchard and Laura Ediger[1]

Over the last decade many businesses have begun to measure, reduce and disclose greenhouse gas (GHG) emissions. By 2009 over 80 per cent of the world's largest 500 companies were reporting their GHG emissions to the Carbon Disclosure Project (CDP).[2] Efforts to report emissions continue to spread rapidly around the world, particularly in Brazil, Russia, India and China.[3] Today, however, corporate best practice is moving beyond merely tracking and reporting GHG emissions, to addressing publicly the risks and opportunities presented by climate change.[4]

As business has become more responsive to climate change, corporate involvement in climate policy has also skyrocketed: in the US the number of interests lobbying on climate change grew 400 per cent between 2003 and 2008 and estimated lobbying expenditures topped US$90 million annually in 2008.[5] For business, policy engagement presents an opportunity to shape the rules, incentives and institutions that define the overall operating context for companies. The promotion by business of systemic changes in climate-related public policy can help business move in a coordinated manner and on a large scale towards low-carbon investments.

As corporate involvement with climate change policy grows, however, so too must the scope of corporate reporting so as to enable stakeholders to understand the potential impacts of these activities. Comprehensive reporting on climate policy engagement must not only incorporate disclosure on political financing, but outline the process of identifying activities for engagement, demonstrate how corporate decisions about policy direction are taken and highlight areas for improvement. Such disclosure enhances accountability, creates a starting point for dialogue, and arms stakeholders with the tools necessary to distinguish public relations exercises from long-term, positive climate engagement.

The business case for involvement in climate policy

For many companies, involvement in climate change policy is seen as a critical investment. The absence of predictable and effective public policy can create bottlenecks in efforts to scale up investments in renewables and energy efficiency initiatives. For example, Google's programmes to help consumers save electricity may be reliant on US legislation that would attach a price to carbon and trigger interest in low-carbon technologies.[6]

Current uncertainty over the shape of future climate policy provides further motivation for companies to seek involvement on policy matters. Companies such as Ford and Hong-Kong-based power company CLP are calling on governments to provide the regulatory certainty they need to make multi-decade investments. Timberland CEO Jeff Swartz has argued, 'I just want to know what the facts are, and I'll get around to innovating in order to make a profit against them.'[7]

Corporate engagement in public policy: consequences for mitigation

Corporate engagement in climate policy can have direct consequences on whether – and how – national lawmakers and the international community find effective techniques for mitigating climate change. Business participation can add valuable technical expertise and generate significant investment capital for new initiatives. When corporate interests fail to align with mitigation goals, however, involvement may dampen or halt legislative attempts towards emissions reductions or low-carbon development.

In early 2010, for example, the powerful US Chamber of Commerce petitioned the US Environmental Protection Agency (EPA) over its finding that GHGs endanger public health.[8] 'Astroturf' organizations – supposed grassroots groups actually formed and funded by business – can also muddy the policy debate. In 2009 Greenpeace USA accused a major trade association for oil and natural gas companies of planning 'Energy Citizen' rallies to discourage support for a federal climate change bill.[9] In Europe intense lobbying from select sectors was believed by some observers to have diluted the EU climate policy targets.[10] Some Australian industries were similarly blamed for trying to weaken that country's attempts at a comprehensive emissions reduction plan (see also contributions 2.2.1 and 2.2.2, in this volume).[11]

Business interests do not always run contrary to the public good, however. Business involvement in initiatives such as Combat Climate Change, Caring for Climate and the Copenhagen Communiqué support calls for climate policy that puts the world on a path for climate stabilization. By early 2010 over 1000 global companies comprising some US$11 trillion in market capitalization and 20 million employees were calling on policy-makers to enact climate legislation,[12] along with over 5000 US-based companies.[13] Encouragingly, reporting on climate policy engagement also seems to be on the rise. A BSR assessment of 150 global industry leaders shows that the vast majority of them are voluntarily reporting on some level of climate policy engagement.[14]

Reporting responsibly and comprehensively on public policy engagement

Environmental groups, consumers and investors are increasingly adding policy engagement to issues that companies are already reporting on, such as corporate emissions and mitigation strategies. At present, however, there is no widely accepted set of indicators for corporate reporting on climate engagement,[15] making it difficult for companies to decide what information to disclose or to compare their reporting practices with peers. It can also be difficult to describe the tangible influence a company has had on a policy process. Communication may occur primarily through informal discussions or indirectly through public statements, making cause and effect unclear.[16]

Nevertheless, there is an opportunity to establish more common definitions and norms around climate policy engagement that would lead to more meaningful discussions, better disclosure to stakeholders and greater incentives for companies to advance systemic climate solutions. Efforts are under way, but they are isolated. The Carbon Disclosure Project investor coalition and the Climate Counts consumer scorecard have both started to include policy engagement as a criterion in their company rankings. Until standards are established, businesses can take the lead in disclosing their engagement with climate change policy by meeting the following stakeholder expectations:

- *Building conceptual and technological links.* These demonstrate the impacts businesses have on climate change through their influence on public policies. In a similar way that British Telecommunications (BT) and Autodesk report emissions in terms of atmospheric share,[17] companies can list what governments they seek to influence, what commitments they seek of them and what this portfolio represents in terms of potential outcomes. They can reference the Climate Interactive C-ROADS platform, which shows the reduction potential of different regimes and the effects that their different commitments are likely to have.
- *Disclosing corporate processes.* The aim here is more comprehensive reporting regarding company activities and their underlying rationale, such as company strategy and, more generally, aspects of governance.[18] Companies can do several things to promote this kind of transparency. They can describe the decision-making process and roles for climate policy efforts, including the teams involved, and how the CEO and the board interact. They can show how the company undergoes decision-making

around issues related to climate change policy engagement – including how the company identifies issues, conducts reviews and pursues dialogue with stakeholders. Finally, they can show evidence that goals and commitments with core business strategy and actions are mutually reinforcing and, at the very least, not in conflict.

- *Creating benchmarks for performance on activities related to climate policy.* Disclosing financial and in-kind support to political parties and politicians, and listing membership in trade groups, are only the first steps in outlining engagement with climate policy. Other efforts, such as funding scientific research on climate change or releasing position statements, should also be included in reporting. The information on involvement in shaping climate policy should be publicly accessible and easily understandable, creating a benchmark against which to assess the impact of corporate efforts on policy outcomes.[19]
- *Engaging the board of directors on policy involvement.* Making boards the decision-takers on climate policy has been positively linked to both high-quality disclosure on climate policy and greater engagement with policy-makers.[20] Commitment at the highest levels not only leads to enhanced reporting but embeds these values throughout an organization, increasing the likelihood that the company's strategy on climate change is far-reaching.
- *Aligning policy efforts internally and externally with company strategy.* A corporation's public stance on climate change should cohere with the private actions it takes to shape policy through 'lobbying, whether as an individual company or as part of a group'.[21] Ensuring a consistent message among all business communications on climate policy and integrating this message into sustainability, marketing and government affairs teams makes it more likely that corporate messaging reflects a real commitment to mitigation strategies.
- *Providing evidence of improvement with each initiative.* Reporting instances of lessons learnt from climate policy engagement – in particular, challenges overcome – makes future engagement more effective.[22] Reporting may also highlight discrepancies between organizational and departmental positions.
- *Seeking independent verification to confirm reporting results.* External confirmation of reporting content can build credibility and bolster consumer and investor confidence in corporate reporting on policy engagement.

Taking the above as a minimum standard for policy engagement on climate change provides stakeholders with a clearer picture of the nature of business engagement in climate change policy and its consequences. Although commitment to combating climate change has grown in the last decade, there is still a long way to go. Comprehensive and comprehensible public disclosure of whom companies engage with in this global discussion, what outcomes they seek to influence and how they make and carry out those decisions is a crucial element in ensuring that corporate engagement carries real, positive and transparent consequences for mitigating climate change through public policy.

Notes

1. Ryan Schuchard is manager of research and innovation and Laura Ediger is environmental manager at BSR.
2. Carbon Disclosure Project, *Carbon Disclosure Project 2009: Global 500 Report* (London: Carbon Disclosure Project, 2009), p. 8.
3. Ibid.
4. Samantha Putt del Pino et al., *Sharpening the Cutting Edge: Corporate Action for a Strong, Low-Carbon Economy* (Washington, DC: World Resources Institute [WRI], 2009).
5. Marianne Lavelle, 'The climate lobby's nonstop growth', Center for Public Integrity (US), 19 May 2009, at www.publicintegrity.org/investigations/climate_change/articles/entry/1376; Marianne Lavelle, 'The climate change lobby explosion', Center for Public Integrity (US), 24 February 2009, at www.publicintegrity.org/investigations/climate_change/articles/entry/1171.
6. *Guardian* (UK), 'Google climate change chief wants price on carbon', 16 April 2010.
7. Politico.com (US), 'Big business pushes for climate action', 5 October 2009, at www.politico.com/news/stories/1009/27896.html.
8. *New York Times* (US), 'US Chamber petitions EPA to reconsider greenhouse gas endangerment finding', 16 March 2010.
9. BusinessGreen.com (UK), 'Greenpeace uncovers "astroturf" campaign to challenge US climate bill', 17 August 2009, at www.businessgreen.com/business-green/news/2247933/greenpeace-uncovers-astroturf.
10. Pew Environment Group, 'The European Union Climate Package' (Arlington, VA: Pew Environment Group), at www.pewglobalwarming.org/ourwork/international/bonn/EUClimatePackage.pdf.
11. Marian Wilkinson et al., '"Brown down" in Australia: Business interests thwart carbon controls on the hottest, driest continent', Center for Public Integrity (US), 6 November 2009, at www.publicintegrity.org/investigations/global_climate_change_lobby/articles/entry/1799.
12. WWF, *Business – The Real Deal* (Washington, DC: WWF, 2009), at http://assets.panda.org/downloads/action_bybusiness_onclimate_paper_corrected.pdf.
13. See www.americanbusinessesforcleanenergy.org/member/listing.
14. Ryan Schuchard, *Communicating on Climate Policy Engagement: A Guide to Sustainability Reporting* (San Francisco: BSR, 2010).
15. Ibid.
16. AccountAbility, *Towards Responsible Lobbying: Leadership and Public Policy* (London: AccountAbility, 2005).
17. For BT, see www.cdproject.net/CDPResults/65_329_219_CDP-The-Carbon-Chasm-Final.pdf; for Autodesk, see http://usa.autodesk.com/adsk/servlet/pc/item?siteID=123112&id=14981941.
18. In a 2010 report, BSR outlines nine elements that should especially be considered in the context of climate change. See Schuchard (2010).
19. Ibid.
20. Carbon Disclosure Project (2009).
21. Simon McRae, *Hidden Voices: The CBI, Corporate Lobbying and Sustainability* (London: Friends of the Earth, 2005); quoted in Schuchard (2010).
22. Schuchard (2010).

4.5.1

Colombia

Measuring transparency policies and mechanisms in public utilities

Alma Rocío Balcázar, Martha Elena Badel and Lorena Roa Barrera[1]

Reforms in the early 1990s opened Colombia's utility sector to private sector participation, creating what is today a blend of private and public management of utilities and presenting new challenges for oversight and accountability.

The management of and demand on public utilities can significantly influence levels of greenhouse gas (GHG) emissions. As large emitters, utilities also possess some of the greatest opportunities to reduce emissions. Energy efficiency in particular currently presents the largest and most cost-effective solution for reducing emissions,[2] a fact recognized in Colombia, which has received endorsement by the Clean Technology Fund for an investment plan proposing abatement measures in energy efficiency.[3]

With the potential to have significant impact on Colombia's carbon footprint, it is essential that utility managers undertake strategies to identify, assess and reduce environmental risks and GHG emissions, while ensuring that consumers understand both pricing structures and opportunities for energy efficiency.

Utilities in Colombia – particularly energy, water and sewage, waste collection and gas – are also beginning to apply for and obtain emissions reduction credits under the Clean Development Mechanism[4] (CDM) (see figure 4.4). The need for accountability and environmental integrity in implementing CDM projects makes a culture of corporate transparency all the more important.

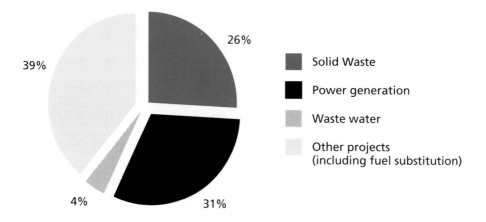

Figure 4.4 Public services in the Colombian CDM portfolio

Source: Adapted from the Colombian Ministry of Environment, Housing and Territorial Development, 2007.

Despite the importance of transparency in the management and provision of basic public services, Colombian utilities demonstrate significant shortcomings, including asymmetries in information that prevent stakeholders from learning how companies manage and deliver public services, and an absence of strong corporate governance practices.[5]

A pilot evaluation

To address some of these issues, Transparencia por Colombia launched a pilot evaluation in 2008, in which 10 public and privately managed utility providers participated.[6] This initiative, the first in the country, assesses the policies and mechanisms used by utility companies in order to support transparency, and seeks to forge an alliance with leading businesses to encourage other utility companies to emulate best practice.[7] Four factors of corporate transparency were measured: disclosure, dialogue, clear rules and voluntary controls (see table 4.2).

Although the model offers only limited insights as to how corporate transparency might influence GHG levels, the study nevertheless establishes a set of baseline expectations for accountability. If the evaluation leads to greater dialogue and information sharing between citizens and utilities, the impacts on consumer choices and long-term business strategy could have positive and direct consequences for emissions reductions.

Factors for transparency	Indicators	What is assessed
Voluntary controls	Additional or self-imposed controls	Assessment mechanisms, procedures, plans and methods adopted voluntarily by the company. Analysis of audit reports, risk management and other voluntary mechanisms.
Clear rules	Corporate ethics	Principles and ethical values are documented within the company, and there is a process for the communication of, and training in, these principles and values. Suppliers and contractors are aligned with the values.
	Corporate governance	Formalization of sound practices of corporate governance and the existence of basic information on concrete policy and measurement on issues including shareholder participation, functions of board of directors, dissemination of financial and non-financial information to stakeholders and periodic evaluation of governance practices.
Dialogue	Customer service systems	Efficacy of response systems and other mechanisms that ensure inclusion and equality meet needs and expectations.
Disclosure	Information to partners, shareholders and investors Information to customers Information to suppliers Information to society	Meets at least minimum standards for information provision and delivers significant information to stakeholders concerning items including corporate risks, profitability, social and environmental sustainability, and information on products and services.

Table 4.2 Colombian utility companies: Factors for corporate transparency, indicators and what is assessed by the pilot study

A mixed record on environmental responsibility

An average overall score of 57 out of 100 suggests a need for utility companies to take additional steps to enhance transparency. Broadly, these include communicating effectively with a diverse group of stakeholders; enhancing the use of information technologies for this purpose; establishing clear policies regarding the dissemination of management activities; and increasing citizen engagement in and oversight of utility services. While utility companies showed greater responsibility regarding environmental impacts and policies than for other issues, the results remain mixed.

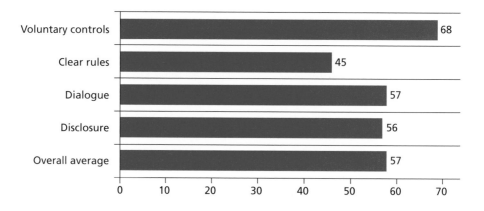

Figure 4.5 Pilot study of Colombian utility company transparency: consolidated results

The evaluation of disclosure revealed some encouraging results. Companies prepared and released reports for stakeholders that discussed environmental management and plans to mitigate their negative impacts on the environment. Many utilities were also found to have posted information on their websites to help consumers use their utilities more efficiently.

What was discouraging, however, was a lack of clarity in pricing and the failure of some companies to help customers understand contracts and invoicing. Consumers therefore face more difficulty in understanding and making decisions about their consumption patterns – a problem that could contribute to energy inefficiency and increased emissions.

The findings on voluntary controls pointed to a lack of corporate promotion of citizen oversight. While companies do make efforts to cultivate dialogue with stakeholders, citizens have access to few effective channels for direct engagement with companies or to solicit information from government oversight bodies.[8] One implication of this is that without access to such information, citizens are limited in their ability to work with utility companies and the government in order to assess companies' impact on Colombia's emissions levels, or collaborate on GHG emissions reduction initiatives.

Setting a standard in utility transparency

Initiatives such as this by Transparencia por Colombia, which has welcomed 13 new utility sector participants for future iterations of the evaluation, have a valuable role to play in encouraging transparency and good governance in utility management and reinforcing minimum standards of disclosure and dialogue.

Inevitably, such an evaluation cannot directly identify how transparency in utility companies affects GHG emissions. Nevertheless, questions of consumer awareness, citizen engagement, and information sharing and collaboration on the long-term strategy of public utilities hold direct relevance for planning emissions reductions. If, over time, the Transparencia por Colombia model and similar initiatives successfully foster widespread standards of transparency and accountability throughout the utility sector, then the ability of citizens to obtain information and engage with business could become not just best practice but common practice. For those who hope to foster dialogue between the public and utilities on climate strategy and energy efficiency, this development would be welcome.

Notes

1. Alma Rocío Balcázar is private sector director, Martha Elena Badel is private sector consultant and Lorena Roa Barrera is private sector professional at Transparencia por Colombia.
2. World Bank, *World Development Report 2010: Development and Climate Change* (Washington, DC: World Bank, 2010), p. 190.
3. In addition to energy efficiency, the plan focuses on abatement in urban transport. See Climate Investment Funds, *Clean Technology Fund Investment Plan for Colombia* (Washington, DC: World Bank, 2010).
4. For up-to-date figures on CDM projects in Colombia, see www.minambiente.gov.co.
5. Departamento Nacional de Planeación, *Prácticas de gobierno corporativo en empresas de servicios públicos domiciliarios: Lineamientos de política*, CONPES Document no. 3384 (Bogotá: Departamento Nacional de Planeación, 2005).
6. These were: Promigas, Telefónica Telecom, ISAGEN, Empresa de Energía de Bogotá, Aguas de Manizales, Empresas Públicas de Medellín, Electrificadora del Caribe and the companies of Grupo Sala: Aseo Emas Pasto, Emas Manizales and Aguas de la Sabana.
7. For the evaluation's complete methodology and results, see Transparencia por Colombia, *Políticas y mecanismos de transparencia en empresas de servicios públicos: Resultados del primer ejercicio de evaluación* (Bogotá: Transparencia por Colombia, 2009).
8. Transparencia por Colombia, 2009.

4.6
Enabling green choices

Ensuring consumers receive accurate, actionable information on the climate impacts of their consumption choices

Fred Pearce[1]

Defining 'greenwash'

A French nuclear power plant trumpets its green credentials by celebrating the award of a certificate for, among other things, using recycled toilet paper at its reactor.[2] A fast-growing airport in Scotland boasts of soaking up carbon dioxide by funding children to plant some trees – never mind the small matter of thousands more planes taking off each year.[3] Private jet companies advertise themselves as carbon-neutral.[4]

There is no agreed definition of 'greenwashing'; but it involves an effort to use publicity to encourage consumers of a product or service to believe that it is more environmentally benign than it really is, or to use the claimed benefits of one 'green' product to improve the reputation of an entire company or industry. Several governments and trade bodies have established guidelines for how to make proper, verifiable environmental claims. Here 'greenwashing' has generally been taken to indicate cases in which companies have hidden environmental impacts by deviating from such guidelines.[5]

Consumers should perhaps be flattered. Many corporations now understand that their customers expect them to have good environmental credentials. Green sells.[6] Such cases also show the potential for abuse of that expectation, however. As suppliers of products and services of every kind, from power to pensions, and cars to copying paper, splatter their advertising and public relations with bogus, misleading and frivolous claims, they threaten to undermine public faith in any kind of environmental progress. Worse still, perhaps, successful greenwashing lets companies off the hook from taking their share of responsibility in confronting a global issue such as climate change. Transparency in terms of green claims, including through independent verification of these claims, is therefore essential to preventing greenwash.

Preventing greenwashing: no easy task

Some governments have tried to impose strict rules on environmental claims. Germany's competition law covers environmental claims in advertising, regulating when phrases such as 'environmentally friendly' can be used. Many have been reluctant to crack down, however. In the US, the Federal Trade Commission (FTC) has guidelines for environmental marketing, but successive administrations have not prioritized acting on them.[7]

In early 2010 the UK government's Department for Environment, Food and Rural Affairs (DEFRA) published guidelines for corporations that want to make credible environmental claims.[8] They boiled down to ensuring that claims were 'clear, accurate, relevant and verifiable'. Ministers refused to adopt a policing role, however, and rejected a proposal that had been made by parliamentarians on the House of Commons Environmental Audit Committee a year beforehand asking ministers to 'intervene directly to remove those [claims] found to be inaccurate or misleading'.[9]

Instead, governments prefer to rely on the growing promotional importance of eco-labelling schemes sponsored by non-governmental organizations (NGOs) and industry, such as those run by the Forest Stewardship Council and Rainforest Alliance to recognize forest-friendly products, and sometimes self-policing from the advertising industry itself.[10] The evidence, however, is that, while the former is growing in popularity, the latter is not working. The UK Advertising Standards Authority (ASA), an industry body, says that, despite a series of tough rulings, it has received a rising tide of public complaints about green claims in advertisements.[11]

The ASA says obviously bogus claims may be diminishing but more subtle propaganda is on the rise. Numerous products make unspecific claims about being 'green', 'eco', 'environmentally friendly', 'sustainable' or even 'carbon-neutral' without any attempt to define what they mean by such terms. Moreover, there is a growing use of images designed to seduce us into imagining that companies and products are green.

The ASA has recently rapped the knuckles of Renault, banning its advertisement of the Twingo – a car with above-average emissions for its size – as an 'eco-car', pictured with leaves blowing out of its tailpipe.[12] It followed up by chastising the Anglo-Dutch oil giant Shell for showing flowers growing out of its refinery chimneys.[13]

The indications are that green image-making is becoming more subtle but more pervasive. Some common tricks are emerging. For example, big companies often green their corporate image by heavily marketing a handful of products with above-average environmental credentials, as if they represented the full range.

Oil companies such as BP and Shell now routinely spend millions of euros a year filling newspapers, billboard hoardings, websites and TV slots with promotion of their investment in renewable energy, when this makes typically around 5 per cent of their budgets.[14] Shell, for instance, has spent millions showing pretty images of a butterfly net catching CO_2 and a pocket calculator with a button marked 'less CO_2,' – at a time when it has been cutting its investment in renewables and when its outgoing chief executive warned of wind, solar and hydrogen power: 'I don't expect them to grow much at Shell from here.'[15]

The Danish power company Dong trades on its green image at home, where it is a major supplier of wind energy, while building coal-fired power stations abroad – in Scotland, for instance.[16] Likewise, German energy giant RWE presents itself as green through its use of wind and water power, even though renewable sources make up only 2.4 per cent of the power generation of what is Europe's largest CO_2 emitter.[17]

A related strategy is to highlight the company's environmental research and development. German car manufacturer Audi promotes its greenness with descriptions of a 'fantasy car' that, it admits, may never be built, while the CO_2 emissions from its real fleet are still way off EU targets.[18]

Such strategies are most common from industries with bad environmental images, such as energy companies, airlines, oil giants, car manufacturers and some major retail chains. Top UK retailer Tesco, for example, claimed in 2009 to be 'setting an example' in tackling climate change, during a year in which it admitted to increasing its CO_2 emissions by almost half a million tonnes. Its argument was that its 'floor space' was increasing more rapidly than its emissions. Furthermore, 'setting an example' went only so far. Like other UK retailers, Tesco refuses to put doors on its store refrigerators, even though this could reduce their energy use by up to 10 per cent, according to one industry source.[19]

Airlines are feeling the heat over their high and fast-growing emissions. Sir Richard Branson's Virgin Atlantic has responded with high-profile investment in trials with biofuel. This cannot disguise the fact that its fleet emissions have been rising rapidly, however – and are higher than those of most African countries.[20]

Spurious statistics are legion in green promotion. European budget airline Easyjet claims prominently on its website that a typical journey on its planes has a smaller carbon footprint than the same journey by a hybrid car – a calculation that is sustainable only on the assumption that the car's passenger seats are empty, while the aircraft's passenger seats are full.[21] Similarly, Lamborghini announced a 35 per cent cut in future CO_2 emissions for one of its vehicles, glossing over the fact that the improvement will still leave it bottom of its class.[22]

A common greenwashing trick is for companies to associate themselves with 'green causes'. During 2009, in the run-up to the Copenhagen Climate Conference, Shell invested widely in funding and promoting special newspaper and magazine supplements on climate change issues.[23] Meanwhile, the French energy company EDF launched an annual 'Green Britain Day', advertised with a green Union Jack. It encouraged its customers to cut their carbon emissions, but made no parallel promises of its own.[24]

Greenwash can hoodwink governments as well as consumers, by encouraging them to make the wrong policy decisions in the belief that they are being 'green'. Arguably, one example is the widespread rebranding of the coal-mining and coal-burning industries with the notion of 'clean coal'. The idea is that, one day, carbon emissions will be tapped before they go up the chimney – a technology known as carbon capture and storage. Planned new coal-fired power stations are routinely advertised as being 'carbon-capture-ready'. This means little, though, since the plants are likely to be nearing the end of their lives before the technology actually becomes available.[25]

Some products may be environmentally benign enough in themselves, but come with huge energy and carbon footprints by the time we consume them. An example is bottled water. It is no more and no less 'green' than tap water at the time the bottle is filled. Trucking those bottles across countries – and often across international borders – gives them a much larger carbon footprint than water delivered by pipeline, however.

Looking for solutions: strengthening standards and empowering consumers

One way out of this quagmire, besides policing the claims themselves, is to circumvent them with agreed standards and to require manufacturers to advertise what standards their products meet. Cars in the European Union (EU) have to undergo a standard test to show their emissions, measured in grams per kilometre, and to include the results in their advertising. This at least allows purchasers to assess the advertising claims against reality.[26] The EU also operates agreed energy efficiency labelling standards for white goods such as refrigerators, for example. Even in this respect, though, industry lobbying has sometimes devalued their transparency. The EU energy label now runs not from G to A, but on to A++, so a product that is graded A – apparently the highest category – turns out to be far from the best.[27]

Moreover, many products have no such standards. The EU has extended its range by introducing its own eco-label, a flower logo, for products that meet its standards of sustainability. More than 3000 products currently carry the flower logo. In Germany some 10,000 products carry the Blue Angel logo.

Even here things can go wrong, however. Two brands of widely sold copying paper, Golden Plus and Lucky Boss, carry the logo across the EU, vouching that the paper comes from sustainable sources. An investigation by an NGO, Forest and European Union Resources Network, in 2010 revealed, however, that significant amounts of the pulp from which the paper was made came, in part at least, from the clear-felling of virgin rainforest in the Indonesian island of Sumatra.[28]

More than showing that not all products carrying the logo live up to their claims, the investigation revealed a web of secrecy behind the EU's verification of claims, meaning, the investigators concluded, that the public could not find out in any detail why some products succeeded while others failed. Transparency is essential for public confidence on the process, and a re-evaluation of the assessments that candidates for the highly prized logo have to undergo is currently taking place.

The EnergyStar programme, run by the US government, aims to assist consumers in making environmentally and cost-friendly choices by awarding the EnergyStar label to energy-efficient products. A good programme in principle, vigilance in implementation appears to be lacking. In 2009 and 2010 the US Government Accountability Office (GAO) submitted products under the guise of fictitious companies and found that the programme was 'vulnerable to fraud and abuse', since many of the GAO's applications for EnergyStar approval were accepted without question, including a proposal for a gas-powered alarm clock.[29]

Until government standards are strengthened, it seems that public exposure remains the best defence against greenwashing, including the important role of the consumer in providing a check against the practice. There are initiatives, by civil society, consumers and, in some cases, the private sector, that work to spot and publicize greenwash. The Greenwashing Index, for example, is operated jointly by a US university and a social marketing agency, and encourages visitors to submit and rate examples of greenwash.[30] Other individual initiatives have also increased the reputational risk of greenwashing; by one estimate, the number of blogs discussing greenwash multiplied by 550 between 2005 and 2008.[31]

There is, of course, a downside to public exposure. Some companies say they now fear making claims about improving the environmental impact of their products in case it prompts critics to charge them with being less than perfect. Businesses should weigh this concern against the cost of doing nothing at all, though; a majority of surveyed consumers in the US and the UK now want companies to provide information on how their products are impacting on climate change, and two-thirds say that business must take global warming more seriously.[32] Consumers can continue to put pressure on businesses to communicate their efforts to become climate-friendly in ways that are honest, measurable and independently verified.

If companies fail to meet these expectations, a rising tide of misleading and frivolous environmental claims will breed confusion and mistrust, and eventually undermine public confidence in efforts to provide green products at all; and, if that happens, the main incentive for companies to clean up their act will be gone.

Notes

1. Fred Pearce is currently environmental consultant to *New Scientist*, an author of several books, including *Confessions of an Eco-Sinner*, and a regular contributor to UK newspapers, including the *Guardian*.
2. See vorort.bund.net/suedlicher-oberrhein/greenwash-kriegspropaganda.html.
3. *Guardian* (UK), 'Edinburgh airport's tree project is trampled by its carbon elephants', 1 April 2010; news.bbc.co.uk/1/hi/scotland/edinburgh_and_east/8585611.stm.
4. *Guardian* (UK), 'Green private jets? Don't make me laugh', 29 October 2009.
5. Typical types of greenwash include: hidden trade-offs, in which one 'green' attribute is highlighted to cover up a bigger environmental problem; unsupported claims that cannot be checked; vague claims, such as 'environmentally friendly' or 'eco'; irrelevant claims, such as 'CFC-free', when no products contain the compound; and misleading images.
6. OgilvyEarth, *From Greenwash to Great. A Practical Guide to Great Green Marketing (without the Greenwash)* (New York: OgilvyEarth, 2010), at http://assets.ogilvy.com/truffles_email/ogilvyearth/Greenwash_Digital.pdf.
7. FTC, *Guides for the Use of Environmental Marketing Claims* (Washington, DC: FTC, 1992), at www.ftc.gov/bcp/grnrule/guides980427.htm; *USA Today*, 'Eco-friendly claims go unchecked: Enforcer blames lack of resources', 22 June 2009.
8. DEFRA, *Green Claims – Practical Guidance: How to Make a Good Environmental Claim* (London: DEFRA, 2003), at www.defra.gov.uk/environment/business/marketing/glc/documents/genericguide.pdf.
9. House of Commons Environmental Audit Committee, *Environmental Labelling: Second Report, Session 2008–09* (London: Her Majesty's Stationery Office, 2009), at www.publications.parliament.uk/pa/cm200809/cmselect/cmenvaud/243/243.pdf.
10. See www.rainforest-alliance.org/agriculture.cfm?id=main.
11. *Guardian* (UK), 'Advertising watchdog receives record complaints over corporate "greenwash"', 1 May 2008; ASA adjudication on Renault (UK) Ltd, Complaint ref: 46093, 26 March 2008.
12. *Guardian* (UK), 'Renault ad banned over green claims', 26 March 2008.

13. *Guardian* (UK), 'Green advertising rules are made to be broken', 23 March 2010.

14. See www.americanprogress.org/issues/2009/03/big_oil_misers.html/#2.

15. See www.treehugger.com/files/2008/12/greenwash-watch-shell-net.php and http://business.
timesonline.co.uk/tol/business/industry_sectors/natural_resources/article5927869.ece.

16. *Guardian* (UK), 'Dong Energy: "clean" Denmark's dirty secret', 17 September2009.

17. See www.rwe.com/web/cms/mediablob/en/315844/data/17906/56684/rwe/responsibility/
performance/energy-climate/security-of-supply/power-generation-structure/RWE-Factbook-
Renewable-Energy-December-2009-.pdf.

18. See www.audi.co.uk/audi-innovation/concept-cars/detroit-showcar-audi-etron.html and
Guardian (UK), 'Has Audi's electric dream already run out of gas?', 21 January 2010.

19. *Guardian* (UK), 'Supermarkets get cold feet over fridge doors', 1 October 2009.

20. *Guardian* (UK), 'Sir Richard Branson's green claims are running on hot air', 27 August 2009.

21. See www.easyjet.com/EN/Environment/carbon_emissions_calculator.asp. This reasoning also
sidesteps the carbon footprint of the most likely alternative: the train journey will almost
certainly have a substantially lower carbon footprint than the car or plane.

22. *Guardian* (UK), 'Lamborghini emits some V12-powered nonsense', 11 June 2009.

23. See www.newstatesman.com/pdf/copenhagen.pdf.

24. *Guardian* (UK), 'Are EDF trying to cut our use of energy? Surely, some mistake', 2 July 2009.

25. The carbon dioxide would be gathered into pipeline networks and buried far from the
atmosphere in old oil wells or salt mines. The system and its required infrastructure, which
would have a large carbon footprint of its own, is untested and several decades away from
becoming commercially viable, however. Even pilot systems have not yet been built.

26. See ec.europa.eu/environment/air/transport/co2/co2_cars_regulation.htm.

27. See www.energylabels.org.uk/eulabel.html.

28. See www.fern.org/sites/fern.org/files/FERN_PindoDeli-final_0.pdf and *Guardian* (UK), 'The
deflowering of the EU's green logo', 15 April 2010.

29. GAO, *Energy Star Program: Covert Testing Shows the Energy Star Program Certification
Process Is Vulnerable to Fraud and Abuse* (Washington, DC: GAO, 2010), pp. 7–15.

30. See www.greenwashingindex.com.

31. Rina Horiuchi et al., *Understanding and Preventing Greenwash: A Business Guide*
(Washington, DC and London: BSR and Futerra, 2009), p. 23.

32. AccountAbility, *What Assures Consumers on Climate Change? Switching on Citizen Power*
(London: AccountAbility, 2007), p. 9.

4.7

Could corruption pose a barrier to the roll-out of renewable energy in North Africa?

Nadejda Komendantova and Anthony Patt[1]

Considerable attention has turned to North Africa as a promising location for the development of renewable energy sources (RES). Egypt, Morocco and Tunisia already produce energy from renewable sources[2] and are eager to increase this share.[3] The European Union (EU) has also committed itself to sourcing 20 per cent of its energy from RES by 2020, part of which is expected to come from solar and offshore wind installations located in North Africa.[4]

Several scientific studies have demonstrated the technical feasibility of developing renewable energy projects in the Sahara Desert for import into Europe,[5] and it is estimated that installations of concentrated solar power (CSP)[6] covering less than 1 per cent of the desert could meet all of Europe's power needs.[7]

RES projects require significant private and public investment, however. The large-scale deployment of CSP in North Africa, including the costs of electricity transmission lines to Europe, would require nearly €400 billion until 2050 to import 700TWh/y (terawatt-hours per year) of solar electricity.[8] Currently, the combination of financing from national budgets and multilateral organizations contributes the major share of investment into renewable energy development in North Africa, focused mainly on wind and solar installations and concentrated in Egypt, Morocco and Tunisia. While private companies have won deals to supply components or to construct plants, significant amounts of financing come from national governments.[9] The involvement of private capital is crucial, however; past experience suggests that, when infrastructure projects reach a large scale, governments may lack the fiscal resources needed to continue funding them.[10]

Unfortunately, European foreign direct investment (FDI) in North Africa remains minimal compared to other regions.[11] According to the World Investment Prospects Survey 2010–2012, after sub-Saharan Africa it was North Africa that was predicted to be the lowest-priority region for FDI in 2010 and 2012.[12] Where it is present, FDI is often linked to the extraction of natural resources.[13]

Some of the challenges for attracting capital have been identified in World Bank studies of regulatory risks in North Africa. One assessment evaluated the business environment across the region and found regulatory shortcomings relating to enforcing contracts, starting a business or dealing with construction permits.[14] In another survey, over 45 per cent of companies involved in FDI in Egypt and Algeria found corruption to be a major constraint.[15]

The International Institute of Applied Systems Analysis (IIASA) conducted research to identify barriers to private investment in RES, focusing on North Africa and on determining the cost of these barriers in terms of investment volumes. IIASA used qualitative methods of research based on structured, semi-structured and in-depth interviews, and quantitative modelling.[16]

Gathering stakeholder perspectives

During the first round of interviews with experts,[17] 52 per cent of all respondents named complexity and corruption in bureaucratic procedures as significant barriers to the deployment of RES in North Africa (figure 4.6). In this context, experts understood corruption primarily as the existence of nepotism, the expectation of hidden payments or gifts to officials as the cost of doing business, or long delays in bureaucratic procedures unless bribes were given.

The following round of interviews presented stakeholders with a list of nine possible risks: regulatory, political, revenue, technical, 'force majeure' (including natural catastrophes and terrorism), financial, construction, operating and environmental. Participants were asked to value these according to the seriousness of their concern and the likelihood of occurrence. As figure 4.7 shows, three types of risk were evaluated as being a high level of concern, with 78 per cent of respondents identifying regulatory risk – defined as complexity or corruption relating to bureaucratic procedures – as a high-level concern.[18]

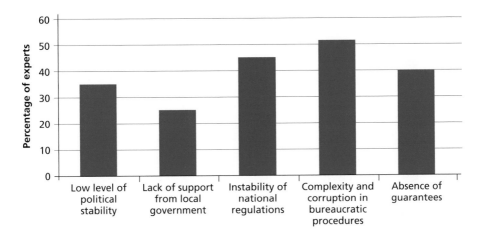

Figure 4.6 Barriers to investment in renewable energy in North Africa

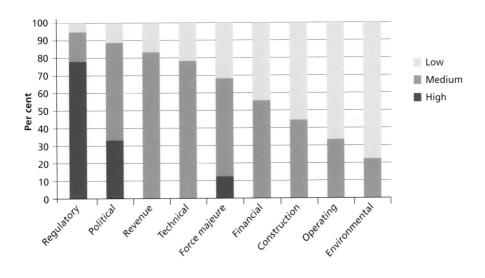

Figure 4.7 Risks perceived as most serious in relation to RES investment in North Africa

Furthermore, 67 per cent of all interviewed stakeholders considered that regulatory risk was very likely to be present in North Africa, while the likelihood of political risk and force majeure was considered to be less (figure 4.8).

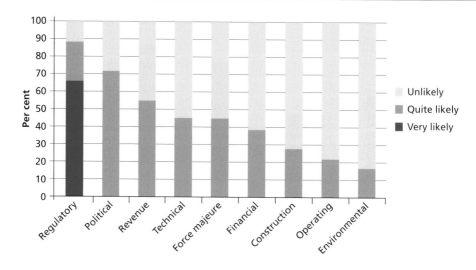

Figure 4.8 Risks perceived as most likely to happen in relation to RES investment in North Africa

Both evaluations demonstrate that the risk of poor-quality bureaucratic procedures was perceived as serious and likely to happen in relation to RES investment in North Africa. Many respondents further noted that investment often does not occur because of complex and lengthy bureaucratic procedures and uncertainty as to whether public officials will expect bribes. Such risks can create difficulties for calculating project budgets and put projects at risk of cost overruns.

The quality of bureaucratic procedures is also a concern for investors in the conventional energy sector, but here the costs of capital are lower, since banks perceive projects with pre-existing track records as less risky and therefore require lower risk premiums for their capital.[19] This is not the case with North African RES projects, and particularly not with CSP, which has no established track record.

The cost of investment

For the second stage of its research, the IIASA used its Mediterranean Area Renewable Generation Estimator (MARGE) to quantify the economic cost that risks of complex or corrupt bureaucratic procedures have on the internal rate of return (IRR).[20] The MARGE model estimated the annual cost of constructing CSP plants, using data from studies on CSP technology and variables input by users, including interest rates and industry growth rates.[21] Investors will generally require a higher IRR for projects they perceive as high-risk because of the technology or the region of operation. MARGE examined the cost of these risks in terms of the overall investment needed between now and 2025 by inputting different IRRs commonly associated with varying levels of risk.

Project developers of conventional thermal power stations generally guarantee an IRR in the range of 6–10 per cent, while developers of large renewable power plants – such as CSP plants in Spain – need to guarantee 15 per cent, due to banks' apparent view that the technology may not yet be commercially viable. Taking into account the perception of bureaucratic risks, it is reasonable to consider that private developers of CSP projects in North Africa could face IRRs as high as 20 per cent.

Taking an IRR of 20 per cent, the MARGE model suggests that the overall investment required by European and North African governments, multilateral organizations and the private sector to develop CSP capacity (including the construction of installations and electricity grids, insurance, operation and management costs) until 2025 could reach €1600 billion (US$2000 billion) with a 20 per cent IRR,[22] in comparison to less than €100 billion (US$130 billion) with a 5 per cent IRR and €580 billion (US$750 billion) with a 15 per cent IRR.

Both the MARGE calculations and the findings of the initial interviews will need to be supported by further research to determine the extent to which perceptions of regulatory risks and complicated bureaucratic procedures reflect concerns over corruption as opposed to legal, though inconvenient, regulatory complications or bureaucratic delays. Nevertheless, the World Bank finding that a substantial percentage of companies operating in the region[23] found corruption to be a significant problem suggests that it could indeed prove an obstacle to the roll-out of renewable energy in the region.

If this is true, a failure to address corruption will result in higher quantities of investment being required for CSP deployment in North Africa. This is just one possible result; another is that investors will simply seek other regions for investment. Given the region's singular potential for solar development, however, this outcome should be avoided. By taking steps to reduce corruption and streamline bureaucratic procedures, North African governments may both fuel their economies and contribute significantly to the reduction of global emissions.

Notes

1. Nadejda Komendantova is a research scholar and Anthony Patt is a team leader of the Decisions and Governance Group at the International Institute of Applied Systems Analysis (IIASA) in Austria.
2. Observatoire Méditerranéen de l'Energie (OME), *Mediterranean Energy Perspectives 2008* (Paris: OME, 2009).

3.   For example, the governments of Egypt and Morocco have committed themselves to achieving 20 per cent and 42 per cent shares of renewable energy by 2020, respectively. Climate Investment Funds (CIFs), *Clean Technology Fund Investment Plan for Concentrated Solar Power in the Middle East and North Africa Region* (Washington, DC: CIFs, 2009), p. 6.

4.   Reuters (UK), 'EU sees solar power imported from Sahara in five years', 20 June 2010.

5.   Gregor Czisch, *Szenarien zur zukünftigen Stromversorgung: kostenoptimierte Variationen zur Versorgung Europas und seiner Nachbarn mit Strom aus erneuerbaren Energien* (Kassel: University of Kassel, 2005).

6.   Concentrated solar power is a promising method of energy generation that uses mirrors to focus sunlight, which heats a transfer liquid that, in turn, generates the steam necessary to power a turbine.

7.   World Bank, *World Development Report 2010: Development and Climate Change* (Washington, DC: World Bank, 2009), p. 221.

8.   By way of comparison, in 2000 Europe's total electricity demand was about 3500 TWh/y for all energy sources. Franz Trieb, *Trans-Mediterranean Interconnection for Concentrating Solar Power* (Stuttgart: German Aerospace Center, 2006), pp. 34 and 102.

9.   UN Environment Programme (UNEP), *Global Trends in Sustainable Energy Investment 2009: Analysis of Trends and Issues in the Financing of Renewable Energy and Energy Efficiency* (Nairobi: UNEP, 2009), p. 56.

10. Clive Harris, *Private Participation in Infrastructure in Developing Countries: Trends, Impacts, and Policy Lessons.* Working Paper no.5 (Washington, DC: World Bank, 2003), p. 40.

11. Marion Mühlberger and Marco Semmelmann, *North Africa: Mediterranean Neighbours on the Rise* (Frankfurt: Deutsche Bank Research, 2010), p. 7.

12. UN Conference on Trade and Development (UNCTAD), *World Investment Report 2010: Investing in a Low-Carbon Economy* (Geneva: UNCTAD, 2010), p. 25.

13. UNCTAD, *World Investment Report 2008: Transnational Corporations and the Infrastructure Challenge* (Geneva: UNCTAD, 2008), p. 43.

14. World Bank, *Doing Business 2008* (Washington, DC: World Bank, 2007), at www.doingbusiness.org.

15. World Bank, 'Enterprise surveys', at www.enterprisesurveys.org. Full survey data are available for Algeria (2007) and Egypt (2008).

16. A more in-depth discussion of the research can be found at Nadejda Komendantova et al., 'Perception of Risks in Renewable Energy Projects: The Case of Concentrated Solar Power in North Africa', *Energy Policy* (forthcoming).

17. Interviews were conducted with participants at an international conference on CSP development that was held in Madrid in 2008; a meeting for the Mediterranean Solar Plan held in Paris in 2009; and a special workshop on barriers to CSP development organized by the IIASA in Austria in 2008.Twenty-three experts were interviewed: five from industry, two from government ministries, seven from the financial sector and nine from the social scientific community. All interviewees worked in Europe and were actively involved in the analysis of CSP projects in North Africa or in the realization or management of these projects.

18. The research assumed that the European feed-in-tariff would be available to support investment into CSP in North Africa for a period of 20 years.

19. See, for example, Edward Kahn, *Comparison of Financing Cost for Wind Turbine and Fossil Powerplants* (Berkeley: University of California, 1995).

20. The internal rate of return means the return on investment capital. It is closely connected with the costs of capital and risk premiums, when investors or banks require higher risk premiums or interest rates for their capital for projects that they perceive as more risky.
21. See www.iiasa.ac.at/Research/RAV/Presentations/MARGE/dist/The_MARGE_Model.html.
22. This investment does not include investment by distribution companies and governments in the purchase of RES electricity.
23. Based on figures from World Bank 'Enterprise surveys': Algeria (64 per cent in 2007), Egypt (45 per cent in 2008) and Morocco (27 per cent in 2007).

4.7.1

Spain

Can incentivizing solar energy invite fraud?

Tono Calleja[1]

In 2008 Spain was a front-runner in the solar market, thanks to a feed-in tariff that mandated that utilities would have to buy solar power at high, government-set rates.[2] The subsidy, introduced in 2007, was the most generous in the world and, with few conditions attached, attracted developers globally.[3] The promise of profits not only set the stage for a boom in photovoltaic (PV) installation, however, but, in the absence of a rigorous oversight mechanism, also proved an incentive for fraud.

By the end of 2007 Spain's goal of producing 400 megawatts (MW) of solar electricity by 2010 had already been met.[4] Hoping to curb this unexpected surge in PV installations, the Spanish government announced reduced electricity rates for solar power plants installed after September 2008 and set a cap of 500MW worth of new projects.[5] Facing the prospect of diminished profits, developers rushed to complete installations by the deadline, challenging the capacity of the regulator and the grid operator to monitor all the new projects.[6] Accompanying the scramble were reports of fraud, with developers allegedly declaring projects to be finished despite the incomplete installation of solar panels or the temporary installation of fake panels.[7]

A 2008 investigation by Spain's national energy commission (Comisión Nacional de Energía: CNE) found that over 4000 PV installations, located in 13 per cent of the country's solar parks, were falsely registered as operational and were making no contribution to the energy grid as at the end of September that year.[8]

In 2009 the government acknowledged that it had been ill-equipped to audit all the solar projects applying for inclusion in the feed-in tariff, and the CNE likewise cited the need for a supervisory mechanism to guarantee that new PV installations meet the requirements necessary to qualify for subsidies.[9] In January of the same year the Ministry of Energy gave PV companies two months to demonstrate that their plants were in fact equipped for connection to the energy grid, with a suspension of payments for those that were not.[10]

From the beginning of investigations in 2008, and throughout 2009, Spain's photovoltaic industry association (Asociación de la Industria Fotovoltaica: ASIF) emphasized that, while completion of the installations by the September deadline was a requirement to qualify for the feed-in tariff, contribution to the energy grid by the deadline was not, and stated that installations that did not contribute to the grid by deadline were not necessarily the result of fraud; for example, some installations may have been completed, but were dependent on local infrastructure for connection.[11] The organization nevertheless welcomed legal action against those found to have committed fraud, as it felt that the ongoing allegations of wrongdoing cast a shadow over the entire sector.[12]

Developers were not the only party to come under scrutiny, however. Spain's recent history of corruption in the real estate market appeared to re-emerge in the solar industry.[13] In 2009 13 civil servants from the region of Castilla y León were found by regional administrators to have inappropriately processed and authorized licences for photovoltaic plants for companies in which they or immediate relatives had a direct stake.[14] According to press accounts, despite decisions taken by regional administrators to suspend the employment and salaries of most of these individuals for one to three years, almost two years later not one had completed these terms, either due to pending appeals or because administrators claimed that postponement of the sanctions was necessary so as not to disrupt the services provided by the employees to the industrial sector.[15] The allegations, spread across four provinces, were dealt with only by regional administrators, to whom those implicated were politically affiliated.[16] Only in the province of Zamora did the public prosecutor open a case, the results of which were pending as of mid-2010.

Such problems are not unique to the solar sector. As in any industry, though, and especially one dealing with a relatively new type of infrastructure, effective oversight is crucial. Government agencies, private sector proponents and environmental advocates cannot succeed in their efforts to introduce renewable forms of energy without strong and meaningful safeguards. In addition to squandering public resources and undermining project success, fraud has a more pernicious effect: if pervasive and persistent, it has the capacity to threaten the fragile trust the public has in the long-term viability of alternative energy.

Notes

1. Tono Calleja is a journalist and researcher specializing in environmental issues and is a member of TI Spain, for which he has contributed this report.
2. *Greentech Media* (US), 'Spain: the solar frontier no more', 29 May 2009.
3. *New York Times* (US), 'Solar industry learns lessons in Spanish sun', 8 March 2010.
4. Ibid.
5. *Greentech Media* (US), 'Solar fraud could eliminate Spanish market', 15 December 2008. Installations that were not operational by the deadline would receive €320 per megawatt-hour (MWh) of capacity for 25 years, rather than the €450 per MWh offered by the feed-in tariff; see Lisa Abend, 'Spanish solar firms accused of fraud', *Nature*, published online 19 December 2008, at www.nature.com/news/2008/081219/full/news.2008.1326.html.
6. *European Daily Electricity Markets* (UK), 'Recession turns up heat on solar subsidies in Spain', 12 March 2010.
7. *Greentech Media* (15 December 2008).
8. *European Daily Electricity Markets* (UK), 'Spanish regulator demands more photovoltaic supervision', 19 May 2009; *Nature* (19 December 2008).
9. Ibid.
10. Ibid.
11. ASIF, 'La inyección de electricidad a la red no era un requisito establecido por el RD 661/2007 para acceder a su régimen retributivo', press release, 29 January 2010; ASIF, 'Las instalaciones solares indebidamente acogidas al RD 661/2007 no deberían percibir la tarifa fotovoltaica', press release, 15 December 2008.
12. ASIF (29 January 2010).
13. Abend (19 December 2008). See, for example, Enriqueta Abad, 'Corruption fuels housing boom and water stress along Spain's coast', in TI, *Global Corruption Report 2008: Corruption in the Water Sector* (Cambridge: Cambridge University Press, 2008), pp. 35–36.
14. *El País* (Spain), 'La energía solar pasa factura al PP', 25 August 2008.
15. *El Mundo* (Spain), '14 expedientados por la trama solar siguen sin cumplir las sanciones', 13 April 2010.
16. Ibid.

4.8

Preventing a resource curse fuelled by the green economy

Stefan Bringezu and Raimund Bleischwitz[1]

Ideally, natural resources should be a boon for any country that possesses them, yet the fraught development paths of many resource-rich countries demonstrate that, under certain conditions, abundant resources can lead to destructive consequences and open the door to corruption.

There are many possible drivers of such a 'resource curse'. Governments that depend primarily on revenues earned from natural resources may not need to rely on citizens to provide a tax base, thus avoiding one important form of accountability. In the absence of accountable governance, funds generated from natural resources may be mismanaged, poorly invested or siphoned off to an elite minority that seeks to concentrate power. Despite signficant additional revenue, social inequity and poverty may rise while long-term economic growth falters. In the worst instances, these conditions can contribute to public unrest or civil war.[2]

Despite all good intentions, a transition to a low-fossil-carbon economy may place increasing demand on land, minerals and other natural resources that had not previously been sought with such intensity. It will be critical to ensure that the scramble for these resources does not trigger a replay of the resource curse. Mapping the geographical hot spots where such green economy resources intersect with weak governance zones may provide a guidepost as to where a push for transparency and public participation will be most crucial, in order to ensure that these resources are utilized properly and the resulting revenues handled responsibly.

Understanding the resources and risks of a low-fossil-carbon economy

Among the most important groups of resources related to the emerging low-fossil-carbon economy are biofuels, which can reduce transportation-related emissions, and metals and minerals that have broad applications in energy efficiency, renewable energy and other green technologies. In both cases, there are accountability concerns that could intensify with expanding markets.

Land resources for biomass

As countries around the world look to biofuels to enhance energy security and mitigate climate change, competition for land and competing land uses will increase. Although biomass cultivation can bring economic opportunity for rural communities, in the absence of transparent governance and public participation, large-scale commercial investments may threaten the security and livelihoods of local landholders.

Many governments, including those in the European Union (EU), China, India, Brazil and the US, have established targets and mandatory quotas for biofuels in transportation.[3] Some calculations suggest, however, that using first-generation biofuels – derived from crops otherwise used for food and feed – to provide a 10 per cent biofuel share towards transport by 2030 would require an additional 118–508 million hectares.[4] For regions such as the EU, models demonstrate that an increased use of biofuels would lead to an overall increase in absolute global cropland requirements.[5] This means that if biofuels are produced on existing cropland, other production – especially for meeting growing food demand – will be displaced to other areas, carrying with it a range of impacts on local communities.

Advanced, or second-generation, biofuels, derived from non-food biomass such as agricultural or forestry residues, or from non-edible plants, may avoid direct competition with food production. Brazil seems to be the only country with considerable potential to produce second-generation biofuels, however, by converting pasture land. In many other countries (such as Cameroon, India, Tanzania and Thailand), significant investments into technological improvements, new infrastructure and capacity-building are necessary to enhance agricultural productivity. If acres of natural or degraded land are eventually cultivated, these too could probably be used for food, again presenting land competition issues.

In 2009, Thailand, Indonesia and Colombia ranked among the most attractive markets for biofuel investment, with Brazil topping the list. African nations, including Egypt, Kenya and Sudan, have notable levels of sugar cane production that could also develop into attractive biofuel markets.[6] Many of these countries rank poorly in governance assessments. Sudan, Egypt, Kenya, Indonesia and Colombia all fall at or below global averages of World Bank indicators measuring the control of corruption, the rule of law, political stability, and voice and accountability.[7] Such indicators could suggest that there is a risk that the influx of substantial revenues from biofuel production or land concessions may not necessarily benefit most citizens of these countries.

Indeed, as the scale of biofuel projects grows, local communities may find themselves increasingly disadvantaged. In recent cases in Asia, Africa and South America, governments and community officials have facilitated land deals with foreign companies that plan to produce crops for export, with limited economic and social value for local communities. A World Bank report on foreign investment in farmland suggests that following the 2008 spike in commodity prices, foreign investors were particularly interested in countries that failed to formally recognize land rights.[8] Biofuel production in countries including Tanzania, Mozambique, India and Colombia has generated reports of land acquisition through illegitimate land titles, water access being denied to local farmers, inadequate compensation agreements and the displacement of local communities by force.[9]

In Indonesia, palm oil production has been linked not only to unsustainable resource management but also to loss of land access for local groups.[10] In February 2010, Sierra Leone signed a US$400 million land deal with a Swiss bioenergy company to cultivate sugarcane for bioethanol production; despite assurances from a project manager that only 'marginal' lands would be used, a visiting reporter cited the pending displacement of dozens of villages.[11]

Mineral resources for microelectronics and large-scale, low-fossil-carbon infrastructure

Mining, a second activity necessary to support the green economy, carries significant opportunities for corruption. The industry is believed to be one of the business sectors most likely to bribe public officials or to influence political processes unduly.[12] The industry is characterized by opacity and confidentiality, which enable companies to conspire with government officials to rig the bidding process. By developing personal relationships with influential members of the political elite, or offering bribes, corporate representatives may secure contracts or political decisions in their favour.[13] Host governments may launder money offshore or direct funds towards spending that benefits the interests of the political elite.

The scaling up of renewable energy will require significant mineral resources for new supply facilities and energy distribution, however. Telecommunication and other information technologies, increasingly used to reduce the need for global travel and transportation, depend on microelectronic devices that require speciality metals. As these and other solutions for reducing greenhouse gas (GHG) emissions are more widely embraced, demand will increase for many types of minerals.

Lithium ion batteries, currently used in electronic devices, are expected to play a growing role in future demand for electric cars. Although forecasts are sensitive to public policy, Credit Suisse's estimate of annual growth rates for lithium demand of about 10 per cent[14] seems conservative but reliable. Increased demand for lithium will lead to additional extraction activities at a limited number of salt lakes, such as in Argentina, Bolivia and Chile. In Bolivia, the government's early planning for joint exploitation projects with international companies and governments has been met with much public approval, but it has also raised concerns from some civil society and environmental organizations regarding the transparency of negotiations and the reliability of environmental assessments[15] (see the Bolivia case study following this section).

Photovoltaic cells for solar arrays and LED-dependent energy-efficient lighting[16] rely on the aluminium by-product gallium. Gallium demand for green technology development is forecast to exceed current total world production by a factor of six by 2030.[17] This could lead to enhanced bauxite mining[18] in countries such as Guinea, China, Russia and Kazakhstan. Mining for tantalum, which is used for capacitors in microelectronics such as mobile phones and PCs, has increased in the Democratic Republic of the Congo (DRC), where the militarization of mining is well documented[19] and illegal trade revenues have been linked to the financing of civil war activities.

Platinum group metals (PGMs) are important chemical catalysts used for pollution control, such as in exhaust catalysts in cars and fuel cells. PGM mining and refining is concentrated in a few regions in the world, though supply is not sufficient to meet expected demand. Platinum is mined in South Africa, and PGMs are produced as a by-product of nickel and copper mining in Russia and Canada.

The market for rare earth metals, used in defence technologies and also crucial for low-fossil-carbon technologies such as wind turbines and hybrid cars, is worth some US$1.3 billion annually. China, one of the few countries currently mining rare earth metals, has considered significantly curbing or ending their export altogether, prompting a rush on mines in Russia, Kazakhstan, South Africa, Botswana, Vietnam and Malaysia.[20]

Rising demand for many of these mineral resources will probably coincide with a shifting pattern of mining activity. Emerging economies such as Brazil, China and India are expected to reach a period of high metal intensity as their development approaches the levels of Organisation for Economic Co-operation and Development (OECD) countries. As mining companies from these countries transition from trading into production, they can be expected to meet domestic demand for raw materials through direct investment throughout the world, and particularly in Africa.

This new buying power may not be matched by high standards in business integrity. In 2008 companies from Brazil, Russia, India and China were perceived by the business community to be among the most likely to engage in bribery when doing business abroad.[21] Indeed, China and India have no law making foreign bribery a criminal offence.[22] With the exception of Brazil, the adoption of international anti-corruption standards is weak. India has ratified neither the UN Convention against Corruption (UNCAC) nor the OECD Convention on Combating Bribery of Foreign Public Officials, while China and Russia have ratified only the former.[23]

Country	Relevance	Use in a low-fossil-carbon economy	ICRG 'Quality of government' indicator[24] 2008 (0–1)
Bolivia	Huge reserves of lithium, antimony and other minerals.	Lithium: used in batteries for electric cars.	0.44
China	Strategic supplier of steel, indium, antimony, molybdenum, neodymium, germanium, tantalum and rare earth metals (more than 90% of world production).	Rare earth metals: used in hybrid cars and wind turbines. Tantalum: used in microelectronics.	0.55
Colombia	Among the most attractive markets for biofuel investment.	Biofuels: used to reduce transportation-related GHG emissions.	0.42
DRC	Large mineral supplier of cassiterite (tin), cobalt, coltan (tantalum) and germanium.	Minerals: used in microelectronics, specifically mobile phones, pagers, PCs, automotive electronics and photovoltaic energy technologies.	0.11
Egypt	Significant sugar cane production; possible future market for biofuels.	Biofuels: used to reduce transportation-related GHG emissions.	0.47
Guinea-Bissau	Largest supplier of bauxite; also important for gallium.	Gallium: used in energy-efficient light infrastructure.	0.38

Country	Relevance	Use in a low-fossil-carbon economy	ICRG 'Quality of government' indicator[24] 2008 (0–1)
Indonesia	Important supplier of biomass (timber and palm oil).	Biomass: used in biofuels to reduce transportation-related GHG emissions.	0.53
Kenya	Significant sugar cane production; possible future market for biofuels.	Biofuels: used to reduce transportation-related GHG emissions.	0.30
Peru	Important supplier of gold and many other minerals, including tellurium.	Minerals used for microelectronics, specifically mobile phones, pagers, PCs, automotive electronics and photovoltaic energy technologies.	0.47
Sudan	Significant sugar cane production; possible future market for biofuels.	Biofuels: used to reduce transportation-related GHG emissions.	0.27

Table 4.3 Selected hot spots of future critical resource supply (in alphabetical order)

Note: scores from *International Country Risk Guide* (ICRG) data (the mean value of the ICRG variables 'Corruption', 'Law and order' and 'Bureaucracy quality', scaled 0–1; higher values indicate higher quality of government).

Source: Authors' compilation.

Towards greener pastures: avoiding a new resource curse

If the resource curse can re-emerge in a low-fossil-carbon economy, so can solutions to prevent it. Various initiatives currently aimed at the oil, gas and mining industries are applicable to the resources necessary for a green infrastructure. Organizations including Publish What You Pay, the Revenue Watch Institute and the Extractive Industries Transparency Initiative promote the public disclosure of industry payments and host government earnings for oil, gas and mining concessions. Such initiatives provide a model that is also applicable to high-demand resources in the green economy. Civil society actors can also make efforts to ensure that mining and land concessions are granted through open bidding processes, with transparent contract design and prior informed consent from affected communities.

The private sector also plays a role. Codes of conduct that commit employees and corporate directors to meet high standards of sustainability and transparency in the mining industry can be used as a model for companies seeking land allocation for biofuel and biomaterial production. Such codes should promote adherence to social and environmental standards, and emphasize the importance of continued consultation with and oversight by affected local communities. While private companies involved in land acquisition thus far have proved to be reluctant to sign up to principles or codes of conduct,[25] multilateral groups and non-governmental organizations (NGOs) should continue to push for this minimum effort and for greater transparency through company reporting on a range of corporate responsibility issues, including anti-bribery measures and governance.

Voluntary efforts can be supported by international legal instruments. The UNCAC calls for criminalizing the bribery of public officials and commits ratifying countries to assist in locating, freezing and confiscating money generated through corruption, making it more difficult to hide stolen resource-related revenues.[26] Encouraging all countries, especially those with growing economic power, to commit themselves to signing and enforcing anti-corruption conventions will help deter gaming by businesses and government officials alike.

National governments are also taking a second look at their legislation. In 2010 Brazil limited the amount of land that foreign investors could purchase by closing a loophole that had allowed foreign investors to operate via Brazilian subsidiaries.[27] The same year, Australian lawmakers debated the merits of an audit or registry of foreign-owned commercial agricultural land.[28]

Regulations aimed at enhancing transparency in the extractive industries will also have an impact. In July 2010 the US government passed legislation requiring oil, gas and mining companies registered with the US Securities and Exchange Commission to disclose tax and revenue payments made to host governments in the countries of operation.[29] This law will affect eight of the world's 10 largest mining companies. One month earlier the Hong Kong stock exchange introduced a similar regulation for listed mining companies, affecting major players on the Asian market.[30]

Also included in the US law is a requirement that companies that manufacture products containing cassiterite, coltan, wolframite or gold disclose whether these are sourced from the DRC or surrounding countries, and to demonstrate what steps are being taken to avoid sourcing from armed groups.[31] Taken together, these legal requirements set a minimum global standard of transparency for extractive companies and manufacturers. If properly enforced and complemented by expanding civil society initiatives, these could set a precedent for greater transparency in mineral and land acquisition for the low-fossil-carbon economy. Improved supply chain management and materials stewardship across industries will further strengthen these efforts.

Consumption and production habits also matter. In 2012 the Rio+20 Earth Summit will provide an opportunity to address open trade for critical metals and recycling. It could facilitate action by establishing an international covenant on improving the recycling of resource-intensive consumer goods. Such a covenant should include the leading countries in terms of the production and final consumption of vehicles and electronic devices, and establish principles of materials stewardship, certification and responsibility. By providing investment opportunities and stability, it could also offer incentives for developing countries to participate. In the long term, the growing strain on many natural resources may be best addressed by an international agreement on sustainable resource management.[32] Such an agreement should be binding, to prevent the circumvention of environmental, social and economic standards, and address the need to reduce demand for natural resources through conservation and efficiency. Any international agreement will be years in the making, but the demands of a green resource economy are already upon us. Enforcing legal requirements, stepping up civil society oversight and demanding business commitments to high governance standards and transparency should help prevent a resource curse in a low-fossil-carbon future.

Notes

1. Stefan Bringezu is director of material flows and resource management at the Wuppertal Institute, Germany, and a member of the International Panel for Sustainable Resource Management; Raimund Bleischwitz is co-director of material flows and resource management at the Wuppertal Institute and professor at the College of Europe, Bruges, Belgium.
2. Macartan Humphreys et al., 'Introduction: What Is the Problem with Natural Resource Wealth', in Macartan Humphreys et al. (eds), *Escaping the Resource Curse* (New York: Columbia University Press, 2007), pp. 1–20; Thorvaldur Gylfason, 'Development and Growth in Mineral-Rich Countries', in Raimund Bleischwitz et al. (eds), *Sustainable Growth and Resource Productivity* (Sheffield: Greenleaf Publishing, 2009), pp. 42–85.
3. Stefan Bringezu et al., *Towards Sustainable Production and Use of Resources: Assessing Biofuels* (Paris: UN Environment Programme [UNEP], 2009).
4. This is between 1.2 and 5 million square kilometres – that is, anywhere from the size of South Africa up to an area twice the size of Sudan. N. H. Ravindranath et al., 'GHG Implications of Land Use and Land Conversion to Biofuel Crops', in Robert Howarth and Stefan Bringezu (eds), *Biofuels: Environmental Consequences and Interactions with Changing Land Use* (New York: Island Press, 2009), pp. 111–125.
5. Bas Eickhout et al., *Local and Global Consequences of the EU Renewable Directive for Biofuels: Testing the Sustainability Criteria*, MNP Report no. 500143001/2008 (Bilthoven: Netherlands Environmental Assessment Agency, 2008); Stefan Bringezu et al., 'Global Implications of Biomass and Biofuel Use in Germany: Recent Trends and Future Scenarios for Domestic and Foreign Agricultural Land Use and Resulting GHG Emissions', *Journal of Cleaner Production*, vol. 17 (2009), pp. 57–68.

6. Ernst & Young, *Biofuels Country Attractiveness Indices*, no. 6 (London: Ernst & Young, March 2009).

7. Daniel Kaufmann et al., *Worldwide Governance Indicators 2008* (Washington, DC: World Bank, 2008).

8. Klaus Deininger et al., *Rising Global Interest in Farmland: Can it Yield Sustainable and Equitable Benefits?* (Washington, DC: World Bank, 2010), p. 55.

9. Lorenzo Cotula et al., *Fuelling Exclusion? The Biofuels Boom and Poor People's Access to Land* (London: International Institute for Environment and Development [IIED], 2008).

10. Ibid.

11. Shepard Daniel and Anuradha Mittal, *(Mis)Investment in Agriculture: The Role of the International Finance Corporation in Global Land Grabs* (Oakland, CA: Oakland Institute, 2010), p. 24.

12. TI, *2008 Bribe Payers Index* (Berlin: TI, 2008).

13. TI, *Corruption and the renegotiation of mining contracts* (Bergen: TI and the Chr. Michelsen Institute, 2007); Global Witness, *Digging in Corruption: Fraud, Abuse and Exploitation in Katanga's Copper and Cobalt Mines* (Washington, DC: Global Witness Publishing, 2006).

14. John McNulty and Alina Khaykin, *Extracting the Details of the Lithium Market* (New York: Credit Suisse US, 2009), p. 18.

15. Rebecca Hollender and Jim Schultz, *Bolivia and Its Lithium: Can the 'Gold of the 21st Century' Help Lift a Nation out of Poverty?* (Cochabamba, Bolivia: Democracy Center, 2010), pp. 42–46.

16. LED stands for light-emitting diode.

17. Gerhard Angerer et al., *Rohstoffe für Zukunftstechnologien* (Stuttgart: Frauenhofer IRB Verlag, 2009)

18. Bauxite contains trace amounts of gallium.

19. Global Witness, *Faced with a Gun, What Can You Do? War and the Militarization of Mining in Eastern Congo* (London: Global Witness, 2008).

20. *Foreign Policy* (US), 'China's ring of power', 9 September 2009; *New York Times* (US), 'China: Earth-friendly elements, mined destructively', 26 December 2009.

21. TI (2008).

22. TI, *Progress Report 2009: Enforcement of the OECD Anti-Bribery Convention* (Berlin: TI, 2009).

23. TI, *Global Corruption Report 2009: Corruption and the Private Sector* (Cambridge: Cambridge University Press, 2009).

24. Jan Teorell et al., *The Quality of Government Dataset Codebook*, version 27 May 2010 (Gothenburg: Quality of Government Institute, University of Gothenburg, 2010), at http:// www.qog.pol.gu.se; PRS Group, *International Country Risk Guide* (Syracuse, NY: PRS Group), time series: 1984–2008, N: 3271, N: 145, N: 131, T: 23).

25. AllAfrica.com (Mauritius), 'Africa: Land grabs continue as elites resist regulation', 13 April 2010.

26. Joseph Siegle, 'Governance Strategies to Remedy the Natural Resources Curse', *International Social Science Journal*, vol. 57 (2009), pp. 45–55.

27. Reuters (UK), 'Brazil curtails land sales to foreigners', 24 August 2010.

28. Senate Select Committee on Agricultural and Related Industries, 'Food Production in Australia' (Canberra: Department of the Senate, 2010), p. 21; ABC (Australia), 'Coalition backs Greens' call for register of foreign farm ownership', 29 July 2010.

29. See Dodd–Frank Wall Street Reform and Consumer Protection Act, HR 4173, US Congress.

30. Publish What You Pay (UK), 'Landmark US legislation sheds light on billions in payments from oil and mineral companies', press release, 16 July 2010; Revenue Watch Institute (US), 'Hong Kong: Stock exchange to require greater transparency', 28 May 2010.
31. Global Witness, 'US passes landmark reforms on resource transparency', press release, 15 July 2010.
32. Raimund Bleischwitz et al., 'Outline of a Resource Policy and Its Economic Dimension', in Stefan Bringezu and Raimund Bleischwitz (eds), *Sustainable Resource Management. Trends, Visions and Policies for Europe and the World* (Sheffield: Greenleaf Publishing, 2009), pp. 216–296; Raimund Bleischwitz and Stefan Bringezu, 'Global Governance for Sustainable Resource Management', *Minerals and Energy*, vol. 23 (2008), pp. 84–101.

4.8.1
Bolivia's lithium
Opportunities and challenges

Marco Octavio Ribera, in collaboration with Cecilia Requena[1]

Because of its potential to serve as a substitute for oil and its role as a promising element for climate change mitigation, interest in lithium is growing. As a widespread technological shift to vehicles that run on lithium batteries would help reduce global greenhouse gas (GHG) emissions, in the coming years global demand for lithium is expected to increase in step with an expanding market for electric vehicles.[2] A boom in lithium demand would carry both the promise of financial prosperity and socio-economic challenges for Bolivia, whose estimated 5 million tonnes of lithium[3] in the Uyuni salt lake may represent up to half of the world's known reserves.[4]

Bolivia's plans for lithium extraction are still in their early stages, but the ultimate success of these plans will depend heavily on the level and quality of civil society participation, the extent to which the government shares information on its development plans, the degree to which there is clarity in how the government grants mining or production contracts, and how it manages revenues derived from lithium exploitation.

As the government seeks to earn revenues from lithium to expand social services[5] (for example, by providing cash incentives to mothers who fulfil requirements for pre- and post-natal care), the legacy of inequity and poverty that accompanies so many resource-rich nations continues to pose challenges. The United Nations Development Programme (UNDP) in Bolivia notes, 'With a long history of dependence on silver, tin, rubber and hydrocarbons, there is a development pattern based on few actors and sectors.'[6] Indeed, with an economy based largely on exporting extractive and raw materials,[7] the country has struggled to transform resource wealth into long-term benefits.

Following a 20-year period characterized by market-driven

economic policies, the Bolivian government has aimed since 2006 to reform the country's extractive policies in order to re-establish state control of the sector and increase public revenues. When his second term started in January 2010, Bolivian president Evo Morales reiterated his desire to develop the country's lithium industry and export value-added lithium products rather than just the raw material. He also referred to the need for foreign investment, emphasizing that these investments should come from 'partners, not patrons'.[8]

While any joint initiative between the Bolivian state and international capital should involve civil society to ensure sustainability and maximize public benefit, early discussions with transnational companies and foreign governments generated little public information. The Bolivian government met with representatives from the automotive and electronics industries and delegations from France, Japan and South Korea[9] yet the outcomes of these events were outlined only generally in press releases.

Nevertheless, the government has made encouraging statements about the importance of public participation and has sought community involvement during the planning phase of a pilot project for lithium exploitation.[10] Despite this, some community groups have claimed that the government reserves its consultation to groups linked to the administration or to Morales' political party.[11]

As plans for lithium exploitation continued to develop at the time of publishing,[12] questions of environmental sustainability, public access to information, public debate and participation remained. These issues will have to be carefully addressed. For example, the new Bolivian constitution refers to mining and hydrocarbons but makes no mentions directly related to environmental precautions, though references to environmental considerations are scattered throughout the rest of the text. Moreover, although the constitution establishes a mechanism for prior consultation with indigenous peoples, the mechanism lacks procedures to ensure transparency. State oil companies run in association with public and private partners, for instance, do not always adhere to public procurement processes[13] and have in some cases failed to consult with indigenous groups prior to oil exploration.[14] Civil society groups in Bolivia are intent on making sure that the same does not happen with lithium exploitation.

Some groups have enjoyed initial victories in response to local and regional concerns: in mid-2010 the government reversed a decree to create a state-owned lithium extraction company after a civic group in Potosí, where the Uyuni salt lake is located, complained that the company had been established without citizen consultation and was intended to be based in the country's capital rather than in the affected region.[15] Still, these organizations need to significantly improve their existing capacities to build a network and mobilize a wider spectrum of citizens by developing a clear and shared vision of common good.

Establishing clear and consistent regulation and incorporating public consultation in the negotiations for and operation of lithium exploitation is especially important given the potential environmental and social impacts. Lithium-processing could threaten local communities and damage the surrounding ecosystem. If not managed properly, mining could affect the growing and promising tourism industry in what is one of Bolivia's poorest areas and also threaten scarce water supplies.[16] Lithium exploitation in Argentina, for example, has led to complaints of chemically contaminated water.[17] In Bolivia, some local environmental groups are doubtful that the government has seriously considered these risks.[18]

Creating the infrastructure necessary to make Bolivia a leading provider in lithium and lithium-based products will take considerable financial resources and technical expertise. This ambitious project will have a much greater chance of sustainability and providing long-term benefits to the Bolivian population if it has buy-in from local communities – especially from indigenous communities – and broader citizen participation. The government can take a number of steps to ensure that lithium exploitation is undertaken responsibly and with public support. Among these steps is the need to clarify and enforce mining and environmental regulations and to provide greater information on the criteria that will be used to assess public and private sector partnerships for lithium-related projects. The public dissemination of high-quality, interpretable information relating to financing and contracting should be matched by proactive moves to engage a wide spectrum of civil society to contribute to the process.

To create a transparent process for lithium exploitation is one of the most significant challenges Bolivia will have to surmount in order to benefit from its lithium in a sustainable manner.

Notes

1.   Marco Octavio Ribera is an environmental researcher with the Liga de Defensa del Medio Ambiente, Bolivia. He has written this article in collaboration with Cecilia Requena, technical secretary at Transparencia Bolivia.
2.   *Financial Times* (UK), 'Surge in lithium demand expected', 22 May 2010.
3.   US Geological Survey, *Mineral Commodity Summaries 2007* (Washington, DC, US Government Printing Office, 2007).
4.   Lawrence Wright, 'Lithium dreams', *The New Yorker* (US), 22 March 2010.
5.   *Guardian* (UK), 'Lithium: The gift of Pachamama', 8 August 2010.

6.   UNDP, *Human Development Report: The Other Frontier: Alternative Uses of Naturales* [sic] *Resources in Bolivia* (La Paz: UNDP, 2008), p. 3.
7.   World Bank, *Strengthening Bolivian Competitiveness: Export Diversification and Inclusive Growth* (Washington, DC: World Bank, 2009).
8.   Reuters (UK), 'Morales to firm state grip, exploit Bolivia lithium', 22 January 2010.
9.   In August 2010 the Bolivian and South Korean governments agreed to work jointly on developing the Uyuni's lithium.
10. Rebecca Hollender and Jim Shultz, *Bolivia and Its Lithium: Can the 'Gold of the 21st Century' Help Lift a Nation out of Poverty?* (Cochabamba: Democracy Center, 2010), p. 46.
11. Ibid.
12. In mid-October 2010, President Morales delivered a formal public presentation on the Bolivian Strategy for Lithium Exploitation. According to this presentation, the Bolivian State will assume all the investment costs related to the production of lithium carbonate and potassium chloride in the pilot phase (2010–2011) as well as the second phase (2012–2014) and will only look for joint ventures in order to gain access to technology for the production of lithium batteries during the third phase of the process, announced to begin in 2014. See *La Razón* (Bolivia), 'Bolivia inicia sola el proceso para industrializar el litio' (22 October 2010).
13. *La Prensa* (Bolivia), 'Petroandina firma contratos que eluden el control de la Ley Safco', 4 October 2009.
14. *La Prensa* (Bolivia), 'Las organizaciones señalan que aún no existe un rechazo a la exploración porque no se consultó', 22 July 2009.
15. *Latin American Herald Tribune* (Venezuela), 'Bolivian government backs off plan to create state lithium firm', 22 March 2010.
16. Robert Moran, *Minando el Agua: La Mina San Cristóbal, Bolivia* (La Paz: FRUTCAS, FSUMCAS and CGIAB, 2009).
17. Hollender and Shultz (2010), p. 41.
18. Ibid., pp. 41–43.

4.9

Engineering the Earth

Considering accountability and the last resort

Graeme Wood[1]

Geoengineering – the intentional alteration of the Earth and its atmosphere on a planetary scale – first appeared on the climate change agenda in 1965.[2] Since then, however, no efforts to develop geoengineering have moved past the early experimental phase. Scientists – even those who support geoengineering research – have been reluctant to consider the technology because it could distract from reducing emissions and lull the public into a false sense of security about a technology that is untested and has significant drawbacks.

As carbon reduction programmes have proved to be politically difficult, however, geoengineering has emerged as an undesirable but possible tool if the climate reaches a catastrophic tipping point. Although geoengineering projects could be undertaken locally, the consequences would be global. The near-total lack of a regulatory apparatus presents significant accountability challenges.

Potential geoengineering technologies fall into two categories. The first and most technically feasible today would be to blot out or dim the Sun with a haze of sulphur dioxide,[3] artificially enhanced cloud cover[4] or ceramic discs suspended in space between the Earth and the Sun.[5] Scientists claim that the swiftest of these proposals could arrest global temperature increases in a year or less.[6] The stratospheric sulphur proposals have the most traction, in part because we already understand the similar effects of volcanic eruptions on global temperatures (Mt Pinatubo's 1991 eruption lowered them by 0.5°C in a matter of months). Obstacles remain, however. The intentional dispersion of sulphur dioxide could potentially increase acid rain[7] or exacerbate ozone depletion. Moreover, none of the Sun-dimming schemes would have any effect on atmospheric CO_2 levels or the vast array of chemical problems (such as ocean acidification) that they present for the biosphere.

A second category involves removing and storing atmospheric carbon, often by changing the ecosystem and enlisting plants to assist with the removal. Efforts are already under way to stimulate blooms of marine phytoplankton, which constitute a significant natural carbon reservoir. It is difficult, however, to predict the consequences of depositing, for example, nitrogen or iron into a complex oceanic ecosystem. While some scientists believe the consequences would be minimal, or even positive, others have expressed concern that harmful algae could thrive or that more CO_2 may ultimately be released than sequestered.[8]

Even though geoengineering remains a 'break glass in case of emergency' response to runaway climate change, its consequences must be considered. Unlike emissions mitigation, geoengineering responses could be speedy and unilateral. If optimistic efficacy and cost estimates hold true, many proposed projects would be within the financial capability of small countries or wealthy private actors.

This raises a number of accountability challenges. First, there is no distinct controlling authority for geoengineering projects. Some multilateral institutions and agreements that have tangential jurisdiction over the effects of geoengineering[9] contain the beginnings of an international control structure. There are no institutions or agreements to govern geoengineering per se, however, and, on the very few occasions when law and geoengineering have intersected, the results have been messy. In 2009 rival German government ministries clashed over whether to stop Lohafex, a pilot effort to fertilize phytoplankton blooms with iron salts.[10] The experiment proceeded, although less CO_2 was sequestered than expected.

The lack of public oversight raises a second area of concern, which is the unclear role of private enterprise in climate engineering. Private companies have developed business plans to try to profit from iron fertilization by earning and selling carbon credits.[11] These activities, which currently involve substantial externalities and occur in an environment of extreme regulatory ambiguity, have the potential to give private entities substantial roles in developing geoengineering technologies, and to distort the research environment in ways that favour private entities over public interest.[12]

The third challenge is still theoretical. Many have pointed out that the effects of climate change will be uneven, with some regions expected to profit from a general rise in temperatures.[13] Since only one country is needed for geoengineering to work, there will be significant incentives for any adversely affected country to pursue geoengineering even if it is to the detriment of other countries. Depending on the type of geoengineering pursued, the global effects could be extremely varied, with some areas experiencing worse climatic effects than they suffer in a warming but ungeoengineered world. Central Africa, for example, is likely to experience drought in the case of stratospheric sulphur injection, and Asian monsoons will probably decline in intensity, with negative effects on agriculture there.[14]

Avoiding such outcomes by introducing a global moratorium on geoengineering would require verification of a country's compliance. Some geoengineering projects, such as constructing a space shade or the mass planting of crops with large root mass, would be easily detectable. Others, such as sulphur aerosol dispersion or iron fertilization, require very few special materials, however, and in principle could be deployed very quickly.

Although a governance regime for geoengineering is essential, its precise form is difficult to predict, in part because the technology and science are relatively young, and the appropriate form of regulation depends on still unknown scientific facts. UN-based, unilateral and consortium-based scenarios are all possible,[15] but each carries significant downsides. The UN-based approach would enjoy broad-based legitimacy and probably have more success at ensuring responsible research. The need for consensus could slow action in the face of an immediate climate crisis, however.[16] Unilateral approaches or cooperation between a small number of countries would allow more scientific exploration, but without international legitimacy and with less chance of preventing irresponsible or egoistic geoengineering by an individual private or national actor.[17]

It is important to acknowledge that because of the significant risks it poses, some civil society groups are calling for research into and consideration of geoengineering to stop altogether. Yet if geoengineering research moves forward – as it likely will – it is important for the foundations of transparent regulation and the highest research standards to be laid out now. Principles are starting to be considered. In early 2010 the UK's House of Commons Science and Technology Committee explored the need for geoengineering to be regulated as a public good, with the following requirements: public participation in decision-making; the disclosure of research and publication of results; independent assessment of impacts; and a robust governance structure prior to any deployment.[18]

These early principles will require greater discussion and development, and should be based on debate that involves not just governments and scientists, but a broad representation of civil society. Regardless of one's belief in the dangers or benefits of geoengineering, a future without clear rules governing research and implementation leaves society ill-prepared to ensure that, if climate change induces acute catastrophes, geoengineering takes place – or is prevented from taking place – in an accountable way.

Notes

1. Graeme Wood is a correspondent and contributing editor at *the Atlantic*, based in Washington, DC.
2. President's Science Advisory Committee (PSAC), *Restoring the Quality of Our Environment: Report of the Environmental Pollution Panel* (Washington, DC: US Government Printing Office, 1965).
3. Paul Crutzen, 'Albedo Enhancement by Stratospheric Sulfur Injections: A Contribution to Resolve a Policy Dilemma?', *Climatic Change*, vol. 77 (2006), pp. 211–219.
4. Stephen Salter et al., 'Sea-Going Hardware for the Cloud Albedo Method of Reversing Global Warming', *Philosophical Transactions of the Royal Society A*, vol. 366 (2008), pp. 3989–4006.
5. Roger Angel, 'Feasibility of Cooling the Earth with a Cloud of Small Spacecraft near the Inner Lagrange Point (L1)', *Proceedings of the National Academy of Sciences*, vol. 103 (2006), pp. 17184–17189.
6. Jason Blackstock et al., *Climate Engineering Responses to Climate Emergencies* (Santa Barbara, CA: Novim, 2009).
7. Ben Kravitz et al., 'Sulfuric Acid Deposition from Stratospheric Geoengineering with Sulfate Aerosols', *Journal of Geophysical Research – Atmospheres*, vol. 114 (2009), pp. D14109.1–D14109.7.
8. Brandon Keim, 'Enviros challenge dumping urea in ocean to sink carbon', *Wired*, 7 November 2007.
9. These are the UN Environmental Modification Convention and the UN Convention on Biological Diversity.
10. *Sydney Morning Herald* (Australia), 'Germany OKs Atlantic global warming experiment', 26 January 2009.
11. *Washington Post* (US), 'Iron to plankton to carbon credits', 20 July 2007.
12. David Victor et al., 'The Geoengineering Option: A Last Resort against Global Warming?', *Foreign Affairs*, vol. 88 (2009), pp. 64–76, p. 72.
13. Gregg Easterbrook, 'Global Warming: Who Loses – and Who Wins?', *the Atlantic*, vol. 299 (April 2007), pp. 52–64.
14. Alan Robock et al., 'The Benefits, Risks, and Costs of Stratospheric Geoengineering', *Geophysical Research Letters*, vol. 36 (2009), pp. L19703.1–L19703.9.
15. See John Virgoe, 'International Governance of a Possible Geoengineering Intervention to Combat Climate Change', *Climatic Change*, vol. 95 (2009), pp. 103–119.
16. Ibid.
17. Ibid.
18. House of Commons Science and Technology Committee, *The Regulation of Geoengineering* (London: Stationery Office, 2010), pp. 29–35; see also Steve Rayner et al., 'Memorandum on Draft Principles for the Conduct of Geoengineering Research' (Oxford: Saïd Business School, 2009).

PART 5

Adaptation to climate change

Building accountable, sustainable resilience

5.0
Adaptation to climate change
Building accountable, sustainable resilience

Adaptation to climate change involves 'adjustment in natural or human systems in response to actual or expected climatic stimuli or their effects, which moderates harm or exploits beneficial opportunities'.[1] This adaptation will take place within the limits of the global structure, which has so far determined that those who have the least responsibility for climate change – in the poorest, least industrialized nations – will suffer the worst consequences.[2]

Funding for adaptation derives from a variety of sources, and flows through a number of streams. Money for adaptation comes mainly from donor countries and, to a lesser extent, charitable foundations, developing country budgets and the private sector. It is channelled through the United Nations Framework Convention on Climate Change (UNFCCC), multilateral banks and bilateral donors in the form of development aid and dedicated national climate change funds.

At the national level, inevitably, developed and developing countries will both continue to take precautions to protect their citizens and economies from the effects of climate change through national plans to improve infrastructure, diversify economies and cope with emergencies. The focus of international interest in adaptation, however, is on the transfer of funds to and the implementation of projects and programmes in developing countries.

A fragmented framework means that separate funds function under their own governance structures, potentially undermining the efforts of the UNFCCC. Furthermore, different operating systems mean that it is difficult to trace what comes into the system and where it goes, thereby compromising transparency and weakening requirements that pledges should be 'new and additional' to development aid.

The opening contribution, by Richard Klein, illustrates how UNFCCC-mandated funds are generated, governed, delivered and used, and highlights the multiple governance issues yet to be resolved, including the considerable structural power imbalances and the influence of developed nations in determining to a large extent where money is spent. Transparency International complements this piece with a discussion on the governance of bilateral and multilateral funds for climate change. It questions whether the preferences of donor countries for these channels signal a parallel structure to the UNFCCC – and one that could potentially undermine it.

Adil Najam assesses the lack of transparency in adaptation financing and the limited access to financial information, and proposes an internationally managed registry to tag and track funds accurately for both adaptation and development. He demonstrates the difficulties surrounding the monitoring of flows to ensure that they are truly 'new and additional' and the complexity of establishing criteria to disaggregate adaptation benefits from the traditional costs of development projects.

Britta Horstmann's section on the Adaptation Fund considers the corruption risks in one of the most innovative and equitable models for funding concrete adaptation projects and programmes. The features of the Adaptation Fund, such as the ability of national implementing agencies to access funds directly, highlight the importance of investing in national-level governance capacity, and provide a lens through which to consider broader governance challenges at the national level.

The implementation of activities that will be funded through the newly established adaptation funds may be new and innovative to some extent, but they will largely involve 'adaptations' to ongoing development activities. The following sections look at some of the current forms of development and suggest ways in which climate change may increase or change some of the corruption risks.

James Lewis highlights the many corruption risks inherent in the building of new structures and maintaining old ones. He provides insight into some of the risks that may be enhanced as large amounts of public funds flow into projects and increased technical specialization makes infrastructure more difficult to monitor. Accompanying this piece, TI UK presents the Project Anti-Corruption System (PACS) standards, an anti-corruption tool to assist in identifying risks in particular construction projects, and Segundo Romera and Aileen Laus highlight the shortcomings in the Philippines' structural preparations for extreme weather events, suggesting that corruption is one reason why disaster preparedness and response are under-funded.

Providing a special focus on the most vulnerable communities, Ingrid Boas and Rebecca Dobson identify migration as a particular form of climate adaptation and highlight the risks for migrants and the organizations that may seek to assist them.

They call for recognition of climate migrants as a specific group under the UNFCCC and for a fund to assist in their relocation and resettlement. This is followed by an illustration by TI Kenya, which shows how climate change and deforestation can lead to large-scale corruption and migration.

As a crucial aspect of adaptation activity, the Water Integrity Network puts forward Bangladesh as a case study to illustrate how water can be integrated into adaptation programming and how corruption can be avoided and water resources managed equitably.

In the final section, Roslyn Hees provides an assessment of the corruption risks surrounding humanitarian aid programmes and the additional stress that they will face as a result of climate change. She suggests that, while the risks will not alter dramatically, the increased pressure under which agencies will operate may intensify already existing corruption. The piece concludes with a set of recommendations for humanitarian aid agencies to prepare for corruption in the context of climate change.

Notes

1. Martin L. Parry et al., *Contribution of Working Group II to the Fourth Assessment Report of the Intergovernmental Panel on Climate Change* (Cambridge: Cambridge University Press, 2007).
2. Ibid.

5.1

Show me the money

Ensuring equity, transparency and accountability in adaptation finance

Richard J. T. Klein[1]

> *We see there is money put before us. Can I suggest, in biblical terms: it looks like we are being offered thirty pieces of silver to betray our people and our future. Mr President, our future is not for sale.*

So said Ian Fry, lead negotiator of Tuvalu, on the last night of the 2009 United Nations Climate Change Conference in Copenhagen. During the final plenary session the mistrust between developed and developing countries over money was starker than ever. Prior to the conference, Benito Müller, a long-term observer of the climate negotiations, had already noted that the history of financial support for developing countries was littered with disappointments and broken promises, which have eroded trust to an unprecedented level.[2] What happened in the closing hours of the Copenhagen conference didn't help to restore this trust.

A small group of countries – Brazil, China, India, South Africa and the US – negotiated and agreed the Copenhagen Accord. Other countries were then asked to adopt it in plenary without transparent or inclusive deliberations. Countries that expressed reservations, such as Tuvalu, were told that the financial support referred to in the Copenhagen Accord would not be available to them.

This section provides context to illustrate some of the reasons behind the mistrust that continues to affect discussions on adaptation funding, and submits that there is a fundamental difference between developing and developed countries' interpretations of 'equity, transparency and accountability'. After presenting an overview of the current adaptation funding 'landscape', the piece discusses these concepts of equity, transparency and accountability with respect to the generation, governance, delivery and use of adaptation money under the UN Framework Convention on Climate Change (UNFCCC). A shared perspective of countries on these issues is important not only so that they can begin to rebuild trust but also to ensure that money is used effectively and efficiently.

Funds for adaptation: an embarrassment of riches

The 2001 United Nations Climate Change Conference in Marrakesh established three funds to support adaptation activities in developing countries: the Least Developed Countries Fund (LDCF) and the Special Climate Change Fund (SCCF), under the UNFCCC, and the Adaptation Fund, under the Kyoto Protocol.

The two funds under the UNFCCC are managed by the Global Environment Facility (GEF) and rely on voluntary contributions from developed countries. The GEF provides funding to eligible developing countries to meet the 'additional' or 'incremental' costs of adaptation; the baseline costs of a project or programme are borne by the recipient country, by other bilateral or multilateral donors, or both.[3] As of May 2010 US$315 million had been pledged for adaptation under these two funds (US$221 million to the LDCF and US$94 million to the SCCF); of this amount, US$220 million has been allocated (US$135 million from the LDCF and US$85 million from the SCCF).[4] In addition, the GEF used its Trust Fund to establish the Strategic Priority on Piloting an Operational Approach to Adaptation (SPA); it has allocated all US$50 million it had made available to it.[5] In 2008 the GEF Council agreed to await the recommendations of the independent evaluation of the SPA and guidance to the GEF from the Conference of the Parties (COP) before making a decision on the future use of the Trust Fund for adaptation activities. No adaptation support is foreseen as part of the fifth replenishment cycle of the GEF (2010–2014).[6]

The Adaptation Fund, which became operational only in 2009, is managed by a special Adaptation Fund Board (AFB), but is also administered by the GEF. It is the first financial instrument under the UNFCCC and its Kyoto Protocol that is not based solely on voluntary contributions from developed countries. It receives a 2 per cent share of proceeds from project activities under the Clean Development Mechanism (CDM), but can also receive funds from other sources to fund concrete adaptation projects and programmes. The actual amount of money that will be available from the Adaptation Fund depends on the extent to which the CDM is used and on the price of carbon. As of July 2010 the Adaptation Fund had received US$160 million, of which US$112.5 million was generated through CDM activities. Estimates of potential resources available for the Adaptation Fund from 31 August 2010 to 31 December 2012 range from US$317 million to US$434 million.[7]

In addition to the funds that operate within the context of the UNFCCC, money for adaptation is provided through several other channels. These may be through domestic national, sectoral and local budgets of developing countries; bilateral and multilateral development assistance; or private sector flows and investments. This makes for an adaptation financing landscape that is highly fragmented, resulting in a proliferation not only of funds but also of policies, rules and procedures.

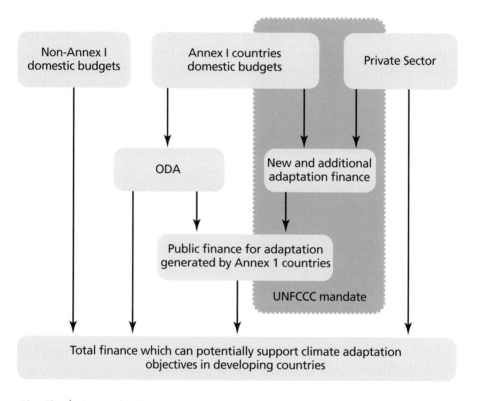

Source: Adapted from Åsa Persson et al., *Adaptation Finance under a Copenhagen Agreed Outcome* (Stockholm: SEI, 2009).

Figure 5.1 Overview of adaptation funding channels

There are a number of anti-corruption and corporate responsibility initiatives that set standards for private flows of money, such as the UN Global Compact and the Equator Principles.[8] Flows coming through bilateral or multilateral development assistance have relevant policies, such as the 2005 Paris Declaration on Aid Effectiveness, which includes measures and standards of performance and accountability, and action to address corruption and a lack of transparency. These were made more concrete in the 2008 Accra Agenda of Action, committing countries to greater transparency in public financial management, including disclosing regular, detailed and timely information on the volume, allocation and – when possible – results of development expenditure. There is also a commitment to ensure that mutual assessment reviews are in place by 2010 to strengthen accountability mechanisms and fight corruption.[9]

This plethora of policies, rules and procedures for financial flows outside the UNFCCC system contributes towards transparency in their separate streams, but they are not coherent and none has a specific focus on ensuring the accountability of adaptation funds. The remainder of this section, therefore, focuses on the specific adaptation funds that have been created under the UNFCCC (the GEF-managed funds and the Adaptation Fund), and on the provisions for funding included in the Copenhagen Accord and the subsequent Cancún Agreements. It follows the template provided in table 5.1, which presents an overview of the most pertinent issues in the negotiations on adaptation finance.

	Generation	Governance	Delivery	Use
Equity	Effort-sharing between providers of adaptation funding, taking into account the principle of common but differentiated responsibilities and respective capabilities.	Equitable representation of developed and developing countries.	Eligibility criteria and prioritization among countries based on their level of vulnerability.	Prioritization within countries based on the level of vulnerability and other nationally defined criteria.
Transparency	Transparent flow of finance stemming from various sources and generated through various mechanisms.	Transparent decision-making in line with just rules of procedures of governing bodies.	Transparent operational policies and guidelines.	Adherence to the principle of subsidiarity and a transparent selection process.
Accountability	Monitoring and reviewing of the provision of new and additional finance.	Provisions in rules of procedures to prevent conflicts of interests and deter corruption.	Adherence to operational policies and guidelines in delivering resources.	Monitoring and reviewing of the implementation of adaptation actions.

Table 5.1 Overview of issues related to equity, transparency and accountability in the generation, governance, delivery and use of adaptation finance

Generating adaptation finance

Article 4.4 of the UNFCCC commits developed countries 'to assist developing countries that are particularly vulnerable to the adverse effects of climate change in meeting costs of adaptation to those adverse effects'. According to article 4.3, this assistance is understood to come in the form of 'new and additional' funding – that is, beyond what developed countries are already planning to provide as official development assistance (ODA).

This funding is to be provided on the basis of equitable effort-sharing; acknowledging the 'common but differentiated responsibilities and respective capabilities' of all parties – meaning that developed countries should lead in efforts to combat climate change and its effects. Developing countries have expressed a preference for nationally assessed contributions from developed countries to provide the lion's share of adaptation finance, reflecting their historic responsibilities for greenhouse gas (GHG) emissions. Developed countries, on the other hand, see a primary role for market-based approaches in generating resources for adaptation, in particular the auctioning of emissions allowances.[10]

The GEF-managed funds depend on voluntary contributions from developed countries, while the GEF Trust Fund is replenished every four years through a negotiation process that takes the 'responsibilities and capabilities' of donors into account. The 2 per cent share of proceeds from the CDM that provides resources for the Adaptation Fund has been seen as a 'solidarity tax' imposed on those developing countries in which CDM projects are implemented. These countries are not necessarily the same as those that are being prioritized for funding; the levy on CDM projects in countries such as India and China will, in effect, be channelled to least developed countries for adaptation projects under the Adaptation Fund. A country's contribution to the Adaptation Fund is thus not related to its 'responsibility' for climate change, but to its ability to attract CDM projects.

The Copenhagen Accord created a Green Climate Fund, which was further refined and agreed at COP 16 in Cancún, with the goal of mobilizing US$100 billion a year by 2020 to be allocated in a balanced manner between adaptation and mitigation, in order to address the needs of developing countries. The accord also mentions the provision of 'new and additional' resources approaching US$30 billion for the period 2010–2012 (so-called 'fast-start' funding), with equal allocation between adaptation and mitigation actions. It does not mention where the money might come from or how this is to be decided, but it could come from a variety of sources, including public and private, bilateral and multilateral and alternative sources of finance. This issue remains to be resolved by a high-level panel set up by

UN Secretary-General Ban Ki-moon. The panel began deliberations in February 2010 to 'study potential sources of revenue that can be used to help developing countries carry out activities to mitigate and adapt to climate change'.[11] The final report, which was presented in Cancún in 2010, concluded that raising US$100 billion per year is challenging but feasible. It discusses a variety of means to raise funds, which still need to implemented by decision-makers.[12]

At least four different definitions of what constitutes 'new and additional' funding make it difficult to ensure accountability in the generation of money.[13] By and large, developing countries consider 'new and additional' resources to be those provided by developing countries over and above the ODA targets of 0.7 per cent of GNI, agreed in the 1970s.[14] These targets are yet to be met by the majority of countries, however, making it difficult to set a baseline above which 'new and additional' funding can be counted.[15] As such, most developed countries interpret new and additional resources as those going beyond current financial flows, but consider ODA as a possible component of these resources.

Developed countries report their bilateral and multilateral financial contributions in their national communications to the UNFCCC Secretariat.[16] The quality of these reports is mixed, however, and there is no common standard for determining the extent to which resources are specifically dedicated to climate change or what constitutes 'new and additional' funding.[17] At the same time, these contributions are also reported to the Organisation for Economic Co-operation and Development's Development Assistance Committee (OECD-DAC) as ODA, which has similarly imprecise and incomparable means of distinguishing climate change funding from development aid.[18] In the absence of clear guidance it will be difficult to prevent the double-counting of money as both adaptation finance and development assistance. According to the Fourth Overall Performance Study of the GEF, '77 percent of contributions to the GEF were recorded as ODA. However, the reality was recently recognized when the ODA percentage for GEF contributions was increased to 96 percent for the purposes of OECD/DAC reporting. If "new and additional" was meant to refer to being beyond regular ODA, only 4 percent of current funds can now be described as such.'[19]

The Copenhagen Accord states that the delivery of funds by developed countries will be measured, reported and verified in accordance with existing and any further guidelines adopted by the Conference of the Parties, and will ensure that the accounting of such targets and finance is rigorous, robust and transparent. Exactly how this will be done remains unclear. This lack of clarity has led to considerable discretion on the part of developed countries to do as they choose. In January 2010 it was found that the UK government's £1.5 billion (approximately US$2.4 billion)

Copenhagen pledge for fast-start funding would be reallocated from existing overseas aid programmes.[20] This discovery was seen to 'undermine repeated government pledges that such climate aid should be additional to existing overseas development aid'.[21] Not only was the money to be reallocated, but much of the pledge included 'already existing commitments' and despite being allocated for climate change would count as ODA, in effect double-counting UK contributions.[22]

In an attempt to enhance transparency in the generation of climate finance, the Dutch government has set up a website to record the money pledged as fast-start funding.[23] The website 'aims to provide transparency about the amount, direction and use of fast-start climate finance, in turn building trust in its delivery and impact'. Although this will serve as a useful device to track funds it is likely to be subject to the same shortcomings as other financial tracking mechanisms.[24]

Governance of adaptation finance

Article 11 of the UNFCCC states that '[t]he financial mechanism shall have an equitable and balanced representation of all Parties within a transparent system of governance'. As such, the composition of the institutions managing the funds and their levels of accountability to the Conference of the Parties under the UNFCCC are crucial for ensuring that they live up to these standards.

The GEF-managed funds and the Adaptation Fund are both accountable to varying degrees to the COP; the Adaptation Fund in particular is considered to be 'under the authority of the COP', meaning that the Conference of the Parties serving as the Meeting of the Parties (MOP) to the Kyoto Protocol has the authority to select the members of its executive body, and approve rules and guidelines.[25] This set-up is seen as a means of instilling trust in the Adaptation Fund and as a response to developing country dissatisfaction with the performance of the GEF as an operating entity under the UNFCCC,[26] which works with 'limited means of accountability' on the basis of 'a loosely worded Memorandum of Understanding'.[27]

The LDCF and the SCCF are governed by members of the GEF Council that have contributed to the funds and form the LDCF/SCCF Council.[28] The members of the council represent 32 constituencies (16 from developing countries, 14 from developed countries and two from countries with economies in transition). Decisions are normally taken by consensus, but if consensus cannot be achieved then decisions can be adopted by a double-weighted majority – that is, an affirmative vote representing both a 60 per cent majority of council members and a 60 per cent majority of the total contributions to the funds.[29] Votes are 'modified to reflect each [country's] relative contributions to these funds'.[30] The latter majority requirement favours the donors rather than the recipients, which undermines the concept of 'equitable and balanced representation' and, consequently, developing countries' trust in the GEF.

The Adaptation Fund is managed by the Adaptation Fund Board. This board consists of 16 members: 10 from developing countries and six from developed countries. This gives a majority on the board to developing countries. The rules of procedure state that decisions of the board are to be taken by consensus whenever possible. If all efforts to reach consensus have been exhausted and no agreement has been reached, decisions are taken by a two-thirds majority of the members present at the meeting, on the basis of one member, one vote. The rules of procedure also contain a section on confidentiality and conflicts of interest. As such, it has been suggested that 'the [Adaptation Fund] represents an important step towards real ownership by developing countries'.[31]

The emphasis on consensus decision-making in all three of the funds has meant that a constituency vote has never been taken. A key concern is that 'de facto consensus-based representative decision-making is, quite generally, susceptible to "backroom deals" by the representatives of the powerful countries (across the "North/South divide") beyond the control of weaker constituents'.[32] Furthermore, such undue influence on decisions goes undetected, as consensus is reached when the chair of a meeting is convinced that there is no opposition to a decision; in effect, consensus is reached on a no-objection basis.[33] In this context it is interesting to note that even the GEF's highly controversial Resource Allocation Framework, set up to allocate funds for mitigation to individual countries, was not voted on.[34] Indeed, the decision was 'pushed forcibly by donors, without authorization of the COP', indicating the political nature of decision-making at the GEF.[35]

The governance of multilateral funding for adaptation under the Copenhagen Accord is to be delivered through effective and efficient funding arrangements, with a governance structure providing for equal representation for developed and developing countries. Channelling the funds through the Adaptation Fund is not specifically mentioned, however, raising concerns on the part of many developing countries, which consider this to be the most equitable avenue for adaptation funding. Indeed, one of the most likely channels for the fast-start funding committed under the accord was the World Bank Climate Investment Funds (CIFs), which are completely outside (and therefore not accountable to) the UNFCCC process. This is a proposal that is favoured by many donor countries, some of which also advocate a role for the CIFs in managing the more long-term Copenhagen Green Climate Fund.[36]

In Cancún, countries agreed that the Green Climate Fund will be governed by a board of 24 members comprising an equal number of members from developing and developed country Parties taking into account regional groups. The World Bank was invited to serve as Trustee on an interim basis, a position that would be reviewed within three years. Given the lack of detail on the Fund, countries decided to establish a Transitional Committee to design the Fund, including its legal and institutional arrangements, rules of procedures, and financial instruments. While the governing board has equal representation, the Committee has a majority of developing countries, which could result in a fund design that is favourable to developing countries.

Delivery of adaptation finance

Article 4.4 (cited above) can be read as defining the countries that would be eligible to receive adaptation finance: developing countries that are 'particularly vulnerable' to the adverse effects of climate change.

This use of the phrase 'particularly vulnerable' has led to much debate. The question of what it means to be particularly vulnerable and how to decide which countries fall into this category remains unanswered. The Preamble to the UNFCCC appears to give at least a partial answer by recognizing 'that low-lying and other small island countries, countries with low-lying coastal, arid and semi-arid areas or areas liable to floods, drought and desertification, and developing countries with fragile mountainous ecosystems are particularly vulnerable to the adverse effects of climate change'.[37]

The 2007 Bali Action Plan, which provided the road map for negotiations towards Copenhagen, is more restrictive and mentions only 'the least developed countries and small island developing States, and further taking into account the needs of countries in Africa affected by drought, desertification and floods'.[38] The negotiating text prepared for the Conference of the Parties in Copenhagen 2009 complicated the issue further by stating that priority 'shall' or 'should' be given to 'particularly vulnerable populations, groups and communities, especially the poor, women, children, the elderly, indigenous peoples, minorities and those suffering from disability'.

Decisions on the allocation of funds for the LDCF, the SCCF and the Adaptation Fund are made by the LDCF/SCCF Council and the Adaptation Fund Board, respectively, and are thus subject to the governance limitations discussed above. In order for them to be equitable, transparent and accountable, however, decisions 'must be guided by an assessment based on agreed, objective and measurable criteria'.[39]

The Adaptation Fund's allocation is guided by the following principles, among others: the level of vulnerability, level of urgency and risks arising from delay; and ensuring access to the fund in a balanced and equitable manner'.[40] What remains unresolved, however, is how to measure levels of 'vulnerability' and 'urgency', and then the successful prioritization of projects that are being funded with scarce resources.

The resulting ambiguity has made it impossible for developing countries to reach agreement on which countries to prioritize for adaptation funding. Some countries have suggested the development of a 'vulnerability index', assuming that such an index could provide an objective answer to the question. As argued by Klein, however, a vulnerability index will not resolve the ambiguity; because the 'level of vulnerability' is not a measurable and quantifiable attribute that can be objectively determined.[41] In fact, parties have experience with the use of indices to guide resource allocation decisions for mitigation. The former Resource Allocation Framework of the GEF combined two indices to facilitate objective and transparent decisions on a politically sensitive issue, but there has been much criticism over the framework. At the 25th GEF Council Meeting in June 2005, countries raised strong objections to the proposal of a Resource Allocation Framework. Among other things, they stated, '[w]e specifically oppose the ranking and categorization of recipient countries through non-transparent assessments based on questionable criteria. GEF resources should not be pre-allocated on such a basis'.[42] It remains unclear whether or not any vulnerability index will receive a warmer welcome.

Use of adaptation finance

While the prioritization of resources among countries should be informed by countries' level of vulnerability, prioritization within countries is country-driven – i.e. based on criteria set by the countries themselves. These criteria should be developed through a transparent and participatory process. The UNFCCC has provided some guidance for in-country prioritization related to the preparation of national adaptation programmes of action (NAPAs), which states that, along with the level or degree of the adverse effects of climate change, least developed countries should consider poverty reduction to enhance adaptive capacity, synergy with other multilateral environmental agreements and cost-effectiveness when selecting priority adaptation activities.[43]

Ensuring that, once adaptation finance has been delivered, it is used for the intended purpose and has a valuable impact raises the issue of the monitoring and evaluation of adaptation outputs and outcomes. Measuring the performance of mitigation activities is not uncontroversial, but it can be expressed in more or less comparable measures of CO_2 equivalents. Adaptation, on the other hand, lacks such a common metric. A careful choice of indicators for adaptation is therefore important in order to 'improve transparency and avoid conflict'.[44] A number of indicators have been suggested, including measuring adaptive capacity and both results-oriented and process-oriented adaptation activities.[45] How these indicators are implemented and how the baselines for measurement are established will significantly affect the effectiveness of the measures.[46]

The GEF has developed a results-based management framework that monitors and reports the LDCF and the SCCF at the programme level, at the level of funding areas and at the project level. This framework will incorporate both process- and results-based indicators to reduce vulnerability to the adverse impacts of climate change and increase resilience.[47] The Adaptation Fund is also developing a results-based management framework to link the strategic objectives and priorities of the fund to the various programmes and projects that it finances.[48] While the Copenhagen Accord does not mention accountability for adaptation finance, it does see transparent implementation as a prerequisite for the provision of funds, and the new Transitional Committee of the Green Climate Fund shall recommend to the COP 'mechanisms to ensure financial accountability and to evaluate the performance of activities supported by the fund ... [and] ensure the application of environmental and social safeguards, as well as internationally accepted fiduciary standards and sound financial management to the fund activities.'

Although results-based frameworks have long been considered one of the most effective ways of measuring the impact of development aid, they are also difficult to establish and are prone to manipulation. For example, project developers have been known to distort the baselines from which progress is measured, amplifying the apparent benefits of projects.[49] Such manipulation is even more risky when the indicators for measuring adaptation actions are so difficult to establish, baselines are so variable and subjective and the impacts of adaptation measures may be felt in the long, medium or short term.[50]

What comes next?

Adaptation financing to date has been in the order of millions of dollars, but it is soon expected to amount to billions. This raises the importance of ensuring equity, transparency and accountability in the generation, governance, delivery and use of the money. The standards set by the UNFCCC, in particular the Adaptation Fund, promote higher levels of country ownership, impose less conditionality and allow more direct access to funds in order to ensure a more equitable distribution of resources when compared to adaptation funding provided through other channels. As we have seen above, however, there remain challenges to their implementation.

The promise of substantially scaled-up finance for adaptation was an important outcome of the Copenhagen and Cancún conferences. It will take time to set up and make operational the Green Climate Fund, but the management of the fast-start adaptation funding mentioned in the Copenhagen Accord is likely to set the tone for future systems of finance. If this money is delivered only or primarily as official development assistance and through existing institutions, such as the World Bank, it is likely to fuel the current mistrust between developed and developing countries. Any future scheme for adaptation finance must exhibit and ensure good governance, including an equitable and transparent allocation of burdens and benefits based on need, capacity and responsibility, and a system of accountability adopted by all countries.

Notes

1. Richard Klein is a senior research fellow at the Stockholm Environment Institute (SEI) and an adjunct professor at the Centre for Climate Science and Policy Research of Linköping University.
2. See www.oxfordenergy.org/comments.php.
3. For more information see http://thegef.org/gef/adaptation.
4. GEF, *Status Report on the Least Developed Countries Fund and the Special Climate Change Fund* (Washington, DC: GEF, 2010).
5. GEF, 'Report on the Completion of the Strategic Priority on Adaptation' (Washington, DC: GEF, 2008).
6. For more information on replenishment, see http://thegef.org/gef/replenishment.
7. Adaptation Fund, *Financial Status of the Adaptation Fund Trust Fund* (Washington, DC: Adaptation Fund, August 2010).
8. See www.unglobalcompact.org and www.equator-principles.com/principles.shtml.
9. See www.oecd.org/document/18/0,3343,en_2649_3236398_35401554_1_1_1_1,00&&en-USS_01DBC.html.
10. Persson et al. (2009), p. 25.
11. For more information, see www.un.org/wcm/content/site/climatechange/pages/financeadvisorygroup.
12. Report of the Secretary-General's High-level Advisory Group on Climate Change Financing, at http://www.un.org/wcm/webdav/site/climatechange/shared/Documents/AGF_reports/AGF%20Report.pdf.
13. Jessica Brown et al., *Climate Finance Additionality: Emerging Definitions and Their Implications*, Climate Finance Policy Brief no. 2 (Berlin and London: Heinrich Böll Stiftung and Overseas Development Institute [ODI], 2010).
14. UN General Assembly Resolution 2626 (xxv), 1970, paragraph 43.

15. Martin Stadelmann et al., *Baseline for Trust: Defining "New and Additional" Climate Funding* (London: International Institute for Environment and Development [IIED], 2010). This briefing paper lists eight possible ways of defining a baseline and their pros and cons.

16. According to the guidelines for the preparation of national communications, developed countries shall indicate what 'new and additional' financial resources they have provided pursuant to article 4.3, and provide information on any financial resources related to the implementation of the convention provided through bilateral, regional and other multilateral channels (UNFCCC guidelines on reporting and review, at http://unfccc.int/resource/docs/cop5/07.pdf).

17. Clare Breidenich and Daniel Bodansky, *Measuring, Reporting and Verification in a Post-2012 Climate Agreement* (Arlington, VA: Pew Center on Global Climate Change, 2009), p.16.

18. See Adil Najam, section 5.1.2 in this volume.

19. GEF, *Progress toward Impact: Fourth Overall Performance Study of the GEF* (Washington, DC: GEF, 2010).

20. David Adam, 'Climate fund "recycled" from existing aid budget, UK government admits', *Guardian* (UK), 29 January 2010.

21. Ibid.

22. Ibid.

23. See www.faststartfinance.org and *Guardian* (UK), 'UN debuts website for tracking climate aid', 3 September 2010.

24. See Adil Najam, section 5.1.2 in this volume.

25. Benito Müller, *'Under the Authority of the COP'?* (Oxford: Oxford Institute for Energy Studies [OIES], November 2009).

26. Ibid.; Richard Klein and Annett Möhner, 'Governance Limits to Effective Global Financial Support for Adaptation', in W. Neil Adger et al. (eds), *Adapting to Climate Change: Thresholds, Values, Governance* (Cambridge: Cambridge University Press, 2009), pp. 465–475.

27. Athena Ballesteros et al., *Power, Responsibility, and Accountability: Re-Thinking the Legitimacy of Institutions for Climate Finance*, working paper (Washington, DC: World Resources Institute [WRI], 2009).

28. GEF, 'Governance of Climate Change Funds' (Washington, DC: GEF, August 2006).

29. Ibid.

30. Ballesteros et al. (2009), p.19.

31. Jan Cedergren, Chair, Adaptation Board, October 2009, quoted on www.climate-l.org.

32. Benito Müller, 'Nairobi 2006: Trust and the Future of Adaptation Funding' (Oxford: OIES, January 2007), p. 5.

33. Ballesteros et al. (2009).

34. Müller (January 2007), p. 5. The resource allocation framework has subsequently been replaced by the System for Transparent Allocation of Resources (STAR), which is considered to be a more equitable framework.

35. Ballesteros et al. (2009), p. 24.

36. European Network on Debt and Development (Eurodad), 'Why the World Bank Is Ill-Fitted for Climate Finance: Key Principles and Recommendations for Equitable Climate Finance Governance', position paper (Brussels: Eurodad, April 2010), p. 3. See also Rebecca Dobson, section 5.1.1 in this volume.

37. See www.un-documents.net/unfccc.htm.

38. See Bali Action Plan, at http://unfccc.int/files/meetings/cop_13/application/pdf/cp_bali_action. pdf.

39. Persson et al. (2009), p. 3.

40. Adaptation Fund, 'Initial Funding Priorities' (Bonn: Adaptation Fund, November 2009).

41. Klein and Möhner (2009).

42. Annex A (untitled) of Joint Summary of the Chairs, 1 July 2005 (revised), GEF Council Meeting, Washington, DC, 3–8 June 2005, p. 19.

43. UNFCCC decision 28/CP.7, 'Guidelines for the preparation of national adaptation programmes of action'.

44. Merylyn McKenzie Hedger et al., 'Evaluating Climate Change Adaptation from a Development Perspective' (Brighton: IDS, November 2008).

45. UNFCCC, *Synthesis Report on Efforts Undertaken to Monitor and Evaluate the Implementation of Adaptation Projects, Policies and Programmes and the Costs and Effectiveness of Completed Projects, Policies and Programmes, and Views on Lessons Learned, Good Practices, Gaps and Needs* (New York: UNFCCC, 2010).

46. This has been acknowledged by the GEF and the Adaptation Fund in the development of their programmes for results-based management.

47. GEF, *Results-Based Management Framework for Least Developed Countries (LDCF) and Special Climate Change Fund (SCCF)* (Washington, DC: GEF, 2009).

48. The framework was approved by the Adaptation Board in June 2010, see http://adaptation-fund.org/node/561.

49. Baselines have been inflated in order to increase the apparent value of projects. See Devi Sridhar and Tami Tamashiro, *Vertical Funds in the Health Sector: Lessons for Education from the Global Fund and GAVI* (Paris: United Nations Educational, Scientific and Cultural Organization [UNESCO], 2009).

50. See Adil Najam, section 5.1.2 in this volume.

5.1.1

Fast-start funding

Is there an emerging parallel structure for climate finance?

Rebecca Dobson[1]

The 2009 Copenhagen Accord calls for 'scaled up, new and additional, predictable and adequate funding as well as improved access' for adaptation and mitigation actions in developing countries. In the short term this has resulted in a pledge of US$30 billion in fast-start funding from developed countries between 2010 and 2012. The accord does not determine the channels through which funding should flow, however. The 2010 Cancún Agreement formally endorsed this pledge and confirmed that there would be balanced allocation between adaptation and mitigation funding.

Although it may seem reasonable that financial pledges made at a United Nations Framework Convention on Climate Change (UNFCCC) conference would naturally flow through the UNFCCC-mandated funds,[2] in 2010 it looked increasingly likely that fast-start funds would be channelled either bilaterally or through the multilateral development banks (MDBs) alongside the UNFCCC funds.[3] This preference of donor countries for financing streams outside the UNFCCC process is linked to the belief that the MDBs are better placed to govern funds and facilitate greater donor control over development aid.

There are concerns, however, that the bilateral climate initiatives – since 2006 at least six new bilateral funds have been announced by donor countries[4] – and multilateral funds, such as the World Bank Climate Investment Funds (CIFs),[5] constitute a parallel structure for climate finance. It is feared that progress that has been made under the UNFCCC in terms of equity between parties in participation, decision-making and governance will be undermined by the bilateral and multilateral structures which, for many, represent a continuation of the old power relationships between donor and recipient countries.

According to analyses of the fast-start funds pledged at Copenhagen, donor countries appear to be favouring the CIFs as a major channel through which the funds will flow.[6] Over a half of the UK's pledge of US$800 million per year has already been disbursed to the World Bank. Of the 2010 US pledge, 39 per cent will be channelled to the World Bank, and in 2011 this share is projected to increase to 47 per cent.[7] It has also been suggested that the World Bank and other MDBs made a 'massive sales pitch' at Copenhagen 'to persuade the ministers and heads of state present to channel the promised fast track financing ... through the CIFs'.[8] As a result, the World Bank received new pledges of US$90 million to start up the CIF project 'Scaling up Renewable Energy Program in Low Income Countries'.[9]

Although no funds have been explicitly created to challenge or compete with the UNFCCC funds – indeed, the CIFs have a self-imposed 'sunset clause' to conclude operations in 2012 – the likely allocation of the Copenhagen fast-start funds to and considerable donor support for the CIFs may suggest that their lives will be extended,[10] and that they could possibly divert funding that would otherwise have gone to the UNFCCC funds. Along with bilateral funds, they currently wield considerable power in the international financing

arena: of the approximately US$5 billion that flows outside the UNFCCC system, the CIFs are expected to disburse US$1.5 billion.[11]

As discussed in the previous section,[12] climate funds managed by the GEF and the Adaptation Fund are accountable to the UNFCCC Conference of the Parties (COP) to varying degrees. The CIFs, by contrast, are run by the World Bank, which has been criticized for its decision-making structure, dubbed 'exclusive, offering many member countries too little voice and too few opportunities for participation'.[13] Bilateral funds also appear to have been designed with 'limited involvement of potential recipient countries'.[14] Other concerns include the fact that funding is provided as a mixture of loans and grants, which count towards countries' ODA commitments,[15] and that direct or indirect conditionalities may be imposed on recipients of the funds.[16]

These features put many bilateral and multilateral funds at odds with the general principles of climate finance: that the polluter pays; that funding should be 'new and additional', adequate and predictable; and that it would be administered with 'equitable and balanced representation of all Parties within a transparent system of governance'. Indeed, donor country preferences for bilateral aid and channelling multilateral funds through the World Bank have not increased levels of trust among developing countries when it comes to the financing of climate projects. In early 2010 Bangladesh rejected the terms of a £60 million grant of climate aid from the UK, because it was to be channelled through the World Bank.[17] The government stated an unequivocal preference for the funds to go through the UN, fearing that the current terms would 'attach unfavourable "strings and conditions"'. Civil society commentators saw this as an example of the UK government attempting to 'weaken the argument for channelling funds through the United Nations or national funds'. Following a two-day meeting between the governments, however, Bangladesh accepted both the terms and the funds.[18]

As an example of a fund set up to pilot programmes for climate change resilience (i.e. adaptation), the CIF's Pilot Program for Climate Resilience (PPCR) does not appear to measure up to the standards of the Kyoto Protocol's Adaptation Fund, which has long been developing countries' preferred channel for the funds.[19] The PPCR has been accused of 'competing' with the Adaptation Fund for pledges[20] and of having what could be considered a 'retrograde governance structure',[21] and on the grounds that its implementing agencies, as MDBs, have a 'poor record of community participation and consultation'.[22]

As in the Adaptation Fund, the PPCR's governing body enjoys 'North–South parity' in its decision-making.

The Strategic Climate Fund, under which it works, however, has a governance structure that leaves 'room for improvement' in terms of controlling interests on the board. Although country participation conforms with the PPCR, there is the addition of a World Bank representative and another representing MDBs, and the stipulation that the permanent co-chair be a World Bank vice president, while the 'country' co-chair rotates.[23] Indeed, it has been suggested that, as the secretariat and an implementing agency of the funds, the World Bank has 'significant influence over priorities'.[24] In terms of participation by civil society, there are now formal observer roles in the governance of the trust funds and, while there was little involvement of civil society in the development of the Clean Technology Fund, the Forest Investment Program under the CIFs has encouraged considerably more participation.[25] It has been criticized, however, as being under-resourced and lacking redress mechanisms to ensure that concerns are addressed.[26]

Although it is important to acknowledge that donor countries are beginning to take their commitments to fund climate change seriously, successful adaptation and mitigation will require the participation, cooperation and collaboration of all parties and demand trust on all sides. The UNFCCC process has striven for equity in decision-making between North and South and for meaningful participation by civil society actors. Indeed, progress was made in Cancún in 2010, where the parties agreed to establish the Green Climate Fund, through which a 'significant share of new multilateral funding for adaptation' should flow.[27] Significantly the Fund will have equal representation of developing and developed countries on its board, signalling considerable progress in the long-term. However, no such agreement was made in relation to fast-start funds. These parallel funding structures outside the UNFCCC risk eroding trust in the system if they are seen to undermine the success of internationally agreed mechanisms to combat climate change.

Notes

1. Rebecca Dobson works for the TI Secretariat in Berlin and is a contributing editor to the *Global Corruption Report*.
2. For adaptation, these would include the funds managed under the Global Environment Facility (GEF) and the Adaptation Fund. See Richard Klein, section 5.1 in this volume.
3. The World Resources Institute (WRI) has produced the 'Summary of Developed Country Fast-Start Climate Finance Pledges', available on its website at www.wri.org.
4. See Gareth Porter et al., *New Finance for Climate Change and the Environment* (Washington, DC: WWF and Heinrich Böll Stiftung North America, 2008) and Neil Bird and Leo Peskett, 'Recent Bilateral Initiatives for Climate Financing: Are They Moving in the Right Direction?', Opinion no. 112 (London: Overseas Development Institute [ODI], September 2008).
5. The CIFs consist of two funds, the Clean Technology Fund and the Strategic Climate Fund, and have been designed to pilot low-carbon and climate-resilient development. The Strategic Climate Fund houses the Pilot Program for Climate Resilience (PPCR – focusing on adaptation actions), the Forest Investment Program and the Scaling up Renewable Energy Program in Low Income Countries.
6. Liane Schalatek et al., *Where's the Money? The Status of Climate Finance post-Copenhagen*, Climate Finance Policy Brief no. 1 (Washington, DC, and London: Heinrich Böll Stiftung North America and ODI, 2010), p. 2.
7. WRI, 'Summary of climate finance pledges put forward by developed countries', as at 18 February 2010. Updated figures from November 2010 state that the UK has pledged £430 million to the World Bank and the US will channel 60 per cent of its funds through multilateral channels and the rest bilaterally. See: http://pdf.wri.org/climate_finance_pledges_2010-11-24.pdf.
8. Schalatek et al. (2010), p. 3.
9. Ibid.
10. European Network on Debt and Development (Eurodad), 'Why the World Bank Is Ill-fitted for Climate Finance: Key Principles and Recommendations for Equitable Climate Finance Governance', position paper (Brussels: Eurodad, 2010).
11. Frank Ackerman, *Financing the Climate Mitigation and Adaptation Measures in Developing Countries*, G-24 Discussion Paper no. 57 (Geneva: UN Conference on Trade and Development [UNCTAD], 2009), p. 7.
12. See Richard Klein, section 5.1 in this volume.

13. Yale Center for the Study of Globalization, *Repowering the World Bank for the 21ˢᵗ Century: Report of the High Level Commission on Modernization of the World Bank Group Governance* (New Haven, CT: Yale Center for the Study of Globalization, 2009), p. ix.

14. Porter et al. (2008), p. 8.

15. Benito Müller, *International Adaptation Finance: The Need for an Innovative and Strategic Approach* (Oxford: Oxford Institute for Energy Studies [OIES], 2008).

16. Eurodad (2010), p. 2. While no specific conditions are placed on countries receiving climate finance, they are often required to have World Bank programmes in place to be eligible for the funds, 'effectively establishing cross-conditionality between general bank lending and climate finance'.

17. David Adam and John Vidal, 'Bangladesh rejects the terms for £60m of climate aid from UK', *Guardian* (UK), 15 February 2010.

18. Ibid.

19. See Richard Klein and Britta Horstmann articles in this chapter. See Richard Klein, section 5.1 and Britta Horstmann, section 5.2, in this volume.

20. Bretton Woods Project, 'Update on the Climate Investment Funds' (London: Bretton Woods Project, March 2010), p. 5.

21. Müller (2008), p. 10.

22. Bretton Woods Project (March 2010), p. 5.

23. Müller (2008), p. 10.

24. Athena Ballesteros et al., *Power, Responsibility, and Accountability: Re-Thinking the Legitimacy of Institutions for Climate Finance*, working paper (Washington, DC: WRI, 2009), p. 26.

25. Ballesteros et al. (2009), p. 27.

26. See Bretton Woods Project, 'Update on the Climate Investment Funds' (London: Bretton Woods Project, July 2010), p. 1, and Anju Sharma, *The Reformed Financial Mechanism of the UNFCCC: Renegotiating the Role of Civil Society in the Governance of Climate Finance* (Oxford: OIES, 2010), pp. 21–25.

27. Draft decision -/CP.16, Outcome of the work of the Ad Hoc Working Group on Long-Term Cooperative Action under the Convention, paragraph 102.

5.1.2

Climate change funds and development

How to ensure transparency and access to information on funding streams for adaptation

Adil Najam[1]

The international community has stated a commitment to provide 'new and additional'[2] funding to make adaptation to climate change a reality. It is still unclear, though, how much funding will be required, how much of it will be raised or from whom and on what principle, and – most importantly – how and what spending decisions will be made. What is clear is that, to be effective, any funding mechanism(s) to emerge from the current structure of fragmented agencies will have to be both transparent and accountable.[3] Reducing corruption, increasing transparency and getting the system right from the beginning means making sure that financial flows are traceable and that information is available on where they come from, where they go and how they are spent.[4]

Although there are specific funds dedicated to funding adaptation activities,[5] a large proportion of adaptation need is currently met and will continue to be catered for through the deployment of existing and future development funds.[6] At the level of implementation, the merging of development and adaptation is necessary, as the aims of the two are often the same; levels of development are one of the most reliable indicators of vulnerability or resilience to climate change. At the point at which money flows into the system, however, it is important that funding earmarked for adaptation is disaggregated from traditional development aid, in order to ensure that it is truly 'new and additional' and does not divert funding away from other priorities. As such, the climate change and development communities will need to collaborate to meet their common goals, requiring common reporting guidelines and internationally agreed criteria to measure adaptation and development outcomes. Increasing access to information and ensuring transparency in both adaptation and development funding will be the surest way to ensure that both adaptation and development funds are accountable and effective.

Designing effective and 'countable' adaptation financing

The next stage, therefore, is to propose a modest but meaningful first step towards a more effective system of adaptation financing.

A good beginning would be to set up a *global adaptation funding tracking system,* which would become a central pivot in any future adaptation-funding architecture.[7] There has been considerable debate on how this can be done most effectively. Developing country proponents have suggested a centralization of adaptation funds under the United Nations Framework Convention on Climate Change (UNFCCC), so as to ensure a harmonized governance of funding, while developed countries have for the most part advocated a more decentralized system relying on existing institutions.[8] This impasse is unlikely to be resolved in the near future, but the need to track development and adaptation funds is urgent. As such, a common system to 'tag' and 'track' the whole range of funding available for adaptation funding would be a step towards addressing the 'lack of confidence' in the current structure, and would provide reliable data on what flows of finance actually contribute to climate change adaptation.[9]

Currently, there is no effective way of tracking such funds. A 2009 study on EU members' commitments for providing financial aid under the 2001 Bonn Declaration has found that the implementation of the declaration was 'difficult to monitor'.[10] The study found flaws in the 'quality and comparability' of national communications to the UNFCCC and that a 'higher quality and consistency of information' would be required to determine whether the Bonn targets had actually been met.[11] As with the Bonn Declaration, recent commitments from donor countries, such as those in the Copenhagen Accord, will come from a number of sources: 'public and private, bilateral and multilateral, including alternative sources of finance'.[12] As such, it is likely that, unless a more transparent and robust system of monitoring and reporting funds is established, it will be similarly 'difficult' to determine whether or not funding commitments have been met.

As recognized by Benito Müller, Director, Energy and Environment at the Oxford Institute for Energy Studies (OIES), in order for financial flows to be monitored and to ensure that donor countries live up to their commitments, the COP will have to list conditions under which contributions can be included.[13] Clarity on what constitutes 'new and additional' funding and what forms of private finance can be counted needs to be established. In the absence of such criteria, however, some experimental tracking of funds has begun. For example, the Global Environment Facility (GEF) and the World Bank Climate Investment Funds have sought to track their climate investments. Some rudimentary tagging of development aid for climate adaptation has also been done by various donor countries, both in terms of their reporting to international agencies such as the UNFCCC and for domestic purposes.[14] These efforts tend to be fairly simple estimations of the 'ins and outs' of monetary flows in well-defined and relatively small systems, however; they lack a common accounting framework and sometimes are internally inconsistent, and the data they report can be 'limited and incomplete'.[15]

Perhaps the most interesting, but very recent, international experiment is the Organisation for Economic Co-operation and Development's Development Assistance Committee (OECD-DAC) Rio Markers, refined in January 2010, which attempt to tag OECD aid flows in relation to the objectives of the Rio Declaration on Environment and Development, and now include a marker for climate adaptation.[16] Although the OECD data are generally considered reliable and comparable, they are not universal and limited to official development assistance (ODA) flows. More importantly, however, the system is rather crude; the markers are still very broad, they tend to be applied inconsistently and they measure intention in use rather than actual deployment.[17] As such, even the OECD-DAC recognizes that this 'does *not* represent an exact quantification of aid towards climate change adaptation'.[18]

Although these experiments are limited in scope and have obvious imperfections in terms of measurability and comparability, they emerge from a need for transparent, accessible and comparable information on climate financing. Expanding these experiments to encompass all development flows and to disaggregate climate adaptation and development clearly and track both simultaneously will require a larger institutional infrastructure and significant investments in methodological innovation. Such initiatives do give us a set of ideas on which to build a more comprehensive system, however.

Comprehensive tagging

It is clear that a methodology needs to be established to monitor the flow of adaptation funding through multiple channels. The system should encourage climate investments to be tagged for their developmental benefits, in the same way that adaptation benefits are tagged on development funding. This will involve collaboration between the climate change and development fields in order to develop consistent criteria that can be used in both realms, to ensure that all channels of financing are measured in a coordinated, coherent and comparable manner.

A unified system of tracking

With clearly defined criteria, multiple institutions and reporting sources will have to be registered under a *global adaptation funding tracking system*. The system should be agreed, supported and managed by a consortium of international organizations. This could be led by institutions such as the UN Environment Programme (UNEP), the UN Development Programme (UNDP) and the World Bank (similar to the current composition of the GEF), with advisory roles for the UNFCCC, in terms of its climate expertise, and OECD-DAC, in terms of its financial tracking expertise.

Certifying and reporting funds

The current format for development funding under the OECD-DAC and the reporting requirements under the UNFCCC national communications would have to be adapted to report consistently on flows of finance. Whereas at present funds such as those tracked by the OECD-DAC are reported and certified by donor countries as a form of 'self-certification', certification and reporting could be done jointly by donor and recipient countries.[19] With clear and transparent criteria for the certification of both climate and development activities, the risk of recipient countries being pressured to overlook certain criteria at the risk of losing donor funding would be reduced.[20] Furthermore, reporting by recipients would ensure that not only declarations and 'intentions' are accounted for, but also the disbursement of funds.

Oversight and compliance

Once funds are reported consistently, a system to verify and oversee the funds should be open to as many stakeholders as possible. In order to encourage wide participation, the format of the global adaptation funding tracking system could be structured in a 'wiki-style' format, with open access to enable interested and informed actors to validate the information provided on the funding streams. The role of civil society and independent experts in monitoring funds through a system of cross-checking would enhance the system by reducing opportunities for corruption, including the diversion of funds to other sectors.[21]

With clear criteria, tracking systems, coherent reporting and independent oversight, donors' compliance with funding commitments, particularly their pledges that are additional to development aid, will be easier to identify. In the event that compliance mechanisms are put in place to ensure that donors live up to their commitments, access to information and transparency will be crucial to monitoring this compliance.

Conclusions

A centralized global register that can track all funds – climate and development alike – and tag them for both their development and adaptation benefits would enable better coordination of activities, reduce duplication and fund fragmentation, and enhance transparency. This calls for the emerging system to go beyond the boundaries of traditional climate financing:

- *Beyond declarations.* Given the long history of unfulfilled commitments on climate financing, donor countries must be held accountable. The current sense of impunity that prevails in the climate regime, whereby commitments are declaratory rather than a legal obligation, needs to be turned on its head.[22]
- *Beyond additionality.* Ensuring that adaptation funding is 'new and additional' is fundamental, but it is clear that the scale of the adaptation challenge is greater than anything that can be addressed by specific adaptation funds alone. Effective adaptation

financing will require the notion of simple additionality to give way to a more nuanced concept of complementarity: adaptation funds must be utilized in ways that ensure that developing countries' adaptation goals are met without compromising their development priorities.

- *Beyond the UNFCCC.* Although climate institutions, principally the UNFCCC, will inevitably be one of the main channels through which adaptation resources will flow, they are unlikely to be – and should not be – the only channels for such funds. Additional capacity will be needed in both development and climate change institutions, so that needs are met transparently and effectively in both domains.
- *Beyond carbon.* Adaptation benefits cannot be measured with the same currencies that are used for mitigation: money and carbon. It is necessary, therefore, to develop a currency with which to measure and account for adaptation actions and ensure that funds are being spent effectively.

Without consensus on what these metrics should be there is the potential for institutional turf battles between the climate and development community over how funding should be classified.

In the absence of a collaborative, transparent and accountable system with clear criteria for measuring and systems for tracking adaptation and development benefits, it will be impossible to ensure that donor commitments to both adaptation and development are met. Instituting a *global adaptation funding tracking system* in the context of current institutions and funding flows would be a first step on the path to ensuring the transparency, accountability and effectiveness of adaptation measures.

Notes

1. Adil Najam is the Frederick S. Pardee professor of global public policy at Boston University. He also serves as the director of the Pardee Center for the Study of the Longer-Range Future and a professor of international relations and of geography and environment.
2. It is still unresolved how baselines for 'new and additional' finance should be established, but in essence the term means that finance flowing to climate change activities should be 'new and additional' to already pledged development aid. For a discussion on how such baselines could be established, see Martin Stadelmann et al., *Baseline for Trust: Defining 'New and Additional' Climate Funding* (London: International Institute for Environment and Development [IIED], 2010).
3. See Adil Najam et al., *Global Environmental Governance: A Reform Agenda* (Winnipeg: International Institute for Sustainable Development [IISD], 2006). There have been a number of suggestions as to what kind of institutional arrangements should be made for the governance of climate funds, principally whether these should be consolidated funds managed by the UNFCCC or whether the current multiple flows of money should be maintained with a registry to track funds allocated to climate change activities. See Benito Müller, *The Reformed Financial Mechanism of the UNFCCC*, part II, *The Question of Oversight: Post-Copenhagen Synthesis Report* (Oxford: Oxford Institute for Energy Studies [OIES], 2010), and David Reed, *The Institutional Architecture for Financing a Global Climate Deal: An Options Paper* (Washington, DC: Technical Working Group on the Institutional Architecture for Climate Finance, 2009).
4. Remi Moncel et al., *Counting the Cash: Elements of a Framework for the Measurement, Reporting and Verification of Climate Finance*, working paper (Washington, DC: World Resources Institute [WRI], 2009).
5. See Richard Klein, section 5.1 in this volume.
6. It is estimated that US$4–37 billion a year will be required to climate-proof adaptation-related activities in developing countries. See World Bank, *Development and Climate Change: A Strategic Framework for the World Bank Group*, technical report (Washington, DC: World Bank, 2008), p. 65.
7. For a related proposal, see Adil Najam and Miquel Muñoz, *Tracking Global Environmental Financing: A Proposal*, Global Environmental Governance (GEG) Briefing Paper no. 1 (Winnipeg: IISD, 2008).

8. For a discussion on the different approaches to managing global climate finance, see Reed (2009).
9. Ibid., p. 2.
10. Marc Pallemaerts and Jonathan Armstrong, *Financial Support to Developing Countries for Climate Change Mitigation and Adaptation: Is the EU Meeting Its Commitments?* (London: Institute for European Environmental Policy [IEEP], 2009), pp. 5–6.
11. Ibid., pp. 15–16.
12. Article 8, Copenhagen Accord, December 2009.
13. Müller (2010), p. 73.
14. For example, the UK's development agency, the Department for International Development (DfID), allocates sector codes to funding projects and programmes, as do many other development assistance agencies around the world, for their domestic reporting purposes.
15. Jessica Brown and Nanki Kaur, 'Financing Adaptation: Matching Form with Function', background note (London: Overseas Development Institute [ODI], 2009); and J. Timmons Roberts et al., 'Has Foreign Aid Been Greened?', *Environment*, vol. 50 (2009), pp. 24–35, at www.environmentmagazine.org/Archives/Back%20Issues/January-February%202009/RobertsParksTierneyHicks-full.html.
16. World Bank, 'Monitoring Climate Finance and ODA', Issues Brief no. 1 (Washington, DC: World Bank, 2010).
17. Moncel et al. (2009).
18. OECD, 'OECD Development Assistance Committee Tracks Aid in Support of Climate Change Mitigation and Adaptation', information note (Paris: OECD, December 2009); emphasis added.
19. Müller (2010), p. 76, discusses both recipient and self-certification of funds.
20. Müller (2010), p. 76, argues that 'simplicity and transparency' are the keys to 'avoid recipients feeling that they are compelled to certify'.
21. Alex Wilks, *Climate Adaptation Funding: Lessons from Development Finance,* discussion paper (Brussels: European Network on Debt and Development [Eurodad], 2010).
22. Adil Najam and Mark Halle, *Global Environmental Governance: The Challenge of Accountability*, Sustainable Development Insights no. 5 (Boston: Frederick S. Pardee Center for the Study of the Longer-Range Future, 2010).

5.2

Promoting an effective and transparent use of funds through the Adaptation Fund

Britta Horstmann[1]

As a new financing institution under the Kyoto Protocol, the Adaptation Fund is about to begin disbursing funds to help developing countries adapt to the adverse effects of climate change. It has the objective of financing concrete adaptation activities, especially in those countries that are 'particularly vulnerable' to the effects of climate change. It is estimated that the amount of available finance under the fund will be in the range US$297–438 million between 2010 and the end of 2012.[2]

The Adaptation Fund marks a change in the international climate change financing architecture, by introducing unique institutional features that meet the long-standing demands of developing countries in climate change negotiations. These features comprise independence from official development assistance, the possibility for developing countries to access funds directly and a governance structure that provides for a majority of developing countries on its board.[3] The Adaptation Fund still needs to pass an on-road test, however, and demonstrate that it can successfully channel funds from the global level to the national level for the implementation of adaptation activities. In particular, it has the task of demonstrating that the current institutional provisions will promote good governance – in this case the use of entrusted power and resources for purposes mandated by Parties to the Kyoto Protocol and the Adaptation Fund Board.

The question of how the Adaptation Fund can promote the effective use of funds becomes fundamental to ensuring that it meets its objectives. To disclose possible risks of corruption as well as entry points for its prevention, this brief analysis looks at the fund's mandate and goals, its institutional arrangements and responsibilities, and its current provisions and entry points to promote the goal-oriented use of resources. Drawing on experiences from similar funding institutions and development cooperation, it concludes by proposing ideas as to how the policies and guidelines of the fund could be improved with regard to the transparent and effective use of its resources.

Mandate and goals of the Adaptation Fund

The ultimate objective of the Adaptation Fund is to provide international financial assistance to developing countries to adapt to the adverse effects of climate change. It pursues the implementation of a central commitment made by developed country Parties to the UNFCCC and the Kyoto Protocol to support developing country parties that are particularly vulnerable to the adverse effects of climate change to meet the costs of adaptation.[4] To finance this, the Adaptation Fund receives a 2 per cent share of the proceeds from the Clean Development Mechanism (CDM).[5]

The Adaptation Fund will finance concrete adaptation projects and programmes,[6] thereby distinguishing it from past adaptation funding under the UNFCCC, which had for a long time been directed at financing national communications and the preparation of national adaptation programmes of action (NAPAs), but not the implementation of adaptation projects. A concrete adaptation project is defined as 'a set of activities aimed at addressing the adverse impacts of and risks posed by climate change', and projects 'concern discrete activities with a collective objective(s) and concrete outcomes and outputs that are more narrowly defined in scope, space, and time'.[7] The support of adaptation activities is guided by principles and modalities with a clear focus on transparency and accountability,[8] and only those activities for which sufficient information is available to warrant the adaptation activity will be financed.[9] The challenge will be to ensure that these principles are considered and implemented by the institutions and actors involved.

Institutional arrangement and responsibilities

As a new institution, the Adaptation Fund cannot draw on existing institutional arrangements, rules and procedures that support these goals and principles. To establish the necessary arrangements, the Adaptation Fund Board, as the operating entity of the fund, has the mandate to operationalize the fund and elaborate the necessary documents under the guidance of Kyoto Protocol parties, to whom it is accountable.[10] The board supervises and manages the fund and decides on the allocation of funds and project proposals, supported by two committees: the Projects and Programme Review Committee (PPRC) and the Ethics and Finance Committee (EFC).

The board is responsible for the development of criteria to ensure that the entities that implement adaptation activities at the national level 'have the capacity to implement the administrative and financial management guidelines of the Adaptation Fund', for monitoring and reviewing the implementation of the fund's operations and for regularly reviewing performance reports on activities, including their independent evaluation and auditing.[11]

Although the Adaptation Fund Board decides on allocation criteria between countries to ensure balanced and equitable access,[12] it is up to national governments to decide on allocation criteria within their country. Funding can be made available for national-, regional- and community-level activities.[13] As the fund adopts a country-driven approach,[14] it will be the responsibility of governments or national-level stakeholders to define the characteristics of an adaptation project or programme in more detail.

The responsible institution at the national level that can endorse funding proposals on behalf of a government will be either a national implementing entity (NIE) or a multilateral implementing entity (MIE), which are designated by the government in question and approved by the Adaptation Fund Board (see also figure 5.2). The implementing entity bears the 'full responsibility for the overall management of the projects and programmes', including 'all financial, monitoring, and reporting responsibilities' (such as for project performance reports).[15] Furthermore, it also oversees the executing entities (EEs), such as non-governmental organizations (NGOs) or government agencies that execute adaptation projects and programmes.

The option to access resources directly through a national-level entity, the NIE, is a new and innovative funding modality in the international climate change finance architecture. In the past, it was possible to access funding under the UNFCCC only by using the services and established institutional structures of certain multilateral banks or organizations. The introduction of the direct access modality requires the board to set up new safeguards for the effective use of funds. To this end, the operational policies, guidelines and standards that have been introduced by the board are particularly important.

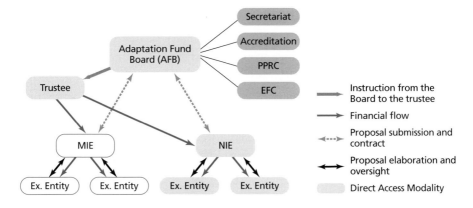

Source: Adapted from AFB/Operation Policies and Guidelines.

Figure 5.2 Institutional structure of the Adaptation Fund

Current guidelines and standards

The operational guidelines and standards delineate important aspects of funding procedures and are important for safeguarding the quality of operations. In particular, those concerning the assessment of funding proposals, the governance processes and institutional capacities at the national level and the monitoring of projects and programmes deserve specific attention.

Transparency and assessment of funding proposals

Although the governance of the Adaptation Fund is guided by the principle of transparency, there are relatively few specific provisions to promote transparency in decision-making in terms of funding proposals and the related processes of proposal elaboration, fund management and reporting. Usually, transparency is enhanced by two important approaches: stakeholder participation and the disclosure of information. The Adaptation Fund Board has two related, but weak, requirements in this regard.

The template for project and programme proposal requires a description of the consultative process, including a list of stakeholders that have been consulted during the project preparation phase.[16] This is not, however, an explicit criterion for project assessment according to the strategic priorities and guidelines of the Adaptation Fund,[17] and is therefore unlikely to be included in the technical review of the proposal by the secretariat, which is then forwarded to the PPRC for further assessment. There is also no assessment of the quality of the stakeholder participation. These weaknesses reduce the onus on implementing entities to ensure transparency and participation in fund allocation and decision-making processes. The participation of national and local stakeholders can be important in improving the quality of funded activities, as many criteria for the assessment of funding proposals and eligibility[18] are very broad and/or need further scrutiny than would be possible by the secretariat or the PPRC. This includes, for example, the assessment of economic, social and environmental benefits or the quality of information an activity is based on.

A related challenge for interested stakeholders is that information about the consultative process may be made available only after this process has been concluded and project proposals have been presented to the board. Under the current operational policies and guidelines, funding proposals have to be made available online only after they are approved by the board.[19] As a result, interested or affected stakeholders who have not been involved in the formal consultation process may not be able to comment on proposals until the process has been completed. The level of detail provided by the Adaptation Fund Board would also have to be comprehensive enough to enable informed judgements on the quality of project proposals. The level of detail to be disclosed online by the Adaptation Fund Board is not specified in the guidelines. Without such guidelines or requirements for stakeholder participation or disclosure of information, transparency may very well vary according to national-level guidelines and practices.

It is likely that the rules will be changed in the near future. At the request of NGOs, the board has already decided to post funding proposals online once they have been received and screened by the secretariat. A facility allows the public to comment on the proposals until a decision has been taken by the board.[20]

Fund allocation at the national level

A crucial issue at the national level will be how projects and programme proposals are selected for presenting to the Adaptation Fund Board. The definition of a 'concrete adaptation project or programme' provided by the board is very broad and does not provide practical guidance for prioritization. The implementing entity or national government will still need to define what 'collective objectives' and 'concrete outcomes' of an adaptation activity are, what and who they are for, or where and when they take place.

A strategic priority of the fund is that eligible parties have to give special attention to the particular needs of the most vulnerable communities.[21] There is no agreed-upon metric or criteria for assessment,[22] however, and the board has not further defined the concept of vulnerability. As such, concepts of 'adaptation activity' and 'vulnerability' both require political decision-making at the national level. It is important, therefore, that the governance processes and the information and criteria a decision is based on are considered legitimate by society, made transparent to the public and allow for the participation of relevant stakeholders.[23]

Institutional capacities of implementing entities

Central to the process of fund allocation and management at the national level are the implementing entities.[24] The requirements for the accreditation of these entities to access funding from the Adaptation Fund concentrate on fiduciary risk management. These comprise competence in financial management, international-standard auditing capacity, institutional capacity (for example, for internationally recognized procurement practices or for independent monitoring and evaluation), transparency, self-investigative powers and anti-corruption measures.[25] The standards are a prerequisite for accreditation to the fund, are checked by an accreditation panel and are valid for five years.[26]

Project- and programme-level monitoring

The implementing entities play a central role in the monitoring and evaluation of project and programme implementation and results.[27] To be accredited, implementing entities have to demonstrate their capacities for monitoring and prove that relevant systems are in place. The arrangements for monitoring and evaluation must be outlined in the funding proposal and are part of the technical review. Evaluations are conducted after the funded activities have taken place; evaluation is obligatory for activities above US$1 million, but small-scale projects below this amount are subject to terminal evaluation only if it is deemed necessary by the board.[28]

Implementing entities have to contract external evaluators to conduct independent evaluations.[29] The quality of the reports depends heavily on what the evaluator is asked to evaluate and what kind of methodology is used, however. A related challenge for the evaluation of projects is the ambiguity of the terms 'adaptation' and 'vulnerability' and the difficulty in establishing an objective metric, which renders any evaluation a difficult task. As to judging whether or not an activity leads to greater adaptive capacity, evaluations are unlikely to be conclusive.

The board intends to put in place a results-based management framework for the fund and consider the process by which this framework will support projects and programmes.[30] This is not yet finalized,[31] but when it is it will be an important step in bolstering the effectiveness of financial support, as it will establish objectives and indicators as well as baselines for activities, drawing, for example, on information from vulnerability and needs assessments.

Conclusions and outlook

This analysis has shown that the institutional capacities and the governance framework at the national level play a pivotal role in the effective implementation of adaptation activities financed by the Adaptation Fund. The provisions of the fund on efficiency, transparency and effectiveness are therefore necessary, but they are not sufficient to promote a goal-oriented use of funds. The collaboration of various stakeholders, particularly national-level stakeholders, will be necessary to make sure that the provisions are implemented effectively.

The Adaptation Fund is at an early stage, and this brief analysis can only highlight some possible entry points for corruption and its prevention. As there are few general formulae for reducing corruption in a sustained way and little empirical evidence to inform the effectiveness of anti-corruption activities at the outset,[32] a successful approach to good governance will require continuous attention and a process of 'learning by doing' to ensure that strategies are appropriate in different national contexts.

Based on the experience of development cooperation and anti-corruption measures in similar institutions, the Adaptation Fund Board may wish to consider the following recommendations to promote the transparent and effective use of funds:

- Provide information on corruption on the Adaptation Fund website, including analytical toolkits, best-practice examples or procurement procedures that meet audit requirements. There are many existing guidelines that could be adapted for this purpose, such as the OECD-DAC Joint Venture for Procurement's guidance notes.
- Liaise with other stakeholders and offer support for NIEs regarding their duties and operations, for example to meet the fiduciary risk management standards throughout the accreditation period.
- Disclose the necessary information and data for project monitoring, evaluation and the tracking of financial flows so as to ensure that independent oversight can take place. This should also include contact persons at the national level or information on the institutional arrangements and responsibilities at the national level that might be provided by eligible Parties to the Adaptation Fund Board.
- Check the independence of monitoring and evaluation specialists who are contracted by implementing entities.
- Facilitate the exchange of views by various stakeholders on lessons learnt as to how to improve effectiveness and transparency in the use of funds, including the question of how vulnerable communities should be considered.
- Introduce a complaints mechanism for funded projects and programmes.
- Liaise with stakeholders and donors to facilitate or support the engagement of civil society, journalists or independent research institutes. An example of international support is the Partnership for Transparency Fund.

Notes

1. Britta Horstmann is a research associate at the German Development Institute.
2. Adaptation Fund Board, 'Financial Status of the Adaptation Fund Trust Fund and the Administrative Trust Fund (as at 30 April 2010)', document code AFB/EFC.1/5 (Bonn: UNFCCC, 20 May 2010).
3. Further analysis on the institutional governance framework of the Adaptation Fund can be found in Richard Klein, section 5.1 in this volume. See also Britta Horstmann, 'Operationalizing the Adaptation Fund: Challenges in Allocating Funds to the Vulnerable' (forthcoming in *Climate Policy*).
4. Article 4.4, UNFCCC, and article 12.8, Kyoto Protocol.
5. Decision 10/CP.7, annex 2; see also decision 5/CP.6. See Richard Klein, section 5.1 in this volume.
6. Decisions 10/CP.7, 1/CMP.4, 1/CMP.3, 5/CMP.2 and 28/CMP.1.
7. Adaptation Fund Board, *Operational Policies and Guidelines for Parties to Access Resources from the Adaptation Fund* (Bonn: UNFCCC, 2009), paragraph 10. The Adaptation Fund can also use the share of proceeds to support activities laid down in paragraph 8 of decision 5/CP.7 or to cover administrative expenses of the fund; see decision 10/CP.7.
8. These include: transparency and openness in the governance of the fund; accountability in the management, operation and use of the funds; efficiency and effectiveness in the management, operation and governance of the fund; sound financial management, including the use of international fiduciary standards; clearly defined responsibilities for quality assurance, management and implementation; independent monitoring, evaluation and financial audits; and no duplication with other sources of funding for adaptation in the use of the Adaptation Fund (decision 5/CMP.2, paragraphs 1 and 2).
9. Decision 5/CP.7, paragraph 8.
10. Decisions 28/CMP.1 and 1/CMP.3, paragraph 4. This operationalization started in 2008 and is close to being completed.
11. Decision 1/CMP.3, paragraph 5.
12. Decision 1/CMP.4, annex IV, paragraph 16 (c).
13. Decision 5/CMP.2, paragraph 2.
14. Decisions 2/CMP.1 and 5/CMP.2, paragraph 2.
15. Adaptation Fund Board (2009), paragraphs 27 and 48.
16. See www.adaptation-fund.org/node/7.
17. See paragraph 15.
18. Adaptation Fund Board (2009), annex 3.
19. Adaptation Fund Board (2009), paragraphs 40 and 41.
20. Adaptation Fund Board, 'Draft Report of the Adaptation Fund Board to the Conference of the Parties Serving as the Meeting of the Parties to the Kyoto Protocol at Its Sixth Session', document code AFB/B.11/7/Rev.1 (Bonn: UNFCCC Adaptation Fund Board, 17 September 2010).
21. Strategic Priorities, Policies and Guidelines, decision 1/ CMP.4 annex IV.
22. Jörn Birkmann (ed.), *Measuring Vulnerability to Natural Hazards: Towards Disaster Resilient Societies* (Tokyo: United Nations University Press, 2006); Gilberto C. Gallopín, 'Linkages between Vulnerability, Resilience and Adaptive Capacity', *Global Environmental Change*, vol. 16 (2006), pp. 293–303; Horstmann (forthcoming).

23. On concepts of 'adaptation' and related institutional challenges, see Britta Horstmann, *Framing Adaptation to Climate Change: A Challenge for Building Institutions*, Discussion Paper no. 23/2008 (Bonn: German Development Institute, 2008).
24. For an overview of accredited implementing entities, see www.adaptation-fund.org/node/9.
25. Adaptation Fund Board (2009), annex 2, paragraphs 53 and 54.
26. Adaptation Fund Board (2009), paragraphs 33–38.
27. Adaptation Fund Board (2009), paragraphs 48 and 49.
28. Adaptation Fund Board, (2009), paragraph 49.
29. Ibid.
30. Adaptation Fund Board (2009), paragraphs 47 and 50.
31. It is scheduled to be ready by Adaptation Fund Board meeting 12.
32. Organisation for Economic Co-operation and Development (OECD), *Synthesis of Lessons Learned of Donor Practices in Fighting Corruption* (Paris: OECD, 2003); Jens Andig and Odd-Helge Fjeldstad, *Corruption: A Review of Contemporary Research* (Bergen: Chr. Michelsen Institute, 2001); Robert Klitgaard, *Controlling Corruption* (Berkeley: University of California Press, 1988).

5.3
Climate-proofing development
Corruption risks in adaptation infrastructure

James Lewis[1]

Building climate-resistant infrastructure – whether flood walls, drainage systems or storm shelters – is one of the main tasks of adapting to climate change. Estimated annual costs could top US$100 billion by 2030.[2] Such massive flows of money being directed towards infrastructure projects – mainly in the developing world – combined with the fact that construction and public works constitute one of the world's most corrupt sectors,[3] make strong governance in this component of climate change adaptation essential.

Climate change adaptation, corruption and vulnerable populations are strongly interlinked. Corruption acts as an engine of poverty and vulnerability – creating weaknesses that are exacerbated by the changing climate.[4] Climate extremes are greatest in poorer countries, where, along with weak governance institutions, there is often endemic corruption. Within 10 years there will be a global slum population of some 1.4 billion living with inadequate water supplies, consequent unsanitary conditions and disease – making clean water and sanitation facilities an attractive target for corruption, greed, collusion and exploitation.[5] Where corruption heightens community vulnerability, it exacerbates the need for adaptation measures. In regions plagued by weak governance, adaptation responses themselves may be particularly prone to corruption.

It is of particular concern that the construction industry, long considered among the most corrupt industrial sectors,[6] will be entrusted with reducing human vulnerability. The World Bank estimates that anything from 5 to 20 per cent of construction costs are currently lost to corruption, burdening developing countries with some US$18 billion a year.[7] Much of this will be lost in countries that are vulnerable to climate change impacts; 'Baby Doc' Duvalier, for example, the former dictator of poverty-ridden and cyclone- and earthquake-prone Haiti, is reported to have amassed a private account equivalent to US$7 million.[8] In this context, it is not surprising that adaptation responses are slow.

The high levels of corruption in the construction industry are not limited to initial financial losses, but have much wider-reaching implications. The fact that corruption often leads to skewed spending priorities and substandard construction and operation has a particular poignancy for climate change adaptation, which seeks to address human vulnerability urgently and efficiently.[9] Corruption and the way its proceeds are used not only may slow down adaptation actions but may fundamentally undermine the process, by diverting funds to illegitimate projects or reducing construction standards and contributing to vulnerability.

Big budgets, big companies – big corruption risks?

Infrastructure and the procurement of public works can be either reactive projects that respond to disasters or other extreme events, or proactive in the form of climate-proofing and new infrastructure to reduce vulnerability. Such efforts will incur colossal investments, mainly from the public sector, and will need to be protected by transparent and accountable systems with rigorous safeguards at the national and local levels.

According to one estimate, annual adaptation-related costs for agriculture, water, health, coasts and ecosystems could reach US$315 billion per year, plus US$16–63 billion for upgraded infrastructure and a possible US$50 billion for extreme weather impacts not avoided by adaptation.[10] Urban infrastructure, including drainage and public buildings, together with roads account for 77 per cent of infrastructure adaptation costs.[11] Such figures are already attracting considerable notice.

Large international construction firms are already gearing up to become an integral part of mitigation and adaptation projects – the very companies that often have rather dubious records of environmental unsustainability and corruption. The 'green power building spree' is demanding planning expertise and capital that only large international engineering companies can provide.[12] In infrastructure adaptation projects, contracts are likely to go the same way. British multinational Mott MacDonald, for example, is positioning itself as a leading specialist in both adaptation and mitigation, stating that it has 'long experience, advanced expertise and international reach' in areas such as coastal zone management, infrastructure engineering and water resource management.[13]

Many such companies have faced allegations of corruption in these very same types of projects, however. In 2003 Betchel was exposed as allegedly having a 'legacy of unsustainable and destructive practices that have reaped permanent human, environmental and community devastation around the globe'.[14] Mott MacDonald faced allegations of corruption in relation to the infamous Lesotho Highlands Water Project.[15]

While the involvement of large infrastructure companies does not necessarily foreshadow corrupt corporate activities in adaptation projects, they do highlight some of the risks that have to be considered when partnering with the construction industry.

When 'business-as-usual' meets adaptation projects

There is ample reason to believe that adaptation-related infrastructure will suffer the same corruption risks inherent in any public works projects. The sector is particularly prone to corruption because it generally builds large, long-term projects for the public sector using complex supply chains.[16] Furthermore, when international companies vie for contracts abroad, the corruption risks grow larger and more difficult to detect and prosecute, as different laws and business cultures come into play.[17]

Corruption in infrastructure projects can pervade all levels and sectors of investment, rural and urban areas, projects of all sizes, and small firms and large contractors. Corruption is a risk at every point, starting with a project's needs assessment, through the preparation and bid design phases, to contractor selection and contract award, and to contract implementation and the final accounting and auditing phase.[18]

Some of the 'business-as-usual' risks in the industry have particular implications for climate adaptation projects. For example, corruption or undue influence in needs assessment can lead to skewed priorities. Governments and officials are already prone to favour grand infrastructure projects, as size itself creates opportunities for corruption and bribery. Such prestige projects can displace projects higher on the scale of social need, are often left unfinished and unused and, ultimately, can end up as environmentally destructive 'monuments to corruption'.[19]

How adaptation needs will be determined and prioritized is still unclear. As of 2010 some 6 per cent of national adaptation programme of action (NAPA) projects were classified as purely infrastructural, with many others including infrastructure or construction elements.[20] Although these projects have been devised in what is considered a participatory manner, they have yet to be implemented and there is no guidance as to which should be built most urgently. The potential for projects to be prioritized for reasons other than urgent adaptation needs is therefore very real.

Another inherent risk in infrastructure projects is the tendency for corruption to raise the price of projects while simultaneously reducing quality.[21] Designs may be manipulated to raise costs or ensure that only a few contractors can comply, or specifications can be made overly sophisticated. This can inflate both the cost and the duration of a project. When bribes are used to conceal quality defects, the result is substandard work. As many infrastructure projects are large, complex and non-standard, they are difficult to assess.[22] Moreover, governments' dual role as customer and regulator[23] of many such projects makes them particularly prone to corruption or fraud – on account of deceitful or insufficient regulatory capacity.

The impact of weak regulation leading to substandard work would be a heavy price to pay in the context of urgent adaptation needs, as the cost would probably be calculated in lives. Past experiences of environment-proofing infrastructure have demonstrated this, but further concerns are likely as climate-proofing projects are rolled out in countries with inadequate regulations or experience.

In Turkey, where an earthquake killed some 11,000 people in 1999, more than a half of all structures failed to comply with building regulations.[24] Similar scenarios can be foreseen for climate-related disasters if adaptation measures do not meet the necessary standards. Rather than increasing people's resilience to climate change, poorly managed adaptation may actually decrease it.

The many risks for adaptation projects

As governments move to build flood walls and embankments, robust drainage systems and cyclone centres for displaced persons, they will also need to ensure that old structures are retrofitted to meet new standards. Governments also need to invest in 'green' technologies so as to ensure that adaptation projects do not unduly exacerbate climate change, as the construction industry accounts for 33 per cent of CO_2 emissions.[25] These interdependent priorities must be addressed in order to preserve scarce resources, and will add to the complexity of planning and building projects.

High-pressure environments, unrealistic deadlines, urgency and haste all characterize the response to rapidly emerging climate change and may lead to multiple excuses for camouflaging corrupt practices. Pressure to complete projects could undermine planning processes, including safeguarding against projects that do not take mitigation considerations into account, such as reducing CO_2 emissions.

Corruption in the planning stages – including land acquisition, development permits and the letting of contracts – is facilitated by haste and fragmented procedures.[26]

The increased specialization that climate-proofing infrastructure entails may serve to limit the number of firms with the perceived expertise to tackle such projects, thereby limiting competition. This is worrisome, because high levels of competition are considered to be 'the single most important fact towards auction efficiency and anti-corruption'.[27] Collusion through anti-competitive cartels, bid-rigging and bribery may seriously diminish infrastructure funding, slowing down construction and skewing development so that it fails to perform as planned, thus wasting entire investments.

Furthermore, when specialist construction firms are few, competition is reduced and opportunities for inexperienced contractors and traders increase. When contracts are allocated by obligation, favour, partisanship, sectarianism or nepotism, not only does this constitute corruption but it can lead to substandard work that jeopardizes the original aims of climate-proofing to protect communities.

As mentioned, infrastructure projects often include non-standard activities that are difficult to assess and measure. This is even more so the case with adaptation projects: establishing whether a cyclone centre is 'cyclone-resistant' or an embankment is strong enough to withstand predicted floods are not simple equations. Quality control is an opportunity to determine the outcome and performance of adaptation projects and is essential for sustained investment. Governments, often responsible for assessing such projects, are frequently too ill-equipped, biased or corrupt to act effectively. Indeed, it has been acknowledged that 'it is often far easier to monitor and deter the outcomes of corruption (a collapsed building) than the act of corruption itself (the theft of resources or a payment to avoid correcting a regulatory infraction)'.[28]

In the case of adaptation projects – which are intended to save lives – this is far too late. Strategies and strict controls against endemic corruption in contexts of increased climate extremes demand correspondingly rigorous procedures for quality control. Site works need informed, alert, independent and authoritative inspectors and supervisors with clear criteria on which they base their assessments.

Finally, for climate-proof infrastructure to remain effective, it needs to be maintained. Corruption has been cited as a factor behind high levels of investment in new infrastructure with no emphasis on maintaining it.[29] The consequences of construction and maintenance failures were shockingly illustrated in New Orleans following Hurricane Katrina in 2005.[30] The breach of the sea defences – meant to protect the city – was due to the negligence of the city government, and incurred losses totalling US$71 billion.[31] This kind of structural failure, which can bring a city in the US to its knees, is surely a glimpse of the future in developing countries if adaptation measures do not succeed in increasing resilience.

Reconstruction: building it better

Increasing resilience with climate-proof infrastructure is essential, but it will never entirely alleviate the risks of catastrophe. When disasters strike, the rebuilding of infrastructure will play a large part in reconstruction efforts. The objective of post-disaster adaptation must be to 'build back better', in order to resist the increased risks inherent in climate change.

A bold illustration of the 'build back better' approach was the reconstruction of the Macedonian capital of Skopje after it was destroyed by an earthquake in 1963. Not only was all the infrastructure rebuilt so as to be earthquake-resistant, but city planning also ensured that the river Vardar was routed in order to control future flooding.[32] An achievement of this scale requires strong governance and management, and transparent sectoral and local administrations.

In cases in which there were weak and fallible institutions before a disaster, they are likely to be weaker to the point of ineffectiveness in the aftermath, when sound planning and reconstruction are needed. Without adequate and consistent measures against corruption, failed reconstruction will further weaken vulnerability to subsequent extremes, and corruption risks will be as great as those that contributed to the original destruction. In the post-conflict reconstruction in Iraq, large portions of construction budgets disappeared entirely as a result of corruption.[33] The close parallels between corruption reduction and disaster reduction have been observed by the UN International Strategy for Disaster Reduction, but little progress has been made to mainstream disaster risk reduction into social, economic, environmental and infrastructure planning and development.[34]

Conclusions: anti-corruption strategies

Taking a step back from questions of accountability and corruption, one could ask why a major emphasis of adaptation efforts is on large-scale construction projects, and whether there are any lower-cost alternatives that might actually be more effective in protecting vulnerable populations.

The answer to the first question may be because many donors and development agencies tend to distribute funds quickly and need to show tangible results, lack the capacity and willingness to oversee many small projects and are perhaps unaware of lower-cost options. The answer to the second question may well lie in improved strategic thinking and better and more participatory planning processes. What is clear is that there are considerable risks in adaptation related to large- and small-scale construction, which could undermine the whole process, making people more vulnerable rather than less. As discussed in the following section, anti-corruption strategies in the form of clear procurement guidelines and the responsible oversight of projects would be a good start.

Notes

1. James Lewis is principal of Datum International, an architectural and environmental writer and a visiting fellow in development studies at the University of Bath.
2. Anthony G. Patt et al., 'Estimating Least-Developed Countries' Vulnerability to Climate-Related Extreme Events over the Next 50 Years', *Proceedings of the National Academy of Sciences of the United States of America*, vol. 107 (2010), pp. 1333–1337.
3. See TI's Bribe Payers Index, at www.transparency.org/bpi.
4. James Lewis and Ian Kelman, 'Places, People and Perpetuity: Community Capacities in Ecologies of Catastrophe', *ACME*, vol. 9 (2010), pp. 191–220, p.199.
5. UN-HABITAT, *State of the World's Cities 2010/2011: Bridging the Urban Divide* (Nairobi: UN-HABITAT, 2010), p. 30; Kings College London, 'Humanitarian Crisis Drivers of the Future – Urban Catastrophes: the Wat/San Dimension', Humanitarian Futures Programme, October 2009, p.10.
6. Bribe Payers Index.
7. Charles Kenny, *Measuring and Reducing the Impact of Corruption in Infrastructure,* Policy Research Working Paper no. 4099 (Washington, DC: World Bank, 2006), p.4.
8. *Observer* (UK), 'Dictators have their plunder confiscated years after they were deposed', 22 November 2009.
9. Charles Kenny (2006).
10. Martin Perry et al., *Assessing the Costs of Adaptation to Climate Change: A Review of the UNFCCC and Other Recent Estimates* (London: International Institute for Environment and Development [IIED], 2009).
11. World Bank, *The Economics of Adaptation to Climate Change: A Synthesis Report* (Washington, DC: World Bank, 2010), p. 11.
12. Reuters (UK), 'Engineering giants follow the money to green power', 29 September 2009.
13. See Mott MacDonald, 'Climate change: how Mott MacDonald is developing solutions to this challenge', at www.sustainability.mottmac.com/expertise/climatechange/adaptation.
14. CorpWatch, Global Exchange and Public Citizen, 'Bechtel: Profiting from Destruction: Why the Corporate Invasion of Iraq Must Be Stopped' (San Francisco: CorpWatch, 2003).
15. For an overview of the Lesotho Highlands Water Project, see TI, *Global Corruption Report 2008: Corruption in the Water Sector* (Cambridge: Cambridge University Press, 2008). For an overview of Mott MacDonald's involvement, see *Guardian* (UK), 'No investigation into UK company over alleged corruption in Lesotho', 7 November 2008.
16. PricewaterhouseCoopers (PwC), 'Corruption Prevention in the Engineering and Construction Industry' (London: PwC, July 2009).
17. U4 Anti-Corruption Resource Centre, 'Grand Designs: Corruption Risk in Major Water Infrastructure Projects' (Bergen: Chr. Michelson Institute, November 2009).

18. TI, *Procurement Handbook: Curbing Corruption in Public Procurement – Experiences from Indonesia, Malaysia and Pakistan* (Berlin: TI, 2006). For a comprehensive list of examples of corrupt behaviour in the industry, see Catherine Stansbury and Neill Stansbury, 'Examples of Corruption in Infrastructure' (Amersham: Global Infrastructure Anti-Corruption Centre, 2008).

19. James Lewis, 'The Worm in the Bud: Corruption, Construction and Catastrophe', in Lee Bosher (ed.), *Hazards and the Built Environment* (Abingdon: Taylor & Francis, 2008), pp. 238–263.

20. UNFCCC, 'National Adaptation Programmes of Action', March 2010, at http://unfccc.int/cooperation_support/least_developed_countries_portal/submitted_napas/items/4585.php.

21. Charles Kenny, *Construction, Corruption and Developing Countries,* Policy Research Working Paper no. 4271 (Washington, DC: World Bank, 2007).

22. Ibid.

23. Ibid.

24. Ibid.

25. Chartered Institute of Building (UK), 'Industry statistics', www.ciob.org.uk/document/industry-statistics.

26. Jim Kennedy et al., 'The Meaning of "Build Back Better": Evidence from Post-Tsunami Aceh and Sri Lanka', *Journal of Contingencies and Crisis Management*, vol. 16 (2008), pp. 24–36.

27. Antonio Estache and Atsushi Iimi, 'Auctions with Endogenous Participation and Quality Thresholds: Evidence from ODA Infrastructure Procurement', ECARES Working Paper no. 2009-006 (Brussels: Université Libre de Bruxelles, 2009).

28. Kenny (2007), p. 9.

29. Ibid., p. 6.

30. *New York Times* (US), 'Ruling on Katrina flooding favors homeowners', 19 November 2009; Ed Pilkington, 'Victims of flooding during Hurricane Katrina win compensation', *Guardian* (UK), 19 November 2009.

31. *National Underwriter* (US), 'Cat losses dropped 52% over last year', 2 December 2009.

32. Vladimir B. Ladinski, 'Post 1963 Skopje Earthquake Reconstruction: Long Term Effects', in Adenrele Awotona (ed.), *Reconstruction after Disaster: Issues and Practices* (Aldershot: Ashgate, 1997), pp. 73–107; *New York Times* (US), 'Rebuilding in Haiti', 2 April 2010.

33. *New York Times* (US), 'Idle contractors add millions to Iraq rebuilding', 25 October 2006.

34. UN, *2009 Global Assessment Report on Disaster Risk Reduction: Risk and Poverty in a Changing Climate* (New York: UN, 2009).

5.3.1

Climate change, infrastructure and corruption

Chandrashekhar Krishnan[1]

Climate change and sea-level rise will have major impacts on infrastructure, particularly in the developing world. Adaptation to these impacts could include: reconstructing key infrastructure destroyed by hurricanes, cyclones and floods; constructing new or strengthening existing sea defences to protect low-lying areas; enhancing the resilience of bridges and highways to climate change; redesigning major infrastructure projects to take account of climate-related risks; and building new infrastructure, such as airports, in areas that are less vulnerable to sea-level rise.

As a result, the infrastructure industry will have a major part to play in adaptation to climate change, but it is also considered one of the most corrupt industries in the world.[2] It would therefore be prudent to ensure that corruption risks are factored into infrastructure sector responses to climate change.

It is unlikely that corruption risks in such projects will be very different from those seen traditionally. Corruption can occur during all phases of a construction project: a representative of the project owner may bribe a government or local authority official to obtain approval for a design that does not meet relevant building regulations; a qualified bidder may be rejected at the pre-qualification stage as a result of a bribe paid to a representative of the owner or engineer by another bidder; a bidder that is not necessarily the best may win a contract as a result of a bribe paid to the tender evaluation manager or a government official; a contractor may pay a bribe to the owner's representative in return for the owner issuing a variation that materially increases the contractor's scope of work; defective works may be covered up, or claims for payment may be submitted for inferior or non-existent equipment or materials; or bribes may be paid to win operation and maintenance contracts, and fraudulent practices can lead to inflated operation and maintenance costs.[3]

Transparency International has developed practical tools to reduce corruption risks in infrastructure projects, which would be applicable to projects initiated in response to climate change. TI-UK and the Global Infrastructure Anti-Corruption (GIAC) Centre have developed and disseminated a Project Anti-Corruption System (PACS) for the construction sector.[4] PACS, which targets both bribery and fraud, sets out a variety of anti-corruption standards and templates to assist project participants to implement these standards, which include independent monitoring, due diligence, contractual commitments, procurement requirements, government commitments, corporate programmes, rules for individuals, training, transparency, reporting and enforcement.[5]

The PACS standards can be used by either public- or private-sector project owners to assess their anti-corruption measures. Each PACS standard has a number of recommended measures; for example, under transparency PACS recommends that information should be 'provided in a free, easily accessible and comprehensible form, and on a prompt and regular basis'. Thus, even if certain standards are being met, the recommended measures may not be implemented in full, and PACS can highlight areas for improvement.

PACS is a highly flexible tool that can be used to assess and improve projects with the aim of reducing corruption. It is comprehensive in its coverage, but is voluntary and so may be taken in part or as a whole. As such, it could be an essential tool for emerging adaptation projects, as PACS users can adapt the measures to their local requirements, taking into consideration local laws and procedures. The integration of such anti-corruption initiatives into the climate change agenda is crucial.[6] We must not let corruption add additional costs to the burden of responding effectively to the climate change impacts in the infrastructure sector. We have the tools to fight it!

Notes

1. Chandrashekhar Krishnan is executive director of TI UK.
2. TI's 2008 Bribe Payers' Index showed that public works and construction was perceived to be one of the most corrupt industries in the world. See www.transparency.org/policy_research/surveys_indices/bpi.
3. Neill Stansbury and Catherine Stansbury, *Preventing Corruption on Construction Projects: Risk Assessment and Proposed Actions for Project Owners* (Berlin: TI, 2005).
4. See www.giaccentre.org/project_anti_corruption_system_home.php.
5. Ibid.

6.   See the GIAC Centre (http://www.giaccentre.org/) for more information on other anti-corruption programmes in the sector. For more information about the Construction Sector Transparency Initiative (CoST), which has completed its pilot phase and focuses on public sector contracting and the disclosure of information, see http://www.constructiontransparency.org/.

5.3.2

Climate-proofing and political influence in the Philippines

Segundo Romero and Aileen Laus[1]

The Philippines is an archipelago located in the typhoon belt and is visited each year by around 20 typhoons. In September 2009 Typhoon Ketsana (Ondoy) resulted in some of the worst flooding in Metro Manila in recorded history. Some 46,000 homes were completely destroyed and 261,000 were partially damaged.[2] Jerry Velasquez reported that, as '[t]he Philippines is one of the very hotspots for climate change ..., what happened during [typhoons] Ondoy and Pepeng was not the worst. The worst is still to come.'[3]

Strategies and actions: how effective are they?

Although the government has not been blind to the need for addressing climate change, it has been slow to act. In a positive step, in 2009 the government enacted the Climate Change Act, which seeks to mainstream mitigation and adaptation measures into government policy and creates a Climate Change Commission to coordinate plans for extreme weather events.[4] Local initiatives have also shown some success: the Albay Public Safety and Emergency Management Office had recorded 'zero casualties' since it began operating in 1994, despite dealing with a number of typhoons and volcanic eruptions between 1995 and 2005.[5] Assistance to local communities is also being provided through the Integrating Disaster Risk Reduction and Climate Change Adaptation project,[6] which provides local governments with training in order to anticipate the damaging effects of extreme weather.[7]

Despite these encouraging developments, the poor response following Typhoon Ketsana made it clear that preparations for climate change are lacking: thousands of people were left marooned on rooftops for hours without food, water or protection; people were swept away in the floods; and there were too few boats and amphibian trucks to rescue the thousands of people.[8] In Marikina, the worst-hit city, only two rubber boats were available for rescue operations.[9] Such experiences indicate that the country is ill-prepared and poorly resourced to deal with extreme weather events. In the area of infrastructure development for disaster risk management alone, it is estimated that Southeast Asian nations should budget amounts equivalent to 5–6 per cent of their GDP; at present they budget only 2–3 per cent. With such resource challenges, it will be difficult to fill the gap, particularly in the face of more extreme weather as a consequence of climate change.[10]

Like elsewhere in the world, much of the required adaptation in the Philippines is related to new climate-proof infrastructure that will stand the test of future typhoons and floods – a sector particularly susceptible to corruption.[11] In 2008 the Department of Public Works and Highways reported that it had completed 1189 flood control projects amounting to Philippine peso (P) 4.655 billion (approximately US$105.9 million), bringing the total completed flood control projects to 9796 since 2001.[12] Many badly needed projects have not even begun or have been severely delayed, however.

The Department of Public Works and Highways was supposed to begin the US$14 million Pasig-Marikina River Improvement Project in 2007, but three years later, in 2010, it has still to be implemented. Similarly, the Kamanava Area Flood Control and Drainage System Improvement Project in northeast Metro Manila, worth US$15 million, has also been delayed, due to 'right of way' compensation issues.[13]

Those that are built may suffer from neglect, as officials fail to maintain crucial disaster risk management facilities. The Effective Flood Control System, a P1.1 billion (approximately US$25 million) project funded by a Japanese loan, was reported to have failed on account of the neglect of the Metropolitan Manila Development Authority.[14] The chairperson of the authority denied the allegations, stating that the equipment was 'operational, but obsolete'.[15]

Many projects are built that increase dangers rather than reduce them. Corruption in the granting of permits and licences means that they may be issued for the construction of buildings in violation of zoning and building codes. In the case of Marikina and Cainta, the flood line was 17 metres above sea level, but a land development project, which had to pass through 32 signatories before being approved, allowed construction at a mere 9 metres.[16]

The result when such building regulations are flouted is increased vulnerability of communities to extreme weather conditions. This becomes even more damaging if, once a disaster strikes, situations are not managed adequately. While people were perishing in Typhoon Ketsana, the government declared a state of calamity, even in areas not affected by the storm.[17] This was extended for a year and a P10 billion supplemental budget was proposed. This led to suspicions, however, that the extended period would lead to the juggling of funds and the circumvention of laws on government procurement; indeed, it is not clear how the amusement tax that had been earmarked for flood control was spent.[18]

As the cases above illustrate, corruption has the potential to undermine adaptation efforts. The unusual access that the government has to funds, particularly in light of its implication in a number of recent corruption scandals,[19] may serve as one explanation as to why climate change adaptation strategies have been inadequate. It appears that it may be true that 'there is one factor hampering government efforts to provide relief to flood victims and improve the nation's disaster preparedness: public distrust. The distrust is fueled by suspicions that funds set aside for disaster mitigation and improvement of flood control infrastructure might end up in the pockets of the corrupt, or in the campaign kitties of potential 2010 candidates.'[20]

Notes

1. Segundo Romero, Professional Lecturer of De La Salle University, and Aileen Laus, The Asia Foundation – Philippines.
2. Inquirer.net (Philippines), 'Conditions still critical for RP typhoon victims – UN', 26 November 2009.
3. Jerry Velasquez is a senior coordinator with the UN International Strategy for Disaster Reduction body. Typhoon Pepeng hit the Philippines in late 2009. See Stephen de Tarczynski, 'Guarded optimism for new climate change law', *Global Issues*, 10 November 2009, at www.globalissues.org/news/2009/11/09/3444.
4. Ibid.
5. *Philippine Star*, 'Albay bags "Galing Pook" for disaster management', 12 February 2009.
6. The project is funded and implemented by the National Economic and Development Authority (NEDA), the UN Development Programme (UNDP) and the Australian Agency for International Development (AusAID).
7. The project has a budget of P107.89 million (A$2.5 million). See Joel Escovilla, 'Disaster risk reduction efforts started', *Business World Online*, 23 November 2009.
8. *Philippine Daily Inquirer*, 'Ondoy exposed flaws in gov't disaster system', 10 September 2009.
9. *Philippine Daily Inquirer*, 'Survivors seethe with anger', 28 September 2009.

10. Ishaan Tharoor, 'The Manila floods: why wasn't the city prepared?', Time.com, 29 September 2009.
11. See James Lewis, section 5.3 in this volume.
12. Lynda B. Valencia, 'Driving development through progressive public works projects', Positive News Media, 28 December 2009, at http://positivenewsmedia.net/am2/publish/Main_News_1/Driving_development_through_progressive_public_works_projects.shtml.
13. See Shay Cullen, 'The Scourge of Climate Change', *Impact*, vol. 43 (2009), p. 11.
14. Aries Rufo, 'P1-B flood warning system wasted due to neglect', ABS-CBNnews.com, 7 October 2009.
15. Allison Lopez, 'MMDA: flood control system working: operational but obsolete P1.1-B equipment', *Philippine Daily Inquirer*, 11 October 2009.
16. Ador Paglinawan, 'Paradox's tell all: typhoon-caused deaths and destruction were not God's acts but were results of criminal negligence', Mabuhay Radio (Philippines), 25 October 2009.
17. *Philippine Star*, 'Hindrance to disaster preparedness', 8 October 2009.
18. Ibid.
19. The excessive control that the executive has over the country's finances, without adequate oversight, has led to high levels of corruption. In contrast to the 'graft-ridden' pork barrel, which averaged P8 billion from 2004 to 2008, appropriations under the control of the president in 2009 amounted to P224.44 billion, equivalent to 16 per cent of the national budget. See Philip Tubeza, 'Graft due to Palace "holding power of purse"', Inquirer.net (Philippines), 21 May 2009.
20. *Philippine Star*, 8 October 2009.

5.4

Disrupting lives

Climate migration and corruption

Ingrid Boas and Rebecca Dobson[1]

As climate change has become a defining feature of world politics in the 21st century, international deliberations have begun to focus on adaptation: finding ways to increase resilience and decrease vulnerability to the changing climate. Corruption is a factor that could worsen climate change impacts and negatively affect the effectiveness of adaptation strategies. The adverse effects of corruption on development have long been acknowledged: corruption increases stresses on a whole range of socio-economic challenges, exacerbating political instability, weakening governance capacity, political effectiveness and law enforcement and diverting financial resources.[2] As corruption has not been extensively examined in relation to climate change, this section contributes to the analysis of the corruption risks in adaptation strategies by looking at the case of climate migration — an important illustration, as it is likely to become an inevitable adaptation strategy for many when other forms of adaptation fail.[3]

The impact of climate change and the role of corruption – migration as an example

The impact of climate change will depend on the capacity of governments, local communities and the international community to adapt to changes such as drought, flooding and desertification.[4] In some regions these changes will have an effect on the abundance of resources. It is estimated that with a 1–2°C increase in temperature an additional 800–1800 million people may be exposed to water stress by 2085.[5] Furthermore, sea-level rise could threaten millions of people living in coastal regions – a threat that is already being felt by small island states such as the Maldives.[6] Although there remains uncertainty about the scale of these effects on human communities, what is clear is that '[c]limate change will affect the basic elements of life for people around the world – access to water, food production, health and the environment'.[7]

Climate change that leads to an increasing scarcity of resources also has the potential to trigger knock-on effects. These may include increased inequality; insecurity and lawlessness; the potential for violent conflict; and large-scale population displacement.[8] The UN High Commissioner for Refugees (UNHCR) has highlighted the linkages between climate change and migration, acknowledging climate change as one of the 'biggest driver[s]' of future displacement.[9] It is estimated that, by 2050, 200 million people, mainly from the South, will be forced to leave their homes because of climate change.[10] These estimates remain debated, and many cite such figures as overly pessimistic,[11] particularly as they rely on climatic projections and tend not to include the adaptive capacity of communities in their calculations. It is also important to note that migration is a multicausal phenomenon of push and pull factors that do not all originate with climate change.[12] The combination of the economic, social and ecological influences on migratory patterns is likely to be profoundly shaped by the changing climate, however.

When considering the socio-economic processes surrounding the flight of climate refugees, it is noteworthy that many of the countries that are vulnerable to climate migration are also those that are challenged with corruption. The main climate migration hot spots are found in Africa and Asia, in particular sub-Saharan Africa, and South and East Asia.[13] These are also areas of the world that tend to have low scores on Transparency International's Corruption Perceptions Index – indicating that they are perceived as having high levels of corruption, and that they are likely to face various governance challenges.[14] Moreover, with the increased pressure of climate change and the consequent inequality and insecurity that this can bring, there is a greater potential for corruption to flourish. A recent report on climate change and conflict, for instance, highlights how, in times of scarcity, resources could be expropriated by the elite at the expense of marginalized communities.[15]

Climate migration: a new governance challenge?

The governance of climate migration at a global level is weak, as there are no strong institutional mechanisms in place at present to deal effectively with climate refugees.[16] Furthermore, different types of governance measures may be required depending on whether climate refugees are displaced within their country of origin or across international borders, and on whether they move as a result of slow-onset climate change or are forced to move because of natural disasters.[17] Moreover, as no strong governance mechanisms have been created so far to assist climate refugees, and as current standards in refugee and human rights law vary considerably depending on the source and type of the flight, 'many climate victims [are left] unprotected and vulnerable to abuse'.[18]

Corruption may aggravate the already challenging situation in terms of coping with climate migration and posing additional governance needs. Climate migration and corruption interact in complex ways. Corruption may first of all be an aggravating factor, pushing populations to migrate as a result of elite capture of their resources.[19] Secondly, adaptation measures could be rendered ineffective as a result of corrupt activities, either directly through the potential for the embezzlement of development funds or indirectly when national law enforcement, political will and regulatory systems are weak. It is precisely these latter socio-economic factors that make states vulnerable to climate change, and subsequent climate migration, and make them less effective in dealing with migration when it occurs. Finally, the process of climate migration itself may increase opportunities for corruption, as climate refugees may become vulnerable victims of corrupt activities as they move to unfamiliar environments with their own socio-economic challenges.

The sorts of challenges created by corruption will also depend on the type of migration patterns, as different circumstances may pose different kinds of problems and opportunities with respect to corruption. The remainder of this contribution analyses the specific corruption challenges for two different forms of climate migration, namely internal migration and displacement, and international migration.

Internal migration and displacement

The internal displacement of large parts of a population due to climate change may trigger enormous challenges for national governments. At present, when natural disasters occur, governments have the primary obligation to protect their citizens, and to provide assistance to internally displaced communities,[20] even though aid agencies and the international community also share obligations related to humanitarian aid.[21] Effective management of internal climate migration will therefore depend on how prepared governments are to cope with climate change impacts and possible sudden and gradual climate migration.

If populations are displaced without warning or if migration is poorly managed, migration has the potential to increase vulnerability and exposure to corruption. For example, checkpoints may be set up on local roads to levy bribes from vulnerable groups; in Côte d'Ivoire, populations moving from the rebel-controlled north to the government-controlled south have been forced to pay US$40–60[22] – a considerable burden for poor travellers. Bribes may also be extorted to process applications to change places of residence.[23] Moreover, once settled, migrants living in urban slums may be exposed to 'threats of clearance, eviction and rent-seeking from government officials'.[24]

Although the Guiding Principles on Internal Displacement[25] have raised awareness about the needs of internally displaced people, they are still not afforded the same rights as refugees.[26] As a result, only half of the world's internally displaced people – estimated at around 26 million at the end of 2008 – receive assistance.[27] Humanitarian aid can be extremely political, and 'sovereignty is often invoked as a justification for restricting international aid efforts'.[28] In 2007, countries such as Sudan, Myanmar and Zimbabwe restricted humanitarian assistance to almost 1.5 million people.[29]

The International Organization for Migration (IOM) has recommended that migration and displacement should not be forgotten in the international negotiations on climate change. It suggests the development of 'integrated solutions that link migration and climate change adaptation'.[30] The national adaptation programmes of action (NAPAs), which have been completed by 38 of the least developed countries, indicate that there is a level of awareness in the climate change adaptation community that climate change could lead to inevitable large-scale migration, and that this requires government planning for resettlement.[31] The NAPAs do not provide consistent detail on implementation of such plans, however, and previous experience of resettlement programmes raises concerns about the effectiveness of such initiatives.[32]

Relocation programmes, including arrangements to build temporary shelters, homes and villages, and those that provide aid or compensation to relocated populations, often operate under weak governance and provide opportunities for corruption. Such programmes may trigger the embezzlement of funds. In addition, bureaucratic procedures surrounding the allocation of land and registration may be subject to bribery and preferential treatment. In Kenya, where some 500,000 people fled their homes following the post-election violence in 2007–2008, government resettlement programmes have been blighted by corruption, resulting in 350,000 people living in temporary camps for extended periods of time.[33] It is estimated that, of the Kenya shilling (Sh) 2 billion (approximately US$28 million) allocated to these internally displaced people, as much as Sh500 million has been 'embezzled'.[34] Furthermore, land bought by the government in the Rift Valley to resettle internally displaced people has been sold to the 'highest bidder'.[35] Similar scenarios are likely to play out in government relocation programmes related to climate change, unless they are well planned and governed appropriately. As argued by Koko Warner, the resettled rely heavily on international and governmental assistance,[36] which leaves them particularly vulnerable to the vagaries of corrupt officials.

International migration

There is limited protection for climate refugees in international law, as they are not considered refugees under the 1951 Geneva Convention or its 1967 Protocol. Other provisions, such as the 1969 Convention on Specific Aspects of Refugee Problems in Africa and the 1984 Cartagena Declaration on Refugees directed to refugees in Central America, Mexico and Panama, may cover climate refugees in as much as they extend their remit to those affected by a serious disturbance in 'public order', but are unlikely to be sufficient to include victims of slow-onset climate change, such as drought.[37] Indeed, these conventions were not originally intended for this population, which raises uncertainty as to whether climate refugees could be protected this way.[38] Climate refugees may also be eligible for temporary protected status; Denmark, for example, provides humanitarian asylum for victims of drought.[39] It is clear that these exceptions are rather narrow and applied at the discretion of individual countries, however, leaving the system with fragmented legislation and legal loopholes.

The crossing of borders is rife with corruption risks, and immigration offices have long been considered a hot spot for corrupt practices. Transparency International's 2009 East African Bribery Index reveals that the immigration departments in Kenya, Uganda and Tanzania are considered to be some of the most corrupt institutions in the region.[40] More generally, the *2009 Human Development Report* suggests that 'a labyrinth of procedures and regulation, often exacerbated by corruption, causes excessive delays and compounds the costs of leaving'.[41] Migrants may also be regarded as 'easy targets by corrupt officials' for the extortion of bribes.[42] The report highlights how police may 'destroy or refuse to recognize documents in order to justify arrest' with the hope of extorting bribes from migrants.[43] Furthermore, when migrants are repatriated, schemes may be subject to corruption. This may cause unequal treatment and delays, or victims may be asked to pay unofficial fees for appropriate travel documentation or be subjected to risks similar to those mentioned for internal resettlement programmes.

Particularly pernicious forms of international migration include the smuggling of migrants[44] and human trafficking.[45] The IOM suggests that millions of people are transported illegally across borders each year, 'under false pretences, or, allegedly, by corrupt government officials'.[46] Increased vulnerability due to climate change could increase the prevalence of both smuggling and trafficking, and corruption is a key factor in understanding both these processes.[47] The industry would not thrive without the complicity of corrupt officials in border patrols, consulates or the police, who may either be actively involved in the issuing of travel documents, or passively tolerate or ignore illegal activities.[48] In 2009 the UN Office on Drugs and

Crime (UNODC) launched a survey, which identified the most vulnerable elements of the human trafficking chain to corruption. Of the respondents, 65 per cent referred to border control, immigration and customs, 50 per cent to law enforcement and police, and 25 per cent to civil society organizations as being most susceptible to corruption.[49]

Climate change may increase the incentives, density and complexity of these illegal circuits, as it has the potential to make smuggling and human trafficking activities very lucrative. In situations in which there is weak governance, climate refugees' vulnerability to these two industries increases. Such a situation was seen in Bangladesh following the flooding in 2007. As the livelihoods of families were destroyed by the floods, the promise of temporary work in India was taken up by many male breadwinners. Instead, the climate refugees became victims of torture and slavery.[50] Meanwhile, the women that they left behind were left with no economic resources, without the expected remittances from the men in India. As a consequence they became vulnerable to human trafficking, forced labour or prostitution.[51]

Conclusions and recommendations

If migration is not managed adequately, some of the most dire predictions of displacement, smuggling and human trafficking may actually become a reality for those forced to migrate due to climate change. The discussion above illustrates that there are corruption risks inherent in the different forms of displacement and migration and that both national and international forms of governance are largely inadequate to cope with the climate change challenge. It is clear that, without effective safeguards and mechanisms for accountability, vulnerability to corruption and the most egregious forms of migration, such as human smuggling and trafficking, may thrive. For these reasons, it is crucial for national and international policy to integrate climate migration as a component of well-governed adaptation programmes.

In order to cope with the challenge of climate migration in an effective and fair manner, climate refugees require legal recognition, political support and financial assistance.[52] Rather than extending the remit of refugee status, the particular nature of climate refugees asks for a unique regime, tailored to their needs, appropriately supported and financed by the international community.[53] This could be realized through an additional protocol to the UNFCCC for the recognition, protection and resettlement of climate refugees, as suggested by Frank Biermann and Ingrid Boas, which includes a specific funding mechanism and an overall framework through which international action can be taken.[54]

At the institutional level, this protocol would be managed by an executive committee functioning under the authority of the Conference of the Parties (COP) to the United Nations Framework Convention on Climate Change (UNFCCC). Rather than providing support through post-disaster assistance, the protocol allows for planned and organized voluntary resettlement programmes.[55] It is envisaged that these resettlements take place largely within the home countries of the affected communities, but would receive international assistance. At the organizational level, various international agencies, such as the UNHCR and the United Nations Development Programme (UNDP), would be involved in the management of resettlement programmes; that they would be accountable to the UNFCCC COP will help ensure a balanced and equitable governance structure.

The protocol also allows for financial support to be provided by the international community, through a climate refugee protection and resettlement fund.[56] This fund is based on the principle of 'common but differentiated responsibilities and respective capabilities', ensuring that developed countries bear most of the costs. As a specialized fund for activities, it would be easier to trace donations and verify that developed countries meet their commitments in this area.

In sum, there is an urgent need for research and policy action to focus on the governance of climate migration through adaptation measures. Some progress was made in the UNFCCC negotiating text at Cancún in 2010, when a paragraph on the relocation of climate change migrants was included.[57] At this nascent stage in the negotiations, it is pivotal that governance and corruption risks are acknowledged and included in policy designs. We simply cannot cope with climate migration effectively and humanely without fighting corruption.

Notes

1. Ingrid Boas is a PhD student at the University of Kent and a guest researcher at the Department of Environmental Policy Analysis of the Institute for Environmental Studies of the VU University Amsterdam. Rebecca Dobson works for Transparency International.
2. Robert Smith and Mathew Walpole, 'Should Conservationists Pay More Attention to Corruption?', *Oryx*, vol. 39 (2005), pp. 251–256; and German Advisory Council on Global Change, *World in Transition: Climate Change as a Security Risk* (London: Earthscan, 2007), p. 43.
3. It is important to note that migration could be identified, 'not only as one of the problems, but also one of the solutions to the challenges presented by climate change': Boncour (2008) Philippe Boncour, Head of the International Dialogue on Migration, International Organisation for Migration, Side Event at the 14th Conference of the Parties to the UNFCCC, 8 December 2008.

4. See discussion in Frank Biermann and Ingrid Boas, 'Preparing for a Warmer World: Towards a Global Governance System to Protect Climate Refugees', *Global Environmental Politics*, vol. 10 (2010), pp. 60–88, pp. 67.

5. Rachel Warren et al. 'Understanding the regional impacts of climate change', Working Paper no. 90 (Norwich: Tyndall Centre for Climate Change Research, 2006), ch. 2. It is important to note that, under such circumstances, between 2074 and 2239 million people may experience an increased run-off. Nonetheless, 'this extra runoff would probably increase flood risks, and because it would occur during the wet season would not alleviate shortages during the dry season in the absence of storage' (Warren et al., 2006, p. 16).

6. Reuters (UK), 'For Maldives, climate deal is a survival issue', 28 November 2009.

7. Nicholas Stern, *The Economics of Climate Change (The Stern Review)* (Cambridge: Cambridge University Press, 2006), ch. 3.5, p. 56.

8. German Advisory Council on Global Change (2007).

9. See UNHCR, 'Climate change could become the biggest driver of displacement: UNHCR chief', 16 December 2009, at www.unhcr.org/4b2910239.html.

10. Norman Myers, 'Environmental Refugees: A Growing Phenomenon of the 21st Century', *Philosophical Transactions of the Royal Society: Biological Sciences*, vol. 357 (2002), pp. 609–613; see also discussion in Stern (2006, ch. 3.5).

11. See Richard Black, *Environmental Refugees: Myth or Reality?*, New Issues in Refugee Research Working Paper no. 34 (Geneva: UNHCR, 2001); Stephen Castles, *Environmental Change and Forced Migration: Making Sense of the Debate*, New Issues in Refugee Research Working Paper no. 70 (Geneva: UNHCR, 2002). Norman Myers and Jennifer Kent have provided a figure for environmental refugees, based on population scenarios, vulnerable areas, etc. Norman Myers and Jennifer Kent, *Environmental Exodus – An Emergent Crisis in the Global Arena* (Washington DC: Climate Institute, 1995). As argued by Stephen Castles, however, they have done so without providing 'figures on people who have actually been displaced by such problems. Rather, the linkage appears simply as "common sense" – if water levels rise, or forests disappear, it seems obvious that people will have to move' (Castles, 2002, p. 3). Nevertheless, the study does provide a basis from which one may depart. In this regard, *The Stern Review* states that Myers and Kent's prediction of 150–200 million environmental refugees 'has not been rigorously tested, but it remains in line with the evidence presented throughout this chapter that climate change will lead to hundreds of millions more people without sufficient water or food to survive or threatened by dangerous floods and increased disease' (Stern, 2006, p.77).

12. Black (2001), p.13.

13. German Advisory Council on Global Change (2007), p. 163. See also Biermann and Boas (2010), p. 69.

14. Many countries in these areas score below 3.6 on a scale of 1 to 10 on TI's Corruption Perceptions Index 2009 (10 meaning that the country is perceived as 'highly clean'): see www.transparency.org/policy_research/surveys_indices/cpi/2009.

15. Jennifer Smith, *The Rough Guide to Climate Change and Conflict* (London: CAFOD, 2008).

16. See discussion in Biermann and Boas (2010); see also Frank Biermann and Ingrid Boas, 'Global Adaptation Governance: Setting the Stage', in Frank Biermann et al. (eds), *Global Climate Governance beyond 2012: Architecture, Agency and Adaptation* (Cambridge, Cambridge University Press, 2010), pp. 223–234.

17. Michelle Leighton, 'Climate Change and Migration: Key Issues for Legal Protection of Migrants and Displaced Persons' (Washington, DC: German Marshall Fund of the United States, 2010); Koko Warner, 'Global Environmental Change and Migration: Governance Challenges', *Global Environmental Change,* vol. 20 (2010), pp. 402–413.
18. Leighton (2010).
19. Smith (2008).
20. Leighton (2010), p.2.
21. Ibid. See Roslyn Hees, section 5.5 in this volume.
22. UN Development Programme (UNDP), *Human Development Report 2009: Overcoming Barriers: Human Mobility and Development* (New York: Palgrave Macmillan, 2009), p. 40.
23. Ibid.
24. Ibid.
25. See www.idpguidingprinciples.org.
26. UNDP (2009), p. 63.
27. Ibid.
28. Ibid.
29. Ibid. The report estimates around 500,000 people in each of the countries.
30. William Lacy Swing, director general IOM, speaking at a side event, 'Climate Adaptation Continuum, Migration and Displacement: Copenhagen and Beyond', COP 15, 16 December 2009.
31. Susan Martin, *Climate Change, Migration and Adaptation* (Washington, DC: German Marshall Fund of the United States, 2010).
32. Ibid.
33. Andrew Teyie, 'IDPs top 2009 list of shame', AllAfrica.com (Mauritius), 5 January 2010.
34. Ibid.
35. Phillip Ngunjiri, 'Want a piece of IDP land? That will be US$866 only', AllAfrica.com (Mauritius), 28 December 2009.
36. Warner (2010), p. 406.
37. Leighton (2010).
38. Biermann and Boas (2010: 'Preparing for a Warmer World'), p. 73.
39. Leighton (2010).
40. The impact of bribery is the proportion of those who report having interacted with a particular organization and being provided with the service after paying a bribe that was demanded of them within the previous 12 months. See TI, 'East African Bribery Index 2009', TI Kenya.
41. UNDP (2009), p. 40.
42. Ibid., p.61.
43. Ibid.
44. UN, *Protocol against the Smuggling of Migrants by Land, Sea and Air, Supplementing the United Nations Convention against Transnational Organized Crime* (New York: UN, 2000).
45. UN, *Protocol to Prevent, Suppress and Punish Trafficking in Persons, Especially Women and Children, Supplementing the United Nations Convention against Transnational Organized Crime* (New York: UN, 2000).
46. IOM, *In Pursuit of the Southern Dream: Victims of Necessity: Assessment of the Irregular Movement of Men from East Africa and the Horn to South Africa* (Geneva: IOM, 2009).

47. See Sheldon Zhang and Samuel Pineda, 'Corruption as a Causal Factor in Human Trafficking', in Dina Siegel and Hans Nelen (eds), *Organized Crime: Culture, Markets and Policies* (Berlin: Springer, 2008), pp. 41–55.

48. Ibid.

49. Anti-Slavery International, TI and UNODC, *The Role of Corruption in Trafficking in Persons* (London: Anti-Slavery International, 2009).

50. Alice Poncelet, 'Bangladesh Case-Study Report: 'The Land of Mad Rivers'', in *Environmental Change and Forced Migration (EACH-FOR)* (Brussels: European Commission, 2009), pp. 19–20.

51. Ibid.

52. Biermann and Boas (2010: 'Preparing for a Warmer World').

53. Ibid.

54. Ibid.

55. Ibid.

56. Ibid.

57. UNFCC (2010) 'Outcome of the work of the Ad Hoc Working Group on long-term Cooperative Action under the Convention', 16th Conference of the Parties, Cancún, Mexico, 29 November to 10 December, paragraph 14(f).

5.4.1

The plunder of Kenya's forests

Resettling the settlers and holding the loggers accountable

Sheila Masinde and Lisa Karanja[1]

Never before had forestry issues hit the headlines as hard as they did in 2009. The destruction of the 400,000 hectare (ha) Mau Forest Complex in the heart of Kenya's Rift Valley brought the issues of deforestation, environmental degradation and conservation to the public consciousness. The Kenya Forestry Working Group has estimated that Kenya stands to lose more than Kenya shilling (Sh) 24 billion (approximately US$300 million) each year from the tourism, tea and energy sectors if the devastation continues at the current rate.[2] In 1963 Kenya had forest cover of some 10 per cent; by 2006 this figure had fallen to a meagre 1.7 per cent.[3]

The devastation of forests, such as the Mau Forest, by slash and burn techniques results in previously dense, green and lush forest becoming choked with parched land and tree stumps. These forests form the basis of water catchments throughout Kenya; their destruction increases pressure on a population grappling with hunger and water and power shortages. The destruction of the forests also has implications for climate change, in terms of both mitigation and adaptation. Forests are important for protecting ecological diversity, regulating climate patterns and acting as carbon sinks: Nobel laureate Wangari Matthai has suggested that 20 per cent of greenhouse gas (GHG) emissions are due to deforestation and forest degradation.[4]

The rate of deforestation in Kenya has spiralled in the last three decades, with the incidence of excisions of forest land, logging including charcoal burning, the harvesting of forest products, cultivation and forest fires all increasing.[5] A report published by the Kenya Forest Service in 2007 suggested that this is the result of forest guards from the Ministry of Forestry being under-resourced, and therefore unable to manage the forests effectively, or due to 'abuse of office, dereliction of duty and/or corruption'.[6] Weak governance has made it difficult to address deforestation in terms of the irregular issuance of logging licences, bribery to forgo arrests or prosecution following forestry offences, and the illegal parcelling out of land by officials to repay or gain political favours.[7]

The nub of the forestry problem in Kenya, precipitated by the allocation of land, is the tension between the necessity to conserve the forests and, at the same time, the need to ensure that settlers on the land are treated fairly and equitably. Among the human factors driving the destruction of the forests are poverty, unsustainable livelihoods, a lack of land and population pressure on the areas surrounding the forest reserves. Successive governments have carved out the forests in an attempt to accommodate communities living near wooded areas, but this has been accompanied by the illegitimate allocation of land.[8]

The government set up a Commission of Inquiry into the Illegal/Irregular Allocation of Land in Kenya, and in 2004 it produced a report.[9] The chair of the commission, Paul Ndung'u, suggested that the grabbing of the Mau Forest had begun as a genuine effort to settle landless members of the Ogiek community, but that in the process of allocating land for these settlements 'corruption crept in'.[10] For instance, instead of carving out the agreed 2000ha to allocate to the Ogiek community, public officials took around 10,000ha and allocated the extra land to 'themselves and other influential individuals in government'.[11]

It is clear that the mass depletion of forests in Kenya could herald an environmental catastrophe for a country dealing with the effects of climate change. What is not so clear is how to conserve the forest, prevent illegal logging, resettle the people and ensure that this process is not also marred by corruption. The resettlement of vulnerable communities, who consider their land to be their own, is of particular concern given that, between 2004 and 2006, it is estimated that more than 100,000 people were forcibly evicted from their homes in forested areas in Kenya.[12] The lack of trust was further heightened in August 2009 when the Kenya Forestry Service issued a 14-day eviction notice on people living in the Mau Forest,[13] which was subsequently overturned by the prime minister, Raila Odinga, after only a few days.[14]

Debate on the resettlement of the Mau Forest inhabitants has been affected by political and tribal undertones, but Rift Valley leaders have stuck to their guns, demanding that their constituents should not be evicted without adequate reparations.[15] The question for the government now is how to determine who have valid claims that need to be compensated. Furthermore, once the evictions and resettlements have taken place, there will be a need to ensure that forestry laws are enforced to stop the situation returning to its current state.[16]

In September 2009, in a move to protect the forest, the government launched an appeal to save the Mau Forest Complex.[17] The Interim Coordinating Secretariat, set up to implement the recommendations of the Mau Forest Task Force, identified a 10-point intervention plan, which includes the creation of institutional frameworks.[18] The plan deals with both the relocation and settlement of communities, including helping them 'to adjust to their new homes', and calls for the 'restoration and replanting of degraded sites'.[19]

It will take years to restore the depleted forests of Kenya to their past glory. If Kenyans are to be protected from the onset of climate change, while avoiding even harsher water shortages than they have already experienced, and at the same time play their part in mitigating climate change's progression, however, the rehabilitation of Kenya's forests is the key; and it will turn only if it is unimpeded by corruption.

Notes

1. Sheila Masinde and Lisa Karanja work for Transparency International Kenya.
2. UN Environment Programme (UNEP), 'Forest fires destroy Kenya's key water catchments', press release, 25 March 2009.
3. UNESCO, 'Fighting desertification in Kenya, one tree at a time', *Courier*, 3, 2006.
4. See www.greenbeltmovement.org/a.php?id=431.
5. Winston Mathu, *Forest Law Enforcement and Governance in Kenya* (Nairobi: Kenya Forest Service, 2007), p. 6.
6. Ibid.
7. Ibid., p. 17.
8. James Makori, 'Mau Compensation: The Corruption and Land Politics in Kenya', *Adili* no. 116 (2010), pp. 1–4.
9. Republic of Kenya, *Report of the Commission of Inquiry into the Illegal/Irregular Allocation of Public Land* (Nairobi: Government Printer, 2004).
10. *Sunday Nation* (Kenya), 'How grabbing of forest land started', on African News Online, 31 July 2009.
11. Ibid.
12. Amnesty International, *Nowhere to Go: Forced Evictions in Mau Forest* (London: Amnesty International, 2007), citing Centre on Housing Rights and Evictions (COHRE) and Hakijamii, 'Forest Evictions: A Way Forward', *Kenya Housing Rights Update,* August 2006. The total number of evictions is disputed, and no accurate numbers are available.
13. *Sunday Nation* (Kenya), 'Rift Valley MPs' fury on new Mau deadline', 25 August 2009.
14. *Sunday Nation* (Kenya), 'Kenya PM tells Mau settlers to ignore quit notice', 26 August 2009.
15. *Daily Nation* (Kenya), 'Raila softens stance on Rift Valley "rebels"', 16 August 2009.

16. Other than the Forest Act (2005), Kenya has over 77 statutes pertaining to forestry. They include the Draft Land Use policy, Environmental Management and Conservation Act (1999), the Wildlife (Conservation and Management) Act 1976 and the Agriculture/National Food Policy (Sessional Paper no. 2, 1994).

17. Environment News Service (US), 'Kenya seeks millions to save Mau Forest, avert water crisis', 14 September 2009.

18. Ibid.

19. Ibid.

5.4.2

Climate change adaptation and water integrity

A global challenge to address local realities

Grit Martinez and Teun Bastemeijer[1]

'Climate adaptation *is* water adaptation': so says the consortium of the Co-operative Programme on Water and Climate (CPWC), the World Water Council (WWC) and the International Union for the Conservation of Nature (IUCN).[2] Climate change can be observed very clearly in the form of increases in water stress and scarcity cutting across sectors and regions. Vulnerability to these impacts is not evenly distributed; often those affected most by climate change have the lowest capacity to cope.[3] As such, a focus on water as a component of any adaptation measure is essential, particularly in developing countries, where low levels of resilience to the effects of climate change mean higher risks for people and the economy.

Climate change interacts with other political, social, economic and environmental phenomena, and these multiple stresses, such as population growth and the unsustainable use of land and natural resources, combine to increase water scarcity and damage by extreme weather events. For example, it is estimated that, by 2020, 75–250 million people in Africa will be exposed to increased water stress as a result of climate change.[4]

There is a perception that adaptation measures under-represent water in 'national plans or in international investment portfolios'.[5] A significant focus on water can be identified in the national adaptation programmes of action (NAPAs) developed by least developed countries under the UN

Framework Convention on Climate Change (UNFCCC), however. In an analysis of the sectors covered by NAPAs, 13 per cent are related to water resources and 9 per cent cover coastal zones and marine ecosystems.[6] There remains concern, however, that NAPAs have not taken 'a holistic approach to adaptation responses in the water sector and its development'.[7]

Although climate change contributes to increased water stress, scarcity in the sector is largely due to weak governance and the absence of regulatory frameworks and law enforcement. Corruption is estimated to increase the cost of achieving the UN Millennium Development Goal on water and sanitation by US$48 billion.[8] In this context, an important element of any adaptation effort should be the promotion of water integrity at all levels. The case study below, which looks at the integration of water and adaptation activities, will serve as an important litmus test for addressing corruption risks in implementing strategies at the national level.

A country-specific approach: adaptation and water challenges in Bangladesh

Bangladesh is on the climate change front line, with a reduction in its vulnerabilities related to water being its highest priority.[9] The UN Development Programme (UNDP) has ranked Bangladesh as the country in the world most at risk in relation to tropical cyclones and the sixth most at risk in the world in relation to floods.[10] Its high level of vulnerability has been recognized by the UNFCCC[11] and is high on the agenda of the Bangladesh government.[12]

In 2005 the Bangladesh government completed its NAPA. Of the 15 projects recommended as urgent in the final report, nine of them were directly related to water.[13] The Bangladesh Climate Change Strategy and Action Plan,[14] prepared following extensive consultation, recognizes water as an essential component of the hazards the country is likely to face as a consequence of climate change.[15] It was estimated that some US$500 million will be necessary in the first two years for strengthening disaster management, research and knowledge management, capacity-building and public awareness, and urgent investment in cyclone shelters and selected drainage programmes.[16]

In June 2010 the government of Bangladesh and development partners reached an agreement to establish a national climate change resilience fund. The development partners will provide an initial contribution of US$100 million.[17] This fund is to be managed and implemented by the government with the involvement of development partners and civil society.[18] The involvement of the

World Bank, in terms of providing 'technical support for implementation', aims to 'help ensure that due diligence requirements are met'.[19]

It seems that Bangladesh is taking climate change and its relationship to water seriously and that there are safeguards in place to ensure good governance of the funds. It is unlikely that this will be enough, however, as corruption is deeply rooted in society and affects the water sector particularly. With facilitating support from the Water Integrity Network (WIN), a core group of organizations recently launched the Bangladesh Water Integrity Initiative (BAWIN).[20] One of its areas of focus is to explore ways to curb corruption in the

areas affected by Cyclone Aila in 2009. BAWIN conducted an investigation into the reasons for delays and specified measures that are needed to ensure transparency and accountability. The study identified the following as areas of particular vulnerability:

- planning, tendering and contracting processes;
- the monitoring and repair of dykes and embankments; and
- the provision of freshwater and the flow of resources to affected people.

These findings will be particularly relevant in the context of the government's plans for water adaptation projects and programmes in the future.

Notes

1. Grit Martinez and Teun Bastemeijer work for the Water Integrity Network (WIN).
2. WWC, *Don't Stick Your Head in the Sand! Towards a Framework for Climate-Proofing* (Marseilles: WWC, 2009).
3. Ibid.
4. UN Educational, Scientific and Cultural Organization (UNESCO), *World Water Development Report 3: Water in a Changing World* (Paris: UNESCO, 2009).
5. UN-Water, 'Climate Change Adaptation: The Pivotal Role of Water' (New York: UN, 2010), p. 1.
6. UN, *Least Developed Countries under the UNFCCC* (New York: UN, 2009).
7. Gunilla Björklund et al., *Water Adaptation in National Adaptation Programmes for Action: Freshwater in Climate Adaptation Planning and Climate Adaptation in Freshwater Planning* (Paris: UNESCO, 2009), p. 8.
8. TI, *Global Corruption Report 2008: Corruption in the Water Sector* (Cambridge: Cambridge University Press, 2008), p. 12.
9. A ranking of key climate change impacts and vulnerabilities for Bangladesh conducted by the Organisation for Economic Co-operation and Development (OECD) identified water and coastal resources as being of the highest priority for adaptation. See Shardul Agrawala and Maëlis Carraro, *Assessing the Role of Microfinance in Fostering Adaptation to Climate Change*, Environmental Working Paper no. 15 (Paris: OECD, 2010).
10. Ministry of Environment and Forests (MoEF), *Bangladesh Climate Change Strategy and Action Plan 2008* (Dhaka: MoEF, 2008), p. 4, at www.moef.gov.bd/moef.pdf.

11. Report of the Conference of the Parties on its 15th session (COP 15), held in Copenhagen 7–19 December 2009. See http://unfccc.int/resource/docs/2009/cop15/eng/11a01.pdf.
12. MoEF, *National Adaptation Programme of Action (NAPA) Final Report* (Dhaka: MoEF, 2005); see http://unfccc.int/resource/docs/napa/ban01.pdf.
13. Ibid.
14. MoEF (2008).
15. Ibid., p. 13.
16. Ibid., p. 29. The total cost of programmes for the first five years could be in the order of US$5 billion.
17. See http://beta.worldbank.org/content/bangladesh-economics-adaptation-climate-change-study.
18. Ministry of Foreign Affairs of Denmark, 'Building resilience to address climate change', 23 September 2010, at www.ambdhaka.um.dk/en/menu/TheEmbassy/News/BuildingResilienceToAddressClimateChange.htm.
19. *Daily Star* (Bangladesh), 'Bangladesh gets US$110m climate fund', 2 June 2010.
20. Kathy Shordt, 'BAWIN concept note' (Berlin: WIN, July 2010).

5.5
When disaster strikes

Corruption and rapid response in climate-related relief and recovery

Roslyn Hees[1]

Efforts to help developing countries adapt to climate change are doomed to failure unless good governance and ethics are integral elements of financial assistance.

(Wangari Maathai, Nobel Peace Prize laureate)[2]

Climate change and natural disasters: nature and scale of the problem

The humanitarian community is well aware of the recent and projected growth in climate-related disasters or extreme weather events and the implications that this will have for the resources needed for emergency responses. Climate change would increase emergency response requirements through both a higher frequency and/or intensity of sudden-impact disasters and expanded coverage of slow-impact disasters. Increased emergency aid will be required because of the loss of agricultural production and food supplies, economic infrastructure, freshwater sources and shelter, and to deal with the immediate and medium-term health problems that result from disasters. The resulting increased demand for emergency aid is likely to offer greater opportunities for the corrupt diversion of aid resources.

The UN's Office for the Coordination of Humanitarian Affairs (OCHA) estimates that the number of recorded disasters has increased from 200 to 400 per year over the past two decades, and that 90 per cent of them are climate-related.[3] An average of about 240 million people are affected by climate-related disasters every year, a number that has about tripled since 1980 and is projected to grow by over 50 per cent to an average of 375 million by 2015.[4] The World Health Organization

(WHO) has calculated that 315,000 deaths per year were due to climate change between 2004 and 2008, substantially greater than the death toll attributable to the 2004 Asian tsunami.[5]

Are disaster response programmes particularly vulnerable to corruption?

Humanitarian aid is generally delivered in challenging environments, and climate change emergency responses will be no different. According to several studies commissioned by Transparency International,[6] the incidence of corruption in disaster response appears to be related to the external environment as well as the effectiveness of internal humanitarian agency controls. As could be expected, corruption risks are higher in countries with endemic pre-crisis corruption, fragile public institutions with low absorptive capacity and weak rule of law, and low levels of independent civil society or media scrutiny and, as a consequence, government accountability to its citizens.

The World Bank has identified some of the most likely climate-related disaster hot spots, and in most cases these countries score poorly regarding both perceptions of government effectiveness and the level of perceived corruption (see Table 5.2). This makes it likely that aid responses will be vulnerable to corruption risks.

The sudden injection of massive resources into a resource-poor environment following a disaster presents particular temptation and opportunities for corrupt behaviour in the form of, for example, 'survival corruption' among disaster victims desperate for emergency aid. Aid is also sometimes captured by 'gatekeepers' – local authorities, community leaders or militias controlling communication with target beneficiaries – who use aid to enhance their own political, social, economic or personal agendas. This 'aid capture' may also serve to prolong conflict or perpetuate dependence, creating a vicious humanitarian cycle.[7] Gatekeepers and aid workers have been known to extort sexual favours in return for food, shelter or admittance to official refugee camps, as reported in several African countries.[8] Corruption also undermines the trust that disaster victims have in aid organizations, whether governmental or non-governmental, which is essential for effective recovery.

Aid resources can be corruptly diverted in a wide variety of ways. Contracts, invoices, employee payroll records and beneficiary numbers or aid packages can be falsified or inflated, and the extra resources pocketed or sold for profit. Bribes, kickbacks or threats can distort the choice of suppliers of goods and services, resulting in higher contract costs or the supply of substandard goods. In all such cases, less aid reaches the beneficiaries.

Climate-related event	Country/hot spot (high risk)*	Government effectiveness score**	Corruption Perceptions Index score***
Drought	Malawi	30.3	3.3
	Ethiopia	39.8	2.7
	Zimbabwe	2.4	2.2
Floods	Bangladesh	22.7	2.4
	China	63.5	3.6
	India	53.6	3.4
Storms	Philippines	55.0	2.4
	Bangladesh	22.7	2.4
	Madagascar	33.2	3.0
Sea-level rise	Maldives	44.1	2.5
	Vietnam	45.5	2.7
	Egypt	43.1	2.8
Reduced agricultural production	Sudan	5.2	1.5
	Senegal	51.2	3.0
	Mali	21.8	2.8

Notes:

* Examples taken from World Bank Environment Department, *Convenient Solutions to an Inconvenient Truth* (Washington, DC: World Bank, 2009), p.19.

** Daniel Kaufman et al., *Governance Matters VIII: Aggregate and Individual Governance Indicators 1996–2008*, Policy Research Working Paper no. 4978 (Washington, DC: World Bank, 2009).

***TI, Corruption Perceptions Index 2009; see www.transparency.org/policy_research/surveys_indices/cpi/2009.

Table 5.2 Climate change hot spots and vulnerability to corruption

'Non-financial corruption', which does not show up in agency accounts and is thus not detected by audits, can also have a damaging effect on the humanitarian mission, however. Practices such as nepotism/cronyism, the diversion of aid to non-target groups and the expropriation of aid resources for political, social or military purposes may not be considered forms of corruption but 'business-as-usual' in some countries. They constitute abuses of power nonetheless and divert resources from the intended beneficiaries.

The massive humanitarian response to the Asian tsunami saw numerous allegations of corruption, such as contractors accused of building housing that did not meet the quality specifications for which they were paid in Aceh, or the claim that reconstructed houses in Sri Lanka were allocated to government officials' friends and family rather than to other victims who had greater need.[9] It has been reported recently – although challenged by the aid agency – that in Somalia close to 50 per cent of the main food aid programme did not reach targeted beneficiaries, but was divided among local implementing partners, transporters and armed militias.[10] The near-total breakdown of political, economic and social institutions in Somalia means that this particular case cannot be considered representative of all aid programmes, but it does illustrate an extreme example of the corrupt diversion of emergency aid.

Existing disaster risk reduction plans

The humanitarian community has formulated various action plans to promote climate-related disaster preparedness and adaptation, such as the Hyogo Framework for Action 2005–2015.[11] These focus mainly on technical risk reduction measures, however, such as improved infrastructure, land-use planning and better disaster prediction and early warning systems. Governance is addressed as regards improving disaster management and response coordination, or strengthening affected communities' ability to anticipate and respond to disaster, but the impact of corruption has, to a large extent, not been considered.

To date, insufficient thought seems to have been given to the expected costs of implementing these action plans, or to the expanded financial resources that will be required to address the human needs created by increased climate-related crises. One such rare analysis estimates that annual international spending on humanitarian aid could grow over the next 20 years (in nominal terms) by anything from 32 per cent (if only estimated increases in disaster frequency are included), to 134 per cent (if disaster frequency and intensity are included) to up to 1600 per cent (if past disaster trends are projected linearly).[12]

The increased resources required, combined with pressure from donors, the media and the general public on public and non-governmental aid organizations to scale up operations and disburse aid rapidly, could stress already overstretched systems and staff, and weaken vigilance and controls. The limitations posed by low absorptive capacity in many at-risk countries (as measured, for example, by government effectiveness in table 5.2) mean that, when aid is scaled up, existing systems may not be able to absorb large increases in resources without leading to more waste, leakage or corruption.[13] In view of this massive potential growth in humanitarian resource flows, it is surprising that so little analysis has been done of the associated corruption risks.

What can be done?

Extensive field research undertaken in partnership with several leading international humanitarian non-governmental organizations culminated in the publication of TI's *Preventing Corruption in Humanitarian Operations: Handbook of Good Practices* in January 2010.[14] The handbook outlines several areas in which improved policies and systems can help prevent and mitigate corruption in disaster responses.

Corruption seems to remain a taboo topic within the humanitarian and climate change community. Discussion of the impact of corruption on climate-related disasters needs to be brought into the open and reflected in the research and advocacy documentation in these fields.

It is important to understand that perceptions of what constitutes corruption vary within and between cultures, and are often limited to financial mismanagement and fraud. '*Non-financial corruption*' (described above) is less often understood as a corrupt practice, and in some cultures may not be considered corrupt at all. Ensuring that affected communities as well as humanitarian aid providers share clear understandings about what constitutes corrupt behaviour and its damaging effects is an important part of preventing it.

Integrating the analysis of corruption risks and the external political and institutional environment into *emergency preparedness*, an essential element in disaster risk reduction, is vital to anticipating and preventing corruption. It is particularly important that both the absorptive capacity of institutions in the affected area and the formal and informal political, economic and social power structures are well understood when formulating disaster response programmes, so that these programmes do not exacerbate corruption risks. On the basis of such analysis, context-specific measures to reduce corruption can be built into the response. As many of the areas that are likely to suffer from climate-related disasters can already be identified, this analysis can be undertaken well in advance of such disasters.

On-site monitoring deters and detects corruption, particularly with regard to non-financial corrupt practices, and needs to be given greater importance in humanitarian responses. Monitoring how corruption can affect aid outcomes should be built into the disaster response at the planning phase. If crisis-prone local communities take the lead in preparing for and responding to climate-related disasters, as many experts recommend, they can also monitor the humanitarian aid responses, including the incidence of corruption. Greater *transparency* in the information on response programmes made available to local governments, recipient communities and civil society organizations will also be essential for effective monitoring and genuine accountability.

Notes

1. Roslyn Hees is senior advisor for the TI Secretariat.
2. Reuters AlertNet (UK), 11 December 2009.
3. EM-DAT: the International Disaster Database, Centre for Research on the Epidemiology of Disasters (CRED), Université Catholique de Louvain, Brussels.
4. Tanja Schuemer-Cross and Ben Heaven Taylor, *The Right to Survive: The Humanitarian Challenge for the Twenty-First Century* (Oxford: Oxfam International, 2009), p. 27.
5. WHO, 'Protecting the Health of Vulnerable People from the Humanitarian Consequences of Climate Change and Climate-Related Disasters' (Geneva: WHO, 2009).
6. Pete Ewins et al., *Mapping the Risks of Corruption in Humanitarian Action* (London: Overseas Development Institute [ODI], 2006); Daniel Maxwell et al. *Preventing Corruption in Humanitarian Assistance: Final Research Report* (Berlin: TI, 2008).
7. Fiona Terry, *Condemned to Repeat: The Paradox of Humanitarian Action* (Ithaca, NY: Cornell University Press, 2002).
8. Corinna Csáky, *No One to Turn to: The Under-Reporting of Child Sexual Exploitation and Abuse by Aid Workers and Peacekeepers* (London: Save the Children, 2008).
9. IPS News (Thailand), 'Tsunami recovery hit by corruption, apathy', 26 December 2006.
10. UN Security Council, 'Report of the Monitoring Group on Somalia pursuant to Security Council Resolution 1853', 10 March 2010.
11. UN International Strategy for Disaster Reduction (ISDR), 'Hyogo Framework for Action 2005–2015: Building the Resilience of Nations and Communities to Disasters' (Geneva: ISDR, 2005).
12. Mackinnon Webster et al., *The Humanitarian Costs of Climate Change* (Medford, MA: Feinstein International Center, Tufts University, 2008).
13. ODI, 'Scaling up versus Absorptive Capacity: Challenges and Opportunities for Reaching the MDGs in Africa', briefing paper (London: ODI, 2005), p. 2.
14. TI, *Preventing Corruption in Humanitarian Operations: Handbook of Good Practices* (Berlin: TI, 2010).

PART 6

Forestry governance

A key issue for climate change

6.0

Forestry governance

A key issue for climate change

Forests cover 31 per cent of the Earth's surface, but they are shrinking at a rate of 13 million hectares (ha) each year.[1] They play a fundamental role in regulating CO_2 levels in the atmosphere, and, as a result, they naturally mitigate the effects of climate change by acting as carbon sinks. Conserving forests and promoting reforestation rather than deforestation or forest degradation has a twofold benefit: the preservation of the carbon already stored and the maintenance or enhancement of the forests' ability to act as a carbon sink and absorb atmospheric CO_2.

Forest resources are very lucrative, however, and have the potential to be an important element of countries' economic development. The sector is prone to illegal logging and corruption, which strips forests at unprecedented rates and does not provide revenue to governments for development purposes. REDD – Reducing Emissions from Deforestation and Forest Degradation – is a mechanism to offer financial incentives for developing countries to reduce forest-related emissions. This special section discusses the governance risks associated with the implementation of REDD in a sector that is vulnerable to corruption.

In the first section, Patrick Alley provides a compelling critique of the drivers of corruption in forestry, including the international demand for timber, shortfalls in legislation regulating illegally sourced forest products and the emphasis on forests as a component of economic development rather than conservation. In a complementary piece, Iftekhar Zaman and Manzoor-e-Khuda analyse the effects of localized corruption in Bangladesh in response to revenue-centric government policy, which encourages the erosion of essential mangroves.

Jeffrey Hatcher and Luke Bailey go on to discuss the implications of implementing REDD in countries and forest environments with poor governance records, particularly in relation to the impact on and participation of indigenous communities. This piece is supplemented by a contribution from Ana Murillo Arguello that highlights the need for supportive government legislation in Nicaragua to ensure that forest communities participate in forest-related policy.

In an assessment of the governance risks associated with the measuring, reporting and verification of REDD, Christopher Barr highlights aspects of the process that could be particularly susceptible to corruption, such as the inappropriate validation of projects, the overestimation of carbon benefits and the misappropriation of carbon rights. Sarah Dix supports this assessment with an example of the illegitimate sale of forest carbon certificates in Papua New Guinea, emphasizing the importance of robust systems for managing the revenue created through REDD+. Finally, Manoj Nadkarni illustrates, with the example of Indonesia, how, even before a REDD mechanism was agreed, the game plan itself was changing rapidly, potentially at the expense of good governance safeguards.

Notes

1.   Food and Agriculture Organization of the UN (FAO), 'Global Forest Resources Assessment 2010: Key Findings' (Rome: FAO, 2010), p. 3.

6.1

Corruption

A root cause of deforestation and forest degradation

Patrick Alley[1]

Corruption and illegality are not uncommon in the resource extraction industry. It is arguable, however, that they are most visible and pervasive in the tropical timber industry. The World Bank estimates US$10–23 billion worth of timber is illegally felled or produced from suspicious origins annually, of which some US$5 billion enters international trade. Governments are deprived of the same amount in lost taxes and royalties.[2] Ironically, much of these losses are in the formal forestry sector, which has been promoted as a key economic driver of development.

Recent findings that land-use changes, including deforestation, are responsible for about 18 per cent of annual greenhouse emissions have raised the stakes and elevated forestry issues onto the international agenda.[3] Key United Nations Framework Convention on Climate Change (UNFCCC) negotiations now include a mechanism to provide incentives to developing countries for the Reducing Emissions from Deforestation and Forest Degradation initiative – a concept known as REDD, and several billion US dollars have been earmarked for REDD and multilateral REDD-related efforts. Some US$17–33 billion per year could flow as a result, making forests worth more standing up than cut down.[4]

The combination of significant corruption risks in the timber industry and the fact that many forest-rich countries suffer very high levels of corruption and poor governance of resource revenues represents one of the greatest threats to the success of any REDD agreement. Interpol warns that the sheer scale of REDD may make it impossible to monitor.[5]

A sector prone to corruption

The forestry sector is one in which large-scale illegality both thrives and depends on widespread corruption. It pervades every step of the logging process, especially in the bidding processes for concessions, forest management (or the lack of it) related to these concessions, over-harvesting, under-declaring timber volumes, cutting outside permitted areas, tax evasion and state failure to prosecute perpetrators. The capacity of some interests to capture forest resources and revenue flows, in the context of an industry that has up to now effectively avoided international regulation, has condemned most reform efforts to failure.

This corruption is enabled in part because most of the world's tropical forests are classified as public land,[6] and can be therefore controlled by relatively few politicians and civil servants, who are in a position to wield great discretionary power in return for bribes. Furthermore, forests are remote and beyond the public gaze, and the populations most affected – more than a billion forest-dependent people – can be effectively excluded from the decision-making processes that determine the fate of forests, due to a lack of information, resources, capacity and influence.[7]

Private land ownership is not a guarantee that corruption can be warded off. Nevertheless, the collective self-interest represented by community or local control of forests, which is itself not immune to corruption, can act as a powerful check on it.

Since the late 1980s the international donor community has spent tens of billions of US dollars trying to reduce deforestation and harness forests for economic growth in developing countries.[8] The international forestry community usually portrays tropical forests as a renewable resource, but industrial-scale logging of tropical forests cannot be simultaneously economically and ecologically sustainable.[9] Most investments have focused on trying to improve forest management, governance, technical capacity, and legal mechanisms and compliance. Nonetheless, the tropical regions of Africa, Latin America and Southeast Asia lost around 1.2 million km^2 of forest from 1990 to 2005 – an area the size of France, Germany and the UK combined.[10]

The typical 30-year harvest rotation required by most tropical forest management plans does not allow enough time for trees to regenerate, so logging companies tend to log far beyond sustainable limits. Now that stricter legal, governance and enforcement systems are being introduced, companies can make money only by seeking subsidies – continually extending their operations into new areas containing high-value virgin forests – or by bucking the system.[11] To maximize profits, companies are tempted either to over-harvest within permitted areas or to cut outside them.[12]

An alarming number of logging companies appear to rely on subterfuge, intimidation of observers and corruption. Transporting timber to export points and evading various taxes and royalties require bribes in order to obtain the necessary paperwork. Once this paperwork is in place the job becomes much easier, because, with the exception of the US (see below), no countries have laws that ban the importation of illegally sourced timber, so it can be laundered onto the international market with ease.[13]

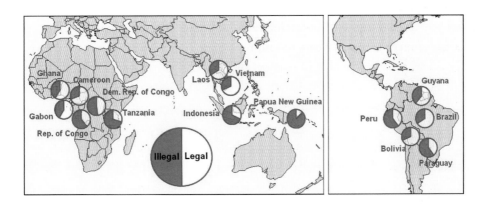

Source: Produced by Global Witness based on estimates from www.globaltimber.org.uk/IllegalTimberPercentages.doc.

Figure 6.1 Estimated proportion of timber exports from 14 REDD countries and Brazil that was illegal in 2007

The engines of corruption

Corruption can be driven by politicians, government officials and their business patrons, who make discretionary timber deals without following due process; by the international donor community, which often drives and bankrolls national forest strategies and individual logging operations, but fails to address adequately the corruption that condemns virtually all these ventures to failure; and by the unrelenting international demand for cheap timber.

The tropical timber industry has both driven and fuelled grand corruption in virtually every country it has operated in. Brazil, home to the world's largest tropical forest block, scores 3.7 (out of 10) on TI's Corruption Perceptions Index. The Democratic Republic of Congo (DRC), with the second largest block, scores 1.9, while Congo Basin countries in general, which together possess Africa's richest forests, have an average score of 2.3. Papua New Guinea, which shares the third largest forest block with West Papua, scores 2.1.

Country	Area of forest ('000 ha)	% total forest area of countries given	TI Corruption Perception Index rating 2008 (rank, out of 180)	World Bank Ease of Doing Business rating 2009 (rank, out of 181)	OECD Country Credit Risk rating 2008 (1 = best; 7 = worst)	Country Indicators for Foreign Policy Fragile States Index rating 2007 (1 = best; 7 = worst)	Freedom House Political Rights rating 2008 (1 = best; 7 = worst)	Freedom House Civil Liberties rating 2008 (1 = best; 7 = worst)	World Bank Government Effectiveness rating 2007 (-2.5 = worst; +2.5 = best)	World Bank Political Stability/Absence of Violence rating 2007 (-2.5 = worst; +2.5 = best)	World Bank Regulatory Quality rating 2007 (-2.5 = worst; +2.5 = best)	World Bank Rule of Law rating 2007 (-2.5 = worst; +2.5 = best)
Ecuador	10,853	0.9	151	136	7	5.18	3	3	-1.04	-0.91	-1.09	-1.04
Vietnam	12,931	1.0	121	92	4	5.11	7	5	-0.41	0.31	-0.43	-0.53
Thailand	14,520	1.2	80	13	3	4.68	6	4	0.16	-1.07	0.11	-0.06
Suriname	14,776	1.2	72	146	n/a	4.46	2	2	-0.03	0.23	-0.40	-0.24
Guyana	15,104	1.2	126	105	n/a	5.09	2	3	-0.09	-0.32	-0.46	-0.57
Laos	16,142	1.3	151	165	7	5.88	7	6	-0.81	0.00	-1.08	-0.96
Malaysia	20,890	1.7	47	20	2	4.41	4	4	1.07	0.20	0.53	0.53
Cameroon	21,245	1.7	141	164	7	5.85	6	6	-0.87	-0.39	-0.71	-1.09
Congo, Rep.	22,471	1.8	158	178	7	6.05	5	5	-1.34	-0.83	-1.20	-1.26
Central African Rep.	22,755	1.8	151	180	7	6.12	5	5	-1.38	-1.78	-1.24	-1.52
Gabon	26,767	2.1	96	151	6	5.13	6	4	-0.66	0.20	-0.49	-0.60
Papua New Guinea	29,437	2.3	151	95	5	5.55	3	3	-0.74	-0.76	-0.51	-0.85
Burma	32,222	2.6	178	n/a	7	5.90	7	7	-1.67	-1.22	-2.23	-1.41
Venezuela	47,713	3.8	158	174	6	5.13	4	4	-0.87	-1.23	-1.56	-1.47
Bolivia	58,740	4.7	102	150	7	5.13	3	3	-0.83	-0.99	-1.18	-0.96
Colombia	60,728	4.8	70	53	4	5.24	3	3	0.03	-1.65	0.21	-0.57
Mexico	64,238	5.1	72	56	2	4.68	2	3	0.13	-0.57	0.39	-0.58
Peru	68,742	5.5	72	62	3	4.92	2	3	-0.44	-0.83	0.20	-0.71
Indonesia	88,495	7.0	126	129	5	5.46	2	3	-0.41	-1.13	-0.30	-0.71
Congo, Dem. Rep.	133,610	10.6	171	181	7	6.50	5	6	-1.68	-2.26	-1.35	-1.67
Brazil	477,698	37.9	80	125	3	4.63	2	2	-0.12	-0.22	-0.04	-0.44
TOTAL	1,260,077											
Average			118	119	5	5.29	4	4	-0.57	-0.72	-0.61	-0.80

Source: Simon Counsell, REDD-Monitor Risk Table, http://www.redd-monitor.org/2008/12/05/risk-the-fatal-flaw-in-forest-carbon-trading/, REDD-Monitor, 2008.

Table 6.1   REDD-Monitor 'Rainforest Risk' tables, December 2008

Politicians, public officials and the timber industry

In some countries, natural resources seem to be treated as the personal fiefdom of the ruling elite, to be 'sold' as they see fit, regardless of national laws. Such elite capture means that corruption has become systemic across entire nations or resource sectors. Over and above the desire for personal wealth, political leaders bestow money or exploitation rights on key ministers and military or business elites in return for political, military or financial support. Capturing state resources effectively requires both coordination and patronage, and the connivance of key officials.

High-level appointments in some places are 'sold' to key allies, who can then run these ministries or departments, making important decisions that favour their patrons rather than the constituencies they are paid to serve. In turn, corrupt officials can ensure that corrupt revenues trickle down the hierarchy so that everyone at the head office benefits.[14]

At the bottom of the 'food chain', field-level forestry enforcement officers are typically very poorly paid and equipped. Their salaries are often augmented by the very logging companies they are meant to oversee, and through bribes and checkpoint fees.[15] Moreover, in remote areas where logging generates vast unofficial revenues, only a very brave person would dare to blow the whistle on the people with whom he or she lives and works. This is the sharp end, where corruption and physical intimidation go hand in hand.

Corruption hot spots

In the early 2000s Cameroon joined the front line in the battle against corruption and illegal logging, as forestry reforms would make the country eligible for international debt relief.[16] Logging companies indulged in illegal logging on a massive scale, following the example of the president's son, Frank Biya, who extended a 1000ha permit[17] so that he eventually controlled about 130,000ha of forest.[18]

In a similar vein, Teodorin Obiang, the agriculture and forests minister of neighbouring Equatorial Guinea and also the son of a president, has a multimillion-dollar car collection and owns a US$35 million beachfront home in Malibu, California – while earning a monthly salary of US$4000.[19] With one of the highest levels of per capita GDP in the world, Equatorial Guinea has little to show for its oil and timber wealth.[20] The timber sector is dominated by Shimmer International, a subsidiary of Malaysian timber conglomerate Rimbunan Hijau, which according to a document obtained in 1999, also acted as a logging contractor for Obiang's own timber concession.[21]

Major reviews of Papua New Guinea's (PNG's) forest sector have found it to be one of the most corrupt in the world. In an unusually blunt governmental report from 1989, corruption was shown to be 'pervasive', including bribery, non-compliance with regulations, extensive violations of landowners' rights and extreme environmental destruction. Logging companies have been reported to be 'roaming the countryside with the self assurance of robber barons; bribing politicians and leaders, creating social disharmony and ignoring laws in order to gain access to, rip out, and export valuable timber'.[22] A 2006 report found that PNG's logging industry 'is synonymous with political corruption, police racketeering and the brutal repression of workers, women and those who question its ways. Its operations routinely destroy the food sources, water supplies and cultural property of those same communities. They provide a breeding ground for arms smuggling, corruption and violence across the country.'[23]

The enablers of corruption, deforestation and degradation

The unsustainable logging of tropical forests is not simply the economic equation of supply and demand. The faith of the international development community in industrial-scale logging as a key economic driver of and contributor to sustainable development and poverty alleviation has been promoted by the international forestry community. It has been seized upon by the tropical timber industry, which portrays itself as a key development partner: the websites of the companies concerned highlight their contributions to national economies, employment and the building of schools and clinics.

Multinational timber companies

Timber companies are seeking to improve their credentials and their eligibility to receive concessions. Another intention is to attract financial support from bilateral development funds and endorsements from large conservation non-governmental organizations (NGOs) to improve the forest management practices that should really be a core part of their business already. In many cases these attempts would appear to be a cynical mechanism to maximize profit at taxpayers' expense, as their actual practices belie their commitment to their publicly stated developmental aims.

The ultimate possessor of the largest timber concession in Africa, Swiss–German timber conglomerate Danzer, is at the forefront of this public relations campaign, stating on its website: 'Responsible forest management means also contributing to the sustainable development of the region and countries [in which] we operate, in particular combating poverty. Danzer Group … has [a] skilled … workforce and has generated tax and export revenues. Also, Danzer Group has built schools, roads and small hospitals at its operations.'[24]

Meanwhile, DRC-based Danzer subsidiary SIFORCO (Société Industrielle et Forestière du Congo) was accused by Greenpeace in 2008 of systematically avoiding taxes through transfer pricing, thus depriving the DRC and Republic of Congo governments of at least €7.8 million.[25] Danzer denied the allegations even though they were based on internal company documentation, citing an audit carried out on its behalf by Ernst & Young, the findings of which have not been made public.[26] While tax avoidance is not necessarily illegal, it does not reflect well on an industry that plays the development card in its international lobbying.

Moreover, along with Danish logging multinational DLH, Danzer companies were also major buyers of timber from Liberia during the presidency of Charles Taylor. Despite extensive evidence linking the timber trade and trafficking of arms into Liberia,[27] human rights abuses, illegal logging and corruption, these companies imported Liberian logs up until the moment that UN Security Council sanctions brought this trade to a halt, in July 2003.[28] From December 2001, long before Security Council sanctions came into force, the most notorious Liberian logging company and a major supplier to DLH and Danzer, the Oriental Timber Company, exported logs to Europe as the Evergreen Trading Company, in an effort to disguise the origin of the timber, and also replaced company markings on logs with a secret code in the form of a series of coloured dots.[29]

In Papua New Guinea the website of Rimbunan Hijau (PNG) proclaims: 'RH is a significant contributor to the nation's economic and social wellbeing. [...] RH is Papua New Guinea's industry leader on environmentally responsible and 100 per cent legal management of forests. [...] RH has prided itself on an economically, environmentally and socially sustainable future for Papua New Guinea.'[30] In fact, in October 2008 it admitted in court that it had been awarded logging rights in PNG illegally.[31] Eight months later its website reported the company's participation in TI's 'Walk against Corruption' in Port Moresby. In an extremely retrogressive step, on 28 May 2010 PNG's Parliament amended the Environment and Conservation Act, removing the rights of indigenous people to challenge deals concerning the country's natural resources.[32]

Multilateral and bilateral donors

In an effort to end corrupt practices, international donors have taken a series of actions, ranging from placing conditions on aid, funding the creation or improvement of forest laws, providing technical assistance for law enforcement activities, funding independent forest monitoring and, in its ultimate manifestation, helping to shape the entire forest sector. Examples include the creation of the Liberia Forest Initiative in post-conflict Liberia and a reform process that cost US$20 million, funded equally by the World Bank and the United States Agency for International Development (USAID).[33]

As is often the case when the root of corruption is at a high level, however, donors have failed to achieve the desired results. A World Bank funding programme in Cambodia and international debt relief in Cameroon gave way to business-as-usual corruption. Essential political support from the donor community for Global Witness, which served as an independent forest monitor in these countries, shrivelled in the face of diplomatic awkwardness caused by the organization's field-based findings that suggested there was top-level corruption.[34] International donors have yet to comprehend that failing to match anti-corruption rhetoric with action actually entrenches corruption, sending a clear message that, when push comes to shove, they will not act.

In Liberia the process of forestry reform entered the implementation phase after five years of work in 2008, with the start of concession auctions and sales of old timber stockpiles. Almost immediately the regulations, guidelines and various checks and balances that had been built in to the reform process were allegedly routinely broken or ignored.[35] In early 2009 the country's Forest Development Authority unilaterally altered the tax structure for the concessions after the bidding process was under way, reducing the requirement for 25 annual payments to one initial payment. This would have cost the government up to US$150 million in revenues.[36] Behind-the-scenes protests from the donor community prevented this from going through, but no one was held accountable and no investigation was conducted. Although no investigation has been carried out as to whether corruption played a role in this process, a Special Presidential Committee established to investigate a forest carbon deal recently released its report which documented various allegations of corruption, and recommended the dismissal of and further investigation into various officials, some of whom were involved in both processes.[37] So while there is no evidence that corruption played a role in the concession allocation process, the Forest Development Authority's decision to unilaterally give up millions of dollars in a sector specifically reformed to bring economic and social benefit is questionable.

Such examples illustrate that the tropical forest sector's ability to deliver economic and social benefits can be undermined in practice by the failure of governments and their aid partners to solve problems. Indeed, the international donor community has displayed a remarkably tolerant attitude towards illegality. Significantly, until 2008, no country had a law that made it illegal to import illegally sourced timber. In May 2008 the US led the way by passing an amendment to the Lacey Act[38] that not only bans the importation of illegally sourced timber but firmly places the burden of proof of legality on the importers and imposes severe penalties for non-compliance, including fines of up to US$500,000, seizure of merchandise and up to five years' imprisonment.

In contrast, the European Union (EU), where it is estimated that the market for illegal tropical timber may comprise between 16 and 19 per cent of total imports,[39] has been considering legislation since 2003. Belatedly, in July 2010 the European Parliament voted to approve a regulation, the aim of which is '...to halt the trade in illegally harvested timber and products made from such timber in the EU ...'. The move was approved by the European Council in October 2010, but the law will not come into force until 2012. Although this regulation is welcome, it falls short of the stringent requirements of the Lacey Act in that it relies on due diligence carried out by the importers themselves, only applies to those who first place timber on the market, rather than the whole supply chain, and there are no minimum penalties across the EU, with sanctions left to member states.[40]

Despite this appalling record, the development community continues to champion industrial-scale logging under the label of 'sustainable forest management'.[41] This includes pressure for countries to factor the forest sector into their national Poverty Reduction Support Programmes; and financial support (bilateral aid and World Bank grants and loans) to improve technical capacity, subsidize logging companies to produce forest management plans, and to fund certification schemes and infrastructure investments. Overall, 'aid' money has bankrolled the forest sector to the tune of around US$750 million per year.[42] Despite these vast sums, the global gross loss of primary forest between 2000 and 2005 averaged 13 million ha per year, 7.3 million ha of which returned as plantations.[43]

In sum, countless initiatives and billions of dollars have been spent trying to curb illegal activities in the industrial logging sector. The question must be asked whether success is actually achievable before the world's remaining tropical forests are commercially logged out – doing little to serve the communities that depend on forests for their livelihoods and next to nothing to mitigate the effects of climate change.

The future of sustainable forestry: seeing REDD?

If forest management regimes that protect the rights of forest-dependent people and are ecologically sustainable are not economically viable, logging companies have incentive to engage in illegal practices to make profits. In countries already given over to concession logging, everything possible must be done to improve transparency and good governance. In countries that still have forests not yet allocated to concessions, such as the DRC and Liberia, the only sensible option is to seek new, alternative uses for forests that are socially, ecologically and economically equitable, or perhaps learn from traditional forest uses that make possible a symbiotic relationship between people and forest ecosystems.

REDD offers the opportunity to preserve these forests. Although preventing illegal practices within REDD and managing forests under a REDD mechanism will face many of the same challenges that have dogged the industrial logging sector, a good REDD agreement must have at its core the protection of natural forests rather than promoting the logging of them. It will be easier to detect criminality in 'no-logging zones' than to spot illegally felled trees among the legally felled ones as the logging trucks roll towards ports in Africa, Asia and Latin America.

Under a REDD regime, forests will still need to be managed. Illegal logging will need to be prevented, social and environmental issues will need to be monitored and carbon will need to be accounted for. Enabling legal mechanisms will need to be created and enforced. REDD revenues will need to be captured and equitably distributed, because REDD cannot work if forest-dependent populations do not realize any benefits. It is, of course, forest-dependent communities that have the best record in conserving forests, but this fact, and the lessons that could be learned from it, are usually ignored by the policy-makers who determine future forest use.

Corruption poses risks to REDD, as illustrated when an Interpol official noted: 'Organised crime syndicates are eyeing the nascent forest carbon market. I will report to the [World Bank] that [REDD] schemes are open to wide abuse... [REDD] fraud could include claiming credits for forests that do not exist or were not protected or by land grabs. It starts with bribery or intimidation of officials, then there's threats and violence against those people.'[44]

In late 2009 the president of the Republic of Congo, Denis Sassou Nguesso, in his role as the African Union's spokesperson on climate change, made various heartfelt pleas to the international community – including US President Barack Obama in particular[45] – for international financial support to help poor but forest-rich countries protect their forests for the global good. This indeed must happen, but his sentiments ignore his country's abysmal record.[46]

Furthermore, the Republic of Congo is a member of the Coalition for Rainforest Nations (CfRN),[47] which is a major force in the drive to obtain financial benefits through a REDD mechanism. CfRN describes itself as 'forested tropical countries collaborating to reconcile forest stewardship with economic development'.[48] Despite these laudable aims, many of the coalition members have egregious records in achieving this reconciliation.[49] Until there is genuine political will in such countries to tackle corruption, a major driver of deforestation, it is unlikely that any forest management regime can be effective. Rhetoric will achieve nothing.

Corruption in tropical forestry has thrived in large part because, although it has been publicly condemned, it has also been tolerated – and it has been tolerated because naive policy-makers have come erroneously to believe that industrial logging is simultaneously ecologically and economically sustainable and good for development as well. The reality is that the world must enter a new phase of zero tolerance for forest-related corruption. The world's remaining forests are at stake, and without them the battle against climate change cannot be won.

Notes

1. Patrick Alley is a director of Global Witness.
2. World Bank, *Strengthening Forest Law Enforcement and Governance: Addressing a Systemic Constraint to Sustainable Development* (Washington, DC: World Bank, 2006), p. xi.
3. Nicholas Stern, *The Economics of Climate Change (The Stern Review)* (Cambridge: Cambridge University Press, 2006). See also: Guido van der Werf et al., 'CO$_2$ Emissions from Forest Loss', *Nature Geoscience*, vol. 2 (2009), pp. 737–738.
4. See Johannes Ebeling and Maï Yasue, 'Generating Carbon Finance through Avoided Deforestation and its Potential to Create Climatic, Conservation and Human Development Benefits', *Philosophical Transactions of the Royal Society B*, vol. 363 (2008), pp. 1917–1924; The Eliasch Review, *Climate Change: Financing Global Forests* (London: Her Majesty's Stationery Office, 2008).
5. *Guardian* (UK), 'UN's forest protection scheme at risk from organized crime, experts warn', 5 October 2009.
6. Food and Agriculture Organization of the UN (FAO), *State of the World's Forests 2007* (Rome: FAO, 2007), p. 70.
7. See International Union for Conservation of Nature (IUCN), 'Indigenous Peoples and REDD-plus: Challenges and Opportunities for the Engagement of Indigenous Peoples and Local Communities in REDD-plus' (Gland: IUCN, 2010).
8. See Anand Madhvani, *An Assessment of Data on ODA Financial Flows in the Forest Sector* (New York: UN Development Programme [UNDP], 1999); Uma Lele et al., *The World Bank Forest Strategy: Striking the Right Balance* (Washington, DC: World Bank, 2000).
9. See Brendan Mackey et al., *Green Carbon: The Role of Natural Forests in Carbon Storage* (Canberra: ANU [Australian National University] E Press, 2008), pp. 17–18.
10. Global Witness, *Trick or Treat? REDD, Development and Sustainable Forest Management* (London: Global Witness, 2009).
11. See http://www.idrc.ca/en/ev-28721-201-1-DO_TOPIC.html.
12. See www.globalwitness.org for reports on Cambodia and Cameroon that are illustrative of these issues; Royal Government of Cambodia, Ministry of Agriculture Forestry and Fisheries, Department of Forestry & Wildlife, *Cambodian Forest Concession Review Report* (Asian Development Bank, 28 April 2000).
13. Dependent on approval by the European Council, an EU regulation is set to take effect from 2012.

14. Global Witness, *Cambodia's Family Trees, Illegal Logging and the Stripping of Public Assets* (Global Witness, June 2007).

15. Numerous interviews conducted by the author in both Cambodia and Cameroon between 1995 and 2002.

16. World Bank, 'Aide-mémoire_Evaluation Mission_Forestry Component of CAS III_FESP: List of conditionalities for HIPC funding and level of achievement' (World Bank, July 2002); World Bank, 'International Development Association and International Finance Corporation interim strategy note for the Republic of Cameroon, FY07-08', Report no. 37897-CM (World Bank, November 2006).

17. Autorisation de Récupération de Bois (ARB), 'NGO accuses Biya's son of plundering Cameroon's rainforests', Afrique en Ligne, 25 July 2009; Project of Independent Observation in Support of Forest Law Enforcement in Cameroon, Joint mission: Central Control Unit – Independent Observer, Global Witness, 30 July 30–2 August, 2002.

18. See Forest Law Enforcement in Cameroon 2nd Summary Report of the Independent Observer December 2001–June 2003, Global Witness, October 2003. Global Witness, an independent forest monitor in Cameroon at the time, found its enquiries into the case blocked by the authorities, and was even asked by the World Bank, UK Department for International Development and other donors to omit mention of these familial links in its reports in order to avoid 'diplomatic' discomfort. Global Witness did not comply with the requests (personal communication with a World Bank official, June 2002).

19. *Financial Times* (UK), 'Taking a cut acceptable, says African minister', 25 October 2006; Global Witness, *The Secret Life of a Shopaholic: How an African Dictator's Playboy Son Went on a Multi-Million Dollar Shopping Spree in the US* (London: Global Witness, November 2009).

20. A special rapporteur to the UN Commission on Human Rights reported that '80 per cent of national income is in the hands of 5 per cent of the population'; see UN Commission on Human Rights, 'Question of the Violation of Human Rights and Fundamental Freedoms in any Part of the World', 27 January 2000. The rapporteur also stated that '[t]he exceptional economic boom which followed the discovery of major oilfields in the mid-1990s has not led to any improvement in the economic, social and cultural rights of the population, more than 65% of which lives in conditions of extreme poverty'. See UN Commission on Human Rights, *UN Report on the Human Rights Situation in Equatorial Guinea – 2001*, 2001.

21. Proyecto Conservación y Utilización Racional de los Ecosistemas Forestales (*CUREF*), 'Situación de las Concesiones Forestales' (document obtained 1999); Greenpeace International, *The Untouchables: Rimbunan Hijau's World of Forest Crime and Political Patronage* (Amsterdam: Greenpeace International, 2004).

22. Government of Papua New Guinea, *Commission of Inquiry into Aspects of the Forest Industry: Final Report* (2 vols) (Waigani: Department of the Prime Minister, 1989).

23. Centre for Environmental Law and Community Rights (CELCOR) and Australian Conservation Foundation (ACF), *Bulldozing Progress: Human Rights Abuses and Corruption in Papua New Guinea's Large Scale Logging Industry* (Port Moresby and Carlton, Victoria: CELCOR and ACF, 2006).

24. Danzer Group website, davidrwebb.com/Africa.2790.0.html.

25. Greenpeace International, *Conning the Congo* (Amsterdam: Greenpeace International, 2008).

26. Danzer Group, 'Danzer Group: Subsidiary IFO in the Republic of Congo obtains FSC certificate' press release, March 2009. When asked, Danzer releases this audit only on receipt of a 'declaration of confidentiality': e-mail from Olof von Gagern, Danzer, to Global Witness, 20 July 2009.

27. This is extensively documented. See, for example, Report of the Panel of Experts appointed pursuant to UN Security Council Resolution 1306 (2000), paragraph 19 in relation to Sierra Leone, paragraph 215.

28. See www.globalwitness.org for numerous reports about the Liberian timber industry.

29. Oriental Timber Company internal company documents in Global Witness's possession.

30. Rimbunan Hijau (PNG) website, www.rhpng.com.pg.

31. For example, www.eventpolynesia.com/newsroom/common/CO2_page_newsroom08088.htm.

32. IRIN News (Papua New Guinea), 'Indigenous people lose out on land rights', 1 June 2010, at http://ww.irinnews.org/Report.aspx?ReportId=89322.

33. See Liberia Forest Initiative website: http://www.fao.org/forestry/lfi/en/.

34. Reform of the Forest Crime Monitoring and Reporting Project, CMB/99/A05, Global Witness, March 2002.

35. Global Witness, 'Credibility of Liberia's forestry reform programme at point of collapse, warns Global Witness', press release, 28 August 2009.

36. SGS/Liberfor, 'Fiscal Year Summary of Forestry Fees Up to 1 June 2010'.

37. Executive Mansion, Government of Liberia, 'Special Statement by President Ellen Johnson Sirleaf on the Report of the Special Presidential Investigative Committee on Alleged Carbon Credit Deal', 12 October 2010. See http://www.emansion.gov.lr/press.php?news_id=1679.

38. The Lacey Act protects plants and wildlife through civil and criminal penalties for violations, including trade in wildlife, fish and plants that have been illegally taken, possessed, transported or sold.

39. WWF, *Illegal Wood for the European Market: An Analysis of the EU Import and Export of Illegal Wood and Related Products* (Brussels: WWF, 2008).

40. European Parliament, 'MEPs vote to cut illegal timber out of the EU market', press release, 7 July 2010. See http://www.illegal-logging.info/uploads/l29520101112en00230034.pdf.

41. The term 'sustainable forest management' is poorly defined. Although on the surface it sounds a reasonable concept, in practice it is usually used by the timber industry to describe conventional, industrial-scale logging. See Global Witness, September 2009.

42. Richard Rice et al., *Sustainable Forest Management: A Review of Conventional Wisdom* (Washington, DC: Center for Applied Biodiversity Science, Conservation International, 2001).

43. FAO, *Global Forest Resources Assessment 2005* (Rome: FAO, 2006).

44. *Guardian* (UK), 5 October 2009.

45. Government of the Republic of Congo, 'Congo–Brazzaville president calls on US to support financial mechanism to preserve Congo Basin', 1 October 2009; Republic of Congo, 'Open letter to President Obama'.

46. This is well documented. See, for example, Judgement in the High Court of Justice, Queen's Bench Division, before Justice Stanley Burnton, Long Beach Limited and Denis Christel Sassou Nguessou and Global Witness Ltd, case no. HQ07X02371, 15 August 2007.

47. For the full composition of the coalition, see www.rainforestcoalition.org.

48. CfRN website, www.rainforestcoalition.org/eng/about/index.php.

49. CfRN member states have a collective average rank of 113 out of 180 on the Corruption Perceptions Index (not including Fiji).

6.1.1

Climate change and corruption leave the world's largest mangrove forest in peril

Iftekhar Zaman and Manzoor-e-Khuda[1]

The Sundarban, off the southwest coast of Bangladesh, is the largest contiguous mangrove forest in the world. It constitutes 51 per cent of the total reserved forest in Bangladesh, contributes 41 per cent to the total forest revenue and accounts for about 45 per cent of all timber and fuel output.[2] Significantly, it also serves as an essential 'bio-shield' against cyclones and high tidal surges, providing protection against coastal erosion and stabilizing land by trapping sediment. In effect, the belt of mangroves is capable of absorbing 30–40 per cent of the total force of a tsunami- or cyclone-generated shock wave before it reaches the inhabited area behind it.[3]

Not only is the Sundarban threatened by the onset of climate change and rising sea levels – it is estimated that a 45cm sea-level rise would inundate 75 per cent of the mangrove, with a 1m rise covering it completely – but it has the additional threat of corruption to contend with. The mangrove is highly vulnerable to illegal logging, particularly in the logging of its precious trees – the sundari. Illegal logging takes place with impunity, involving the collusion of business syndicates, corrupt forest officials and the local administration.[4] The common form of smuggling these trees involves labourers operating under the guise of transporting Nypa leaves in rafts that are in fact full of illegal logs. It has been estimated that, with this form of trafficking alone, the value of the logs smuggled out of the mangrove each year is equal to Bangladeshi taka (Tk) 60 million.[5] Logs are also illegally transported by fishermen and bawalis (official collectors of Nypa leaves); through this process an estimated Tk1.35 billion worth of logs are smuggled each year.[6]

In order for this illegal trade to function unchallenged it demands the complicity of local officials. It is estimated that corrupt forest officials extort almost Tk62.5 million from the bawalis each year, in addition to the regular revenue coming from permits issued to them. In order to cope with such demands they have to collect almost four times their permitted volume of Nypa leaves. Similarly, fishermen have to pay unofficial tolls to officials for each trip, make payments at different checkpoints on their transportation routes and pay bribes when they renew their boat permits. It is estimated that, in total, forest officials extort around Tk230 million a year from the fishermen.[7] In addition, officials often allow entry into wildlife sanctuaries in exchange for bribes, encouraging further degradation of the ecosystem.[8]

Illegal logging has a substantial impact on the mangrove's ability to protect settlements from environmental threats, which are likely to become more severe and frequent with the onset of climate change. Bangladesh's policies can themselves have the effect of encouraging illegal logging practices. Bangladesh follows a revenue-oriented forest policy rather than one focused on conservation. Each year a revenue target is set by the government, which progressively increases over time. The achievement of these targets is the principal criterion on which the performance of forestry officials is evaluated. As a result, officials are under pressure to meet targets, and often resort to unauthorized means of collecting the revenue.

The combination of illegal practices – some of them encouraged by the government's emphasis on revenues rather than conservation – is likely to degrade the Sundarban significantly and, in turn, have cumulative impacts on climate change, environmental sustainability and development. The degradation of the mangrove will mean that it will not be able to play its carbon storage role, further contributing to climate change. Its loss as a bio-shield against cyclones and tidal waves and its weakened capacity to trap land sediments and stabilize the coastline will have severe consequences for the 3.5 million people who depend directly or indirectly for their livelihoods on the mangrove's resources.[9]

The role of illegal practices and wrong-headed policies in accelerating the degradation of the mangrove highlights the need for tackling governance issues in any climate change adaptation plan. The government's first step should be to reorient forestry policy away from concentrating on revenues to one of promoting sustainable extraction and conservation and mainstreaming these initiatives into national development and planning. This, coupled with adequate monitoring by Forest Department officials, the police, army and border guards, who are themselves held accountable, and effective incentives and enforcement powers, would have a twofold impact on the Sundarban: it would contribute to mitigation through the preservation of a carbon sink, and be an effective contributor to adaptation by maintaining the natural bio-shield, which will become all the more important for human development as the effects of inevitable climate change become more severe.

Notes

1. Iftekhar Zaman and Manzoor-e-Khuda work for Transparency International Bangladesh.
2. Food and Agriculture Organization (FAO), quoted in Saidur Rahman (undated), 'Ecology and Management of Sundarban: A Rich Biodiversity of the World's Largest Mangrove Ecosystem'.
3. *Daily Star* (Bangladesh), 28 December 2007.
4. This section draws from a diagnostic study by TI Bangladesh, *Transparency and Accountability in Forest Conservation and Management: Problems and Way Out* (Dhaka: TI Bangladesh, 2008). See www.ti-bangladesh.org/research/Eng-ex-summary-forest.pdf.
5. Ibid. US$1 = taka 68 (approximately).
6. Ibid.
7. Ibid.
8. Ibid.
9. See www.unnayan.org/env.unit/paper3.pdf.

6.2

Governance in the world's tropical forests

Where will REDD+ land?

Jeffrey Hatcher and Luke Bailey[1]

Despite the disappointing outcome of the United Nations Framework Convention on Climate Change's (UNFCCC's) 2009 climate change conference in Copenhagen, an initiative known as Reducing Emissions from Deforestation and Forest Degradation (REDD) remains one of the strongest points of international political consensus. REDD was formally introduced at the UNFCCC's 2007 conference, held in Bali, Indonesia, as an incentive-based mechanism to slow or stop deforestation and forest degradation, which is a major source of global greenhouse gas emissions. As thinking on REDD – now expanded and known as REDD+[2] – has matured over the past few years, a more sophisticated dialogue has developed on the links between governance and better forest management.

International climate negotiators and national policy-makers have begun to appreciate that REDD+ is not just about counting carbon but, rather, the complex social, ecological and economic relations in the forest areas where that carbon is found. REDD+ has the potential to drastically alter the way the world's forests are governed. At its core it is a restrictive land-use regulation, and thus it harbours the potential to infringe on local peoples' rights to access, use and manage the forests on which their livelihoods depend.[3] This concern is all the more pressing given that many countries eligible for World Bank or REDD+ readiness[4] programmes have been deemed 'fragile states', with poor governance and little economic growth.[5] Weak institutions, powerful vested interests and pervasive corruption pose acute challenges to efforts to reduce deforestation in these countries.

REDD+ has the potential to improve forest governance through increased funding for governance reforms, greater scrutiny of national forest sectors and the creation of new opportunities for forest communities to claim their rights from central governments. Although REDD+ is moving towards implementation at the national scale, the cause for optimism should not hinder measures to ensure that REDD+ does not inadvertently weaken local or national governance or exacerbate political and economic inequalities.

The risks of REDD+ should be examined by pursuing two objectives. The first is to assess the status quo of governance in potential REDD+ countries in relation to the governance requirements needed to reduce emissions from deforestation and degradation. The second is to highlight the governance and accountability mechanisms needed to ensure that any REDD+ programme enhances the rights of forest communities and indigenous peoples. The world's tropical forests are remote, and they have long been poorly governed resource bases for national development where corruption and human rights abuses are commonplace.[6] REDD+ can change things for the better if it pays adequate attention to the governance issues that plague tropical forests. Otherwise it has the potential to worsen the situation.

Governance in potential REDD+ countries today

Aside from some small voluntary carbon market activities and readiness activities, an international REDD+ programme does not exist today. Funds and programmes have been established to prepare a set of countries to eventually participate in REDD+, either by selling carbon credits from verified emissions reductions in carbon markets or through more direct bilateral or multilateral compensation. The most prominent programmes[7] have identified a set of countries – often overlapping[8] – that will be prepared for REDD+ through a variety of technical and political interventions. These countries are mostly found in the tropics. While most of the world's forest carbon emissions come from just two countries – Indonesia and Brazil – REDD+ proponents argue that, without involving other smaller deforesters such as Liberia and Panama, there is a risk that deforestation will shift from one country to another.[9]

Examples of weak governance, corruption and rights abuses are not hard to find in potential REDD+ countries and their forests.[10] National forest agencies, which will be responsible for much of the REDD+ programme implementation, are not immune from such problems. A recent report, for example, uses allegations of financial mismanagement in Indonesia's Reforestation Fund as a warning.[11] Similarly, reports of missing Norwegian bilateral funds granted to Tanzania provide just a hint at the potential for corruption should a massive influx of REDD+ cash occur.[12] More directly related to REDD+, examples in Papua New Guinea (PNG) of forest owners being conned into selling away their carbon rights, and perceptions of government collusion with carbon brokers, paint a bleak picture for the future of REDD+.[13]

To achieve its aims and protect the rights of forest-based populations, REDD+ will require improvements on two levels: national institutional governance and forest governance.

Institutional governance

This relates to political stability, rent-seeking, clear and enforceable property rights, transparency, contract enforcement and effective judicial systems. These considerations are particularly important if REDD+ is to be funded through market- or fund-based financing to compensate for verified emissions reductions through the issuance and purchase of certified emission reduction (CER) credits. For example, sellers of credits originating in a country with limited rule of law will face the challenge of assuring buyers of the existence and persistence of the reductions purchased on paper. Unfortunately, most tropical forest countries, especially those with some of the highest deforestation rates, do not score well on relevant governance parameters.

The series of governance indicators in table 6.2 provides some parameters relevant to market- and fund-based REDD+ schemes for comparison across primary emitting countries. Most forest carbon emissions originate from a handful of countries. According to the best available figures, 61 per cent of all 2005 carbon emissions from land-use changes and forestry[14] came from Indonesia and Brazil. The nine next largest emitters totalled 23 per cent – less than Indonesia alone. While not all the countries in table 6.2 currently participate in REDD+ programmes, they will probably participate in REDD's voluntary carbon market.

A glance at the list of top emitters shows the serious governance challenges they face. The political context in some of these countries may pose insurmountable challenges to any new initiative to combat deforestation, let alone one as complicated as REDD+, with its requirements for new forest-monitoring technologies, standardized forest carbon inventories and consultations with remote communities.

The countries in table 6.2 generally score poorly on quantitative estimates of the corruption, transparency, government capacity and business environment:

- Eleven countries fall in the bottom half of TI's Corruption Perceptions Index, six of them in the bottom quartile.
- The countries fare somewhat better in Freedom House's ranking of political and civil liberties, with five in the lower half.

- All but two countries rank above 100 on the World Bank's 'Doing business' ranking of 183 countries, with six in the bottom quartile. According to the World Bank's 'Governance indicators', only Malaysia ranks well on 'government effectiveness' and 'control of corruption', with three and two countries in the bottom quartile, respectively.
- Eight of the 11 countries received a 'C' or 'D' rating from the French export credit rating agency Coface.[15]

From an environmental or climate perspective, these considerations are worrying, because the level of these countries' institutional capacity, corruption and transparency could potentially prevent the accurate reporting of emissions reductions upon which the REDD+ scheme depends. Thus an independent monitoring system is needed to measure both carbon and non-carbon outcomes of REDD+, as advocated by Global Witness. Additionally, there are doubts about the accuracy of government-reported data in the only existing global database of forest cover, the FAO's commonly cited Global Forest Resources Assessments.[16]

These data point out the potential difficulty in establishing, maintaining and monitoring national REDD+ programmes. A number of organizations have already voiced concern over the manner in which national consultations with civil society and indigenous peoples on REDD+ planning have been conducted.[17] Such critiques highlight the difficulty of implementing REDD+ in countries with a long-standing record of human rights abuse and a disregard for engaging local peoples in natural resource management plans. The fact that governments have been spurred to establish national working groups on REDD+ and attempt consultations can be seen as a positive development, however, insofar as governments are now reflecting on these issues and will probably report their performance for donor scrutiny.

Forest governance

This includes the conditions of forest tenure, forest management, land-use planning, and revenues and incentives.[18] The drivers of deforestation and degradation – mostly logging, agriculture and fire, as well as the interactions between them – are complex and difficult to address effectively through national policies.[19] Examples from history, however, show that certain basic conditions, such as secure land tenure and devolved management authority to local communities, have led to improvements in forest condition, carbon sequestration and local livelihoods.[20]

Unfortunately, for most of the world's forests these basic conditions do not exist. Weak governance affects the poor in particular, making their tenure over land insecure, creating additional costs to access administrative services, undermining systems of justice and dispute resolution and corroding social relations.[21]

Country	CAIT – 2005 yearly emissions		FAO Global Forest Resource Assessments, 2000–5	TI CPI, 2009	Freedom House ranking, 2009	World Bank, Doing Business 2010	World Bank 'Governance indicators' (−2.5 to 2.5, 2.5 = best governance)		COFACE 'Country risk' ratings (A1–D)	
	MtCO₂e	Share of world total (%)	Annual change in forest cover (Mha/yr)	Corruption Perceptions Index (1 – 10, 1 = most corrupt)	Combined average rating (1 – 7, 1 = free)	Ease of doing business ranking (out of 183)	Government effectiveness	Control of corruption	Country rating	Business climate rating
1 Brazil	1830	34.0	−3.10	3.7	2	129	0.0	0.0	A4	A4
2 Indonesia	1459	27.1	−1.87	2.8	2.5	122	−0.3	−0.6	B	C
3 Venezuela	187	3.5	−0.29	1.9	4	177	−0.9	−1.1	C	C
4 DRC	176	3.3	−0.32	1.7	6	182	−1.3	−1.3	D	D
5 Myanmar	158	2.9	−0.47	1.4	7	-	−1.7	−1.7	D	D
5 Nigeria	158	2.9	−0.41	2.5	4.5	125	−1.0	−0.9	D	D
7 Bolivia	139	2.6	−0.27	2.7	3	161	−0.8	−0.5	D	C
7 Malaysia	139	2.6	−0.14	4.5	4	23	1.1	0.1	A2	A3
9 Zambia	106	2.0	−0.45	3.0	3.0	90	−0.7	−0.5	C	C
10 Cambodia	84	1.6	−0.22	2.0	5.5	145	−0.8	−1.1	D	D
10 Ecuador	84	1.6	−0.20	2.2	3	138	−1.0	−0.8	C	C
Mean				2.6	4	129	−0.7	−0.8		
Total	4520	84								

Notes: TI's Corruption Perceptions Index measures poll results on the perceived level of corruption in 180 countries. The index is based on a 10-point scale, with 1 being most corrupt, and seeks to illustrate the effects of corruption specifically, apart from political instability and decentralization difficulties.

Freedom House's ranking of countries is a combined average of scores from a questionnaire on political rights and civil liberties, answered by in situ analysts. Countries are rated in increments of 0.5, with 1 representing the most free and 7 the least.

The World Bank's *Doing Business Report 2010* ranks 183 countries in terms of the ease of doing business, taking into account factors such as regulatory burdens, taxes and contract enforcement. The ranking is focused on domestic, small and medium-sized enterprises in the formal sector.

The World Bank's 'Governance indicators' compile survey results from businesses, researchers, citizens and non-governmental organizations (NGOs) on the 'rule of law' (the perceived degree of confidence that actors have in the laws of society, including property rights regimes, policing, judiciary and prevalence of crime). 'Control of corruption' illustrates the perceived extent of patronage, bribery, elite capture and other forms of corruption.

The 'Country risk' ratings developed by Coface, a French export credit agency, provide a standardized qualitative assessment of countries' overall stability and the business climate. Ratings range from A1 to A4, followed by B, C and D. An A1 rating denotes political stability and a positive business climate with strong institutions. In D-rated nations, corporate default rates are high, information and institutions are weak and the political and economic situation makes entrepreneurial activity highly risky.

Sources: CAIT Version 7.0 (WRI, 2010); TI, *Corruption Perceptions Index 2008*; Freedom House, *Freedom in the World 2009: Setbacks and Resilience* (Washington, DC: Freedom House, 2009); World Bank, *Doing Business 2010* (Washington, DC: World Bank, 2009), p. 4, tab. 1.3; Daniel Kaufmann et al., *Governance Matters VIII: Aggregate and Individual Governance Indicators, 1996–2008*, Policy Research Working Paper no. 4978 (Washington, DC: World Bank, 2009); Coface, 'Country risk' ratings, 2009.

Table 6.2 Governance indicators in key forest-carbon-emitting countries

Furthermore, the overwhelming majority of the world's tropical forests are legally owned by governments, despite the long-standing and legitimate claims of indigenous peoples and local communities, who have only minimal legal authority over managing the forests where they live and on which they depend.[22]

Latin America has done the most to legally recognize community forest ownership and management, with about 32 per cent of the region's forests under community and indigenous peoples' ownership or designated use (figure 6.2). In Asia the figure is about 27 per cent. In Africa, however, nearly 98 per cent of forests are claimed by the state. Moreover, there is a high degree of uncertainty and contestation in each region over statutory and customary ownership rights to forest and forest resources. In most countries the ownership rights to carbon remain unclear, and the creation of a new asset class – forest carbon – is likely to engender even more contestation in the forest landscape.

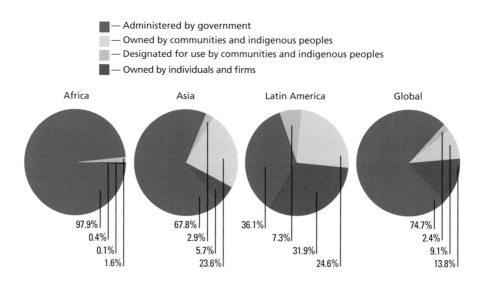

Figure 6.2 Regional forest tenure distribution, 2008

Source: Rights and Resources Initiative, *The End of the Hinterland*, 2010.

Governance requirements: ensuring REDD+ promotes the rights and well-being of forest communities and indigenous peoples

Effectively reducing emissions from deforestation and forest degradation, and promoting enhanced carbon sequestration capacities in the world's tropical forests, will require better forest governance and national institutional governance. The funding being touted by REDD+ proponents – US$3.5 billion was committed in

Copenhagen for REDD readiness – presents some hope that the world is serious about tackling deforestation. Nonetheless, there is also cause for concern, given the institutional environment in which this money will be injected. Governance reforms are lengthy processes, and funding increases alone are not adequate to guarantee their success. Without strong coordination and oversight, aid influxes may even exacerbate corruption.[23]

Basic governance reforms, including establishing a foundation of institutions and systems, are necessary for REDD+ target countries to make the most out of funding without negatively affecting the lives of forest communities and indigenous peoples. Such reforms should include:

- clarifying and securing the customary and statutory rights to land, carbon and forest for communities and indigenous, forest-dependent peoples;
- establishing independent, national and international oversight, recourse and auditing mechanisms to review impacts, realign REDD+ programmes and provide redress when rights are violated;
- directing compensation towards communities that have long depended upon and maintained forests; and
- ensuring that REDD+ programmes do not just monitor carbon but also include a robust measuring, reporting and verification (MRV) system to monitor rights impacts and flows of finances.[24]

Table 6.3 presents some considerations for REDD+ governance at the international, national and local levels. These parameters of good governance must be embedded within a national and local context in order for them to be relevant and effective.

From an optimistic perspective, it is worth noting that the costs of improving forest governance are relatively low compared to projected REDD funding. Recognizing forest tenure rights, for example, while politically strenuous, carries a relatively low direct cost.[25] A 2008 report commissioned by the UK prime minister estimates the governance cost of reducing forest emissions in 25 countries at US$2.3 billion over five years.[26] Merely securing financing does not guarantee results, however. As the report notes, such ambitious global projects 'have not always been successful... due to too little being spent, poor project design and management, or to lack of political will'.[27]

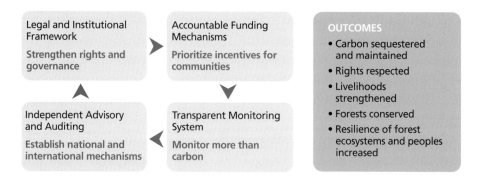

Figure 6.3 Framework of actions for ensuring effective climate change adaptation and mitigation in forest areas

Source: Adapted from Rights and Resources Initiative and Rainforest Foundation Norway, Foundations for Effectiveness, 2008.

Conclusion

Where does an examination of governance in REDD+ countries leave us? If one were pessimistic, one would conclude that the governance obstacles to reducing emissions from deforestation and forest degradation – or even just to set up a REDD+ programme – are too great to overcome. The challenges are all the more daunting given the short timeframe in which REDD+ proponents are expecting to disburse fast-start financing: nearly US$3.5 billion from 2010 to 2012.[28]

On the other hand, some national governments have taken dramatic steps to clarify property rights while making steady, incremental progress in strengthening governance.[29] It is important to recognize, given the momentum behind REDD+ and the support it received at the 2009 Copenhagen conference and subsequent inter-ministerial meetings,[30] that projects and financing will probably proceed despite governance challenges. This means that the world must act to ensure the money is directed towards the policies and governance reforms necessary to achieve long-term emissions reductions, enhanced sequestration and protection of the rights of forest communities.

Achieving forest carbon emissions reductions will mean realigning forest economies towards more sound governance of resources that includes greater local decision-making authority. Wholesale improvement to national governance is not likely to be the short-term outcome of REDD+ as these changes are likely beyond the scope of REDD+ itself – i.e. functioning court systems and political stability. Forest governance can be improved, though, by seizing this moment to secure the rights and tenure of forest communities, and improving decision-making processes related to forest management and land use.

	Transparency	Accountability	Equity	Participation	Coordination
International REDD+ governance (e.g. UNFCCC decision-making processes, global carbon market regulatory bodies, multilateral and bilateral funds)	Understandable information on negotiation processes, market regulatory bodies and fund governance is made accessible (e.g. funds allocated/ transferred).	Actions by investors, market regulatory bodies and funds are subject to independent audit, oversight and recourse (e.g. World Bank Inspection Panel).	Responsibilities, risks and benefits of participating in REDD+ programmes and markets are made clear and shared equitably.	Negotiations, market regulatory bodies and funds include effective participation from those affected by REDD+ markets and programmes. Refusing to participate in REDD+ remains an option.	Market regulations, funds and related readiness activities are coordinated to avoid creating multiple standards for protection of rights and interests of those affected.
National (e.g. national land-use planning decision-making structures, forest agencies, REDD+ working groups)	Understandable information related to land-use policy decisions, participation in REDD+ markets and funds, and REDD+ working group governance is made freely accessible (e.g. funds received/ disbursed).	Actions taken by national decision-makers and REDD+ programmes are subject to independent audit, oversight and recourse (e.g. through national courts or specialized land courts).	Responsibilities, risks and benefits for participating in REDD+ programmes and markets are made clear. Decisions on sharing responsibilities, risks and benefits are made through transparent and participatory processes.	Decision-making processes regarding land use and REDD+ programmes include representation from all sectors of society affected, including marginalized groups, customary authorities and indigenous peoples. Refusing to participate in REDD+ remains an option.	National land-use policies and REDD+ programmes are coordinated with other sectors, local governments and customary authorities, while respecting traditional/ customary decision-making processes.

	Transparency	Accountability	Equity	Participation	Coordination
Local (e.g. local government administration, forest agencies, customary authorities)	Information on decision-making structures and decisions regarding land-use planning and REDD+ and land rights is made available in local languages and proactively disseminated (e.g. funds received).	Local implementation of land-use policies and REDD+ programmes are subject to local oversight and recourse mechanisms where appropriate and linked with national and international recourse mechanisms.	Responsibilities, risks and benefits for participating in REDD+ programmes are made clear to all those potentially affected. Local benefit-sharing mechanisms are developed in transparent and participatory processes.	Decision-making processes regarding land use and REDD+ programmes include representation from all sectors of society affected, including marginalized groups, customary authorities and indigenous peoples. Refusing to participate in REDD+ remains an option.	Local REDD+ actions are coordinated with local and customary authorities to avoid restricting livelihoods and ensure coherence in government policy implementation and respect for traditional/ customary decision-making processes.

Table 6.3 Levels and dimensions of good governance for REDD+

Notes

1. Jeffrey Hatcher is global programmes manager and Luke Bailey is senior associate for policy analysis at the Rights and Resources Initiative (RRI), based in Washington, DC.
2. The '+' sign denotes the eligibility of sustainable forest management, afforestation/ reforestation, restoration and conservation activities.
3. Deutsche Gesellschaft für Technische Zusammenarbeit (GTZ), *Making REDD work: A Practitioner's Guide for Successful Implementation of REDD* (Eschborn: GTZ, 2009).
4. The term readiness can be loosely defined as the process leading to the point at which a country is deemed (or deems itself) ready to engage in REDD+. The assessment of whether a country is ready for REDD+ can be made against technological, economic, institutional or governance related criteria. Many of the REDD+ programmes operating today are preparing countries to engage in REDD+ by, for example, strengthening the national institutions that will implement REDD+ activities.
5. Centre d'Analyse Stratégique, *La lutte contre la déforestation dans les 'États fragiles': une vision renouvelée de l'aide au développement'* Briefing Note no. 180 (Paris: Centre d'Analyse Stratégique, 2010).
6. RRI, *Seeing People through the Trees: Scaling Up Efforts to Advance Rights and Address Poverty, Conflict and Climate Change* (Washington, DC: RRI, 2008).
7. These are the Forest Carbon Partnership Facility (FCPF), UN-REDD Programme, Forest Investment Program (FIP), Amazon Fund, Congo Basin Forest Fund (CBFF), Norway International Climate and Forest Initiative (NICFI) and Governors' Climate and Forests (GCF) Task Force.

8. Better coordination of donor efforts is among the goals of the REDD+ Partnership, which was established in May 2010.

9. Current REDD+ country participants of the FCPF are: Argentina, **Bolivia**, Cameroon, **Cambodia**, the Central African Republic, Chile, Colombia, **the Democratic Republic of the Congo (DRC)**, the Republic of Congo, Costa Rica, El Salvador, Equatorial Guinea, Ethiopia, Gabon, Ghana, Guatemala, Guyana, Honduras, **Indonesia**, Kenya, Laos, Liberia, Madagascar, Mexico, Mozambique, Nepal, Nicaragua, **Panama**, **Papua New Guinea (PNG)**, **Paraguay**, Peru, Suriname, **Tanzania**, Thailand, Uganda, Vanuatu, **Vietnam**.
    Names in bold, plus the Philippines, the Solomon Islands and Zambia, are also members of UN-REDD. Current FIP recipient countries are: Brazil, the DRC, Indonesia, Morocco, Nepal and Romania. Norway is involved in bilateral programmes with Brazil and Tanzania, and is looking to expand efforts in Indonesia, Guyana, Gabon and PNG, among others. The GCF is a coalition of state governors in the US, Brazil, Indonesia, Mexico and Nigeria pursuing a subnational approach to REDD.

10. See, for instance, Environmental Investigation Agency (EIA) and Telapak, *Up for Grabs: Deforestation and Exploitation in Papua's Plantations Boom* (London: EIA, 2009); Global Witness, *Country for Sale: How Cambodia's Elite Has Captured the Country's Extractive Industries* (London: Global Witness, 2009); RRI, *The End of the Hinterland: Forest Conflict and Climate Change* (Washington, DC: RRI, 2010).

11. Christopher Barr et al., *Financial Governance and Indonesia's Reforestation Fund during the Soeharto and Post-Soeharto Periods, 1989–2009: A Political Economic Analysis of Lessons for REDD+*, Occasional Paper no. 52 (Bogor, Indonesia: Center for International Forestry Research [CIFOR], 2010).

12. *Development Today* (Norway), 'UN channels Norwegian funds through corruption-tainted ministry', 31 December 2009.

13. SBS World News Australia, 'PNG climate woes continue', 12 December 2009.

14. Climate Analysis Indicators Tool (CAIT) data provide yearly CO_2e emissions from forestry and land use, showing that the vast majority of these carbon dioxide emissions are from forestry (a small portion of carbon is released by 'agricultural energy use' – e.g. tractors). While greenhouse gas emissions from crops and livestock are significant in many countries, they are virtually all methane and nitrous oxide. See cait.wri.org/figures/World-FlowChart.pdf.

15. For further discussion of Coface and World Bank 'Governance indicators' ratings of REDD+ country governance, see Global Witness, *Building Confidence in REDD: Monitoring beyond Carbon* (London: Global Witness, 2009).

16. Alan Grainger, 'Difficulties in Tracking the Long-term Global Trend in Tropical Forest Area', *Proceedings of the National Academy of Sciences of the USA*, vol. 105 (2008), pp. 818–823.

17. Accra Caucus on Forests and Climate Change, *Realizing Rights, Protecting Forests: An Alternative Vision for Reducing Deforestation* (Accra: Accra Caucus on Forests and Climate Change, 2010).

18. Brenda Brito et al., *The Governance of Forests Tool Kit (Version 1): A Draft Framework of Indicators for Assessing Governance of the Forest Sector* (Washington, DC: World Resources Institute [WRI], 2009).

19. Helmut. Geist and Eric Lambin, 'Proximate Causes and Underlying Driving Forces of Tropical Deforestation', *BioScience*, vol. 52 (2002), pp. 143–150.

20. Jeffrey Hatcher, *Securing Tenure Rights and Reducing Emissions from Deforestation and Degradation (REDD): Costs and Lessons Learned*, Social Development Working Paper no. 120 (Washington, DC: World Bank, 2009).

21. FAO, *Good Governance in Land Tenure and Administration*, Land Tenure Study no. 9 (Rome: FAO, 2007).

22. International Tropical Timber Organization (ITTO) and RRI, *Tropical Forest Tenure Assessment: Trends, Challenges and Opportunities* (Washington, DC: ITTO and RRI, 2009).

23. Lisa Chauvet and Paul Collier, 'What Are the Preconditions for Turnarounds in Failing States?', *Conflict Management and Peace Science*, vol. 25 (2008), pp. 332–348.

24. Global Witness is developing tools to monitor the non-carbon dimensions of REDD+.

25. ITTO and RRI, 2009.

26. Included in this estimate are land tenure reforms, monitoring systems and capacity building. Johan Eliasch, *Climate Change: Financing Global Forests (The Eliasch Review)* (Richmond: UK Office of Public Sector Information, 2008), p. 219.

27. Ibid.

28. Press kit, International Conference on the Major Forest Basins, 11 March 2010, Paris.

29. Bolivia, Brazil and Mozambique, for example, have all begun recognizing and clarifying property rights to lands and forests. See William Sunderlin et al., *From Exclusion to Ownership: Challenges and Opportunities in Advancing Forest Tenure Reform* (Washington, DC: RRI, 2008).

30. International Conference on the Major Forest Basins, 11 March 2010, Paris; Oslo Forest and Climate Conference, 27 May 2010, Oslo.

6.2.1

Bosawás

The 'Lung of Central America' under threat

Ana Murillo Arguello[1]

The natural reserve of Bosawás in Nicaragua is the most extensive forested area north of the Amazon and covers 15.25 per cent of the country.[2] Despite the forest's natural wealth, the native Miskito and Mayangna inhabitants have been confronted with the destruction of their environment. As a result, Nicaragua has lost 27 per cent of its forest cover in the last 17 years.[3]

The unsustainable exploitation of the forest – including the advancing agricultural frontier, the expansion of animal husbandry and incentives to extract wood indiscriminately – is coupled with the difficulties experienced by the local people in enforcing their rights.[4] The destruction of the forest has affected its inhabitants negatively, effectively keeping them in extreme poverty and exacerbating food and water scarcity. The farmers who live on the borders of the forest zone have begun promoting sustainable resource extraction, agriculture and ecotourism,[5] but there have been few public policies to support those who practice conservation.

By the first half of 2010, however, all reported 23 allegations related to the Bosawás in that year had been resolved by the courts.[6] This shows an improvement in capacity to deal with illegal practices related to the environment, which had been exacerbated by insufficient laws and lack of coordination between the local and central governments.[7]

The degradation of the forests in Nicaragua increases the people's vulnerability to climate change and natural disasters. The country needs an improved regulatory framework, management capacity, and adequate resources to follow up on the legal claims of the local people. The participation of local actors in these processes is fundamental to ensuring that their rights are upheld.

Notes

1. Ana Murillo Arguello works for Grupo Cívico Ética y Transparencia.
2. The Bosawás was designated a Biosphere Reserve and World Heritage Site by UNESCO in 1997.
3. See http://elac.uca.edu.ni/pd/economia/files/82/332/01+-+Recursos.pdf.
4. 'Environmental Report of the year 2003', Managua, Nicaragua. See also, IPS News, 'Nicaragua: Can army protect plundered forest reserves?', 1 February 2010.
5. Master conference, Climate Days, 25–26 March 2009, Managua.
6. TI-Nicaragua interview Ana Isable Sequeira, Fiscal Department of the Public Ministry.
7. 'Governance analysis of the forestry sector in Nicaragua', CATIE Verifor, 2006.

6.3

Governance risks for REDD+

How weak forest carbon accounting can create opportunities for corruption and fraud

Christopher Barr[1]

In the global effort to mitigate climate change, investments aimed at slowing the pace of deforestation and forest degradation, particularly in tropical regions, are believed to be a cost-effective approach to reduce CO_2 emissions.[2] Through the UN-sponsored initiative Reducing Emissions from Deforestation and Forest Degradation (REDD), institutional mechanisms are being designed to provide policy and financial incentives for developing countries to protect standing forests and rehabilitate degraded forests. A version of the programme, known as REDD+, aims to provide further incentives for the conservation and enhancement of carbon stocks.

Significant funds are expected to flow once REDD+ programmes are fully operational – up to US$28 billion per year, to reduce the rate of global deforestation by 50 per cent.[3] An unavoidable challenge for REDD+, however, lies in the fact that some developing countries with the highest rates of deforestation also have high levels of corruption. As described in the preceding sections, weak forest governance in many developing countries has facilitated widespread forest-related corruption and financial fraud, and these in turn are major drivers of illegal and unsustainable forest harvesting.

Accordingly, a number of existential questions for REDD+ must be asked. Will the flow of tens, potentially hundreds, of billions of dollars into tropical forest countries create new opportunities for corruption and fraud for powerful political and economic actors? If this occurs, will such funding significantly exacerbate the deforestation and forest degradation that the initiative is designed to slow?

REDD+ proponents frequently dismiss such possibilities by emphasizing that the payments are designed to be performance-based.[4] If carbon emissions are not reduced, they argue, the money will not flow. Implicit in such assurances is a twofold assumption: first that REDD+ programmes will have effective institutions for the measuring, reporting and verification (MRV) of forest-based emission reductions and carbon stock enhancements; and, second, that REDD+ payments will be guided by the empirical assessments of such MRV processes. It is important to examine these assumptions critically in order to highlight how potential weaknesses in the MRV process itself could pose corruption and fraud risks for REDD+.

The emerging structure of REDD+ payment schemes

The institutional architecture for REDD+ is still in the design phase and, therefore, evolving.[5] Several different approaches are being considered for providing financial incentives to tropical countries to reduce forest-related carbon emissions and/or to enhance carbon stocks. At the global level, the most significant of these include 'fund-based' and 'market-based' models.[6]

Fund-based models are designed to channel REDD+ financing to recipient countries and projects through a dedicated fund established by the UNFCCC's Conference of the Parties (COP).[7] Several alternatives have been proposed for how a COP-mandated fund might be administered, reflecting varying degrees of centralization.[8] A REDD+ fund administered directly by the UNFCCC or a designee could concentrate decision-making at the international level, with a highly centralized secretariat determining how funding is allocated. Under a more decentralized approach, funding procedures could be consolidated at the COP level, but a range of national and international entities could be actively involved in overseeing disbursement and determining the criteria and procedures for performance assessment.

Market-based models are generally designed to link forest-related emissions reductions with the emerging demand for carbon offsets in global carbon markets.[9] Tropical countries would be compensated for reducing forest carbon emissions and/or enhancing carbon stocks relative to a national baseline or reference level. Compensation would be in the form of REDD+ carbon credits, which could, in principle, be traded in either voluntary or formal (including compliance and offset) carbon markets. With the latter being structured around cap-and-trade systems, it is anticipated that carbon emitters in developed countries would purchase REDD+ carbon credits as one way to offset their own emissions. Proponents of market-based models argue that linking REDD+ to compliance carbon markets would enable REDD forest countries to tap substantially larger and more sustainable sources of financing than most fund-based models, which are likely to depend heavily upon public and private donations.[10]

It is likely that a future REDD+ payment mechanism will involve both fund- and market-based models, with variations between participating countries. Brazil, for instance, has shown a preference for a fund-based approach, while Indonesia has advocated a market-based model.[11] Regardless, participating countries have several institutional options through which international REDD+ funding can be channelled:[12] directly to REDD+ projects managed by public or private sector actors; to national REDD+ funds administered by a government or independent body that would coordinate payment distribution; and/or to national governments in the form of budgetary support.[13] Some REDD+ countries may select more than one of these options.

Measuring and verifying forest carbon credits

Under both fund- and market-based models, the vast majority of REDD+ payments are expected to be delivered as compensation for output-based activities – that is, for verified reductions of forest carbon emissions and/or enhancement of carbon stocks.[14] To function effectively, REDD+ institutions will therefore require reliable tools for measuring such changes and assessing the extent to which they resulted from REDD+-funded activities. Key steps in this process include determining national reference levels, validating project methodologies, and measuring, reporting and verification.

Reference levels

A national reference level is a projection of a country's forest-related carbon emissions and removals over a defined period of time, based on documented past and anticipated future levels of deforestation and forest degradation.[15] It is intended to serve as a baseline against which carbon emissions reductions and/or carbon stock enhancements will be credited under REDD+. Significantly, experts have not agreed on a single methodology for setting national reference levels, and at least as of late 2009 the UNFCCC had offered little guidance.[16] To a considerable degree national reference levels are politically negotiated, and they are often strongly contested.[17] Different approaches for calculating reference levels can have far-reaching implications for how much REDD+ funding a country ultimately may receive.[18] A reference level based on substantially overestimated historical forest carbon emissions could potentially lead a country to be compensated for emissions reductions greater than those actually achieved.

Validation

Proposed projects must undergo a validation process to ensure that they qualify for REDD+ funding, including whether the methodologies meet REDD+ requirements and whether the planned activities are likely to generate the projected emissions reductions and/or carbon stock enhancements.[19] Critically, validation is also expected to determine whether 'additionality' will be achieved – that is, whether the projected reductions or enhancements would be above and beyond those that would have occurred without REDD+ funding.[20] If it is likely that the project would have been carried out without REDD+ funding, then the benefits are not 'additional' and the project would presumably not qualify for funding.

Measuring, reporting and verification

National REDD+ programmes are expected to have mechanisms for regularly measuring, reporting and verifying project activities to determine whether the planned carbon benefits are actually being achieved.[21] MRV will be carried out at multiple scales, ranging from the project to the national level. A key objective of national MRV programmes is ensuring that 'leakage' does not occur – that is, the displacement of carbon emissions from REDD+ activity areas to non-REDD+ areas.[22]

Under guidelines formulated by the Intergovernmental Panel on Climate Change (IPCC), the verification process should measure changes in two key variables: the area of deforestation and forest degradation, and carbon stock densities per unit area.[23] These measurements can then be used to estimate net carbon emissions and removals from a particular tract of forest during a specified period of time. Deforestation can often be measured effectively using remote sensing with field-based substantiation, or 'ground-truthing' to verify the analysis. Measuring forest degradation and carbon stock densities, by contrast, is considerably more difficult, and generally requires much higher levels of data collection on the ground.[24]

In spite of significant improvements in technology and methodologies, measuring changes in forest carbon often faces significant informational challenges, including:

- a lack of agreement on key definitions – e.g. forest definition and classification of land types;

- a lack of historical and project-scale information – e.g. satellite images, vegetation cover, soil maps, management;
- a lack of information on local drivers of land-use change;
- dispersed and incomparable information;
- inconsistency between the types of measurement and the monitoring methods used; and
- high information requirements because of the numerous, detailed and complex project methodologies.[25]

Weak capacity and uncertain political support for MRV

Despite the central importance of validation and MRV, the vast majority of countries participating in the interim REDD+ Partnership are poorly prepared to measure and verify changes in forest carbon emissions and carbon stocks. A recent review of forest-carbon-monitoring capacity among 99 non-Annex I (developing) countries found that most have limited abilities to estimate greenhouse gas (GHG) emissions and forest loss completely and accurately. Fewer than one-fifth of them have submitted a complete GHG inventory, and only three have a very good capacity to monitor forest area changes and take forest inventories.[26]

As part of the REDD+ readiness process, bilateral and multilateral donor organizations are working with developing forest countries to build the institutional capacity for national and subnational MRV programmes.[27] Such efforts will take time, however, and many REDD+ countries may not have MRV mechanisms capable of verifying compliance-grade credits for at least a decade.[28]

Often overlooked is the fact that building capacity for forest monitoring and carbon accounting is not simply a technical process. In many contexts it is also a political challenge for government forest management agencies.[29] Indeed, the disorganized and highly opaque state of forestry statistics in many REDD+ countries is symptomatic of more fundamental problems with how forests are administered.[30] By keeping forest monitoring and reporting activities to a minimum, state forestry bureaucracies can evade accountability for widespread corruption, illegal logging and other governance problems. REDD+ efforts to build capacity for forest carbon monitoring could be undermined by bureaucratic resistance on the part of state forestry institutions.[31]

In many countries likely to participate in REDD+, it is also conceivable that powerful state elites may seek to control MRV institutions to influence how payments are allocated. Senior political leaders and military officers in timber-rich countries frequently seek to control the institutional mechanisms through which economic rents associated with forests are distributed – a behaviour known as rent-seizing.[32] By controlling the disbursement of forest rents, for example by distributing timber concessions, they are often able to secure the political support of powerful individuals and institutions both within and outside the state apparatus.[33] To the extent that REDD+ payment schemes generate new opportunities for rent capture, the ability to control MRV decisions would hold considerable strategic significance. Specifically, the ability to influence the validation and verification processes could enable well-placed state elites to channel REDD+ payments to favoured projects, regardless of whether they qualify.

To reduce the risks of biased MRV programmes, REDD+ proponents are considering ways to involve independent third-party auditors in validation and verification – such as creating an international forest-carbon-monitoring body, either as a new entity or under an existing international organization; establishing regional MRV partnerships among forest countries in a shared geographic area;[34] and using independent, private sector carbon-accounting firms.[35]

Each option offers potential benefits for ensuring accurate, objective and reliable MRV processes. None of these approaches is without its own risks, however. In 2008 and 2009, for instance, the UN temporarily suspended two of the world's leading private sector carbon-accounting agencies – Swiss-based SGS and the Norwegian firm Det Norske Veritas (DNV) – because of inadequate oversight of their audits, and insufficient training and qualifications of their auditing staff.[36] Such concerns underline the need for robust oversight of the carbon-accounting bodies involved in REDD+ project validation and verification.[37]

Corruption and fraud risks of compromised MRV

Some REDD+ countries have histories of weak forest governance, including theft of forestry revenues by corrupt government officials and financial fraud by private sector actors involved in commercial forestry. By paying to reduce forest-related carbon emissions, REDD+ aims to change the sector's financial incentives in order to generate a new commodity – forest carbon credits – while slowing deforestation and forest degradation. In countries where MRV mechanisms are not fully functional or are politically compromised, however, REDD+ payments may in fact offer incentives for corruption and fraud by government officials and project sponsors seeking to 'game the system'.

Although REDD+ is still in the planning phase, a growing number of cases suggest how corruption and fraud may undermine forest carbon payment schemes. Some have occurred in countries now undergoing the REDD+ readiness process, while others are associated with Clean Development Mechanism (CDM) projects or global carbon markets not specifically related to forests. Some of the examples below are also largely speculative, although they are based on illicit practices in other types of commercial forestry activities found in developing countries likely to participate in REDD+. Collectively, they are indicative of how REDD+ may become susceptible to corruption and fraud.

Inappropriate validation

It is conceivable that authorized validators could approve projects that should not qualify for REDD+ funding – for example, a project that is unlikely to generate the projected carbon benefits or that cannot demonstrate that the reductions would be 'additional'. This could result from the project sponsor bribing the validator; the sponsor presenting misleading data or inaccurate statements; a conflict of interest on the validator's part; the technical incompetence of those assessing the proposal; or some combination of these.

Numerous examples of inappropriate validations of CDM projects have been documented, offering important lessons for REDD+.[38] A UN official estimated in 2007 that 15–20 per cent of offset credits have been issued inappropriately due to inadequate findings of additionality.[39] 'Validations are an open flame in the system,' the official said. '[The validators] began rubber-stamping what developers were putting into the projects. Then once the projects are up and running – well, it's too late'.[40]

Another critic, estimating that questionable CDM emissions reduction credits may be as high as two-thirds, stated: '[J]udging additionality has turned out to be unknowable and unworkable… One commonly used "scam" is to make a proposed project look like an economic loser on its own, but a profitable earner once offset income is factored in'.[41]

Overestimation of carbon benefits

Once a REDD+ project is under way there may be strong incentives for MRV participants to overestimate carbon emissions reductions and/or carbon stock enhancements. When project sponsors include state elites or their business partners, national MRV agencies or individual staff members may be subject to political pressure or be offered bribes to 'verify' carbon benefits that are higher than a project actually achieves. Project implementers have an interest in both overstating avoided emissions and understating problems with the permanence of carbon stocks.[42] At least over the short term, government carbon-accounting agencies may also find it financially rewarding to over-report emissions reductions and carbon stock enhancements so as to secure higher REDD+ payments.[43]

A recent review of carbon accounting under the CDM also highlights conflicts of interest between verifiers and project sponsors, stating that verifiers and validators are paid by project developers and often have to 'compete vigorously to win business'.[44] This suggests that verification agencies could have a direct, if unstated, financial incentive to assess projects favourably. If it is too harsh in its assessments, a verifier may find it difficult to secure future contracts.

A project's carbon benefits can be overestimated in any number of ways. Most blatantly, data can be intentionally manipulated or misreported. More subtly, verifiers can skew their analyses through their selection of methodologies for measuring key variables; the amount of ground-truthing conducted; the selection of sites for field-based data collection; and the assumptions factored into their calculations. For example, estimates of how much carbon will be sequestered by an afforestation project can vary greatly, depending on assumptions about planting densities, annual growth rates, carbon densities of the species used, seedling mortality, site management practices and other variables.[45]

Verification of fictitious projects

In some countries it is conceivable that MRV governance weaknesses could result in the 'verification' of REDD+ projects that are never actually carried out. Most directly, validation and verification agencies could be persuaded – through political pressure or bribery, perhaps – to sign off on projects that do not even exist.

Hypothetically, unscrupulous project developers or government officials could seek REDD+ payments for forest areas that, in fact, are under no immediate threat of deforestation or degradation. To the extent that they are able to tell a convincing (if misleading) story, these fictitious projects may be difficult to distinguish from legitimate REDD+ projects. Even if field visits are made, the forests could be shown to remain standing over the course of the project period, with carbon emissions presumably averted. This seemingly successful outcome would then be falsely attributed to REDD+ interventions.

Although MRV systems are presumably being designed to inhibit such blatant cases of fraud, the funding of fictitious projects in forestry and other sectors is not uncommon in some countries expected to play a prominent role in REDD+.[46] In Indonesia there have been numerous documented cases of the government's Reforestation Fund financing plantation and forest rehabilitation projects that existed only on paper.[47] To a significant degree, this has been possible because the programme has been administered with limited transparency in the use of funds and very little monitoring of project sites. Similarly, many REDD+ projects are likely to be situated in remote sites where external scrutiny is minimal.

Double-counting and fraudulent trade of carbon credits

With the rapid growth of global carbon markets, commercial fraud in the trading of carbon credits has emerged as a serious crime. In some instances unscrupulous brokers are suspected to have sold fictitious credits for carbon projects that do not actually exist.[48] Companies may have also sold the same credits (often for projects that do exist) to multiple buyers – a practice known as 'double-counting'.[49] Such practices are believed to be particularly prevalent in voluntary carbon markets, as these are poorly regulated and transactions frequently involve little more than an agreement between buyers and sellers.[50]

One of the main reasons that carbon markets are vulnerable to fraudulent trading practices is that the commodity being traded – the carbon credit – is intangible and poorly understood by many buyers. The complexity of carbon offset markets created under the Kyoto Protocol has been so characterized:

> [C]arbon offsets... are unlike any securities ever created... Unlike traditional commodities, which sometime during the course of their market exchange must be delivered to someone in physical form, the carbon market is based on the lack of delivery of an invisible substance to no one.[51]

Within this context, carbon buyers depend heavily on assurances from brokers and project developers that the credits they are purchasing come from legitimate projects. Brokers, in turn, depend heavily on the credibility of the validation and verification processes to determine that these projects have reduced emissions effectively. This dependence on multiple intermediaries often makes it difficult for buyers to know exactly what they are purchasing, thereby making the market ripe for fraud.[52] As one hedge fund manager noted, 'There are plenty of carbon cowboys out there, looking to make a quick buck.'[53]

Anticipating such problems, clearly, proponents of REDD+ have advocated the creation of a national register of forest carbon credits for each country participating in REDD+.[54] A similar register of credits, the UN's International Transaction Log, was established under the Clean Development Mechanism to track the purchase or sale of each credit issued. Significantly, when credits are purchased as carbon offsets they are then supposed to be 'retired' from the registry so they cannot be sold again. It is not yet clear what safeguards will exist to ensure that REDD+ credits will not be sold in voluntary markets once they are listed in the registry and will, in fact, be retired when they are purchased as offsets.

Misappropriation of carbon rights

In a growing list of countries, forest-dependent communities are becoming victims of carbon-related fraud. Anticipating the considerable profits to be made from forest carbon once REDD+ is fully under way, carbon brokers and project developers have moved aggressively to secure the carbon rights for large tracts of tropical forest. Often working closely with government officials, they have frequently negotiated contracts allowing them to sell the carbon sequestered in forests that are owned by local communities.

Representatives of forest peoples' organizations have raised concerns that it is common for these negotiations not to be conducted in a free and open manner, and that the significant disparities of information and power can lead to the fraudulent misappropriation of local landowners' carbon rights.[55] In some instances, project developers and government officials have allegedly made false or misleading claims in order to secure carbon rights on terms that are highly unfavourable to local stakeholders.[56]

'Permanence' risks and the securitization of forest carbon credits

A central challenge for REDD+ lies in the risk that forest carbon emissions reductions may not be permanent. Indeed, there is a very real possibility that carbon benefits achieved by a particular REDD+ project could be reversed if the site is degraded or deforested after verification. This could happen for any number of reasons, including adverse natural causes – e.g. drought, pests, fire; a failure on the part of project sponsors to maintain forest cover; encroachment from other stakeholders; policy changes encouraging the conversion of the site to another land use; or the detrimental effects of climate change.[57]

The risks of non-permanence become especially problematic for REDD+ credits that are traded in carbon markets.[58] Assuming that high standards for verification are met, forest carbon credits are expected to become fungible with mitigation credits and allowance units from other sectors once they enter the market. This becomes particularly important if REDD+ credits are used as offsets for emissions in other sectors. As one analyst explained:

> When you claim an offset and it doesn't work, the climate is screwed twice over – first because the same amount of forest has been cut down after all, and second because a huge amount of additional warming gases has been pumped into the atmosphere on the assumption that the gases will be locked away by the now-dead trees. So the offset hasn't prevented emissions – it [has] doubled them.[59]

From a commercial perspective as well, it is unlikely that carbon offset markets will work efficiently unless buyers have a high level of confidence that the credits they purchase will retain their value over time. If non-permanence is perceived to be a significant risk for credits generated under REDD+, it can be anticipated that buyers will shift to other sectors to purchase compliance-grade offsets.

To manage the commercial risks associated with non-permanence, REDD+ planners are considering various liability mechanisms, including strategies through which these risks can be securitized.[60] Options range from issuing credits for more limited periods and holding a portion of project credits in escrow, on the one hand, to various forms of risk pooling, insurance, and shared liability between developed and developing countries, on the other.[61] By establishing liability for forest carbon emissions, these options will essentially determine who will be responsible for paying compensation to whom in the event that emissions reductions are reversed.

Introducing liability mechanisms into REDD+ could bring with them a certain degree of moral hazard, however.[62] Indeed, to the extent that project owners are aware that the long-term success of their projects is ensured, they may have a perverse incentive to minimize the resources they commit to managing the sites – particularly if substantial portions of the payments are made early in the crediting period. In some cases, project sponsors could walk away from their obligations altogether if this would be more profitable than managing them beyond the initial verification.

Given the generally weak enforcement of commercial and forestry laws in many countries likely to participate in REDD+, it can further be anticipated that national governments may be required to provide guarantees that project owners will fulfil their agreements. If project owners with permanent credits fail to meet their obligations or disappear, the ultimate liability will probably revert to the government of the selling country.[63] In such circumstances, private risk will effectively be assumed by public institutions – a situation ripe for corruption and fraud. Project owners with close ties to state elites may be able to exploit such arrangements to maximize their profits, while transferring liabilities or losses to the government.

More generally, creating new forms of financial securities to address 'permanence' risks related to REDD+, as well as emission credits from other sectors, raises fundamental concerns about systemic weaknesses in the global carbon trade. Indeed, a growing number of analysts are questioning whether the world's rapidly expanding markets for carbon credits may be yet another financial bubble, which at some point is bound to burst.[64] The parallels with the recent US housing bubble, which was catalysed by the emergence of exotic financial instruments, are difficult to miss.

In simple terms, carbon credits are a new type of derivatives contract, in which a supplier agrees to deliver a commodity (carbon emissions reductions) at an agreed point in the future. By packaging the risks associated with carbon credits into novel and complex financial securities, however, the institutions involved are not only spreading these risks among a much larger group of actors but, quite possibly, amplifying these risks as well.[65]

With all credits generated through emissions reductions, the value of the asset is very much contingent on the reliability of validation and verification. Market actors will face particular challenges determining the value of credits generated under REDD+: most project locations are remote; MRV processes in many developing countries are likely to be weak and politically compromised; and the permanence of forest carbon emissions reductions is difficult to ensure. Buyers of securities backed by forest carbon credits may have few available tools to know what they are really worth.[66]

Taken together, these factors should raise red flags as to the possibility of financial fraud and systemic risk. In the absence of transparency and effective regulation, there is a very real chance that many investors could end up owning assets with an actual worth that is much less than they assume. Market actors who know how to 'game the system' are likely to make big profits, while most others suffer substantial losses. Moreover, just as the recent subprime market in housing triggered a financial crisis of global proportions, so too could a subprime market in carbon – with enormous implications for life on this planet.

Notes

1. Christopher Barr is director of Woods & Wayside International and a former senior scientist at the Center for International Forestry Research (CIFOR).
2. Nicholas Stern, *The Economics of Climate Change (The Stern Review)* (Cambridge: Cambridge University Press, 2006).
3. Georg Kindermann et al., 'Global Cost Estimates of Reducing Carbon Emissions through Avoided Deforestation', *Proceedings of the National Academy of Sciences*, vol. 105 (2008), pp. 10302–10307.
4. Lydia Olander et al., *International Forest Carbon and the Climate Change Challenge: Issues and Options* (Durham, NC: Nicholas Institute for Environmental Policy Solutions, Duke University, 2009), pp. 26–27.
5. Forest-related carbon credits are already being issued under the UN-sponsored Clean Development Mechanism and are currently traded in voluntary carbon markets. The failure of the international community to reach a legally binding agreement on REDD+ at the 15th Conference of the Parties (COP 15) in Copenhagen in December 2009 means that negotiations over the structure are expected to continue beyond COP 16, held in Cancún, Mexico, in November/December 2010. In May 2010, however, at the Oslo Climate and Forest Conference, some 58 nations agreed to establish an interim REDD+ Partnership, in which partner countries collaborate on REDD+ activities within a voluntary, non-legally binding framework.

6.   Charlotte Streck et al., *REDD+ Institutional Options Assessment: Developing an Efficient, Effective, and Equitable Institutional Framework for REDD+ under the UNFCCC* (Washington, DC: Meridian Institute, 2009).

7.   Ibid. Such a COP-mandated fund may be initiated specifically to support REDD+ activities, or it may be linked to a broader mechanism to finance climate change mitigation.

8.   Ibid.

9.   Ibid.

10. Ibid.

11. Peter Riggs, 'Foundations for REDD? The Debate on "Avoided Deforestation" at the Bali UNFCCC Conference of Parties', unpublished manuscript, 2008.

12. Sheila Wertz-Kanounnikoff and Arild Angelsen, 'Global and National REDD+ Architecture: Linking Institutions and Actions', in Arild Angelsen et al. (eds), *Realizing REDD+: National Strategy and Policy Options* (Bogor, Indonesia: Center for International Forestry Research [CIFOR], 2009), pp. 13–24.

13. Arild Vatn and Arild Angelsen, 'Options for a National REDD+ Architecture', in Arild Angelsen et al. (eds) (2009), pp. 57–74.

14. According to the UNFCCC guidelines, REDD+ payments may also be made for capacity-building and readiness activities, and for policies and measures aimed at addressing the drivers of forest carbon change. See Vatn and Angelsen (2009).

15. Arild Angelsen 'How Do We Set the Reference Levels for REDD Payments?' in Arild Angelsen (ed.), *Moving Ahead with REDD: Issues, Options and Implications* (Bogor, Indonesia: CIFOR, 2008), pp. 53–64.

16. Martin Herold and Margaret Skutsch, 'Measurement, Reporting and Verification for REDD+: Objectives, Capacities and Institutions', in CIFOR, (2009), pp. 85–100.

17. Louis Verchot and Elena Petkova, *The State of REDD Negotiations* (Bogor, Indonesia: CIFOR, 2010).

18. Wertz-Kanounnikoff and Angelsen (2009).

19. See Avoided Deforestation Partners.org, 'REDD methodology framework: version 1.0', April 2009.

20. Arild Angelsen and Sheila Wertz-Kanounnikoff, 'What Are the Key Design Issues for REDD and the Criteria for Assessing Options?, in Arild Angelsen (ed.), *Moving Ahead with REDD: Issues, Options and Implications* (Bogor, Indonesia: CIFOR, 2008), pp. 11–22.

21. Sheila Wertz-Kanounnikoff and Louis Verchot, 'How Can We Monitor, Report and Verify Carbon Emissions from Forests?', in Angelsen (ed.) (2008), pp. 87–98.

22. Herold and Skutsch (2009).

23. Global Observation of Forest and Land Cover Dynamics (GOFC-GOLD), *A Sourcebook of Methods and Procedures for Monitoring and Reporting Anthropogenic Greenhouse Gas Emissions and Removals Caused by Deforestation, Gains and Losses of Carbon Stocks in Forests Remaining Forests, and Forestation* (Ottawa: Natural Resources Canada, 2008). If the aim is to estimate the net carbon emissions associated with land-use change (i.e. not only the change in forest condition), the level of emissions associated with the new land use must also be measured. As Wertz-Kanounnikoff and Verchot (2009) note, emission levels can vary considerably depending on the specific type of change: converting tropical forest to soybean, maize or rice can produce 60 per cent more emissions than converting to oil palm.

24. Daniel Murdiyarso et al., 'How Do We Measure and Monitor Forest Degradation?', in Angelsen (ed.) (2008), pp. 99–106.

25. Tanja Havemann et al., *Measuring and Monitoring Terrestrial Carbon as Part of "REDD+" MRV Systems: The State of the Science and Implications for Policy Makers*, Policy Brief no. 5 (Washington, DC: Terrestrial Carbon Group, 2009).

26. Martin Herold, *An Assessment of National Forest Monitoring Capabilities in Tropical Non-Annex I Countries: Recommendations for Capacity Building* (Jena: GOFC-GOLD Land Cover Project Office, Friedrich Schiller University, 2009).

27. Herold and Skutsch (2009).

28. Brian Murray et al., *Forging a Path for High-Quality Compliance REDD Credits*, Report no. 09–06 (Durham, NC: Nicholas Institute for Environmental Policy Solutions, Duke University, 2009).

29. William Sunderlin and Stibniati Atmadja, 'Is REDD+ an Idea Whose Time Has Come, or Gone?', in Angelsen et al. (eds) (2009), pp. 45–53.

30. Emily Harwell, *'Wild Money': The Human Rights Consequences of Illegal Logging and Corruption in Indonesia's Forestry Sector* (New York: Human Rights Watch, 2009). A recent CIFOR report on Indonesia's Reforestation Fund describes this dynamic in terms that could apply to many other forest countries as well: 'Throughout the [Soeharto era] (and, in many respects, continuing since then), data collection and record-keeping associated with each stage of commercial timber extraction in Indonesia – from forest inventories, for instance, to harvest planning, timber production reports, forest royalty payments, industrial wood supply plans and forest regeneration monitoring – have been poorly organized. The very limited availability of reliable information has made it extremely difficult for either external observers or stakeholders within the sector to obtain a clear understanding of what is really happening to the nation's forest resources. In this way, the generally low quality of forest record-keeping has played a critical role in enabling high levels of illegal activity to occur within the sector.' Christopher Barr et al., *Financial Governance and Indonesia's Reforestation Fund during the Soeharto and Post-Soeharto Periods, 1989–2009: A Political Economic Analysis of Lessons for REDD+*, Occasional Paper no. 52 (Bogor, Indonesia: CIFOR, 2010).

31. Luca Tacconi et al., 'Anti-corruption Policies in the Forest Sector and REDD+', in Angelsen et al., (eds) (2009), pp. 163–174.

32. Michael Ross, *Timber Booms and Institutional Breakdown in South East Asia* (Cambridge: Cambridge University Press, 2001).

33. Ibid.; David Brown, 'Addicted to Rent: Corporate and Spatial Distribution of Forest Resources in Indonesia; Implication for Forest Sustainability and Government Policy' (Jakarta: Indonesia–UK Tropical Forest Management Program, 1999).

34. One example of such a regional partnership is the Central African Forest Watchdog, now being formed by members of the Central African Forest Commission, including Cameroon, the Democratic Republic of the Congo (DRC), the Republic of Congo, Equatorial Guinea and Gabon; Wertz-Kanounnikoff and Verchot (2009).

35. Murray et al. (2009).

36. Mark Shapiro, 'Conning the Climate: Inside the Carbon-Trading Shell Game', *Harper's Magazine*, February 2010, p. 36.

37. Ibid. Investigative journalist Mark Schapiro argues that these suspensions, however muscular they may seem, in fact underscore the limits of UN oversight of the 'designated operational entities' (DOEs) it has deputized to validate and verify carbon emission reduction projects: 'The only mechanism the UN has for evaluating its DOEs is the evidence they themselves create and present: the validation reports they write and the data they gather onsite. When the UN does spot checks, as it did with DNV (Det Norske Veritas) and SGS, it performs them in

the offices of the validators, not in the field. The increasingly complex and far-flung projects, with developers dredging up thousands of claimed reductions in remote areas all around the world, already far outstrip the UN's ability to police them adequately'.

38. Michael Brown, 'Limiting Corrupt Incentives in a Global REDD Regime', *Ecology Law Quarterly,* vol. 37 (2010), pp. 237–267.
39. Shapiro (2010).
40. Ibid.
41. Patrick McCully, 'Guardian: Kyoto Carbon Trading Strategy discredited', 21 May 2008, at www.internationalrivers.org/node/2851.
42. Luca Tacconi et al., 'Anti-Corruption Policies in the Forest Sector and REDD+', in Angelsen et al. (eds) (2009), pp. 163–174.
43. Although such practices may be difficult to sustain – and, indeed, could result in the interruption of REDD+ payments to these jurisdictions if they are exposed – state actors might have an incentive to maximize resource revenues in the short term because of uncertainties over how long they will remain in office. See Ross (2001).
44. Shapiro (2010). In some cases the conflict of interest between verifiers and project developers may be even more direct: 'In this highly specialized new industry, perhaps a thousand people really understand how onsite CDM projects work … It is not uncommon for validators and verifiers to cross over to the far more lucrative business of developing carbon projects themselves – and then requesting audits from their former colleagues.'
45. Omar Masera et al., 'Modelling Carbon Sequestration in Afforestation, Agroforestry and Forest Management Projects: The CO2FIX V.2 Approach', *Ecological Modelling* 164 (2003), pp. 177–199.
46. Greenpeace, *A Future for Forests: An Amazon Case Study* (Amsterdam: Greenpeace, 2008). Phil Oyono et al., 'Green and Black Gold in Rural Cameroon: Natural Resources for Local Governance, Justice and Sustainability', *Environmental Governance in Africa*, Working Paper 22, 2006.
47. Barr et al. (2010), p.15; *Reuters*, 'Graft threatens Indonesia's carbon offset billions: report', 12 January 2010.
48. Deloitte, *Carbon Credit Fraud: The White Collar Crime of the Future* (Sydney: Deloitte, 2009), p.2: 'Interpol is warning EU member countries of "bogus" carbon credits that are being sold on the market'.
49. *Financial Times* (UK), 'Beware the carbon offsetting cowboys', 26 April 2007.
50. Ibid.
51. Shapiro (2010).
52. Ibid.
53. *Financial Times* (UK), 26 April 2007.
54. Streck et al. (2009).
55. Forest Peoples Programme (FPP), *Indigenous Peoples' Rights and Reduced Emissions from Reduced Deforestation and Forest Degradation: The Case of the Saramaka People v. Suriname* (Moreton-in-Marsh, UK: FPP, 2009); Tom Griffiths, *Seeing "RED"? "Avoided Deforestation" and the Rights of Indigenous Peoples and Local Communities* (Moreton-in-Marsh: FPP, 2007).
56. *The Age* (Australia), 'Carbon scandal snares Australian company', 4 September 2009; *The Age* (Australia), 'PNG's PM nephew "pushing carbon deals"', 3 July 2009.
57. Michael Dutschke, 'How Do We Ensure Permanence and Assign Liability?', in Angelsen (ed.) (2008), pp. 77–86.
58. Ibid.

59. *The Nation* (US), 'The wrong kind of green', 22 March 2010.
60. Dutschke (2008).
61. Ibid.
62. Barr et al. (2010), p. 33.
63. Ibid., p. 80.
64. Michelle Chan, *Subprime Carbon?: Re-thinking the World's Largest New Derivatives Market* (Washington, DC: Friends of the Earth, 2009); Larry Lohmann, 'Neoliberalism and the Calculable World: The Rise of Carbon Trading', in Steffen Böhm and Siddhartha Dabhi (eds), *Upsetting the Offset: The Political Economy of Carbon Trading* (London: Mayfly Books, 2009), pp. 25–40; *Rolling Stone* (US), 'The great American bubble machine', 9–23 July 2009.
65. Ibid.
66. Chan (2009).

6.3.1

Hypothetical offsets

Carbon trading and land rights in Papua New Guinea

Sarah Dix[1]

Papua New Guinea (PNG) has the world's third largest rainforest, and the government has shown considerable interest in turning the asset into carbon-trading revenue within the framework of the Reducing Emissions from Deforestation and Forest Degradation (REDD) programme. The paucity of legislation, controversy surrounding the institutional framework and the complexity of dealing with literally thousands of customary landowners pose significant management and governance challenges, however.[2]

In March 2008 the government signed an agreement with Australia in which Australia undertook to 'cooperate on Reducing Emissions from Deforestation and Forest Degradation (REDD), and assist Papua New Guinea to participate in future international carbon markets', as well as to engage in a 'strategic policy dialogue on climate change.'[3] In June 2009 the Australia–PNG Forestry Memorandum of Understanding was signed, paving the way for greater cooperation in the forest sector.

Despite these agreements, as of mid-2009 there was no domestic policy, or specific legislation on carbon trading in PNG, however.[4] Several REDD strategic plans had been drafted, but none had received the overall endorsement of the government: notably the Draft Forestry and Climate Change Policy Framework for Action prepared by the National Forest Authority, and the interim REDD strategy drafted by the Office for Climate Change and Environmental Sustainability (OCCES). The OCCES was created in 2008 under the Prime Minister's Office, primarily with a view to managing the funds expected from REDD.[5] It has been criticized by the public on many fronts.

Key challenges for REDD in PNG

In 2009 the OCCES issued certificates for at least 40 future REDD credits for 1 million tonnes of carbon each.[6] One of the projects is in the 800,000 hectares (ha) of virgin rainforest in Kamula Duso, which is embroiled in a protracted legal battle over land ownership, and until this is settled in the courts 'nobody is supposed to touch it'.[7]

There are allegations that this is in violation of current law and the constitution,[8] in effect entailing the deprivation of the property and carbon rights of the customary owners of the land. In response, the OCCES has claimed that, because Forest Management Agreements (FMAs) or logging concessions had been acquired by the state in these areas, they have the right to sell the carbon. Although it is true that the Forestry Act does not prohibit FMAs from being used for other purposes, they have only previously been used by the state for logging,[9] and the existing FMAs, under which the REDD credits were issued, made no reference to carbon.

Furthermore, the Forestry Act and forestry policy currently determine the shares of revenue from the forests in PNG. According to one estimate, the timber royalty is generally distributed between landowners and government at a 3:1 ratio.[10] In the case of carbon trade, it is unclear whether landowners will benefit similarly. Environmental groups are concerned that most of the carbon trade money will be used up in the running of OCCES and paying middlemen to do transactions on behalf of landowners. If the high revenues expected from REDD are not managed transparently and with stakeholder oversight, there are high risks that the forest communities will see little of the REDD benefits.

Notes

1. Transparency International Papua New Guinea.
2. On the technical as well as political challenges, see Stephen Howes, 'Cheap but Not Easy: The Reduction of Greenhouse Gas Emissions from Deforestation and Forest Degradation in Papua New Guinea', *Pacific Economic Bulletin*, vol. 24 (2009), pp. 130–143.
3. Papua New Guinea-Australia Forest Carbon Partnership, 6 March 2008. See www. climatechange.gov.au.
4. Draft Papua New Guinea UN-REDD Programme document, as presented to UN-REDD policy board, 9–10 March 2009, Port Moresby, at www.un-redd.org/UNREDDProgramme/ CountryActions/PapuaNewGuinea/tabid/1026/language/enUS/Default.aspx. See also Chalapan Kaluwin, *Understanding Climate Change: Developing a Policy for Papua New Guinea*. Occasional Paper no. 1 (Port Moresby: National Research Institute, 2008).
5. National Executive Council decision 56/2008.
6. *The Economist* (UK), 'Money grows on trees', 6 June 2009.
7. Ibid.

8. The PNG constitution's fourth goal is 'to ensure that the forest resources of the country are used and replenished for the collective benefit of all Papua New Guineans now and for future generations'.
9. Forestry Act (1991, with amendments in 1993, 1996, 2000, 2005 and 2010).
10. Nalau Bingeding, 'Carbon Trade: Do We Know What We Are Doing?', *Spotlight with NRI*, vol. 3, no. 5 (Port Moresby: National Research Institute, 2009).

6.3.2

Is Norway rocking the REDD boat?

Manoj Nadkarni[1]

In the midst of the seesawing Reducing Emissions from Deforestation and Forest Degradation (REDD) negotiations and country positions, REDD funds are beginning to flow. In addition to UN and World Bank funds, there are bilateral financial agreements too. Chief among these is the agreement signed in May 2010 between Norway and Indonesia. Under the US$1 billion deal, Indonesia, among other activities, has pledged to stop issuing new permits to exploit natural forests and carbon peat land areas.[2] Forest civil society organizations, both globally and in Indonesia, claim that this is a game changer.

It could be said that this pre-emptive arrangement – before any global REDD mechanisms have been agreed – is a positive step, in as much as it ups the pace and shows that some countries have faith in REDD and want to see it work. On the other hand, though, there is serious disquiet about the deal. At one level this uneasiness stems from the belief that REDD mechanisms should be based on global consensus and not bilateral agreements, and the Norwegian move may undermine United Nations Framework Convention on Climate Change (UNFCCC) processes. Another, perhaps more immediate concern is the capacity of Indonesia's forestry and other ministries to manage the US$1 billion under the agreement.

Indonesia does not have the cleanest track record when it comes to managing its forests. For example, auditors found that the country's Reforestation Fund, managed by the Department of Forestry, had lost US$5.25 billion between 1994 and 1998, due to 'systematic financial mismanagement and fraud'.[3] Furthermore, Wandojo Siswanto, a leading Indonesian climate negotiator at Copenhagen and a key architect of the Indonesia REDD programme, has also been subject to allegations of corruption by Indonesia's anti-corruption agency.[4] In 2008 Siswanto admitted taking Indonesian rupiah (Rp) 50 million (approximately US$4600) 'as a payoff for favouritism in awarding tenders'.[5]

Another interesting factor is the announcement that Indonesia is planning to set up a special agency to coordinate REDD activities and manage the Norwegian funds. This agency will bypass the forestry ministry and report directly to the president, Susilo Bambang Yudhoyono.[6] This may be a welcome move, but at the same time it may have the effect of concentrating power in the hands of a few officials and lead to overlap in jurisdiction, therefore making decision-making more complicated and bureaucratic. These are all warning signs as far as corruption risks are concerned.

President Yudhoyono suggested in April that an illegal logging mafia was responsible for much of the deforestation in Indonesia, and created a Judicial Mafia Task Force to examine the illegal logging, but the task force itself has come under criticism for alleged conflict of interest issues among its members.[7]

Notes

1. Manoj Nadkarni manages the Forest Governance Integrity Programme at Transparency International.
2. *Jakarta Post* (Indonesia), 'Government may name local firm as fund manager', 16 August 2010.
3. Reuters (UK), 'Graft could jeopardize Indonesia's climate deals ', 17 September 2010; *Jakarta Globe* (Indonesia), 'KPK: corruption jeopardizes lucrative climate-change deals', 17 September 2010.
4. Ibid.
5. *Jakarta Post* (Indonesia), 'Bribes went to Forestry Ministry officials: trial witness', 31 October 2008.
6. *Jakarta Post* (Indonesia), 'SBY's new hard act: to make REDD+ work', 6 October 2010.
7. *Indonesia Today*, 'Judicial mafia eradication task force under pressure', 2 August 2010.

Index